ANCIENT PROPHECIES and their meaning for to-day—and tomorrow . . . the many Christian churches in our time—will they someday unite? . . . the ultimate ordeal that the human race may face—in our own lifetime . . . these and many other matters of the deepest concern are presented in this worldwide best-seller, an unforgettable and enriching book.

From Here to FOREVER

E.G. White

A condensation of

The Great Controversy
Between Christ and Satan

**PACIFIC PRESS
PUBLISHING ASSOCIATION**
Mountain View, California
Oshawa, Ontario

This condensation is not a paraphrase. The author's own words are retained throughout, except when it has been necessary to substitute a proper noun for a pronoun to avoid confusion, to change a verb tense to maintain meaning and continuity, or to supply a word or phrase to make a sentence read more smoothly.

Copyright © 1982 by
Pacific Press Publishing Association
Printed in United States of America
All Rights Reserved

ISBN 0-8163-0511-0

Why You Should Read This Book

To millions of people, life seems both meaningless and absurd. Science, technology, even philosophy and theology, have pictured human beings as mere creatures of chance. Yet, consciously or not, men and women find it difficult to accept a purposeless existence. Violence, protests and rebellion, experimentation with drugs—these are, in many cases, the irrational expressions of people struggling with their appalling lostness. Like orphans they cry out from their loneliness and despair, "Who am I? Who were my parents? Why did they give me up? How can I find them?"

Many turn to science for answers, tuning our great radio telescopes in on the heartbeat of the stars, as if to ask, Is there anyone out there who knows me? Who cares for me? But science has no answer. Science is set up to ask questions: How is an atom constructed? How is it split? How do our minds work? How is the universe constructed?

It cannot tell us why there is an atom, why human beings exist, why there is a universe at all. Nor can it answer those unique questions that concern thinking people:

If there is meaning and justice in the universe, why do the innocent suffer with the guilty?

Is there life after death? Does the human personality live on?

Do today's Christian churches really speak for God? What is truth?

What is the future of the world? Will it end with the whimper of a child struggling for a last breath in polluted atmosphere, or with the bang of atomic hell unleashed from cherry-red ICBM nose cones? Or will humans—who in recorded history never have demonstrated the ability to control their own basic selfishness—suddenly succeed in banishing evil, war, poverty and even death?

This book gives the answers, and they are reassuring. Life does have meaning! We are not alone in the universe. Someone out there cares! Someone, indeed, who has involved Himself in human history, who Himself joined our race, so that we could get through to Him and He to us; Someone whose strong hand has been over this planet and who will guide it back to peace—and soon.

But long years ago a persuasive cosmic being determined to seize control of our world and thwart God's plan for the happiness of His earthly family. In graphic language—indeed, multiplied thousands have called it inspired language—the author of this book tears the curtain from the dim unknown and fearlessly exposes the strategies of this powerful but unseen personality whose hand is stretched out to grasp the sovereignty of our world. On the human scene pagan princes and religious establishments alike are exposed as guilty parties in the conspiracy.

Only in an age of religious freedom could this book be printed and widely circulated, for it cuts hard across some of the most powerful Establishments of our day. It tells why a Reformation was needed, and why it was halted; the sad story of apostate churches, of persecuting alliances, of an emerging coalition of church and state that will yet play its inglorious part before the great controversy between evil and good is ended. And in this conflict every human being is a participant.

Here the author writes of things not yet existing in her day. She speaks with an honesty that disturbs and startles. The issues of the controversy are so great and the stakes so high that somebody had to voice these words of warning and enlightenment.

No reader who turns the pages of this book will put it down without wondering whether it was more than chance that led him to discover it.

The Publishers

Lifting the Veil on the Future*

Before the entrance of sin, Adam enjoyed open communion with his Maker; but since man separated himself from God by transgression, the human race has been cut off from this high privilege. By the plan of redemption, however, a way has been opened whereby the inhabitants of the earth may still have connection with heaven. God has communicated with men by His Spirit, and divine light has been imparted to the world by revelations to His chosen servants. "Holy men of God spake as they were moved by the Holy Ghost." 2 Peter 1:21.

During the first 2500 years of human history, there was no written revelation. Those who had been taught of God communicated their knowledge to others, and it was handed down from father to son, through successive generations. The preparation of the written word began in the time of Moses. Inspired revelations were then embodied in an Inspired Book. This work continued during the long period of 1600 years—from Moses, the historian of creation and the law, to John, the recorder of the most sublime truths of the gospel.

The Bible points to God as its author; yet it was written by human hands; and in the varied style of its different books it presents the characteristics of the several writers. The truths revealed are all "given by inspiration of God" (2 Timothy 3:16); yet they are expressed in the words of men. The Infinite One by His Holy Spirit has shed light into the minds and hearts of His servants. He has given dreams and visions, sym-

* Author's Introduction

bols and figures; and those to whom the truth was thus revealed have themselves embodied the thought in human language.

Written in different ages, by men who differed widely in rank and occupation, and in mental and spiritual endowments, the books of the Bible present a wide contrast in style, as well as a diversity in the nature of the subjects unfolded. Different forms of expression are employed by different writers; often the same truth is more strikingly presented by one than by another. And as several writers present a subject under varied aspects and relations, there may appear, to the superficial, careless, or prejudiced reader, to be discrepancy or contradiction, where the thoughtful, reverent student, with clearer insight, discerns the underlying harmony.

As presented through different individuals, the truth is brought out in its varied aspects. One writer is more strongly impressed with one phase of the subject; he grasps those points that harmonize with his experience or with his power of perception and appreciation; another seizes upon a different phase; and each, under the guidance of the Holy Spirit, presents what is most forcibly impressed upon his own mind—a different aspect of the truth in each, but a perfect harmony through all. And the truths thus revealed unite to form a perfect whole, adapted to meet the wants of men in all the circumstances and experiences of life.

God has been pleased to communicate His truth to the world by human agencies, and He Himself, by His Holy Spirit, qualified men and enabled them to do this work. He guided the mind in the selection of what to speak and what to write. The treasure was entrusted to earthen vessels, yet it is, nonetheless, from Heaven. The testimony is conveyed through the imperfect expression of human language, yet it is the testimony of God; and the obedient, believing child of God beholds in it the glory of a divine power, full of grace and truth.

In His Word, God has committed to men the knowledge necessary for salvation. The Holy Scriptures are to be accepted as an authoritative, infallible revelation of His will. They are the standard of character, the revealer of doctrines, and the test of experience. "Every scripture inspired of God is also profitable for teaching, for reproof, for correction, for instruction which is in righteousness; that the man of God may be complete, furnished completely unto every good work." 2 Timothy 3:16, 17, RV.

Yet the fact that God has revealed His will to men through His Word has not rendered needless the continued presence and guiding of the Holy Spirit. On the contrary, the Spirit was promised by our Saviour, to open the Word to His servants, to illuminate and apply its teachings. And since it was the Spirit of God that inspired the Bible, it is impossible that the teaching of the Spirit should ever be contrary to that of the Word.

The Spirit was not given—nor can it ever be bestowed—to supersede the Bible; for the Scriptures explicitly state that the Word of God is the standard by which all teaching and experience must be tested. Says the apostle John, "Believe not every spirit, but try the spirits whether they are of God: because many false prophets are gone out into the world." 1 John 4:1. And Isaiah declares, "To the law and to the testimony: if they speak not according to this word, it is because there is no light in them." Isaiah 8:20.

Great reproach has been cast upon the work of the Holy Spirit by the errors of a class that, claiming its enlightenment, profess to have no further need of guidance from the Word of God. They are governed by impressions which they regard as the voice of God in the soul. But the spirit that controls them is not the Spirit of God. This following of impressions, to the neglect of the Scriptures, can lead only to confusion, to deception and ruin. It serves only to further the designs of the evil one. Since the ministry of the Holy Spirit is of vital importance to the church of Christ, it is one of the devices of Satan, through the errors of extremists and fanatics, to cast contempt upon the work of the Spirit and cause the people of God to neglect this source of strength which our Lord Himself has provided.

In harmony with the Word of God, His Spirit was to continue its work throughout the period of the gospel dispensation. During the ages while the Scriptures of both the Old and the New Testament were being given, the Holy Spirit did not cease to communicate light to individual minds, apart from the revelations to be embodied in the Sacred Canon. The Bible itself relates how, through the Holy Spirit, men received warning, reproof, counsel, and instruction, in matters in no way relating to the giving of the Scriptures. And mention is made of prophets in different ages, of whose utterances nothing is recorded. In like manner, after the close of the canon of the Scripture, the Holy Spirit was still to continue its work, to enlighten, warn, and comfort the children of God.

Jesus promised His disciples, "The Comforter, which is the Holy Ghost, whom the Father will send in my name, he shall teach you all things, and bring all things to your remembrance, whatsoever I have said unto you." "When he, the Spirit of truth, is come, he will guide you into all truth: . . . and he will show you things to come." John 14:26; 16:13. Scripture plainly teaches that these promises, so far from being limited to apostolic days, extend to the church of Christ in all ages. The Saviour assures His followers, "I am with you alway, even unto the end of the world." Matthew 28:20. And Paul declares that the gifts and manifestations of the Spirit were set in the church "for the perfecting of the saints, for the work of the ministry, for the edifying of the body of Christ: till we all come in the unity of the faith, and of the knowledge of the Son of God, unto a perfect man, unto the measure of the stature of the fulness of Christ." Ephesians 4:12, 13.

For the believers at Ephesus the apostle prayed, "That the God of our Lord Jesus Christ, the Father of glory, may give unto you the *Spirit of wisdom and rev-*

elation in the knowledge of him: *the eyes of your understanding being enlightened;* that ye may know what is the hope of his calling, and . . . what is the *exceeding greatness* of his power to usward who believe.'' Ephesians 1:17-19. The ministry of the divine Spirit in enlightening the understanding and opening to the mind the deep things of God's Holy Word was the blessing which Paul thus besought for the Ephesian church.

After the wonderful manifestation of the Holy Spirit on the Day of Pentecost, Peter exhorted the people to repentance and baptism in the name of Christ, for the remission of their sins; and he said: ''Ye shall receive the gift of the Holy Ghost. For the promise is unto you, and to your children, and to all that are afar off, even as many as the Lord our God shall call.'' Acts 2:38, 39.

In immediate connection with the scenes of the great day of God, the Lord by the prophet Joel has promised a special manifestation of His Spirit. Joel 2:28. This prophecy received a partial fulfillment in the outpouring of the Spirit on the Day of Pentecost; but it will reach its full accomplishment in the manifestation of divine grace which will attend the closing work of the gospel.

The great controversy between good and evil will increase in intensity to the very close of time. In all ages the wrath of Satan has been manifested against the church of Christ; and God has bestowed His grace and Spirit upon His people to strengthen them to stand against the power of the evil one. When the apostles of Christ were to bear His gospel to the world and to record it for all future ages, they were especially endowed with the enlightenment of the Spirit. But as the church approaches her final deliverance, Satan is to work with greater power. He comes down ''having great wrath, because he knoweth that he hath but a short time.'' Revelation 12:12. He will work ''with all power and signs and lying wonders.'' 2 Thessalonians 2:9. For 6000 years that mastermind that once was highest among the angels of God has been wholly bent to the work of deception and ruin. And all the depths of satanic skill and subtlety acquired, all the cruelty developed during these struggles of the ages will be brought to bear against God's people in the final conflict. And in this time of peril the followers of Christ are to bear to the world the warning of the Lord's second advent; and a people are to be prepared to stand before Him at His coming, "without spot, and blameless." 2 Peter 3:14. At this time the special endowment of divine grace and power is not less needful to the church than in apostolic days.

Through the illumination of the Holy Spirit, the scenes of the long-continued conflict between good and evil have been opened to the writer of these pages. From time to time I have been permitted to behold the working, in different ages, of the great controversy between Christ, the Prince of life, the Author of our salvation, and Satan, the prince of evil, the author of sin, the first transgressor of God's holy law. Satan's enmity against Christ has been manifested against His followers. The same hatred of the principles of God's law, the same policy of deception, by which error is made to appear as truth, by which human laws are substituted for the law of God, and men are led to worship the creature rather than the Creator, may be traced in all the history of the past. Satan's efforts to misrepresent the character of God, to cause men to cherish a false conception of the Creator, and thus to regard Him with fear and hate rather than with love; his endeavors to set aside the divine law, leading the people to think themselves free from its requirements; and his persecution of those who dare to resist his deceptions, have been steadfastly pursued in all ages. They may be traced in the history of patriarchs, prophets, and apostles, of martyrs and reformers.

In the great final conflict, Satan will employ the same policy, manifest the same spirit, and work for the same end as in all preceding ages. That which has been, will be, except that the coming struggle will be marked with a terrible intensity such as the world has never witnessed. Satan's deceptions will be more subtle, his assaults more determined. If it were possible, he would lead astray the elect. Mark 13:22.

As the Spirit of God has opened to my mind the great truths of His Word, and the scenes of the past and the future, I have been bidden to make known to others that which has thus been revealed—to trace the history of the controversy in past ages, and especially so to present it as to shed a light on the fast-approaching struggle of the future. In pursuance of this purpose, I have endeavored to select and group together events in the history of the church in such a manner as to trace the unfolding of the great testing truths that at different periods have been given to the world, that have excited the wrath of Satan and the enmity of a world-loving church, and that have been maintained by the witness of those who "loved not their lives unto the death."

In these records we may see a foreshadowing of the conflict before us. Regarding them in the light of God's Word, and by the illumination of His Spirit, we may see unveiled the devices of the wicked one and the dangers which they must shun who would be found "without fault" before the Lord at His coming.

The great events which have marked the progress of reform in past ages are matters of history, well known and universally acknowledged by the Protestant world; they are facts which none can gainsay. This history I have presented briefly, in accordance with the scope of the book and the brevity which must necessarily be observed, the facts having been condensed into as little space as seemed consistent with a proper understanding of their application. In some cases where a historian has so grouped together events as to afford, in brief, a comprehensive view of the subject, or has summarized details in a convenient manner, his words have been quoted; but in some instances no specific credit has been given, since the quotations are not given for the purpose of citing that writer as authority, but because his statement affords a ready and forcible presentation of the subject. In narrating the experience and views of those carrying forward the work of reform in our own time, similar use has been made of their published works.

It is not so much the object of this book to present new truths concerning the struggles of former times, as to bring out facts and principles which have a bearing on coming events. Yet viewed as a part of the controversy between the forces of light and darkness, all these records of the past are seen to have a new significance; and through them a light is cast upon the future, illumining the pathway of those who, like the reformers of past ages, will be called, even at the peril of all earthly good, to witness "for the word of God, and for the testimony of Jesus Christ."

To unfold the scenes of the great controversy between truth and error; to reveal the wiles of Satan and the means by which he may be successfully resisted; to present a satisfactory solution of the great problem of evil, shedding such a light upon the origin and the final disposition of sin as to make fully manifest the justice and benevolence of God in all His dealings with His creatures; and to show the holy, unchanging nature of His law, is the object of this book. That through its influence souls may be delivered from the power of darkness and become "partakers of the inheritance of the saints in light," to the praise of Him who loved us and gave Himself for us is the earnest prayer of the writer.

E.G.W.

Contents

1 / A Forecast of the World's Destiny

From the crest of Olivet, Jesus looked upon Jerusalem. In full view were the magnificent buildings of the temple. The setting sun lighted up the snowy whiteness of its marble walls and gleamed from golden tower and pinnacle. What child of Israel could gaze upon the scene without a thrill of joy and admiration! But other thoughts occupied the mind of Jesus. "When he was come near, he beheld the city, and wept over it." Luke 19:41.

Jesus' tears were not for Himself, though before Him lay Gethsemane, the scene of approaching agony, and not far distant, Calvary, the place of crucifixion. Yet it was not these scenes that cast the shadow upon Him in this hour of gladness. He wept for the doomed thousands of Jerusalem.

The history of more than a thousand years of God's special favor and guardian care, manifested to the chosen people, was open to the eye of Jesus. Jerusalem had been honored of God above all the earth. The Lord had "chosen Zion . . . for his habitation." Psalm 132:13. For ages, holy prophets had uttered their messages of warning. Daily the blood of lambs had been offered, pointing to the Lamb of God.

Had Israel as a nation preserved her allegiance to Heaven, Jerusalem would have stood forever, the elect of God. But the history of that favored people was a record of backsliding and rebellion. With more than a father's pitying love, God had "compassion on his people, and on his dwelling place." 2 Chronicles 36:15.

When entreaty and rebuke had failed, He sent the best gift of heaven, the Son of God Himself, to plead with the impenitent city.

For three years the Lord of light and glory had gone in and out among His people, "doing good, and healing all that were oppressed of the devil," setting at liberty them that were bound, restoring sight to the blind, causing the lame to walk and the deaf to hear, cleansing lepers, raising the dead, and preaching the gospel to the poor. See Acts 10:38; Luke 4:18; Matthew 11:5.

A homeless wanderer, He lived to minister to the needs and lighten the woes of men, to plead with them to accept the gift of life. The waves of mercy, beaten back by those stubborn hearts, returned in a stronger tide of pitying, inexpressible love. But Israel had turned from her best Friend and only Helper. The pleadings of His love had been despised.

The hour of hope and pardon was fast passing. The cloud that had been gathering through ages of apostasy and rebellion was about to burst upon a guilty people. He who alone could save them from their impending fate had been slighted, abused, rejected, and was soon to be crucified.

As Christ looked upon Jerusalem, the doom of a whole city, a whole nation, was before Him. He beheld the destroying angel with sword uplifted against the city which had so long been God's dwelling place. From the very spot afterward occupied by Titus and his army, He looked across the valley upon the sacred courts and porticoes. With tear-dimmed eyes He saw the walls surrounded by alien hosts. He heard the tread of armies marshaling for war, the voice of mothers and children crying for bread in the besieged city. He saw her holy house, her palaces and towers, given to the flames, a heap of smoldering ruins.

Looking down the ages, He saw the covenant people scattered in every land, "like wrecks on a desert shore." Divine pity, yearning love, found utterance in the mournful words: "O Jerusalem, Jerusalem, thou that killest the prophets and stonest them which are sent unto thee, how often would I have gathered thy children together, even as a hen gathereth her chickens under her wings, and ye would not!'' Matthew 23:37.

Christ saw in Jerusalem a symbol of the world hardened in unbelief and rebellion, hastening on to meet the retributive judgments of God. His heart was moved with pity for the afflicted and suffering ones of earth. He yearned to relieve them all. He was willing to pour out His soul unto death to bring salvation within their reach.

The Majesty of heaven in tears! That scene shows how hard a task it is to save the guilty from the consequence of transgressing the law of God. Jesus saw the world involved in deception similar to that which caused the destruction of Jerusalem. The great sin of the Jews was their rejection of Christ; the great sin of the world would be their rejection of the law of God, the foundation of His government in heaven and earth. Millions in bondage to sin, doomed to suffer the second death, would refuse to listen to words of truth in their day of visitation.

Magnificent Temple Doomed

Two days before the Passover, Christ again went with His disciples to the Mount of Olives overlooking the city. Once more He gazed upon the temple in its dazzling splendor, a diadem of beauty. Solomon, the wisest of Israel's monarchs, had completed the first temple, the most magnificent building the world ever saw. After its destruction by Nebuchadnezzar, it was rebuilt about five hundred years before the birth of Christ.

But the second temple had not equaled the first in magnificence. No cloud of glory, no fire from heaven, descended upon its altar. The ark, the mercy seat, and the tables of the testimony were not to be found there. No voice from heaven made known to the priest the will of God. The second temple was not honored with the cloud of God's glory, but with the living presence of One who was God Himself manifest in the flesh. The "Desire of all nations" had come to His temple when the Man of Nazareth taught and healed in the sacred courts. But Israel had put from her the proffered Gift of heaven. With the humble Teacher who had that day passed out from its golden gate, the glory had forever departed from the temple. Already were the Saviour's words fulfilled: "Your house is left unto you desolate." Matthew 23:38.

The disciples had been filled with wonder at Christ's prediction of the overthrow of the temple, and they desired to understand the meaning of His words. Herod the Great had lavished upon it both Roman and Jewish treasure. Massive blocks of white marble, forwarded from Rome, formed part of its structure. To these the disciples had called the attention of their Master, saying: "See what manner of stones and what buildings are here!" Mark 13:1.

Jesus made the solemn and startling reply: "Verily I say unto you, There shall not be left here one stone upon another, that shall not be thrown down." Matthew 24:2. The Lord had told the disciples that He would come the second time. Hence, at the mention of judgments upon Jerusalem, their minds reverted to that coming, and they asked: "When shall these things be? and what shall be the sign of thy coming, and of the end of the world?" Matthew 24:3.

Christ presented before them an outline of prominent events before the close of time. The prophecy He uttered was twofold in its meaning. While foreshadowing the destruction of Jerusalem, it prefigured also the terrors of the last great day.

Judgments were to fall upon Israel for their rejection and crucifixion of the Messiah. "When ye therefore shall see the abomination of desolation, spoken of by Daniel the prophet, stand in the holy place, (whoso readeth, let him understand:) then let them which be in Judea flee into the mountains." Matthew 24:15, 16.

See also Luke 21:20, 21. When the idolatrous standards of the Romans should be set up in the holy ground outside the city walls, then the followers of Christ were to find safety in flight. Those who would escape must make no delay. Because of her sins, wrath had been denounced against Jerusalem. Her stubborn unbelief rendered her doom certain. See Micah 3:9-11.

The inhabitants of Jerusalem accused Christ of being the cause of all the troubles which had come upon them in consequence of their sins. Though they knew Him to be sinless, they declared His death necessary to their safety as a nation. They concurred in the decision of their high priest that it would be better for one man to die than for the whole nation to perish. See John 11:47-53.

While they slew their Saviour because He reproved their sins, they regarded themselves as God's favored people and expected the Lord to deliver them from their enemies!

God's Long-suffering

For nearly forty years the Lord delayed His judgments. There were still many Jews who were ignorant of the character and work of Christ. And the children had not enjoyed the light which their parents had spurned. Through the preaching of the apostles, God would cause light to shine upon them. They would see how prophecy had been fulfilled, not only in the birth and life of Christ, but in His death and resurrection. The children were not condemned for the sins of the parents; but when they rejected the additional light granted to them, they became partakers of the parents' sins and filled up the measure of their iniquity.

The Jews in their stubborn impenitence rejected the last offer of mercy. Then God withdrew His protection from them. The nation was left to the control of the leader she had chosen. Satan aroused the fiercest and most debased passions of the soul. Men were beyond reason—controlled by impulse and blind rage, satanic in their cruelty. Friends and kindred betrayed one another. Parents slew their children, and children their parents. Rulers had no power to rule themselves. Passion made them tyrants. The Jews had accepted false testimony to condemn the innocent Son of God. Now false accusations made their lives uncertain. The fear of God no longer disturbed them. Satan was at the head of the nation.

Leaders of opposing factions fell upon each other's forces and slaughtered without mercy. Even the sanctity of the temple could not restrain their horrible ferocity. The sanctuary was polluted with the bodies of the slain. Yet the instigators of this hellish work declared they had no fear that Jerusalem would be destroyed! It was God's own city. Even while Roman legions were besieging the temple, multitudes held fast to the belief that the Most High would interpose for the defeat of their adversaries. But Israel had spurned the divine protection, and now she had no defense.

Portents of Disaster

All the predictions given by Christ concerning the destruction of Jerusalem were fulfilled to the letter. Signs and wonders appeared. For seven years a man continued to go up and down the streets of Jerusalem, declaring woes to come. This strange being was imprisoned and scourged, but to insult and abuse he answered only, "Woe, woe to Jerusalem!" He was slain in the siege he foretold.[1]

Not one Christian perished in the destruction of Jerusalem. After the Romans under Cestius had surrounded the city, they unexpectedly abandoned the siege when everything seemed favorable for attack. The Roman general withdrew his forces without the least apparent reason. The promised sign had been given to the waiting Christians. Luke 21:20, 21.

Events were so overruled that neither Jews nor Romans should hinder the flight of the Christians. Upon the retreat of Cestius, the Jews pursued, and while both forces were thus fully engaged, the Christians throughout the land were able to make their escape unmolested to a place of safety, the city of Pella.

The Jewish forces, pursuing after Cestius and his army, fell upon their rear. With great difficulty the Romans succeeded in making their retreat. The Jews with their spoils returned in triumph to Jerusalem. Yet this apparent success brought them only evil. It inspired that spirit of stubborn resistance to the Romans which brought unutterable woe upon the doomed city.

Terrible were the calamities that fell upon Jerusalem when the siege was resumed by Titus. The city was invested at the time of the Passover, when millions of Jews were assembled within its walls. Stores of provision had previously been destroyed through the revenge of the contending factions. Now all the horrors of starvation were experienced. Men gnawed the leather of their belts and sandals and the covering of their shields. Great numbers stole out at night to gather wild plants growing outside the city walls, though many were put to death with cruel torture. Often those who returned in safety were robbed of what they had gleaned. Husbands robbed their wives, and wives their husbands. Children snatched the food from the mouths of their aged parents.

The Roman leaders endeavored to strike terror to the Jews and thus cause them to surrender. Prisoners were scourged, tortured, and crucified before the wall of the city. Along the Valley of Jehoshaphat and at Calvary, crosses were erected in great numbers. There was scarcely room to move among them. So was visited that awful imprecation uttered before the judgment seat of Pilate: "His blood be on us, and on our children." Matthew 27:25.

Titus was filled with horror as he saw bodies lying in heaps in the valleys. Like one entranced, he looked upon the magnificent temple and gave command that not one stone of it be touched. He made an earnest appeal to the Jewish leaders not to force him to defile the sacred place with blood. If they would fight in any other place, no Roman should violate the sanctity of the temple! Josephus himself entreated them to surrender, to save themselves, their city, and their place of worship. But with bitter curses, darts were hurled at him, their last human mediator. In vain were the efforts of Titus to save the temple. One greater than he had declared that not one stone was to be left upon another.

Titus at last decided to take the temple by storm, determined that if possible it should be saved from destruction. But his commands were disregarded. A firebrand was flung by a soldier through an opening in the porch, and immediately the cedar-lined chambers about the holy house were in a blaze. Titus rushed to the place and commanded the soldiers to quench the flames. His words were unheeded. In their fury the soldiers hurled blazing brands into the chambers adjoining the temple and then slaughtered those who had found shelter there. Blood flowed down the temple steps like water.

After the destruction of the temple, the whole city fell to the Romans. The leaders of the Jews forsook their impregnable towers. Titus declared that God had given them into his hands; for no engines, however powerful, could have prevailed against those stupendous battlements. Both the city and the temple were razed to their foundations, and the ground upon which the holy house had stood was "plowed like a field." See Jeremiah 26:18. More than a million perished; the survivors were carried away as captives, sold as slaves, dragged to Rome, thrown to wild beasts in the amphitheaters, or scattered as homeless wanderers throughout the earth.

The Jews had filled for themselves the cup of vengeance. In all the woes that followed in their dispersion, they were reaping the harvest which their own hands had sown. "O Israel, thou has destroyed thyself"; "for thou hast fallen by thine iniquity." Hosea

13:9; 14:1. Their sufferings are often represented as a punishment by the direct decree of God. Thus the great deceiver seeks to conceal his own work. By stubborn rejection of divine love and mercy, the Jews had caused the protection of God to be withdrawn from them.

We cannot know how much we owe to Christ for the peace and protection which we enjoy. The restraining power of God prevents mankind from passing fully under the control of Satan. The disobedient and unthankful have great reason for gratitude for God's mercy. But when men pass the limits of divine forbearance, restraint is removed. God does not stand as an executioner of the sentence against transgression. He leaves the rejectors of His mercy to reap that which they have sown. Every ray of light rejected is a seed sown which yields its unfailing harvest. The Spirit of God, persistently resisted, is at last withdrawn. Then there is left no power to control the evil passions of the soul, no protection from the malice and enmity of Satan.

The destruction of Jerusalem is a solemn warning to all who are resisting the pleadings of divine mercy. The Saviour's prophecy concerning judgments upon Jerusalem is to have another fulfillment. In the fate of the chosen city we behold the doom of a world that has rejected God's mercy and trampled upon His law. Dark are the records of human misery that earth has witnessed. Terrible have been the results of rejecting the authority of Heaven. But a scene yet darker is presented in the revelations of the future. When the restraining Spirit of God shall be wholly withdrawn, no longer to hold in check the outburst of human passion and satanic wrath, the world will behold, as never before, the results of Satan's rule.

In that day, as in Jerusalem's destruction, God's people will be delivered. See Isaiah 4:3; Matthew 24:30, 31. Christ will come the second time to gather His faithful ones to Himself. "Then shall all the tribes of the earth mourn, and they shall see the Son of man coming in the clouds of heaven with power and great glory. And he shall send his angels with a great sound of a trumpet, and they shall gather together his elect from the four winds, from one end of heaven to the other." Matthew 24:30, 31.

Let men beware lest they neglect the words of Christ. As He warned His disciples of Jerusalem's destruction that they might make their escape, so He has warned the world of the day of final destruction. All who will may flee from the wrath to come. "There shall be signs in the sun, and in the moon, and in the stars; and upon the earth distress of nations." Luke 21:25. See also Matthew 24:29; Mark 13:24-26; Revelation 6:12-17. "Watch ye therefore," are Christ's words of admonition. Mark 13:35. They that heed the warning shall not be left in darkness.

The world is no more ready to credit the message for this time than were the Jews to receive the Saviour's warning concerning Jerusalem. Come when it may, the day of God will come unawares to the ungodly. When life is going on in its unvarying round; when men are absorbed in pleasure, in business, in money-making; when religious leaders are magnifying the world's progress, and people are lulled in a false security— then, as the midnight thief steals within the unguarded dwelling, so shall sudden destruction come upon the careless and ungodly, "and they shall not escape." See 1 Thessalonians 5:2-5.

Reference
1. Milman, *History of the Jews*, book 13.

2/The First Christians —Loyal and True

Jesus revealed to His disciples the experience of His people from the time when He should be taken from them, to His return in power and glory. Penetrating deep into the future, His eye discerned the fierce tempests that were to beat upon His followers in coming ages of persecution. See Matthew 24:9, 21, 22. The followers of Christ must tread the same path of reproach and suffering which their Master trod. The enmity against the world's Redeemer would be manifested against all who should believe on His name.

Paganism foresaw that should the gospel triumph, her temples and altars would be swept away; therefore the fires of persecution were kindled. Christians were stripped of their possessions and driven from their homes. Great numbers, noble and slave, rich and poor, learned and ignorant, were slain without mercy.

Beginning under Nero, persecutions continued for centuries. Christians were falsely declared to be the cause of famine, pestilence, and earthquake. Informers stood ready, for gain, to betray the innocent as rebels and pests to society. Great numbers were thrown to wild beasts or burned alive in amphitheaters. Some were crucified; others were covered with skins of wild animals and thrust into the arena to be torn by dogs. At public fetes vast multitudes assembled to enjoy the sight and greet their dying agonies with laughter and applause.

The followers of Christ were forced to seek concealment in solitary places. Beneath the hills outside the city of Rome, long galleries had been tunneled through earth and rock for miles beyond the city walls. In these underground retreats the followers of Christ buried their dead; here also, when proscribed, they found a home. Many called to mind the words of their Master, that when persecuted for Christ's sake, they were to be exceeding glad. Great would be their reward in heaven, for so the prophets had been persecuted before them. See Matthew 5:11, 12.

Songs of triumph ascended from the midst of crackling flames. By faith they saw Christ and angels gazing upon them with the deepest interest and regarding their steadfastness with approval. A voice came from the throne of God: "Be thou faithful unto death, and I will give thee a crown of life." Revelation 2:10.

In vain were Satan's efforts to destroy the church of Christ by violence. God's workmen were slain, but the gospel continued to spread and its adherents to increase. Said a Christian: "The oftener we are mown down by you, the more in number we grow; the blood of Christians is seed."[1]

Satan therefore laid his plans to war more successfully against God by planting his banner *in* the Christian church to gain by artifice what he failed to secure by force. Persecution ceased. In its stead were substituted the allurements of temporal prosperity and honor. Idolaters were led to receive a part of the Christian faith, while they rejected essential truths. They professed to accept Jesus, but had no conviction of sin and felt no need of repentance or change of heart. With some concessions on their part they proposed that Christians should make concessions, that all might unite on the platform of "belief in Christ."

Now the church was in fearful peril. Prison, torture, fire, and sword were blessings in comparison with this! Some Christians stood firm. Others were in favor of modifying their faith. Under a cloak of pretended Christianity, Satan insinuated himself into the church to corrupt their faith.

Most Christians at last consented to lower the standard. A union was formed between Christianity and paganism. Although the worshipers of idols professed to unite with the church, they still clung to their idolatry, only changing the objects of their worship to images of Jesus, and even of Mary and the saints. Unsound doctrines, superstitious rites, and idolatrous ceremonies were incorporated into the church's faith and worship. The Christian religion became corrupted, and the church lost her purity and power. Some, however, were not misled. They still maintained their fidelity to the Author of truth.

Two Classes in the Church

There have ever been two classes among those who profess to follow Christ. While one class study the Saviour's life and earnestly seek to correct their defects and conform to the Pattern, the other class shun the plain, practical truths which expose their errors. Even in her best state the church was not composed wholly of the true and sincere. Judas was connected with the disciples, that through the instruction and example of Christ he might be led to see his errors. But by indulgence in sin he invited the temptations of Satan. He became angry when his faults were reproved and thus was led to betray his Master. See Mark 14:10, 11.

Ananias and Sapphira pretended to make an entire sacrifice for God when covetously withholding a portion for themselves. The Spirit of truth revealed to the apostles the real character of these pretenders, and the judgments of God rid the church of the foul blot upon its purity. See Acts 5:1-11. As persecution came upon Christ's followers, those only who were willing to forsake all for truth desired to become His disciples. But as persecution ceased, converts were added who were less sincere, and the way was open for Satan to obtain a foothold.

When Christians consented to unite with those who were half converted from paganism, Satan exulted. He then inspired them to persecute those who remained true to God. These apostate Christians, uniting with half-pagan companions, directed their warfare against the most essential features of the doctrine of Christ. It required a desperate struggle to stand firm against deceptions and abominations introduced into the church. The Bible was not accepted as the standard of faith. The doctrine of religious freedom was termed heresy, and its upholders were proscribed.

After long conflict, the faithful saw that separation was an absolute necessity. They dared not tolerate errors fatal to their own souls and imperil the faith of their children and children's children. They felt that peace would be too dearly purchased at the sacrifice of principle. If unity could be secured only by the compromise of truth, then let there be difference, and even war.

The early Christians were indeed a peculiar people. Few in numbers, without wealth, position, or honorary titles, they were hated by the wicked, even as Abel was hated by Cain. See Genesis 4:1-10. From the days of Christ until now His faithful disciples have excited the hatred and opposition of those who love sin.

How, then, can the gospel be called a message of peace? Angels sang above the plains of Bethlehem: "Glory to God in the highest, and on earth peace, good will toward men." Luke 2:14. There is a seeming contradiction between these prophetic declarations and the words of Christ: "I come not to send peace, but a sword." Matthew 10:34. But rightly understood, the two are in perfect harmony. The gospel is a message of peace. The religion of Christ, received and obeyed, would spread peace and happiness throughout the earth. It was the mission of Jesus to reconcile men to God, and thus to one another. But the world at large is under the control of Satan, Christ's bitterest foe. The gospel presents principles of life wholly at variance with their habits and desires, and they rise against it. They hate the purity which condemns sin, and they persecute those who urge upon them its holy claims. It is in this sense that the gospel is called a sword. See Matthew 10:34.

Many who are weak in faith are ready to cast away their confidence in God because He suffers base men to prosper, while the best and purest are tormented by their cruel power. How can One who is just and merciful and infinite in power, tolerate such injustice? God has given us sufficient evidence of His love. We are not to doubt His goodness because we cannot understand His providence. Said the Saviour, "Remember the word that I said unto you, The servant is not greater than his lord. If they have persecuted me, they will also persecute you." John 15:20. Those who are called to endure torture and martyrdom are but following in the steps of God's dear Son.

The righteous are placed in the furnace of affliction that they themselves may be purified, that their example may convince others of the reality of faith and godliness, and that their consistent course may condemn the ungodly and unbelieving. God permits the wicked to prosper and to reveal their enmity against Him that all may see His justice and mercy in their utter destruction. Every act of cruelty toward God's faithful ones will be punished as though done to Christ Himself.

Paul declares that "all that will live godly in Christ Jesus shall suffer persecution." 2 Timothy 3:12. Why is it, then, that persecution seems to slumber? The only reason is that the church has conformed to the world's standard and therefore awakens no opposition. Religion in our day is not the pure and holy faith of Christ and His apostles. Because the truths of the Word of God are indifferently regarded, because there is so little vital godliness in the church, Christianity is popular with the world. Let there be a revival of the faith of the early church, and the fires of persecution will be rekindled.

Reference
1. Tertullian, *Apology*, paragraph 50.

3 / Spiritual Darkness in the Early Church

The apostle Paul declared that the day of Christ should not come "except there come a falling away first, and that man of sin be revealed, the son of perdition; who opposeth and exalteth himself above all that is called God, or that is worshipped; so that he as God sitteth in the temple of God, shewing himself that he is God." And furthermore, "the mystery of iniquity doth already work." 2 Thessalonians 2:3, 4, 7. Even at that early date the apostle saw, creeping in, errors that would prepare the way for the papacy.

Little by little, "the mystery of iniquity" carried forward its deceptive work. The customs of heathenism found their way into the Christian church, restrained for a time by fierce persecutions under paganism; but as persecution ceased, Christianity laid aside the humble simplicity of Christ for the pomp of pagan priests and rulers. The nominal conversion of Constantine caused great rejoicing. Now the work of corruption rapidly progressed. Paganism, appearing vanquished, became the conqueror. Her doctrines and superstitions were incorporated into the faith of the professed followers of Christ.

This compromise between paganism and Christianity resulted in "the man of sin" foretold in prophecy. That false religion is a masterpiece of Satan, his effort to seat himself upon the throne to rule the earth according to his will.

It is one of the leading doctrines of Romanism that the pope is invested with supreme authority over bishops and pastors in all the world. More than this, the pope has been styled "Lord God the Pope" and declared infallible. (See Appendix.) The same claim urged by Satan in the wilderness of temptation is still urged by him through the Church of Rome, and vast numbers yield him homage.

But those who reverence God meet this assumption as Christ met the wily foe: "Thou shalt worship the Lord thy God, and him only shalt thou serve." Luke 4:8. God has never appointed any man head of the church. Papal supremacy is opposed to the Scriptures. The pope can have no power over Christ's church except by usurpation. Romanists bring against Protestants the charge of willful separation from the true church. But they are the ones who departed from "the faith which was once delivered unto the saints." Jude 3.

Satan well knew that it was by the Holy Scriptures that the Saviour resisted his attacks. At every assault, Christ presented the shield of eternal truth, saying, "It is written." In order for Satan to maintain his sway over men and establish the authority of the papal usurper, he must keep them in ignorance of the Scriptures. Its sacred truths must be concealed and suppressed. For hundreds of years the circulation of the Bible was prohibited by the Roman Church. The people were forbidden to read it. Priests and prelates interpreted its teachings to sustain their pretensions. Thus the pope came to be almost universally acknowledged as the vicegerent of God on earth.

How the Sabbath was "Changed"

Prophecy declared that the papacy was to "think to change times and laws." Daniel 7:25. To afford a substitute for the worship of idols, the adoration of images and relics was gradually introduced into Christian worship. The decree of a general council (see Appendix) finally established this idolatry. Rome presumed to expunge from the law of God the second commandment, forbidding image worship, and to divide the tenth commandment in order to preserve the number.

Unconsecrated leaders of the church tampered with the fourth commandment also, to set aside the ancient Sabbath, the day which God had blessed and sanctified (Genesis 2:2, 3) and in its stead exalted the festival observed by the heathen as "the venerable day of the sun." In the first centuries the true Sabbath had been kept by all Christians, but Satan worked to bring about his object. Sunday was made a festival in honor of the resurrection of Christ. Religious services were held upon it, yet it was regarded as a day of recreation, the Sabbath being still sacredly observed.

Satan had led the Jews, before the advent of Christ, to load down the Sabbath with rigorous exactions, making it a burden. Now, taking advantage of the false light in which he had caused it to be regarded, he cast contempt upon it as a "Jewish" institution. While Christians generally continued to observe Sunday as a joyous festival, he led them to make the Sabbath a day of sadness and gloom in order to show hatred of Judaism.

The emperor Constantine issued a decree making Sunday a public festival throughout the Roman Empire. (See Appendix.) The day of the sun was reverenced by his pagan subjects and honored by Christians. He was urged to do this by the bishops of the church. Inspired by thirst for power, they perceived that if the same day was observed by both Christians and heathen, it would advance the power and glory of the church. But while many God-fearing Christians were gradually led to regard Sunday as possessing a degree of sacredness, they still held the true Sabbath and observed it in obedience to the fourth commandment.

The archdeceiver had not completed his work. He was resolved to exercise his power through his vicegerent, the proud pontiff who claimed to represent Christ. Vast councils were held in which dignitaries were convened from all the world. In nearly every council the Sabbath was pressed down a little lower, while Sunday was exalted. Thus the pagan festival came finally to be honored as a divine institution, while the Bible Sabbath was pronounced a relic of Judaism and its observance declared accursed.

The apostate had succeeded in exalting himself "above all that is called God, or that is worshiped." 2 Thessalonians 2:4. He had dared to change the only precept of the divine law that points to the true and living God. In the fourth commandment, God is revealed as the Creator. As a memorial of the work of creation, the seventh day was sanctified as a rest day for man, designed to keep the living God ever before the minds of men as the object of worship. Satan strives to turn men from obedience to God's law; therefore he directs his efforts especially against that commandment which points to God as the Creator.

Protestants now urge that the resurrection of Christ on Sunday made it the Christian Sabbath. But no such honor was given to the day by Christ or His apostles. The observance of Sunday had its origin in that "mystery of lawlessness" (2 Thessalonians 2:7, RV) which, even in Paul's day, had begun its work. What reason can be given for a change which the Scriptures do not sanction?

In the sixth century, the bishop of Rome was declared to be the head over the entire church. Paganism had given place to the papacy. The dragon had given the beast "his power, and his seat, and great authority." Revelation 13:2. (See Appendix.)

Now began the 1260 years of papal oppression foretold in the prophecies of Daniel and the Revelation. Daniel 7:25; Revelation 13:5-7. Christians were forced to choose either to yield their integrity and accept the papal ceremonies and worship, or to wear away their lives in dungeons, or to suffer death. Now were fulfilled the words of Jesus: "Ye shall be betrayed both by parents, and brethren, and kinsfolks, and friends; and some of you shall they cause to be put to death. And ye shall be hated of all men for my name's sake.'' Luke 21:16, 17.

The world became a vast battlefield. For hundreds of years the church of Christ found refuge in seclusion and obscurity. ''The woman fled into the wilderness, where she hath a place prepared of God, that they should feed her there a thousand two hundred and threescore days.'' Revelation 12:6.

The accession of the Roman Church to power marked the beginning of the Dark Ages. Faith was transferred from Christ to the pope of Rome. Instead of trusting in the Son of God for forgiveness of sins and for eternal salvation, the people looked to the pope and to the priests to whom he delegated authority. The pope was their earthly mediator. He stood in the place of God to them. A deviation from his requirements was sufficient cause for severe punishment. Thus the minds of the people were turned away from God to fallible and cruel men, nay, more, to the prince of darkness himself who exercised his power through them. When the Scriptures are suppressed and man comes to regard himself as supreme, we look only for fraud, deception, and debasing iniquity.

Days of Peril for the Church

The faithful standard-bearers were few. At times it seemed that error would wholly prevail, and true religion would be banished from the earth. The gospel was lost sight of, and the people were burdened with rigorous exactions. They were taught to trust to works of their own to atone for sin. Long pilgrimages, acts of penance, the worship of relics, the erection of churches, shrines, and altars, the payment of large sums to the church—these were enjoined to appease the wrath of God or to secure His favor.

About the close of the eighth century, papists put forth the claim that in the first ages of the church the bishops of Rome had possessed the same spiritual power which they now assumed. Ancient writings were forged by monks. Decrees of councils before unheard of were discovered, establishing the universal supremacy of the pope from the earliest times. (See Appendix.)

The few faithful builders upon the sure foundation (1 Corinthians 3:10, 11) were perplexed. Wearied with the constant struggle against persecution, fraud, and every other obstacle that Satan could devise, some who had been faithful became disheartened. For the sake of peace and security for their property and their lives, they turned away from the sure foundation. Others were undaunted by the opposition of their enemies.

Image worship became general. Candles were burned before images and prayers offered to them. The most absurd customs prevailed. Reason itself seemed to have lost its sway. While priests and bishops were themselves pleasure-loving and corrupt, the people who looked to them for guidance would be sunken in ignorance and vice.

In the eleventh century, Pope Gregory VII proclaimed that the church had never erred, nor would it ever err, according to the Scriptures. But Scripture proofs did not accompany the assertion. The proud pontiff also claimed power to depose emperors. An illustration of the tyrannical character of this advocate of infallibility was his treatment of the German emperor, Henry IV. For presuming to disregard the pope's authority, this monarch was excommunicated and dethroned. His own princes were encouraged in rebellion against him by the papal mandate.

Henry felt the necessity of making peace with Rome. With his wife and faithful servant he crossed the Alps in midwinter, that he might humble himself before the pope. Upon reaching Gregory's castle, he was conducted into an outer court. There, in the severe cold of winter, with uncovered head and naked feet, he awaited the pope's permission to come into his presence. Not until he had continued three days fasting and making confession, did the pontiff grant him pardon. Even then it was only upon condition that the emperor should await the sanction of the pope before resuming the insignia or exercising the power of royalty. Gregory, elated with his triumph, boasted that it was his duty to pull down the pride of kings.

How striking the contrast between this haughty pontiff and Christ, who represents Himself as pleading at the door of the heart for admittance. He taught His disciples: "Whosoever will be chief among you, let him be your servant." Matthew 20:27.

Even before the establishment of the papacy the teachings of heathen philosophers had exerted an influence in the church. Many still clung to the tenets of pagan philosophy and urged its study upon others as a means of extending their influence among the heathen. Serious errors were thus introduced into the Christian faith.

How False Doctrines Came In

Prominent among these was the belief in man's natural immortality and his consciousness in death. This doctrine laid the foundation upon which Rome established the invocation of saints and the adoration of the Virgin Mary. From this sprang also the heresy of eternal torment for the finally impenitent, which was early incorporated into the papal faith.

The way was prepared for still another invention of paganism—purgatory, employed to terrify the superstitious multitudes. This heresy affirmed the existence of a place of torment in which souls of such as have not merited eternal damnation suffer punishment for their sins, and from which, when freed from impurity, they are admitted to heaven. (See Appendix.)

Still another fabrication was needed to enable Rome to profit by the fears and vices of her adherents: the doctrine of indulgences. Full remission of sins, past, present, and future, was promised to all who would enlist in the pontiff's wars to punish his enemies or to exterminate those who dared deny his spiritual suprem-acy. By payment of money to the church, people might free themselves from sin and also release the souls of deceased friends who were confined in the tormenting flames. By such means did Rome fill her coffers and sustain the magnificence, luxury, and vice of the pre-tended representatives of Him who had not where to lay His head. (See Appendix.)

The Lord's supper had been supplanted by the idola-trous sacrifice of the mass. Papal priests pretended to convert the simple bread and wine into the actual "body and blood of Christ."[1] With blasphemous pre-sumption, they openly claimed the power of creating God, the Creator of all things. Christians were re-quired, on pain of death, to avow their faith in this Heaven-insulting heresy.

In the thirteenth century was established that most terrible engine of the papacy—the Inquisition. In their secret councils Satan and his angels controlled the minds of evil men. Unseen in the midst stood an angel of God, taking the fearful record of their iniquitous de-crees and writing the history of deeds too horrible to appear to human eyes. "Babylon the great" was "drunken with the blood of the saints." See Revela-tion 17:5, 6. The mangled forms of millions of martyrs cried to God for vengeance upon that apostate power.

Popery had become the world's despot. Kings and emperors bowed to the decrees of the Roman pontiff. For hundreds of years the doctrines of Rome were im-plicitly received. Its clergy were honored and liberally sustained. Never since has the Roman Church attained to greater dignity, magnificence, or power.

But "the noon of the papacy was the midnight of the world."[2] The Scriptures were almost unknown. The papal leaders hated the light which would reveal their sins. God's law, the standard of righteousness, having been removed, they practiced vice without restraint. The palaces of popes and prelates were scenes of vile debauchery. Some of the pontiffs were guilty of crimes so revolting that secular rulers endeavored to depose them as monsters too vile to be tolerated. For centuries Europe made no progress in learning, arts, or civilization. A moral and intellectual paralysis had fallen upon Christendom.

Such were the results of banishing the Word of God!

References

1. Cardinal Wiseman's Lectures on *"The Real Presence,"* lecture 8, sec. 3, par. 26.

2. Wylie, *History of Protestantism*, book 1, chap. 4.

4/The Waldenses Defend the Faith

During the long period of papal supremacy, there were witnesses for God who cherished faith in Christ as the only mediator between God and man. They held the Bible as the only rule of life, and hallowed the true Sabbath. They were branded as heretics, their writings suppressed, misrepresented, or mutilated. Yet they stood firm.

They have little place in human records, except in the accusations of their persecutors. Everything "heretical," whether persons or writings, Rome sought to destroy. Rome endeavored also to destroy every record of her cruelty toward dissenters. Before the invention of printing, books were few in number; therefore there was little to prevent the Romanists from carrying out their purpose. No sooner had the papacy obtained power than she stretched out her arms to crush all that refused to acknowledge her sway.

In Great Britain primitive Christianity had early taken root, uncorrupted by Romish apostasy. Persecution from pagan emperors was the only gift the first churches of Britain received from Rome. Many Christians fleeing persecution in England found refuge in Scotland. Thence truth was carried to Ireland, and in these countries it was received with gladness.

When the Saxons invaded Britain, heathenism gained control, and the Christians were forced to retreat to the mountains. In Scotland, a century later, the light shone out to far-distant lands. From Ireland came Columba and his colaborers, who made the lonely island of Iona the center of their missionary labors. Among these evangelists was an observer of the Bible Sabbath, and thus this truth was introduced among the people. A school was established at Iona, from which missionaries went out to Scotland, England, Germany, Switzerland, and even Italy.

Rome Meets Bible Religion

But Rome resolved to bring Britain under her supremacy. In the sixth century her missionaries undertook the conversion of the heathen Saxons. As the work progressed, the papal leaders encountered the primitive Christians—simple, humble, and scriptural in character, doctrine, and manners. The former manifested the superstition, pomp, and arrogance of popery. Rome demanded that these Christian churches acknowledge the sovereign pontiff. The Britons replied that the pope was not entitled to supremacy in the church and they could render to him only that submission due every follower of Christ. They knew no other master than Christ.

Now the true spirit of the papacy was revealed. Said the Romish leader: "If you will not receive brethren who bring you peace, you shall receive enemies who will bring you war."[1] War and deception were employed against these witnesses for Bible faith, until the churches of Britain were destroyed or forced to submit to the pope.

In lands beyond the jurisdiction of Rome, for centuries Christian bodies remained almost wholly free from papal corruption. They continued to regard the Bible as the only rule of faith. These Christians believed in the perpetuity of the law of God and observed the Sabbath of the fourth commandment. Churches that held to this faith and practice existed in Central Africa and among the Armenians of Asia.

Of those who resisted the papal power, the Waldenses stood foremost. In the very land where popery had fixed its seat, the churches of Piedmont maintained their independence. But the time came when Rome insisted upon their submission. Some, however, refused to yield to pope or prelate, determined to preserve the purity and simplicity of their faith. A separation took place. Those who adhered to the ancient faith now withdrew. Some, forsaking their native Alps, raised the banner of truth in foreign lands. Others retreated to the rocky fastnesses of the mountains and there preserved their freedom to worship God.

Their religious belief was founded upon the written Word of God. Those humble peasants, shut away from the world, had not by themselves arrived at truth in opposition to the dogmas of the apostate church. Their religious belief was their inheritance from their fathers. They contended for the faith of the apostolic church. "The church in the wilderness," and not the proud hierarchy enthroned in the world's great capital, was the true church of Christ, the guardian of the treasures of truth which God committed to His people to be given to the world.

Among the leading causes that had led to the separation of the true church from Rome was the hatred of the latter toward the Bible Sabbath. As foretold by prophecy, the papal power trampled the law of God in the dust. Churches under the papacy were compelled to honor Sunday. Amid the prevailing error many of the true people of God became so bewildered that while they observed the Sabbath, they refrained from labor also on Sunday. But this did not satisfy the papal leaders. They demanded that the Sabbath be profaned, and they denounced those who dared to show it honor.

Hundreds of years before the Reformation the Waldenses possessed the Bible in their native tongue. This rendered them the special objects of persecution. They declared Rome to be the apostate Babylon of the Apocalypse. At the peril of their lives they stood up to resist her corruptions. Through ages of apostasy there were Waldenses who denied the supremacy of Rome, rejected image worship as idolatry, and kept the true Sabbath. (See Appendix.)

Behind the lofty bulwarks of the mountains the Waldenses found a hiding place. Those faithful exiles pointed their children to the heights towering above them in majesty and spoke of Him whose word is as enduring as the everlasting hills. God had set fast the mountains; no arm but that of Infinite Power could move them. In like manner He had established His law. The arm of man could as readily uproot the mountains and hurl them into the sea, as change one precept of the law of God. Those pilgrims indulged no repining because of the hardships of their lot; they were never lonely amid the mountain solitudes. They rejoiced in their freedom to worship. From many a lofty cliff they chanted praise, and the armies of Rome could not silence their songs of thanksgiving.

Valued Principles of Truth

Principles of truth they valued above houses and lands, friends, kindred, even life itself. From earliest childhood the youth were taught to regard sacredly the claims of the law of God. Copies of the Bible were rare; therefore its precious words were committed to memory. Many were able to repeat large portions of both the Old and the New Testament.

They were educated from childhood to endure hardness and to think and act for themselves. They were taught to bear responsibilities, to be guarded in speech, and to understand the wisdom of silence. One indiscreet word in the hearing of their enemies might imperil the lives of hundreds of brethren, for as wolves hunting prey, the enemies of truth pursued those who dared to claim freedom of religious faith.

The Waldenses with persevering patience toiled for their bread. Every spot of tillable land among the mountains was carefully improved. Economy and self-denial formed a part of the education the children received. The process was laborious but wholesome, just what man needs in his fallen state. The youth were taught that all their powers belonged to God, to be developed for His service.

The Vaudois churches resembled the church of apostolic times. Rejecting the supremacy of pope and prelate, they held the Bible as the only infallible authority. Their pastors, unlike the lordly priests of Rome, fed the flock of God, leading them to the green pastures and living fountains of His Holy Word. The people assembled, not in magnificent churches or grand cathedrals, but in the Alpine valleys, or, in time of danger, in some rocky stronghold, to listen to the words of truth from the servants of Christ. The pastors not only preached the gospel, they visited the sick and labored to promote harmony and brotherly love. Like Paul the tentmaker, each learned some trade by which, if necessary, to provide for his own support.

From their pastors the youth received instruction. The Bible was made the chief study. The Gospels of Matthew and John were committed to memory, with many of the Epistles.

By untiring labor, sometimes in the dark caverns of the earth, by the light of torches, the Sacred Scriptures were written out, verse by verse. Angels from heaven surrounded these faithful workers.

Satan had urged papal priests and prelates to bury the Word of truth beneath the rubbish of error and superstition. But in a wonderful manner it was preserved uncorrupted through all the ages of darkness. Like the ark upon the billowy deep, the Word of God outrides the storms that threaten it with destruction. As the mine has rich veins of gold and silver hidden beneath the surface, so the Holy Scriptures have treasures of truth revealed only to the humble, prayerful seeker. God designed the Bible to be a lessonbook to all mankind as a revelation of Himself. Every truth discerned is a fresh disclosure of the character of its Author.

From their schools in the mountains some youth were sent to institutions of learning in France or Italy, where was a more extended field for study and observation than in their native Alps. The youth thus sent were exposed to temptation. They encountered Satan's agents who urged upon them subtle heresies and dangerous deceptions. But their education from childhood prepared them for this.

In the schools whither they went they were not to make confidants of any. Their garments were so prepared as to conceal their greatest treasure—the Scriptures. Whenever they could they cautiously placed some portion in the way of those whose hearts seemed open to receive truth. Converts to the true faith were won in these institutions of learning, and frequently its principles permeated the entire school. Yet the papal leaders could not trace the so-called corrupting "heresy" to its source.

Young People Trained as Missionaries

The Vaudois Christians felt a solemn responsibility to let their light shine. By the power of God's Word they sought to break the bondage which Rome had imposed. The Vaudois ministers were to serve three years in some mission field before taking charge of a church at home—a fitting introduction to the pastor's life in times that tried men's souls. The youth saw before them, not earthly wealth and glory, but toil and danger and possibly a martyr's fate. The missionaries went out two and two, as Jesus sent forth His disciples.

To have made known their mission would have ensured its defeat. Every minister possessed a knowledge of some trade or profession, and the missionaries prosecuted their work under cover of a secular calling, usually that of merchant or peddler. "They carried silks, jewelry, and other articles, . . . and were welcomed as merchants where they would have been spurned as missionaries."[2] They secretly carried copies of the Bible, in whole or in part. Often an interest to read God's Word was awakened, and some portion was left with those who desired it.

With naked feet and garments coarse and travel-stained, these missionaries passed through great cities and penetrated to distant lands. Churches sprang up in their path, and the blood of martyrs witnessed for the truth. Veiled and silent, the Word of God was meeting a glad reception in the homes and hearts of men.

The Waldenses believed that the end of all things was not far distant. As they studied the Bible they were deeply impressed with their duty to make known to others its saving truths. They found comfort, hope, and peace in believing in Jesus. As the light made glad their hearts, they longed to shed its beams upon those in the darkness of papal error.

Under the guidance of pope and priest, multitudes were taught to trust to their good works to save them. They were ever looking to themselves, their minds dwelling upon their sinful condition, afflicting soul and body, yet finding no relief. Thousands spent their lives in convent cells. By oft-repeated fasts and scourgings, by midnight vigils, by prostration upon cold, damp stones, by long pilgrimages—haunted with the fear of God's avenging wrath—many suffered on, until exhausted nature gave way. Without one ray of hope they sank into the tomb.

Sinners Pointed to Christ

The Waldenses longed to open to these starving souls messages of peace in the promises of God and to point them to Christ as their only hope of salvation. The doctrine that good works can atone for transgression they held to be based upon falsehood. The merits of a crucified and risen Saviour are the foundation of the Christian faith. The dependence of the soul upon Christ must be as close as that of a limb to the body or of a branch to the vine.

The teachings of popes and priests had led men to look upon God and even Christ as stern and forbidding, so devoid of sympathy with man that the mediation of priests and saints must be invoked. Those whose minds had been enlightened longed to clear away the obstructions which Satan had piled up, that men might come directly to God, confess their sins, and obtain pardon and peace.

Invading the Kingdom of Satan

The Vaudois missionary cautiously produced the carefully written portions of the Holy Scriptures. The light of truth penetrated many a darkened mind, until the Sun of Righteousness shone into the heart with healing in His beams. Often the hearer desired some portion of Scripture to be repeated, as if he would assure himself he had heard aright.

Many saw how vain is the mediation of men in behalf of the sinner. They exclaimed with rejoicing, "Christ is my priest; His blood is my sacrifice; His altar is my confessional." So great was the flood of light shed upon them, that they seemed transported to heaven. All fear of death was banished. They could now covet prison if they might thereby honor their Redeemer.

In secret places the Word of God was brought forth and read, sometimes to a single soul, sometimes to a little company longing for light. Often the entire night was spent in this manner. Often would words like these be uttered: "Will God accept *my* offering? Will He smile upon *me*? Will He pardon *me?*" The answer was read, "Come unto me, all ye that labor and are heavy laden, and I will give you rest." Matthew 11:28.

Those happy souls returned to their homes to diffuse light, to repeat to others, as well as they could, their new experience. They had found the true and living way! Scripture spoke to the hearts of those longing for truth.

The messenger of truth went on his way. In many instances his hearers had not asked whence he came or whither he went. They had been so overwhelmed that they had not thought to question him. Could he have been an angel from heaven? they queried.

In many cases the messenger of truth had made his

way to other lands or was wearing out his life in some dungeon or perhaps his bones were whitening where he had witnessed for the truth. But the words he had left behind were doing their work.

The papal leaders saw danger from the labors of these humble itinerants. The light of truth would sweep away the heavy clouds of error that enveloped the people; it would direct minds to God alone and eventually destroy the supremacy of Rome.

This people, holding the faith of the ancient church, was a constant testimony to Rome's apostasy and therefore excited hatred and persecution. Their refusal to surrender the Scriptures was an offense that Rome could not tolerate.

Rome Determines to Destroy the Waldenses

Now began the most terrible crusades against God's people in their mountain homes. Inquisitors were put upon their track. Again and again were their fertile lands laid waste, their dwellings and chapels swept away. No charge could be brought against the moral character of this proscribed class. Their grand offense was that they would not worship God according to the will of the pope. For this "crime" every insult and torture that men or devils could invent was heaped upon them.

When Rome determined to exterminate the hated sect, a bull [edict] was issued by the pope condemning them as heretics and delivering them to slaughter. (See Appendix.) They were not accused as idlers, or dishonest, or disorderly; but it was declared that they had an appearance of piety and sanctity that seduced "the sheep of the true fold." This bull called upon all members of the church to join the crusade against the heretics. As an incentive it "released all who joined the crusade from any oaths they might have taken; it legitimatized their title to any property they might have illegally acquired, and promised remission of all their sins to such as should kill any heretic. It annulled all contracts made in favor of Vaudois, forbade all persons to give them any aid whatever, and empowered all persons to take possession of their property."[3] This document clearly reveals the roar of the dragon, and not the voice of Christ. The same spirit that crucified Christ and slew the apostles, that moved the bloodthirsty Nero against the faithful in his day, was at work to rid the earth of those who were beloved of God.

Notwithstanding the crusades against them and the inhuman butchery to which they were subjected, this God-fearing people continued to send out missionaries to scatter the precious truth. They were hunted to the death, yet their blood watered the seed sown and yielded fruit.

Thus the Waldenses witnessed for God centuries before Luther. They planted the seeds of the Reformation that began in the time of Wycliffe, grew broad and deep in the days of Luther, and is to be carried forward to the close of time.

References
1. J. H. Merle D'Aubigne, *History of the Reformation of the Sixteenth Century*, bk. 17, ch. 2.
2. Wylie, bk. 1, ch. 7.
3. Wylie, bk. 16, ch. 1.

5/ The Light Breaks in England

God had not suffered His Word to be wholly destroyed. In different countries of Europe men were moved by the Spirit of God to search for truth as for hid treasures. Providentially guided to the Holy Scriptures, they were willing to accept light at any cost to themselves. Though they did not see all things clearly, they were enabled to perceive many long-buried truths.

The time had come for the Scriptures to be given to the people in their native tongue. The world had passed its midnight. In many lands appeared tokens of the coming dawn.

In the fourteenth century the "morning star of the Reformation" arose in England. John Wycliffe was noted at college for his fervent piety as well as his sound scholarship. Educated in scholastic philosophy, the canons of the church, and civil law, he was prepared to engage in the great struggle for civil and religious liberty. He had acquired the intellectual discipline of the schools, and he understood the tactics of the schoolmen. The extent and thoroughness of his knowledge commanded the respect of both friends and foes. His enemies were prevented from casting contempt upon the cause of reform by exposing the ignorance or weakness of its supporter.

While Wycliffe was still at college, he entered upon the study of the Scriptures. Heretofore Wycliffe had felt a great want, which neither his scholastic studies nor the teaching of the church could satisfy. In the Word of God he found that which he had sought in vain. Here he saw Christ set forth as the only advocate for man. He determined to proclaim the truths he had discovered.

Wycliffe did not, at the opening of his work, set himself in opposition to Rome. But the more clearly he discerned the errors of the papacy, the more earnestly he presented the teaching of the Bible. He saw that Rome had forsaken the Word of God for human tradition. He fearlessly accused the priesthood of having banished the Scriptures, and demanded that the Bible be restored to the people and that its authority be again established in the church. He was an able and eloquent preacher, and his daily life was a demonstration of the truths he preached. His knowledge of the Scriptures, the purity of his life, and his courage and integrity won general esteem. Many saw the iniquity in the Roman Church. They hailed with unconcealed joy the truths brought to view by Wycliffe. But the papal leaders were filled with rage; this Reformer was gaining an influence greater than their own.

A Keen Detector of Error

Wycliffe was a keen detector of error and struck fearlessly against abuses sanctioned by Rome. While chaplain for the king, he took a bold stand against payment of tribute claimed by the pope from the English monarch. Papal assumption of authority over secular rulers was contrary to both reason and revelation. The demands of the pope had excited indignation, and Wycliffe's teachings influenced the leading minds of the nation. The king and the nobles united in refusing the payment of tribute.

Mendicant friars swarmed in England, casting a blight upon the greatness and prosperity of the nation. The monks' lives of idleness and beggary were not only a drain upon the resources of the people, they brought useful labor into contempt. Youth were demoralized and corrupted. Many were induced to devote themselves to a monastic life not only without the consent of their parents, but even without their knowledge and contrary to their commands. By this "monstrous inhumanity," as Luther afterward styled it, "savoring more of the wolf and the tyrant than of the Christian and the man," were the hearts of children steeled against their parents.[1]

Even students in the universities were deceived by the monks and induced to join their orders. Once fast in the snare it was impossible to obtain freedom. Many parents refused to send their sons to the universities. The schools languished, and ignorance prevailed.

The pope had bestowed on these monks the power to hear confessions and grant pardon—a source of great evil. Bent on enhancing their gains, the friars were so ready to grant absolution that criminals resorted to them, and the worst vices rapidly increased. Gifts that should have relieved the sick and the poor went to the monks. The wealth of the friars was constantly increasing, and their magnificent edifices and luxurious tables made more apparent the growing poverty of the nation. Yet the friars continued to maintain their hold on the superstitious multitudes and led them to believe that all religious duty was comprised in acknowledging the supremacy of the pope, adoring the saints, and making gifts to the monks. This was sufficient to secure a place in heaven!

Wycliffe, with clear insight, struck at the root of the evil, declaring that the system itself was false and should be abolished. Discussion and inquiry were awakening. Many were led to question whether they should not seek pardon from God rather than from the pontiff of Rome. (See Appendix.) "The monks and priests of Rome," said they, "are eating us away like a cancer. God must deliver us, or the people will perish."[2] Begging monks claimed they were following the Saviour's example, declaring that Jesus and His disciples had been supported by the charities of the people. This claim led many to the Bible to learn the truth for themselves.

Wycliffe began to write and publish tracts against the friars, to call the people to the teachings of the Bible and its Author. In no more effectual way could he have undertaken the overthrow of that mammoth fabric which the pope had erected, in which millions were held captive.

Wycliffe, called to defend the rights of the English crown against the encroachments of Rome, was appointed a royal ambassador in the Netherlands. Here he was brought into communicaton with ecclesiastics from France, Italy, and Spain, and had opportunity to look behind the scenes hidden from him in England. In these representatives from the papal court he read the true character of the hierarchy. He returned to England to repeat his former teachings with greater zeal, declaring that pride and deception were the gods of Rome.

After his return to England, Wycliffe received from the king the appointment to the rectory of Lutterworth. This was an assurance that the monarch had not been displeased by his plain speaking. Wycliffe's influence was felt in molding the belief of the nation.

Papal thunders were soon hurled against him. Three bulls were dispatched commanding immediate measures to silence the teacher of "heresy."[3]

The arrival of the papal bulls laid upon all England a command for the imprisonment of the heretic. (See Appendix.) It appeared certain that Wycliffe must soon fall to the vengeance of Rome. But He who declared to one of old, "Fear not: . . . I am thy shield" (Genesis 15:1), stretched out His hand to protect His servant. Death came, not to the Reformer, but to the pontiff who had decreed his destruction.

The death of Gregory XI was followed by the election of two rival popes. (See Appendix.) Each called upon the faithful to make war on the other, enforcing his demands by terrible anathemas against his adversaries and promises of rewards in heaven to his supporters. The rival factions had all they could do to attack each other, and Wycliffe for a time had rest.

The schism, with all the strife and corruption which it caused, prepared the way for the Reformation by enabling the people to see what the papacy really was. Wycliffe called upon the people to consider whether these two popes were not speaking the truth in condemning each other as the antichrist.

Determined that the light should be carried to every part of England, Wycliffe organized a body of preachers, simple, devout men who loved the truth and desired to extend it. These men, teaching in market places, in the streets of the great cities, and in country lanes, sought out the aged, the sick, and the poor, and opened to them the glad tidings of the grace of God.

At Oxford, Wycliffe preached the Word of God in the halls of the university. He received the title of "the Gospel Doctor." But the greatest work of his life was to be the translation of the Scriptures into English, so that every man in England might read the wonderful works of God.

Attacked by Dangerous Illness

But suddenly his labors were stopped. Though not yet sixty, unceasing toil, study, and the assaults of enemies had told upon his strength and made him prematurely old. He was attacked by a dangerous illness. The friars thought he would repent of the evil he had done the church, and they hurried to his chamber to listen to his confession. "You have death on your lips," they said; "be touched by your faults, and retract in our presence all that you have said to our injury."

The Reformer listened in silence. Then he bade his attendant raise him in his bed. Gazing steadily upon them, he said in the firm, strong voice which had so often caused them to tremble, "I shall not die, but live; and again declare the evil deeds of the friars."[4] Astonished and abashed, the monks hurried from the room.

Wycliffe lived to place in the hands of his country-

men the most powerful of all weapons against Rome—
the Bible, the Heaven-appointed agent to liberate, enlighten, and evangelize the people. Wycliffe knew that
only a few years for labor remained for him; he saw the
opposition he must meet; but encouraged by the promises of God's Word, he went forward. In the full vigor
of his intellectual powers, rich in experience, he had
been prepared by God's providence for this, the greatest of his labors. The Reformer in his rectory at
Lutterworth, unheeding the storm that raged without,
applied himself to his chosen task.

At last the work was completed—the first English
translation of the Bible. The Reformer had placed in
the hands of the English people a light which should
never be extinguished. He had done more to break the
fetters of ignorance and to liberate and elevate his
country than was ever achieved by victories on fields
of battle.

Only by wearisome labor could copies of the Bible
be multiplied. So great was the interest to obtain the
book that it was with difficulty that copyists could supply the demand. Wealthy purchasers desired the whole
Bible. Others bought only a portion. In many cases,
families united to purchase a copy. Wycliffe's Bible
soon found its way to the homes of the people.

Wycliffe now taught the distinctive doctrines of
Protestantism—salvation through faith in Christ and
the sole infallibility of the Scriptures. The new faith
was accepted by nearly one half of the people of England.

The appearance of the Scriptures brought dismay to
the authorities of the church. There was at this time no
law in England prohibiting the Bible, for it had never
before been published in the language of the people.
Such laws were afterward enacted and rigorously enforced.

Again the papal leaders plotted to silence the Reformer's voice. First, a synod of bishops declared his
writings heretical. Winning the young king, Richard II,

to their side, they obtained a royal decree consigning to prison all who should hold the condemned doctrines.

Wycliffe appealed from the synod to Parliament. He fearlessly arraigned the hierarchy before the national council and demanded reform of the enormous abuses sanctioned by the church. His enemies were brought to confusion. It had been expected that the Reformer, in his old age, alone and friendless, would bow to the authority of the crown. But instead, Parliament, roused by the stirring appeals of Wycliffe, repealed the persecuting edict, and the Reformer was again at liberty.

A third time he was brought to trial, and now before the highest ecclesiastical tribunal in the kingdom. Here at last the Reformer's work would be stopped. So thought the papists. If they could accomplish their purpose, Wycliffe would leave the court only for the flames.

Wycliffe Refuses to Retract

But Wycliffe did not retract. He fearlessly maintained his teachings and repelled the accusations of his persecutors. He summoned his hearers before the divine tribunal and weighed their sophistries and deceptions in the balances of eternal truth. The power of the Holy Spirit was upon the hearers. As arrows from the Lord's quiver, the Reformer's words pierced their hearts. The charge of heresy, which they had brought against him, he threw back on them.

"With whom, think you," he said, "are ye contending? with an old man on the brink of the grave? No! with Truth—Truth which is stronger than you, and will overcome you."[5] So saying, he withdrew and not one of his adversaries attempted to prevent him.

Wycliffe's work was almost done, but once more he was to bear witness for the gospel. He was summoned for trial before the papal tribunal at Rome, which had so often shed the blood of the saints. A shock of palsy made it impossible for him to perform the journey. But though his voice was not to be heard at Rome, he could speak by letter. The Reformer wrote the pope a letter, which, while respectful and Christian in spirit, was a keen rebuke to the pomp and pride of the papal see.

Wycliffe presented to the pope and his cardinals the meekness and humility of Christ, exhibiting not only to themselves but to all Christendom the contrast between them and the Master whose representatives they professed to be.

Wycliffe fully expected that his life would be the price of his fidelity. The king, the pope, and the bishops were united to accomplish his ruin, and it seemed certain that a few months at most would bring him to the stake. But his courage was unshaken.

The man who for a whole lifetime had stood boldly in defense of the truth was not to fall a victim of the hatred of its foes. The Lord had been his protector; and now, when his enemies felt sure of their prey, God's hand removed him beyond their reach. In his church at Lutterworth, as he was about to dispense the communion, he fell stricken with palsy, and in a short time yielded up his life.

Herald of a New Era

God had put the word of truth in Wycliffe's mouth. His life was protected and his labors prolonged until a foundation was laid for the Reformation. There was none who went before Wycliffe from whose work he could shape his system of reform. He was the herald of a new era. Yet in the truth which he presented there was a unity and completeness which reformers who followed did not exceed and which some did not reach. So firm and true was the framework, that it needed not to be reconstructed by those who came after him.

The great movement that Wycliffe inaugurated to set free the nations so long bound to Rome had its spring in the Bible. Here was the source of that stream of blessing which has flowed down the ages since the fourteenth century. Educated to regard Rome as the infallible authority and to accept with unquestioning reverence the teachings and customs of a thousand years, Wycliffe turned away from all these to listen to God's Holy Word. Instead of the church speaking through the pope, he declared the only true authority to be the voice of God speaking through His Word. And he taught that the Holy Spirit is its only interpreter.

Wycliffe was one of the greatest of the Reformers. He was equaled by few who came after him. Purity of life, unwearying diligence in study and labor, incorruptible integrity, and Christlike love, characterized the first of the Reformers.

It was the Bible that made him what he was. The study of the Bible will ennoble every thought, feeling, and aspiration as no other study can. It gives stability of purpose, courage, and fortitude. An earnest, reverent study of the Scriptures would give the world men of stronger intellect, as well as of nobler principle, than has ever resulted from the ablest training that human philosophy affords.

Wycliffe's followers, known as Wycliffites and Lollards, scattered to other lands, carrying the gospel. Now that their leader was removed, the preachers labored with even greater zeal than before. Multitudes flocked to listen. Some of the nobility, and even the wife of the king, were among the converts. In many places the idolatrous symbols of Romanism were removed from the churches.

But soon pitiless persecution burst upon those who had dared to accept the Bible as their guide. For the first time in the history of England the stake was decreed against the disciples of the gospel. Martyrdom succeeded martyrdom. Hunted as foes of the church and traitors to the realm, the advocates of truth continued to preach in secret places, finding shelter in the humble homes of the poor, and often hiding away even in dens and caves.

A calm, patient protest against the corruption of religious faith continued to be uttered for centuries. The Christians of that early time had learned to love God's

Word and patiently suffered for its sake. Many sacrificed their worldly possessions for Christ. Those permitted to dwell in their homes gladly sheltered their banished brethren, and when they too were driven forth, they cheerfully accepted the lot of the outcast. The number was not small who bore fearless testimony to the truth in dungeon cells and in the midst of torture and flame, rejoicing that they were counted worthy to know "the fellowship of his sufferings."

The papists' hatred could not be satisfied while Wycliffe's body rested in the grave. More than forty years after his death his bones were exhumed and publicly burned, and the ashes thrown into a neighboring brook. "This brook," says an old writer, "hath conveyed his ashes into Avon, Avon into Severn, Severn into the narrow seas, they into the main ocean. And thus the ashes of Wycliffe are the emblem of his doctrine, which now is dispersed all the world over."[6]

Through the writings of Wycliffe, John Huss of Bohemia was led to renounce many of the errors of Romanism. From Bohemia the work extended to other lands. A divine hand was preparing the way for the Great Reformation.

References
1. Barnas Sears, *The Life of Luther*, pp. 70, 69.
2. D'Aubigne, bk. 17, ch. 7.
3. Augustus Neander, *General History of the Christian Religion and Church*, period 6, sec. 2, pt. 1, par. 8. See also Appendix.
4. D'Aubigne, bk. 17, ch. 7.
5. Wylie, bk. 2, ch. 13.
6. T. Fuller, *Church History of Britain*, bk. 4, sec. 2, par. 54.

6 / Two Heroes Face Death

As early as the ninth century the Bible had been translated and public worship was conducted in the language of the people of Bohemia. But Gregory VII was intent upon enslaving the people, and a bull was issued forbidding public worship in the Bohemian tongue. The pope declared that "it was pleasing to the Omnipotent that His worship should be celebrated in an unknown language."[1] But Heaven had provided agencies for the preservation of the church. Many Waldenses and Albigenses, driven by persecution, came to Bohemia. They labored zealously in secret. Thus the true faith was preserved.

Before the days of Huss there were men in Bohemia who condemned the corruption in the church. The fears of the hierarchy were roused, and persecution was opened against the gospel. After a time it was decreed that all who departed from the Romish worship should be burned. But the Christians looked forward to the triumph of their cause. One declared when dying, "There shall arise one from among the common people, without sword or authority, and against him they shall not be able to prevail."[2] Already one was rising, whose testimony against Rome would stir the nations.

John Huss was of humble birth and was early left an orphan by the death of his father. His pious mother, regarding education and the fear of God as the most valuable of possessions, sought to secure this heritage for her son. Huss studied at the provincial school, then repaired to the university at Prague, receiving admission as a charity scholar.

At the university, Huss soon distinguished himself by his rapid progress. His gentle, winning deportment gained him universal esteem. He was a sincere adherent of the Roman Church and an earnest seeker for the spiritual blessings it professes to bestow. After completing his college course, he entered the priesthood. Rapidly attaining eminence, he became attached to the court of the king. He was also made professor and afterward rector of the university. The humble charity scholar had become the pride of his country, his name renowned throughout Europe.

Jerome, who afterward became associated with Huss, had brought with him from England the writings of Wycliffe. The queen of England, a convert to Wycliffe's teachings, was a Bohemian princess. Through her influence the Reformer's works were widely circulated in her native country. Huss was inclined to regard with favor the reforms advocated. Already, though he knew it not, he had entered upon a path which was to lead him far away from Rome.

Two Pictures Impress Huss

About this time, two strangers from England, men of learning, had received the light and had come to spread it in Prague. They were soon silenced, but being unwilling to relinquish their purpose, had recourse to other measures. Being artists as well as preachers, in a place open to the public they drew two pictures. One represented the entrance of Christ into Jerusalem, "meek, and sitting upon an ass" (Matthew 21:5) and followed by His disciples in travel-worn garments and with naked feet. The other picture portrayed a pontifical procession—the pope in his rich robes and triple crown, mounted upon a horse magnificently adorned, preceded by trumpeters and followed by cardinals and prelates in dazzling array.

Crowds came to gaze upon the drawings. None could fail to read the moral. There was great commotion in Prague, and the strangers found it necessary to depart. But the pictures made a deep impression on Huss and led him to a closer study of the Bible and of Wycliffe's writings.

Though he was not prepared yet to accept all the reforms advocated by Wycliffe, he saw the true character of the papacy, and denounced the pride, ambition, and corruption of the hierarchy.

Prague Placed Under Interdict

Tidings were carried to Rome, and Huss was summoned to appear before the pope. To obey would be certain death. The king and queen of Bohemia, the university, members of the nobility, and officers of the government, united in an appeal to the pontiff that Huss be permitted to remain at Prague and answer by deputy. Instead, the pope proceeded to the trial and condemnation of Huss, and declared the city of Prague under interdict.

In that age this sentence created alarm. The people looked upon the pope as the representative of God, holding the keys of heaven and hell and possessing power to invoke judgments. It was believed that until it should please the pope to remove the ban, the dead were shut out from the abodes of bliss. All the services of religion were suspended. The churches were closed. Marriages were solemnized in the churchyard. The dead were interred without rites in ditches or fields.

Prague was filled with tumult. A large class denounced Huss and demanded that he be given up to Rome. To quiet the storm, the Reformer withdrew for a time to his native village. He did not cease his labors, but traveled through the country preaching to eager crowds. When the excitement in Prague subsided, Huss returned to continue preaching the Word of God. His enemies were powerful, but the queen and many nobles were his friends, and the people in great numbers sided with him.

Huss had stood alone in his labors. Now Jerome joined in the reform. The two were hereafter united in their lives, and in death they were not to be divided. In those qualities which constitute real strength of character, Huss was the greater. Jerome, with true humility, perceived his worth and yielded to his counsels. Under their united labors the reform rapidly extended.

God permitted great light to shine upon the minds of these chosen men, revealing to them many of the errors of Rome, but they did not receive all the light to be given to the world. God was leading the people out of the darkness of Romanism, and He led them on, step by step, as they could bear it. Like the full glory of the noontide sun to those who have long dwelt in darkness, all the light would have caused them to turn away. Therefore He revealed it little by little, as it could be received by the people.

The schism in the church continued. Three popes were now contending for supremacy. Their strife filled Christendom with tumult. Not content with hurling anathemas, each cast about to purchase arms and obtain soldiers. Of course money must be had; to procure this, the gifts, offices, and blessing of the church were offered for sale. (See Appendix.)

With increasing boldness Huss thundered against the abominations tolerated in the name of religion. The people openly accused Rome as the cause of the miseries that overwhelmed Christendom.

Again Prague seemed on the verge of a bloody conflict. As in former ages, God's servant was accused as "he that troubleth Israel." 1 Kings 18:17. The city was again placed under interdict, and Huss withdrew to his native village. He was to speak from a wider stage, to all Christendom, before laying down his life as a witness for truth.

A general council was summoned to meet at Constance [southwestern Germany], called at the desire of the emperor Sigismund by one of the three rival popes, John XXIII. Pope John, whose character and policy could ill bear investigation, dared not oppose the will of Sigismund. (See Appendix.) The chief objects to be accomplished were to heal the schism in the church and to root out "heresy." The two antipopes were summoned to appear as well as John Huss. The former were represented by their delegates. Pope John came with many misgivings, fearing to be brought to account for the vices which had disgraced the tiara as well as for the crimes which had secured it. Yet he made his entry into the city of Constance with great pomp, attended by ecclesiastics and a train of courtiers. Above his head was a golden canopy, borne by four of the chief magistrates. The host was carried before him, and the rich dress of the cardinals and nobles made an imposing display.

Meanwhile another traveler was approaching Constance. Huss parted from his friends as if he were never to meet them again, feeling that his journey was leading him to the stake. He had obtained a safe-conduct from the king of Bohemia and one also from Emperor Sigismund. But he made all his arrangements in view of the probability of his death.

Safe Conduct From the King

In a letter to his friends he said: "My brethren, . . . I am departing with a safe-conduct from the king to meet my numerous and mortal enemies. . . . Jesus Christ suffered for His well-beloved; and therefore ought we to be astonished that He has left us His example? . . . Therefore, beloved, if my death ought to contribute to His glory, pray that it may come quickly, and that He may enable me to support all my calamities with constancy. . . . Let us pray to God . . . that I may not suppress one tittle of the truth of the gospel, in order to leave my brethren an excellent example to follow."[3]

In another letter, Huss spoke with humility of his own errors, accusing himself "of having felt pleasure in wearing rich apparel and of having wasted hours in frivolous occupations." He then added, "May the glory of God and the salvation of souls occupy thy mind, and not the possession of benefices and estates. Beware of adorning thy house more than thy soul; and, above all, give thy care to the spiritual edifice. Be pious and humble with the poor, and consume not thy substance in feasting."[4]

At Constance, Huss was granted full liberty. To the emperor's safe-conduct was added a personal assurance of protection by the pope. But, in violation of these repeated declarations, the Reformer was in a short time arrested by order of the pope and cardinals and thrust into a loathsome dungeon. Later he was transferred to a strong castle across the Rhine and there kept a prisoner. The pope was soon after committed to the same prison.[5] He had been proved guilty of the basest crimes, besides murder, simony, and adultery, "sins not fit to be named." He was finally deprived of the tiara. The antipopes also were deposed, and a new pontiff chosen.

Though the pope himself had been guilty of greater crimes than Huss had charged upon the priests, yet the same council which degraded the pontiff proceeded to crush the Reformer. The imprisonment of Huss excited great indignation in Bohemia. The emperor, loath to violate a safe-conduct, opposed the proceedings against him. But the enemies of the Reformer brought forward arguments to prove that "faith ought not to be kept with heretics, nor persons suspected of heresy, though they are furnished with safe-conducts from the emperor and kings."[6]

Enfeebled by illness—the damp dungeon brought on a fever which nearly ended his life—Huss was at last brought before the council. Loaded with chains he stood in the presence of the emperor, whose good faith had been pledged to protect him. He firmly maintained the truth and uttered a solemn protest against the corruptions of the hierarchy. Required to choose whether he would recant his doctrines or suffer death, he accepted the martyr's fate.

The grace of God sustained him. During the weeks of

suffering before his final sentence, heaven's peace filled his soul. "I write this letter," he said to a friend, "in my prison, and with my fettered hand, expecting my sentence of death tomorrow. . . . When, with the assistance of Jesus Christ, we shall again meet in the delicious peace of the future life, you will learn how merciful God has shown Himself toward me, how effectually He has supported me in the midst of my temptations and trials."[7]

Triumph Foreseen

In his dungeon he foresaw the triumph of the true faith. In his dreams he saw the pope and bishops effacing the pictures of Christ which he had painted on the walls of the chapel at Prague. "This vision distressed him: but on the next day he saw many painters occupied in restoring these figures in greater number and in brighter colours. . . . The painters, . . . surrounded by an immense crowd, exclaimed, 'Now let the popes and bishops come; they shall never efface them more!' " Said the Reformer, "The image of Christ will never be effaced. They have wished to destroy it, but it shall be painted afresh in all hearts by much better preachers than myself."[8]

For the last time, Huss was brought before the council, a vast and brilliant assembly—emperor, princes of the empire, royal deputies, cardinals, bishops, priests, and an immense crowd.

Called upon for his final decision, Huss declared his refusal to abjure. Fixing his glance upon the monarch whose plighted word had been so shamelessly violated, he declared: "I determined, of my own free will, to appear before this council, under the public protection and faith of the emperor here present."[9] A deep flush crimsoned the face of Sigismund as the eyes of all turned upon him.

Sentence having been pronounced, the ceremony of degradation began. Again exhorted to retract, Huss replied, turning toward the people: "With what face, then, should I behold the heavens? How should I look on those multitudes of men to whom I have preached the pure gospel? No; I esteem their salvation more than this poor body, now appointed unto death." The priestly vestments were removed one by one, each bishop pronouncing a curse as he performed his part of the ceremony. Finally, "they put on his head a cap or pyramidal-shaped miter of paper, on which were painted frightful figures of demons, with the word 'Archheretic' conspicuous in front. 'Most joyfully,' said Huss, 'will I wear this crown of shame for Thy sake, O Jesus, who for me didst wear a crown of thorns.' "[10]

Huss Dies at the Stake

He was now led away. An immense procession followed. When all was ready for the fire to be lighted, the martyr was once more exhorted to save himself by renouncing his errors. "What errors," said Huss, "shall I renounce? I know myself guilty of none. I call God to witness that all that I have written and preached has been with the view of rescuing souls from sin and perdition; and, therefore, most joyfully will I confirm with my blood that truth which I have written and preached."[11]

When the flames kindled about him, he began to sing, "Jesus, Thou Son of David, have mercy on me," and so continued till his voice was silenced forever. A zealous papist, describing the martyrdom of Huss, and of Jerome, who died soon after, said: "They prepared for the fire as if they were going to a marriage feast. They uttered no cry of pain. When the flames rose, they began to sing hymns; and scarce could the vehemency of the fire stop their singing."[12]

When the body of Huss had been consumed, his ashes were gathered up and cast into the Rhine, and thus borne onward to the ocean to be as seed scattered in all the countries of the earth. In lands yet unknown it would yield abundant fruit in witnesses for the truth.

The voice in the council hall of Constance wakened echoes heard through all coming ages. His example would encourage multitudes to stand firm in the face of torture and death. His execution had exhibited to the world the perfidious cruelty of Rome. The enemies of truth had been furthering the cause which they sought to destroy!

Yet the blood of another witness must testify for the truth. Jerome had exhorted Huss to courage and firmness, declaring that if he should fall into peril, he would fly to his assistance. Hearing of the Reformer's imprisonment, the faithful disciple prepared to fulfill his promise. Without a safe-conduct he set out for Constance. On arriving, he was convinced that he had only exposed himself to peril without the possibility of doing anything for Huss. He fled but was arrested and brought back loaded with fetters. At his first appearance before the council his attempts to reply were met with shouts, "To the flames with him!"[13] He was thrown into a dungeon and fed on bread and water. The cruelties of his imprisonment brought illness and threatened his life; and his enemies, fearing he might escape them, treated him with less severity, though he remained in prison one year.

Jerome Submits to the Council

The violation of Huss's safe-conduct had roused a storm of indignation. The council determined, instead of burning Jerome, to force him to retract. He was offered the alternative to recant or to die at the stake. Weakened by illness, by the rigors of prison and the torture of anxiety and suspense, separated from friends, and disheartened by the death of Huss, Jerome's fortitude gave way. He pledged himself to adhere to the Catholic faith and accepted the action of the council in condemning Wycliffe and Huss, excepting, however, the "holy truths"[14] which they had taught.

But in the solitude of his dungeon he saw clearly what he had done. He thought of the courage and fidelity of Huss and pondered his own denial of the truth. He thought of the divine Master who for his sake endured the cross. Before his retraction he had found comfort amid sufferings in the assurance of God's favor, but now remorse and doubt tortured his soul. He knew that still other retractions must be made before he could be at peace with Rome. The path upon which he was entering could end only in complete apostasy.

Jerome Finds Repentance and New Courage

Soon he was again brought before the council. His submission had not satisfied the judges. Only by unreserved surrender of truth could Jerome preserve his life. But he had determined to avow his faith and follow his brother martyr to the flames.

He renounced his former recantation and, as a dying man, solemnly required opportunity to make his defense. The prelates insisted that he merely affirm or deny the charges brought against him. Jerome protested against such cruel injustice. "You have held me shut up three hundred and forty days in a frightful prison," he said; "you then bring me out before you, and lending an ear to my mortal enemies, you refuse to hear me. . . . Take care not to sin against justice. As to me, I am only a feeble mortal; my life is but of little importance; and when I exhort you not to deliver an unjust sentence, I speak less for myself than for you."[15]

His request was finally granted. In the presence of his judges, Jerome kneeled down and prayed that the divine Spirit might control his thoughts, that he might speak nothing contrary to truth or unworthy of his Master. To him that day was fulfilled the promise, "When they deliver you up, take no thought how or what ye shall speak: for it shall be given you in that same hour what ye shall speak. For it is not ye that speak, but the Spirit of your Father which speaketh in you." Matthew 10:19, 20.

For a whole year Jerome had been in a dungeon, unable to read or even see. Yet his arguments were presented with as much clearness and power as if he had had undisturbed opportunity for study. He pointed his hearers to the long line of holy men condemned by unjust judges. In almost every generation those seeking to elevate the people of their time had been cast out. Christ Himself was condemned as a malefactor at an unrighteous tribunal.

Jerome now declared his repentance and bore witness to the innocence and holiness of the martyr Huss. "I knew him from his childhood," he said. "He was a most excellent man, just and holy; he was condemned, notwithstanding his innocence. . . . I am ready to die. I will not recoil before the torments that are prepared for me by my enemies and false witnesses, who will one day have to render an account of their impostures before the great God, whom nothing can deceive."

Jerome continued: "Of all the sins that I have committed since my youth, none weigh so heavily on my mind, and cause me such poignant remorse, as that which I committed in this fatal place, when I approved of the iniquitous sentence rendered against Wycliffe, and against the holy martyr, John Huss, my master and my friend. Yes! I confess it from my heart, and declare with horror that I disgracefully quailed when, through a dread of death, I condemned their doctrines. I therefore supplicate . . . Almighty God to deign to pardon me my sins, and this one in particular, the most heinous of all."

Pointing to his judges, he said firmly, "You condemned Wycliffe and John Huss. . . . The things which they have affirmed, and which are irrefutable, I also think and declare, like them."

His words were interrupted. The prelates, trembling with rage, cried out: "What need is there of further proof? We behold with our own eyes the most obstinate of heretics!"

Unmoved by the tempest, Jerome exclaimed: "What! do you suppose that I fear to die? You have held me for a whole year in a frightful dungeon, more horrible than death itself. . . . I cannot but express my astonishment at such great barbarity toward a Christian."[16]

Assigned to Prison and Death

Again the storm of rage burst out, and Jerome was hurried away to prison. Yet there were some upon whom his words had made a deep impression and who desired to save his life. He was visited by dignitaries and urged to submit to the council. Brilliant prospects were presented as reward.

"Prove to me from the Holy Writings that I am in error," he said, "and I will abjure it."

"The Holy Writings!" exclaimed one of his tempters, "is everything then to be judged by them? Who can understand them till the church has interpreted them?"

"Are the traditions of men more worthy of faith than the gospel of our Saviour?" replied Jerome.

"Heretic!" was the response, "I repent having pleaded so long with you. I see that you are urged on by the devil."[17]

Erelong he was led out to the same spot upon which Huss had yielded up his life. He went singing on his way, his countenance lighted up with joy and peace. To him death had lost its terrors. When the executioner, about to kindle the pile, stepped behind him, the martyr exclaimed, "Apply the fire before my face. Had I been afraid, I should not be here."

His last words were a prayer: "Lord, Almighty Father, have pity on me, and pardon me my sins; for Thou knowest that I have always loved Thy truth."[18] The ashes of the martyr were gathered up and, like those of Huss, thrown into the Rhine. So perished God's faithful light-bearers.

The execution of Huss had kindled a flame of indignation and horror in Bohemia. The whole nation declared him to have been a faithful teacher of the

truth. The council was charged with murder. His doctrines attracted greater attention than before, and
many were led to accept the reformed faith. The pope
and the emperor united to crush the movement, and
the armies of Sigismund were hurled upon Bohemia.

But a deliverer was raised up. Ziska, one of the
ablest generals of his age, was the leader of the Bohemians. Trusting in the help of God, that people with-
stood the mightiest armies that could be brought
against them. Again and again the emperor invaded
Bohemia, only to be repulsed. The Hussites were
raised above the fear of death, and nothing could stand
against them. The brave Ziska died, but his place
was filled by Procopius, in some respects a more able
leader.

The pope proclaimed a crusade against the Hussites.
An immense force was precipitated upon Bohemia,
only to suffer terrible defeat. Another crusade was proclaimed. In all the papal countries of Europe men,
money, and munitions of war were raised. Multitudes
flocked to the papal standard.

The vast force entered Bohemia. The people rallied
to repel them. The two armies approached each other
until only a river lay between. "The crusaders were in
greatly superior force, but instead of dashing across
the stream, and closing in battle with the Hussites,
whom they had come so far to meet, they stood gazing
in silence at those warriors."[19]

Suddenly a mysterious terror fell upon the host.
Without striking a blow, that mighty force broke and
scattered as if dispelled by an unseen power. The
Hussite army pursued the fugitives, and immense
booty fell into the hands of the victors. The war, instead of impoverishing, enriched the Bohemians.

A few years later, under a new pope, still another
crusade was set on foot. A vast army entered Bohemia.
The Hussite forces fell back before them, drawing the
invaders farther into the country, leading them to
count the victory already won.

At last the army of Procopius advanced to give them battle. As the sound of the approaching force was heard, even before the Hussites were in sight, a panic again fell upon the crusaders. Princes, generals, and common soldiers, casting away their armor, fled in all directions. The rout was complete, and again an immense booty fell into the hands of the victors.

Thus the second time a host of warlike men, trained for battle, fled without a blow before the defenders of a small and feeble nation. The invaders were smitten with a supernatural terror. He who put to flight the armies of Midian before Gideon and his three hundred, had again stretched out His hand. See Judges 7:19-25; Psalm 53:5.

Betrayed by Diplomacy

The papal leaders at last resorted to diplomacy. A compromise was entered into that betrayed the Bohemians into the power of Rome. The Bohemians had specified four points as the condition of peace with Rome: (1) the free preaching of the Bible; (2) the right of the whole church to both the bread and the wine in the communion and the use of the mother tongue in divine worship; (3) the exclusion of the clergy from all secular offices and authority; and, (4) in cases of crime, the jurisdiction of the civil courts over clergy and laity alike. The papal authorities agreed that the four articles should be accepted, "but that the right of explaining them . . . should belong to the council—in other words, to the pope and the emperor."[20] Rome gained by dissimulation and fraud what she had failed to gain by conflict. Placing her own interpretation upon the Hussite articles, as upon the Bible, she could pervert their meaning to suit her purposes.

A large class in Bohemia, seeing that it betrayed their liberties, could not consent to the compact. Dissensions arose, leading to strife among themselves. The noble Procopius fell, and the liberties of Bohemia perished.

Again foreign armies invaded Bohemia, and those who remained faithful to the gospel were subjected to a bloody persecution. Yet their firmness was unshaken. Forced to find refuge in caves, they still assembled to read God's Word and unite in His worship. Through messengers secretly sent to different countries they learned "that amid the mountains of the Alps was an ancient church, resting on the foundations of Scripture, and protesting against the idolatrous corruptions of Rome."[21] With great joy, a correspondence was opened with the Waldensian Christians.

Steadfast to the gospel, the Bohemians waited through the night of their persecution, in the darkest hour still turning their eyes toward the horizon like men who watch for the morning.

References

1. Wylie, bk. 3, ch. 1.
2. *Ibid.*, bk. 3, ch. 1.
3. Bonnechose, vol. 1, pp. 147, 148.
4. *Ibid.*, vol. 1, pp. 148, 149.
5. *Ibid.*, vol. 1, p. 247.
6. Jacques Lenfant, *History of the Council of Constance*, vol. 1, p. 516.
7. Bonnechose, vol. 2, p. 67.
8. D'Aubigne, bk. 1, ch. 6.
9. Bonnechose, vol. 2, p. 84.
10. Wylie, bk. 3, ch. 7.
11. *Ibid.*, bk. 3, ch. 7.
12. *Ibid.*, bk. 3, ch. 7.
13. Bonnechose, vol. 1, p. 234.
14. *Ibid.*, vol. 2, p. 141.
15. *Ibid.*, vol. 2, pp. 146, 147.
16. Bonnechose, vol. 2, pp. 151, 153.
17. Wylie, bk. 3, ch. 10.
18. Bonnechose, vol. 2, p. 168.
19. Wylie, bk. 3, ch. 17.
20. Wylie, bk. 3, ch. 18.
21. Wylie, bk. 3, ch. 19.

7/Luther, a Man for His Time

Foremost among those called to lead the church from the darkness of popery into the light of a purer faith stood Martin Luther. Knowing no fear but the fear of God, and acknowledging no foundation for faith but the Holy Scriptures, Luther was the man for his time.

Luther's early years were spent in the humble home of a German peasant. His father intended him for a lawyer, but God purposed to make him a builder in the great temple that was rising slowly through the centuries. Hardship, privation, and severe discipline were the school in which Infinite Wisdom prepared Luther for the mission of his life.

Luther's father was a man of active mind. His sterling good sense led him to regard the monastic system with distrust. He was displeased when Luther, without his consent, entered a monastery. It was two years before the father was reconciled to his son, and even then his opinions remained the same.

Luther's parents endeavored to instruct their children in the knowledge of God. Their efforts were earnest and persevering to prepare their children for a life of usefulness. They sometimes exercised too great severity, but the Reformer himself found in their discipline more to approve than to condemn.

At school Luther was treated with harshness and even violence. He often suffered from hunger. The gloomy, superstitious ideas of religion then prevailing filled him with fear. He would lie down at night with a sorrowful heart, in constant terror at the thought of God as a cruel tyrant, rather than a kind heavenly Father.

When he entered the University of Erfurt, his prospects were brighter than in his earlier years. His parents, having by thrift and industry acquired a competence, were able to render him all needed assistance. And judicious friends somewhat lessened the gloomy effects of his former training. With favorable influences, his mind rapidly developed. Untiring application soon placed him in the foremost rank among his associates.

Luther did not fail to begin each day with prayer, his heart continually breathing a petition for guidance. "To pray well," he often said, "is the better half of study."[1]

One day in the library of the university he discovered a Latin Bible, a book he had never seen. He had heard portions of the Gospels and Epistles, which he supposed were the entire Bible. Now, for the first time, he looked upon the whole of God's Word. With awe and wonder he turned the sacred pages and read for himself the words of life, pausing to exclaim, "O that God would give me such a book for myself!"[2] Angels were by his side. Rays of light from God revealed treasures of truth to his understanding. The deep conviction of his condition as a sinner took hold upon him as never before.

Peace With God

A desire to find peace with God led him to devote himself to a monastic life. Here he was required to perform the lowest drudgery and to beg from house to house. He patiently endured this humiliation, believing it necessary because of his sins.

Robbing himself of sleep and grudging even the time spent at his scanty meals, he delighted in the study of God's Word. He had found a Bible chained to the convent wall, and to this he often repaired.

He led a most rigorous life, endeavoring by fasting, vigils, and scourgings to subdue the evils of his nature. He afterward said, ''If ever monk could obtain heaven by his monkish works, I should certainly have been entitled to it. . . . If it had continued much longer, I should have carried my mortifications even to death.''[3] With all his efforts, his burdened soul found no relief. He was at last driven to the verge of despair.

When it appeared that all was lost, God raised up a friend for him. Staupitz opened the Word of God to Luther's mind and bade him look away from self and look to Jesus. ''Instead of torturing yourself on account of your sins, throw yourself into the Redeemer's arms. Trust in Him, in the righteousness of His life, in the atonement of His death. . . . The Son of God . . . became man to give you the assurance of divine favor. . . . Love Him who first loved you.''[4] His words made a deep impression on Luther's mind. Peace came to his troubled soul.

Ordained a priest, Luther was called to a professorship in the University of Wittenberg. He began to lecture on the Psalms, the Gospels, and the Epistles to crowds of delighted listeners. Staupitz, his superior, urged him to ascend the pulpit and preach. But Luther felt himself unworthy to speak to the people in Christ's stead. It was only after a long struggle that he yielded to the solicitation of his friends. He was mighty in the Scriptures, and the grace of God rested upon him. The clearness and power with which he presented the truth convinced their understanding, and his fervor touched their hearts.

Luther, still a true son of the papal church, had no thought he would ever be anything else. Led to visit Rome, he pursued his journey on foot, lodging at monasteries on the way. He was filled with wonder at the magnificence and luxury that he witnessed. The monks dwelt in splendid apartments, attired themselves in costly robes, and feasted at a sumptuous table. Luther's mind was becoming perplexed.

At last he beheld in the distance the seven-hilled city. He prostrated himself upon the earth, exclaiming: "Holy Rome, I salute thee!"[5] He visited the churches, listened to the marvelous tales repeated by priests and monks, and performed all the ceremonies required. Everywhere, scenes filled him with astonishment—iniquity among the clergy, indecent jokes from prelates. He was filled with horror at their profanity even during mass. He met dissipation, debauchery. "No one can imagine," he wrote, "what sins and infamous actions are committed in Rome. . . . They are in the habit of saying, 'If there is a hell, Rome is built over it.' "[6]

Truth on Pilate's Staircase

An indulgence had been promised by the pope to all who should ascend upon their knees "Pilate's staircase," said to have been miraculously conveyed from Jerusalem to Rome. Luther was one day climbing these steps when a voice like thunder seemed to say, "The just shall live by faith." Romans 1:17. He sprang to his feet in shame and horror. From that time he saw more clearly than ever before the fallacy of trusting to human works for salvation. He turned his face from Rome. From that time the separation grew until he severed all connection with the papal church.

After his return from Rome, Luther received the degree of doctor of divinity. Now he was at liberty to devote himself to the Scriptures that he loved. He had taken a solemn vow to preach with fidelity the Word of God, not the doctrines of the popes. He was no longer the mere monk, but the authorized herald of the Bible, called as a shepherd to feed the flock of God that were hungering and thirsting for truth. He firmly declared that Christians should receive no other doctrines than those which rest on the authority of the Sacred Scriptures.

Eager crowds hung upon his words. The glad tidings of a Saviour's love, the assurance of pardon and peace through His atoning blood rejoiced their hearts. At

Wittenberg a light was kindled whose rays should increase in brightness to the close of time.

But between truth and error there is conflict. Our Saviour Himself declared: "I came not to send peace, but a sword." Matthew 10:34. Said Luther, a few years after the opening of the Reformation: "God . . . pushes me forward. . . . I desire to live in repose; but I am thrown into the midst of tumults and revolutions."[7]

Indulgences for Sale

The Roman Church made merchandise of the grace of God. Under the plea of raising funds for the erection of St. Peter's at Rome, indulgences for sin were offered for sale by authority of the pope. By the price of crime a temple was to be built for God's worship. It was this that aroused the most successful of the enemies of popery and led to the battle which shook the papal throne and the triple crown upon the pontiff's head.

Tetzel, the official appointed to conduct the sale of indulgences in Germany, had been convicted of base offenses against society and the law of God, but he was employed to further the mercenary projects of the pope in Germany. He repeated glaring falsehoods and marvelous tales to deceive an ignorant and superstitious people. Had they possessed the Word of God they would not have been deceived, but the Bible had been withheld from them.[8]

As Tetzel entered a town, a messenger went before, announcing: "The grace of God and of the holy father is at your gates."[9] The people welcomed the blasphemous pretender as if he were God Himself. Tetzel, ascending the pulpit in the church, extolled indulgences as the most precious gift of God. He declared that by virtue of his certificates of pardon, all the sins which the purchaser should *afterward* desire to commit would be forgiven him and "not even repentance is necessary."[10] He assured his hearers that his indulgences had power to save the dead; the very moment the money should clink against the bottom of his chest, the soul in whose behalf it had been paid would escape from purgatory and make its way to heaven.[11]

Gold and silver flowed into Tetzel's treasury. A salvation bought with money was more easily obtained than that which requires repentance, faith, and diligent effort to resist and overcome sin. (See Appendix.)

Luther was filled with horror. Many of his own congregation had purchased certificates of pardon. They soon began to come to their pastor, confessing sins and expecting absolution, not because they were penitent and wished to reform, but on the ground of the indulgence. Luther refused, and warned them that unless they should repent and reform, they must perish in their sins. They repaired to Tetzel with the complaint that their confessor had refused his certificates, and some boldly demanded that their money be returned. Filled with rage, the friar uttered terrible curses, caused fires to be lighted in the public squares, and declared that he "had received an order from the pope to burn all heretics who presumed to oppose his most holy indulgences."[12]

Luther's Work Begins

Luther's voice was heard from the pulpit in solemn warning. He set before the people the offensive character of sin and taught that it is impossible for man by his own works to lessen its guilt or evade its punishment. Nothing but repentance toward God and faith in Christ can save the sinner. The grace of Christ cannot be purchased; it is a free gift. He counseled the people not to buy indulgences, but to look in faith to a crucified Redeemer. He related his own painful experience and assured his hearers that it was by believing in Christ that he found peace and joy.

As Tetzel continued his impious pretensions, Luther determined upon a more effectual protest. The castle church of Wittenberg possessed relics which on certain holy days were exhibited to the people. Full remission of sins was granted to all who then visited the church and made confession. One of the most important of these occasions, the festival of All Saints, was approaching. Luther, joining the crowds already making their way to the church, posted on its door ninety-five propositions against the doctrine of indulgences.

His propositions attracted universal attention. They were read and repeated in every direction. Great excitement was created in the whole city. By these theses it was shown that the power to grant pardon of sin and to remit its penalty had never been committed to the pope or any man. It was clearly shown that the grace of God is freely bestowed on all who seek it by repentance and faith.

Luther's theses spread through all Germany and in a few weeks had sounded throughout Europe. Many devoted Romanists read the propositions with joy, recognizing in them the voice of God. They felt that the Lord had set His hand to arrest the swelling tide of corruption issuing from Rome. Princes and magistrates secretly rejoiced that a check was to be put upon the arrogant power which denied appeal from its decisions.

Crafty ecclesiastics, seeing their gains endangered, were enraged. The Reformer had bitter accusers to meet. "Who does not know," he responded, "that a man rarely puts forth any new idea without . . . being accused of exciting quarrels? . . . Why were Christ and all the martyrs put to death? Because . . . they advanced novelties without having first humbly taken counsel of the oracles of the ancient opinions."[13]

The reproaches of Luther's enemies, their misrepresentation of his purposes, and their malicious reflections on his character came in upon him like a flood. He had felt confident that the leaders would gladly unite with him in reform. In anticipation he had seen a brighter day dawning for the church.

But encouragement had changed to reproach. Many dignitaries of church and state soon saw that the acceptance of these truths would virtually undermine the authority of Rome, stop thousands of streams now flowing into her treasury, and thus curtail the luxury of the papal leaders. To teach the people to look to Christ alone for salvation would overthrow the pontiff's throne and eventually destroy their own authority. Thus they arrayed themselves against Christ and the truth by opposition to the man He sent to enlighten them.

Luther trembled as he looked upon himself—one man opposed to the mighty powers of earth. "Who was I," he writes, "to oppose the majesty of the pope, before whom . . . the kings of the earth and the whole world trembled? . . . No one can know what my heart suffered during these first two years and into what despondency, I may say into what despair, I was sunk."[14] But when human support failed, he looked to God alone. He could lean in safety upon that all-powerful arm.

To a friend Luther wrote: "Your first duty is to begin by prayer. . . . Hope for nothing from your own labors, from your own understanding: trust solely in God, and in the influence of His Spirit."[15] Here is a lesson of importance to those who feel that God has called them to present to others solemn truths for this time. In the conflict with the powers of evil there is need of something more than intellect and human wisdom.

Luther Appealed Only to the Bible

When enemies appealed to custom and tradition, Luther met them with the Bible only, arguments which they could not answer. From Luther's sermons and writings issued beams of light which awakened and illuminated thousands. The Word of God was like a two-edged sword, cutting its way to the hearts of the people. The eyes of the people, so long directed to human rites and earthly mediators, were now turning in faith to Christ and Him crucified.

This widespread interest aroused the fears of the papal authorities. Luther received a summons to appear at Rome. His friends knew well the danger that threatened him in that corrupt city, already drunk with the blood of the martyrs of Jesus. They requested that he receive his examination in Germany.

This was effected, and the pope's legate was appointed to hear the case. In the instructions to this official, it was stated that Luther had already been declared a heretic. The legate was therefore "to prosecute and constrain without any delay." The legate was empowered "to proscribe him in every part of Germany; to banish, curse, and excommunicate all those who are attached to him," to excommunicate all, of whatever dignity in church or state, except the emperor, who should neglect to seize Luther and his adherents and deliver them to the vengeance of Rome.[16]

Not a trace of Christian principle or even common justice is to be seen in the document. Luther had had no opportunity to explain or defend his position; yet he was pronounced a heretic and in the same day exhorted, accused, judged, and condemned.

When Luther so much needed the counsel of a true friend, God sent Melanchthon to Wittenberg. Melanchthon's sound judgment, combined with purity and uprightness of character, won universal admiration. He soon became Luther's most trusted friend— his gentleness, caution, and exactness a complement to Luther's courage and energy.

Augsburg had been fixed as the place of trial, and the Reformer set out on foot. Threats had been made that he would be murdered on the way, and his friends begged him not to venture. But his language was, "I am like Jeremiah, a man of strife, and contention; but the more their threats increase, the more my joy is multiplied. . . . They have already destroyed my honor and my reputation. . . . As for my soul, they cannot take that. He who desires to proclaim the word of Christ to the world, must expect death at every moment."[17]

The tidings of Luther's arrival at Augsburg gave

great satisfaction to the papal legate. The troublesome heretic exciting the attention of the world seemed now in the power of Rome; he should not escape. The legate intended to force Luther to retract, or failing in this, to cause him to be conveyed to Rome to share the fate of Huss and Jerome. Therefore through his agents he endeavored to induce Luther to appear without a safe-conduct, trusting himself to his mercy. This the Reformer declined to do. Not until he had received the document pledging the emperor's protection did he appear in the presence of the papal ambassador.

As a matter of policy, the Romanists decided to win Luther by an appearance of gentleness. The legate professed great friendliness, but demanded that Luther submit implicitly to the church and yield every point without argument or question. Luther, in reply, expressed his regard for the church, his desire for truth, his readiness to answer all objections to what he had taught, and to submit his doctrines to the decision of leading universities. But he protested against the cardinal's course in requiring him to retract without having proved him in error.

The only response was, "Retract, retract!" The Reformer showed that his position was sustained by Scripture. He could not renounce truth. The legate, unable to reply to Luther's arguments, overwhelmed him with a storm of reproaches, gibes, flattery, quotations from tradition, and the sayings of the Fathers, granting the Reformer no opportunity to speak. Luther finally obtained a reluctant permission to present his answer in writing.

Said he, writing to a friend, "What is written may be submitted to the judgment of others; and second, one has a better chance of working on the fears, if not on the conscience, of an arrogant and babbling despot, who would otherwise overpower by his imperious language."[18]

At the next interview, Luther presented a clear, concise, and forcible exposition of his views, supported by

Scripture. This paper, after reading aloud, he handed to the cardinal, who cast it contemptuously aside, declaring it to be a mass of idle words and irrelevant quotations. Luther now met the haughty prelate on his own ground—the traditions and teaching of the church—and utterly overthrew his assumptions.

The prelate lost all self-control and in a rage cried out, "Retract! or I will send you to Rome." And he finally declared, in a haughty and angry tone, "Retract, or return no more."[19]

The Reformer promptly withdrew with his friends, thus declaring plainly that no retraction was to be expected from him. This was not what the cardinal had purposed. Now, left alone with his supporters, he looked from one to another in chagrin at the unexpected failure of his schemes.

The large assembly present had opportunity to compare the two men and to judge for themselves the spirit manifested by them, as well as of the strength and truthfulness of their positions. The Reformer, simple, humble, firm, having truth on his side; the pope's representative, self-important, haughty, unreasonable, without a single argument from the Scriptures, yet vehemently crying, "Retract, or be sent to Rome."

Escape From Augsburg

Luther's friends urged that as it was useless for him to stay, he should return to Wittenberg without delay, and that utmost caution be observed. He accordingly left Augsburg before daybreak on horseback, accompanied only by a guide furnished by the magistrate. He secretly made his way through the dark streets of the city. Enemies, vigilant and cruel, were plotting his destruction. Those were moments of anxiety and earnest prayer. He reached a small gate in the wall of the city. It was opened for him, and with his guide he passed through. Before the legate learned of Luther's departure, he was beyond the reach of his persecutors.

At the news of Luther's escape the legate was overwhelmed with surprise and anger. He had expected to receive great honor for his firmness in dealing with this disturber of the church. In a letter to Frederick, the elector of Saxony, he bitterly denounced Luther, demanding that Frederick send the Reformer to Rome or banish him from Saxony.

The elector had, as yet, little knowledge of the reformed doctrines, but he was deeply impressed by the force and clearness of Luther's words. Until the Reformer should be proved in error, Frederick resolved to stand as his protector. In reply to the legate he wrote: "Since Doctor Martin has appeared before you at Augsburg, you should be satisfied. We did not expect that you would endeavor to make him retract without having convinced him of his errors. None of the learned men in our principality have informed me that Martin's doctrine is impious, antichristian, or heretical."[20] The elector saw that a work of reform was needed. He secretly rejoiced that a better influence was making itself felt in the church.

Only a year had passed since the Reformer posted his theses on the castle church, yet his writings had kindled everywhere a new interest in the Holy Scriptures. Not only from all parts of Germany, but from other lands, students flocked to the university. Young men coming in sight of Wittenberg for the first time "raised their hands to heaven, and praised God for having caused the light of truth to shine forth from this city."[21]

Luther was as yet but partially converted from the errors of Romanism. But, he wrote, "I am reading the decrees of the pontiffs, and . . . I do not know whether the pope is antichrist himself, or his apostle, so greatly is Christ misrepresented and crucified in them."[22]

Rome became more and more exasperated by the attacks of Luther. Fanatical opponents, even doctors in Catholic universities, declared that he who should kill the monk would be without sin. But God was his defense. His doctrines were heard everywhere—"in cottages and convents, . . . in the castles of the nobles, in the universities, and in the palaces of kings.''[23]

About this time Luther found that the great truth of justification by faith had been held by the Bohemian Reformer, Huss. ''We have all,'' said Luther, ''Paul, Augustine, and myself, been Hussites without knowing it!'' ''The truth was preached . . . a century ago, and burned!''[24]

Luther wrote thus of the universities: ''I am much afraid that the universities will prove to be the great gates of hell, unless they diligently labor in explaining the Holy Scriptures, and engraving them in the hearts of youth. . . . Every institution in which men are not unceasingly occupied with the word of God must become corrupt.''[25]

This appeal was circulated throughout Germany. The whole nation was stirred. Luther's opponents urged the pope to take decisive measures against him. It was decreed that his doctrines should be immediately condemned. The Reformer and his adherents, if they did not recant, were all to be excommunicated.

A Terrible Crisis

That was a terrible crisis for the Reformation. Luther was not blind to the tempest about to burst, but he trusted in Christ to be his support and shield. ''What is about to happen I know not, nor do I care to know. . . . Not so much as a leaf falls, without the will of our Father. How much rather will He care for us! It is a light thing to die for the Word, since the Word which was made flesh hath Himself died.''[26]

When the papal bull reached Luther, he said: ''I despise and attack it, as impious, false. . . . It is *Christ* Himself who is condemned therein. Already I feel greater liberty in my heart; for at last I know that the pope is antichrist, and that his throne is that of Satan himself.''[27]

Yet the mandate of Rome was not without effect.

The weak and superstitious trembled before the decree of the pope, and many felt that life was too dear to be risked. Was the Reformer's work about to close?

Luther was fearless still. With terrible power he flung back upon Rome herself the sentence of condemnation. In the presence of a crowd of citizens of all ranks Luther burned the pope's bull. He said, "A serious struggle has just begun. Hitherto I have been only playing with the pope. I began this work in God's name; it will be ended without me, and by His might. . . . Who knows if God has not chosen and called me, and if they ought not to fear that, by despising me, they despise God Himself? . . .

"God never selected as a prophet either the high priest or any other great personage; but ordinarily He chose low and despised men, once even the shepherd Amos. In every age, the saints have had to reprove the great, kings, princes, priests, and wise men, at the peril of their lives. . . . I do not say that I am a prophet; but I say that they ought to fear precisely because I am alone and that they are many. I am sure of this, that the word of God is with me, and that it is not with them."[28]

Yet it was not without a terrible struggle with himself that Luther decided upon a final separation from the church: "Oh, how much pain it has caused me, though I had the Scriptures on my side, to justify it to myself that I should dare to make a stand alone against the pope, and hold him forth as antichrist! How many times have I not asked myself with bitterness that question which was so frequent on the lips of the papists: 'Art thou alone wise? Can everyone else be mistaken? How will it be, if, after all, it is thyself who art wrong, and who art involving in thy error so many souls, who will then be eternally damned?' 'Twas so I fought with myself and with Satan, till Christ, by His own infallible word, fortified my heart against these doubts."[29]

A new bull appeared, declaring the Reformer's final separation from the Roman Church, denouncing him as accursed of Heaven, and including in the same condemnation all who should receive his doctrines.

Opposition is the lot of all whom God employs to present truths specially applicable to their time. There was a present truth in the days of Luther; there is present truth for the church today. But truth is no more desired by the majority today than it was by papists who opposed Luther. Those who present the truth for this time should not expect to be received with greater favor that were earlier reformers. The great controversy between truth and error, between Christ and Satan, is to increase to the close of this world's history. See John 15:19, 20; Luke 6:26.

References

1. D'Aubigne, bk. 2, ch. 2.
2. *Ibid.*, bk. 2, ch. 2.
3. *Ibid.*, bk. 2, ch. 3.
4. *Ibid.*, bk. 2, ch. 4.
5. D'Aubigne, bk. 2, ch. 6.
6. *Ibid.*, bk. 2, ch. 6.
7. D'Aubigne, bk. 5, ch. 2.
8. See John C. L. Giesler, *A Compendium of Ecclesiastical History,* per. 4, sec. 1, par. 5.
9. D'Aubigne, bk. 3, ch. 1.
10. *Ibid.*, bk. 3, ch. 1.
11. See K. R. Hagenbach, *History of the Reformation,* vol. 1, p. 96.
12. D'Aubigne, bk. 3, ch. 4.
13. *Ibid.*, bk. 3, ch. 6.
14. *Ibid.*, bk. 3, ch. 6.
15. *Ibid.*, bk. 3, ch. 7.
16. *Ibid.*, bk. 4, ch. 2.
17. *Ibid.*, bk. 4, ch. 4.
18. Martyn, *The Life and Times of Luther,* pp. 271, 272.
19. D'Aubigne, London ed., bk. 4, ch. 8.
20. D'Aubigne, bk. 4, ch. 10.
21. *Ibid.*, bk. 4, ch. 10.
22. *Ibid.*, bk. 5, ch. 1.

23. *Ibid.*, bk. 6, ch. 2.
24. Wylie, bk. 6, ch. 1.
25. D'Aubigne, bk. 6, ch. 3.
26. D'Aubigne, 3rd London ed., Walther, 1840, bk. 6, ch. 9.
27. D'Aubigne, bk. 6, ch. 9.
28. *Ibid.*, bk. 6, ch. 10.
29. Martyn, pp. 372, 373.

8 / A Champion of Truth

A new emperor, Charles V, ascended the throne of Germany. The elector of Saxony to whom Charles was in great degree indebted for his crown, entreated him to take no step against Luther until he should have granted him a hearing. The emperor was thus placed in a position of great perplexity and embarrassment. The papists would be satisfied with nothing short of Luther's death. The elector had declared "that Dr. Luther should be furnished with a safe-conduct, so that he might appear before a tribunal of learned, pious, and impartial judges."[1]

The assembly convened at Worms. For the first time the princes of Germany were to meet their youthful monarch in assembly. Dignitaries of church and state and ambassadors from foreign lands all gathered at Worms. Yet the subject that excited the deepest interest was the Reformer. Charles had directed the elector to bring Luther with him, assuring protection and promising free discussion of the questions in dispute. Luther wrote the elector: "If the emperor calls me, I cannot doubt that it is the call of God Himself. If they desire to use violence against me, . . . I place the matter in the Lord's hands. . . . If He will not save me, my life is of little consequence. . . . You may expect everything from me . . . except flight and recantation. Fly I cannot, and still less retract."[2]

As the news was circulated that Luther was to appear before the diet, a general excitement was created. Aleander, the papal legate, was alarmed and enraged.

To inquire into a case in which the pope had already pronounced sentence of condemnation would cast contempt upon the authority of the pontiff. Furthermore, the powerful arguments of this man might turn many of the princes from the pope. He remonstrated with Charles against Luther's appearance at Worms and induced the emperor to yield.

Not content with this victory, Aleander labored to secure Luther's condemnation, accusing the Reformer of "sedition, rebellion, impiety, and blasphemy." But his vehemence revealed the spirit by which he was actuated. "He is moved by hatred and vengeance," was the general remark.[3]

With redoubled zeal Aleander urged the emperor to execute the papal edicts. Overcome by the legate's importunity Charles bade him present his case to the diet. With misgivings those who favored the Reformer looked forward to Aleander's speech. The elector of Saxony was not present, but some of his councilors took notes of the nuncio's address.

Luther Accused of Heresy

With learning and eloquence, Aleander set himself to overthrow Luther as an enemy of the church and the state. "In Luther's errors there is enough," he declared, to warrant the burning of "a hundred thousand heretics."

"What are all these Lutherans? A crew of insolent pedagogues, corrupt priests, dissolute monks, ignorant lawyers, and degraded nobles. . . . How far superior to them is the Catholic party in number, ability and power! A unanimous decree from this illustrious assembly will enlighten the simple, warn the imprudent, decide the waverers, and give strength to the weak."[4]

The same arguments are still urged against all who dare to present the plain teachings of God's Word. "Who are these preachers of new doctrines? They are unlearned, few in numbers, and of the poorer class. Yet they claim to have the truth, and to be the chosen people of God. They are ignorant and deceived. How greatly superior in numbers and influence is our church!'' These arguments are no more conclusive now than in the days of the Reformer.

Luther was not present, with the clear and convincing truths of God's Word, to vanquish the papal champion. There was manifest a general disposition not only to condemn him and the doctrines which he taught, but if possible to uproot the heresy. All that Rome could say in her own vindication had been said. Henceforth the contrast between truth and error would be more clearly seen as they should take the field in open warfare.

Now the Lord moved upon a member of the diet to give a true delineation of the effects of papal tyranny. Duke George of Saxony stood up in that princely assembly and specified with terrible exactness the deceptions and abominations of popery:

''Abuses . . . cry out against Rome. All shame has been put aside, and their only object is . . . money, money, money, . . . so that the preachers who should teach the truth, utter nothing but falsehoods, and are not only tolerated, but rewarded, because the greater their lies, the greater their gain. It is from this foul spring that such tainted waters flow. Debauchery stretches out the hand to avarice. . . . Alas, it is the scandal caused by the clergy that hurls so many poor souls into eternal condemnation. A general reform must be effected.''[5] The fact that the speaker was a determined enemy of the Reformer gave greater influence to his words.

Angels of God shed beams of light into the darkness of error and opened hearts to truth. The power of the God of truth controlled even the adversaries of the Reformation and prepared the way for the great work about to be accomplished. The voice of One greater than Luther had been heard in that assembly.

A committee was appointed to prepare an enumeration of papal oppressions that weighed heavily on the

German people. This list was presented to the emperor, with a request that he take measures for the correction of these abuses. Said the petitioners, "It is our duty to prevent the ruin and dishonor of our people. For this reason we most humbly but most urgently entreat you to order a general reformation, and to undertake its accomplishment."[6]

Luther Summoned to Appear

The council now demanded the Reformer's appearance. The emperor at last consented, and Luther was summoned. With the summons was issued a safe-conduct. These were borne to Wittenberg by a herald commissioned to conduct him to Worms.

Knowing the prejudice and enmity against him, the friends of Luther feared that his safe-conduct would not be respected. He replied: "Christ will give me His Spirit to overcome these ministers of error. I despise them during my life; I shall triumph over them by my death. They are busy at Worms about compelling me to retract; and this shall be my retraction: I said formerly that the pope was Christ's vicar; now I assert that he is the Lord's adversary, and the devil's apostle."[7]

Besides the imperial messenger, three friends determined to accompany Luther. Melanchthon's heart was knit to Luther's, and he yearned to follow him. But his entreaties were denied. Said the Reformer: "If I do not return, and my enemies put me to death, continue to teach, and stand fast in the truth. Labor in my stead. . . . If you survive, my death will be of little consequence."[8]

The minds of the people were oppressed by gloomy forebodings. They learned that Luther's writings had been condemned at Worms. The herald, fearing for Luther's safety at the council, asked if he still wished to go forward. He answered, "Although interdicted in every city, I shall go on."[9]

At Erfurt, Luther passed through the streets he had often traversed, visited his convent cell, and thought

upon the struggles through which the light now flooding Germany had been shed upon his soul. He was
urged to preach. This he had been forbidden to do, but
the herald granted him permission, and the friar who
had once been made the drudge of the convent, now
entered the pulpit.

The people listened as if spellbound. The bread of
life was broken to those starving souls. Christ was
lifted up before them as above popes, legates, emperors, and kings. Luther made no reference to his own
perilous position. In Christ he had lost sight of self. He
hid behind the Man of Calvary, seeking only to present
Jesus as the sinner's Redeemer.

The Courage of a Martyr

As the Reformer proceeded, an eager multitude
thronged about him, and friendly voices warned him of
the Romanists. "They will burn you," said some,
"and reduce your body to ashes, as they did with John
Huss." Luther answered, "Though they should kindle
a fire all the way from Worms to Wittenberg, . . . I
would walk through it in the name of the Lord; I would
appear before them, . . . confessing the Lord Jesus
Christ."[10]

His approach to Worms created great commotion.
Friends trembled for his safety; enemies feared for
their cause. At the instigation of the papists he was
urged to repair to the castle of a friendly knight, where,
it was declared, all difficulties could be amicably
adjusted. Friends described the dangers that threatened him. Luther, still unshaken, declared: "Even
should there be as many devils in Worms as tiles on the
housetops, still I would enter it."[11]

Upon his arrival at Worms, a vast crowd flocked to
the gates to welcome him. The excitement was intense.
"God will be my defense," said Luther as he alighted
from his carriage. His arrival filled the papists with
consternation. The emperor summoned his councilors.
What course should be pursued? A rigid papist de-

clared: "We have long consulted on this matter. Let your imperial majesty get rid of this man at once. Did not Sigismund cause John Huss to be burnt? We are not bound either to give or to observe the safe-conduct of a heretic." "No," said the emperor, "we must keep our promise."[12] It was decided that the Reformer should be heard.

All the city were eager to see this remarkable man. Luther, wearied from the journey, needed quiet and repose. But he had enjoyed only a few hours' rest when noblemen, knights, priests, and citizens gathered eagerly about him. Among these were nobles who had boldly demanded of the emperor a reform of ecclesiastical abuses. Enemies as well as friends came to look upon the dauntless monk. His bearing was firm and courageous. His pale, thin face wore a kindly and even joyous expression. The deep earnestness of his words gave power that even his enemies could not wholly withstand. Some were convinced that a divine influence attended him; others declared, as had the Pharisees concerning Christ: "He hath a devil." John 10:20.

On the following day an imperial officer was appointed to conduct Luther to the hall of audience. Every avenue was crowded with spectators eager to look upon the monk who had dared to resist the pope. An old general, the hero of many battles, said to him kindly: "Poor monk, thou art now going to make a nobler stand than I or any other captains have ever made in the bloodiest of our battles. But if thy cause is just, . . . go forward in God's name, and fear nothing. God will not forsake thee."[13]

Luther Stands Before the Council

The emperor occupied the throne, surrounded by the most illustrious personages in the empire. Martin Luther was now to answer for his faith. "This appearance was of itself a signal victory over the papacy. The pope had condemned the man, and he was now standing before a tribunal which, by the very act, set itself above the pope. The pope had laid him under interdict, and cut him off from all human society; and yet he was summoned in respectful language, and received before the most august assembly in the world. . . . Rome was already descending from her throne, and it was the voice of a monk that caused this humiliation.''[14]

The lowly-born Reformer seemed awed and embarrassed. Several princes approached him, and one whispered: ''Fear not them which kill the body, but are not able to kill the soul.'' Another said: ''When ye shall be brought before governors and kings for my sake, it shall be given you, by the Spirit of your Father, what ye shall say.'' See Matthew 10:28, 18, 19.

A deep silence fell upon the crowded assembly. Then an imperial officer arose and, pointing to Luther's writings, demanded that the Reformer answer two questions—whether he acknowledged them as his, and whether he proposed to retract the opinions therein advanced. The titles of the books having been read, Luther, to the first question, acknowledged the books to be his. ''As to the second,'' he said, ''I should act imprudently were I to reply without reflection. I might affirm less than the circumstance demands, or more than truth requires. For this reason I entreat your imperial majesty, with all humility, to allow me time, that I may answer without offending against the word of God.''[15]

Luther convinced the assembly that he did not act from passion or impulse. Such calmness and self-command, unexpected in one bold and uncompromising, enabled him afterward to answer with wisdom and dignity that surprised his adversaries and rebuked their insolence.

The next day he was to render his final answer. For a time his heart sank. His enemies seemed about to triumph. Clouds gathered about him and seemed to separate him from God. In anguish of spirit he poured out those broken, heart-rending cries, which none but God can fully understand.

"O almighty and everlasting God," he pleaded, "if it is only in the strength of this world that I must put my trust, all is over. . . . My last hour is come, my condemnation has been pronounced. . . . O God, do Thou help me against all the wisdom of the world. . . . The cause is Thine, . . . and it is a righteous and eternal cause. O Lord, help me! Faithful and unchangeable God, in no man do I place my trust. . . . Thou hast chosen me for this work. . . . Stand at my side, for the sake of Thy well-beloved Jesus Christ, who is my defense, my shield, and my strong tower."[16]

Yet it was not the fear of personal suffering, torture, or death that overwhelmed him with terror. He felt his insufficiency. Through his weakness the cause of truth might suffer loss. Not for his own safety, but for the triumph of the gospel did he wrestle with God. In his utter helplessness his faith fastened upon Christ, the mighty Deliverer. He would not appear alone before the council. Peace returned to his soul, and he rejoiced that he was permitted to uplift the Word of God before the rulers of the nations.

Luther thought upon his answer, examined passages in his writings, and drew from Scripture suitable proofs to sustain his positions. Then, laying his left hand on the Sacred Volume, he lifted his right hand to heaven and vowed "to remain faithful to the gospel, and freely to confess his faith, even should he seal his testimony with his blood."[17]

Luther Before the Diet Again

When again ushered into the Diet, he was calm and peaceful, yet brave and noble, as God's witness among the great ones of earth. The imperial officer now demanded his decision. Did he desire to retract? Luther made his answer in a humble tone, without violence or passion. His demeanor was diffident and respectful; yet he manifested a confidence and joy that surprised the assembly.

"Most serene emperor, illustrious princes, gracious

lords," said Luther, "I appear before you this day, in conformity with the order given me yesterday. If, through ignorance, I should transgress the usages and proprieties of courts I entreat you to pardon me; for I was not brought up in the palaces of kings, but in the seclusion of a convent."[18]

Then he stated that in some of his published works he had treated of faith and good works; even his enemies declared them profitable. To retract these would condemn truths which all confessed. The second class consisted of writings exposing corruptions and abuses of the papacy. To revoke these would strengthen the tyranny of Rome and open a wider door to great impieties. In the third class he had attacked individuals who defended existing evils. Concerning these he freely confessed that he had been more violent than was becoming. But even these books he could not revoke, for the enemies of truth would then take occasion to curse God's people with still greater cruelty.

He continued, "I shall defend myself as Christ did: 'If I have spoken evil, bear witness of the evil.' . . . By the mercy of God, I conjure you, most serene emperor, and you, most illustrious princes, and all men of every degree, to prove from the writings of the prophets and apostles that I have erred. As soon as I am convinced of this, I will retract every error, and be the first to lay hold of my books and throw them into the fire. . . .

"Far from being dismayed, I rejoice to see that the gospel is now, as in former times, a cause of trouble and dissension. This is the character, this is the destiny, of the word of God. 'I came not to send peace on earth, but a sword,' said Jesus Christ. . . . Beware lest, by presuming to quench dissensions, you should persecute the holy word of God, and draw down upon yourselves a frightful deluge of insurmountable dangers, of present disasters, and eternal desolation."[19]

Luther had spoken in German; he was now requested to repeat the same words in Latin. He again delivered his speech with the same clearness as at the first. God's providence directed in this. Many princes were so blinded by error and superstition that at first they did not see the force of Luther's reasoning, but the repetition enabled them to perceive clearly the points presented.

Those who stubbornly closed their eyes to the light were enraged at the power of Luther's words. The spokesman of the diet said angrily: "You have not answered the question put to you. . . . You are required to give a clear and precise answer. . . . Will you, or will you not, retract?"

The Reformer answered: "Since your most serene majesty and your high mightinesses require from me a clear, simple, and precise answer, I will give you one, and it is this: I cannot submit my faith either to the pope or the councils, because it is clear as the day that they have frequently erred and contradicted each other. Unless therefore I am convinced by the testimony of the Scripture, . . . *I cannot and I will not retract,* for it is unsafe for a Christian to speak against his conscience. Here I stand, I can do no other; may God help me. Amen."[20]

Thus stood this righteous man. His greatness and purity of character, his peace and joy of heart, were manifest to all as he witnessed to the superiority of that faith that overcomes the world.

At his first answer Luther had spoken with a respectful, almost submissive bearing. The Romanists regarded the request for delay as merely the prelude to his recantation. Charles himself, noting half contemptuously the monk's worn frame, his plain attire, and the simplicity of his address, had declared: "This monk will never make a heretic of me." The courage and firmness which he now displayed, the power of his reasoning, filled all parties with surprise. The emperor, moved to admiration, exclaimed: "This monk speaks with an intrepid heart and unshaken courage."

The partisans of Rome had been worsted. They sought to maintain their power, not by appealing to

Scripture, but by threats, Rome's unfailing argument. Said the spokesman of the diet: "If you do not retract, the emperor and the states of the empire will consult what course to adopt against an incorrigible heretic."

Luther said calmly: "May God be my helper, for I can retract nothing."[21]

He was directed to withdraw while the princes consulted together. Luther's persistent refusal to submit might affect the history of the church for ages. It was decided to give him one more opportunity to retract. Again the question was put. Would he renounce his doctrines? "I have no other reply to make," he said, "than that which I have already made."

The papal leaders were chagrined that their power should be despised by a humble monk. Luther had spoken to all with Christian dignity and calmness, his words free from passion and misrepresentation. He had lost sight of himself and felt only that he was in the presence of One infinitely superior to popes, kings, and emperors. The Spirit of God had been present, impressing the hearts of the chiefs of the empire.

Several princes boldly acknowledged the justice of Luther's cause. Another class did not at the time express their convictions, but at a future time became fearless supporters of the Reformation.

The elector Frederick had with deep emotion listened to Luther's speech. With joy and pride he witnessed the doctor's courage and self-possession, and determined to stand more firmly in his defense. He saw that the wisdom of popes, kings, and prelates had been brought to nought by the power of truth.

As the legate perceived the effect produced by Luther's speech, he resolved to employ every means at his command to effect the Reformer's overthrow. With eloquence and diplomatic skill he represented to the youthful emperor the danger of sacrificing, in the cause of an insignificant monk, the friendship and support of Rome.

On the day following Luther's answer, Charles announced to the diet his determination to maintain and protect the Catholic religion. Vigorous measures should be employed against Luther and the heresies he taught: "I will sacrifice my kingdoms, my treasures, my friends, my body, my blood, my soul, and my life. . . . I shall . . . proceed against him and his adherents as contumacious heretics, by excommunication, by interdict, and by every means calculated to destroy them."[22] Nevertheless, the emperor declared, Luther's safe-conduct must be respected. He must be allowed to reach his home in safety.

Luther's Safe-conduct in Jeopardy

The representatives of the pope again demanded that the Reformer's safe-conduct be disregarded. "The Rhine should receive his ashes, as it had received those of John Huss a century ago."[23] But princes of Germany, though avowed enemies to Luther, protested such a breach of public faith. They pointed to the calamities which had followed the death of Huss. They dared not call down upon Germany a repetition of those terrible evils.

Charles, in answer to the base proposal, said: "Though honor and faith should be banished from all the world, they ought to find a refuge in the hearts of princes."[24] He was further urged by Luther's papal enemies to deal with the Reformer as Sigismund had dealt with Huss. But recalling the scene when Huss in public assembly had pointed to his chains and reminded the monarch of his plighted faith, Charles V declared, "I should not like to blush like Sigismund."[25]

Yet Charles deliberately rejected the truths presented by Luther. He would not step out of the path of custom to walk in the ways of truth and righteousness. Because his fathers did, he would uphold the papacy. Thus he refused to accept light in advance of what his fathers had received.

Many at the present day cling to the traditions of their fathers. When the Lord sends additional light they refuse to accept it because it was not received by their fathers. We shall not be approved of God in looking to our fathers to determine our duty instead of searching the Word of Truth for ourselves. We are accountable for the additional light now shining upon us from the Word of God.

Divine power had spoken through Luther to the emperor and princes of Germany. His Spirit pleaded for the last time with many in that assembly. As Pilate, centuries before, so had Charles V, yielding to worldly pride, decided to reject the light of truth.

The designs against Luther were widely circulated, causing excitement throughout the city. Many friends, knowing the treacherous cruelty of Rome, resolved that the Reformer should not be sacrificed. Hundreds of nobles pledged to protect him. On the gates of houses and in public places placards were posted, some condemning and others sustaining Luther. On one were written the significant words, "Woe to thee, O land, when thy king is a child." Ecclesiastes 10:16. Popular enthusiasm in Luther's favor convinced the emperor and the diet that any injustice shown him would endanger the peace of the empire and stability of the throne.

Efforts for Compromise With Rome

Frederick of Saxony carefully concealed his real feelings toward the Reformer. At the same time he guarded him with tireless vigilance, watching his movements and those of his enemies. But many made no attempt to conceal their sympathy with Luther. "The doctor's little room," wrote Spalatin, "could not contain all the visitors who presented themselves."[26] Even those who had no faith in his doctrines could not but admire that integrity which led him to brave death rather than violate his conscience.

Earnest efforts were made to obtain Luther's consent to a compromise with Rome. Nobles and princes represented to him that if he set up his own judgment against the church and the councils he would be banished from the empire and have no defense. Again he was urged, submit to the judgment of the emperor. Then he would have nothing to fear. "I consent," said he in reply, "with all my heart, that the emperor, the princes, and even the meanest Christian, should examine and judge my works; but on one condition, that they take the word of God for their standard. Men have nothing to do but to obey it."

To another appeal he said: "I consent to renounce my safe-conduct. I place my person and my life in the emperor's hands, but the word of God—never!"[27] He stated his willingness to submit to a general council, but on condition that the council be required to decide according to the Scriptures. "In what concerns the word of God and the faith, every Christian is as good a judge as the pope, though supported by a million councils."[28] Both friends and foes were at last convinced that further effort for reconciliation would be useless.

Had the Reformer yielded a single point, Satan and his hosts would have gained the victory. But his unwavering firmness was the means of emancipating the church. The influence of this one man who dared to think and act for himself was to affect the church and the world, not only in his own time, but in all future generations.

Luther was soon commanded by the emperor to return home. This notice would be speedily followed by his condemnation. Threatening clouds overhung his path, but as he departed from Worms, his heart was filled with joy and praise.

After his departure, desirous that his firmness not be mistaken for rebellion, Luther wrote to the emperor: "I am ready most earnestly to obey your majesty, in honor or in dishonor, in life or in death, and with no exception save the word of God, by which man lives. . . . When eternal interests are concerned, God wills not that man should submit unto man. For such submission in spiritual matters is a real worship, and ought to be rendered solely to the Creator.''[29]

On the journey from Worms, princely ecclesiastics welcomed the excommunicated monk, and civil rulers honored the man whom the emperor had denounced. He was urged to preach, and, notwithstanding the imperial prohibition, he again entered the pulpit. "I never pledged myself to chain up the word of God," he said, "nor will I."[30]

He had not been long absent from Worms when the papists prevailed upon the emperor to issue an edict against him. Luther was denounced as "Satan himself under the form of a man and dressed in a monk's frock."[31] As soon as his safe-conduct should expire, all persons were forbidden to harbor him, give him food or drink, or by word or act, aid or abet him. He was to be delivered to the authorities, his adherents also to be imprisoned and their property confiscated. His writings were to be destroyed, and, finally, all who should dare to act contrary to this decree were included in its condemnation. The elector of Saxony and the princes most friendly to Luther had left Worms soon after his departure, and the emperor's decree received the sanction of the diet. The Romanists were jubilant. They considered the fate of the Reformation sealed.

God Uses Frederick of Saxony

A vigilant eye had followed Luther's movements, and a true and noble heart had resolved upon his rescue. God gave to Frederick of Saxony a plan for the Reformer's preservation. On his homeward journey Luther was separated from his attendants and hurriedly conveyed through the forest to the castle of Wartburg, an isolated mountain fortress. His concealment was so involved in mystery that even Frederick himself knew not whither he had been conducted. This ignorance was with design; so long as the elector knew nothing, he could reveal nothing. Satisfied that the Reformer was safe, he was content.

Spring, summer, and autumn passed, and winter came, and Luther still remained a prisoner. Aleander and his partisans exulted. The light of the gospel seemed about to be extinguished. But the Reformer's light was to shine forth with brighter radiance.

Security at Wartburg

In the friendly security of the Wartburg, Luther rejoiced in release from the heat and turmoil of battle. But, accustomed to a life of activity and stern conflict, he could ill endure to remain inactive. In those solitary days the condition of the church rose up before him. He feared being charged with cowardice in withdrawing from the contest. Then he reproached himself for his indolence and self-indulgence.

Yet at the same time he was daily accomplishing more than it seemed possible for one man to do. His pen was never idle. His enemies were astonished and confused by tangible proof that he was still active. A host of tracts from his pen circulated throughout Germany. He also translated the New Testament into the German tongue. From his rocky Patmos he continued for nearly a whole year to proclaim the gospel and rebuke the errors of the times.

God had withdrawn His servant from the stage of public life. In the solitude and obscurity of his mountain retreat, Luther was removed from earthly supports and shut out from human praise. He was thus saved from the pride and self-confidence so often caused by success.

As men rejoice in the freedom which the truth brings them, Satan seeks to divert their thoughts and affections from God and to fix them upon human agencies, to honor the instrument and to ignore the Hand that directs the events of providence. Too often religious leaders thus praised are led to trust in themselves. The people are disposed to look to them for guidance instead of to the Word of God. From this danger God would guard the Reformation. The eyes of men had been turned to Luther as the expounder of the truth; he was removed that all eyes might be directed to the eternal Author of truth.

References

1. D'Aubigne, bk. 6, ch. 11.
2. *Ibid.*, bk. 7, ch. 1.
3. *Ibid.*, bk. 7, ch. 1.
4. *Ibid.*, bk. 7, ch. 3.
5. *Ibid.*, bk. 7, ch. 4.
6. *Ibid.*, bk. 7, ch. 4.
7. *Ibid.*, bk. 7, ch. 6.
8. *Ibid.*, bk. 7, ch. 7.
9. *Ibid.*, bk. 7, ch. 7.
10. *Ibid.*, bk. 7, ch. 7.
11. *Ibid.*, bk. 7, ch. 7.
12. *Ibid.*, bk. 7, ch. 8.
13. D'Aubigne, bk. 7, ch. 8.
14. *Ibid.*, bk. 7, ch. 8.
15. D'Aubigne, bk. 7, ch. 8.
16. *Ibid.*, bk. 7, ch. 8.
17. *Ibid.*, bk. 7, ch. 8.
18. *Ibid.*, bk. 7, ch. 8.
19. *Ibid.*, bk. 7, ch. 8.
20. *Ibid.*, bk. 7, ch. 8.
21. *Ibid.*, bk. 7, ch. 8.
22. *Ibid.*, bk. 7, ch. 9.
23. *Ibid.*, bk. 7, ch. 9.
24. *Ibid.*, bk. 7, ch. 9.
25. Lenfant, vol. 1, p. 422.
26. Martyn, vol. 1, p. 404.
27. D'Aubigne, bk. 7, ch. 10.
28. Martyn, vol. 1, p. 410.
29. D'Aubigne, bk. 7, ch. 11.
30. Martyn, vol. 1, p. 420.
31. D'Aubigne, bk. 7, ch. 11.

9/ Light Kindled in Switzerland

A few weeks after the birth of Luther in a miner's cabin in Saxony, Ulric Zwingli was born in a herdsman's cottage among the Alps. Reared amid scenes of natural grandeur, his mind was early impressed with the majesty of God. At the side of his grandmother he listened to the few precious Bible stories she had gleaned from the legends and traditions of the church.

At the age of thirteen he went to Bern, which then possessed the most distinguished school in Switzerland. Here, however, a danger arose. Determined efforts were put forth by the friars to lure him into a monastery. Providentially his father received information of the designs of the friars. He saw that his son's future usefulness was at stake and directed him to return home.

The command was obeyed, but the youth could not be long content in his native valley, and he soon resumed his studies, repairing, after a time, to Basel. It was here that Zwingli first heard the gospel of God's free grace. Wittembach, while studying Greek and Hebrew, had been led to the Holy Scriptures, and thus rays of divine light were shed into the minds of the students under his instruction. He declared that the death of Christ is the sinner's only ransom. To Zwingli these words were as the first ray of light that precedes the dawn.

Zwingli was soon called from Basel to enter upon his lifework. His first labor was in an alpine parish. Ordained as a priest, he "devoted himself with his whole soul to the search after divine truth."[1]

The more he searched the Scriptures, the clearer appeared the contrast between truth and the heresies of Rome. He submitted himself to the Bible as the Word of God, the only sufficient, infallible rule. He saw that it must be its own interpreter. He sought every help to obtain a correct understanding of its meaning, and he invoked the aid of the Holy Spirit. "I began to ask God for His light," he afterward wrote, " and the Scriptures began to be much easier to me."[2]

The doctrine preached by Zwingli was not received from Luther. It was the doctrine of Christ. "If Luther preaches Christ," said the Swiss Reformer, "he does what I am doing. . . . Never has one single word been written by me to Luther, nor by Luther to me. And Why? . . . That it might be shown how much the Spirit of God is in unison with itself, since both of us, without any collusion, teach the doctrine of Christ with such uniformity."[3]

In 1516 Zwingli was invited to preach in the convent at Einsiedeln. Here he was to exert an influence as a Reformer that would be felt far beyond his native Alps.

Among the chief attractions of Einsiedeln was an image of the Virgin, said to have the power of working miracles. Above the gateway of the convent was the inscription, "Here a plenary remission of sins may be obtained."[4] Multitudes came to the shrine of the Virgin from all parts of Switzerland, and even from France and Germany. Zwingli seized the opportunity to proclaim liberty through the gospel to these bondslaves of superstition.

"Do not imagine," he said, "that God is in this temple more than in any other part of creation. . . . Can unprofitable works, long pilgrimages, offerings, images, the invocation of the Virgin or of the saints secure for you the grace of God? . . . What efficacy has a glossy cowl, a smooth-shorn head, a long and flowing robe, or gold-embroidered slippers?" "Christ," he said, "who was once offered upon the cross, is the sacrifice and victim, that had made satisfaction for the sins of believers to all eternity."[5]

To many it was a bitter disappointment to be told that their toilsome journey had been in vain. Pardon freely offered through Christ they could not comprehend. They were satisfied with the way Rome had marked out for them. It was easier to trust their salvation to the priests and pope than to seek purity of heart.

But another class received with gladness the tidings of redemption through Christ, and in faith accepted the Saviour's blood as their propitiation. These returned home to reveal to others the precious light they had received. The truth was thus carried from town to town, and the number of pilgrims to the Virgin's shrine greatly lessened. There was a falling off in the offerings, and consequently in the salary of Zwingli, which was drawn from them. But this caused him only joy as he saw that the power of superstition was being broken. The truth was gaining hold upon the hearts of the people.

Zwingli Called to Zurich

After three years Zwingli was called to preach in the cathedral at Zurich, the most important town of the Swiss confederacy. The influence exerted here would be widely felt. The ecclesiastics proceeded to instruct him as to his duties:

"You will make every exertion to collect the revenues of the chapter without overlooking the least. . . . You will be diligent in increasing the income arising from the sick, from masses, and in general from every ecclesiastical ordinance." "As for the administration of the sacraments, the preaching, and the care of the flock, . . . you may employ a substitute, and particularly in preaching."[6]

Zwingli listened in silence to this charge, and said in reply, "The life of Christ has been too long hidden from the people. I shall preach upon the whole of the

Gospel of St. Matthew. . . . It is to God's glory, to the praise of His Son, to the real salvation of souls, and to their edification in the true faith, that I shall consecrate my ministry."

The people flocked in great numbers to listen to his preaching. He began his ministry by opening the Gospels and explaining the life, teachings, and death of Christ. "It is to Christ," he said, "that I desire to lead you—to Christ, the true source of salvation." Statesmen, scholars, artisans, and peasants listened to his words. He fearlessly rebuked the evils and corruptions of the times. Many returned from the cathedral praising God. "This man," they said, "is a preacher of the truth. He will be our Moses, to lead us forth from this Egyptian darkness."[7]

After a time opposition arose. The monks assailed him with gibes and sneers; others resorted to insolence and threats. But Zwingli bore all with patience.

When God is preparing to break the shackles of ignorance and superstition, Satan works with greatest power to enshroud men in darkness and to bind their fetters more firmly. Rome proceeded with renewed energy to open her market throughout Christendom, offering pardon for money. Every sin had its price, and men were granted free license for crime if the treasury of the church was kept well filled. Thus the two movements advanced—Rome licensing sin and making it her source of revenue, the Reformers condemning sin and pointing to Christ as the propitiation and deliverer.

Sale of Indulgences in Switzerland

In Germany the sale of indulgences was conducted by the infamous Tetzel. In Switzerland the traffic was put under the control of Samson, an Italian monk. Samson had already secured immense sums from Germany and Switzerland to fill the papal treasury. Now he traversed Switzerland, despoiling the poor peasants of their scanty earnings and exacting rich gifts from the wealthy. The Reformer immediately set out to oppose him. Such was Zwingli's success in exposing the friar's pretensions that he was obliged to leave for other quarters. At Zurich, Zwingli preached zealously against the pardonmongers. When Samson approached the place, he secured an entrance by stratagem. But, sent away without the sale of a single pardon, he soon left Switzerland.

The plague, or Great Death, swept over Switzerland in the year 1519. Many were led to feel how vain and worthless were the pardons they had purchased; they longed for a surer foundation for their faith. Zwingli at Zurich was smitten down, and the report was widely circulated that he was dead. In that trying hour he looked in faith to the cross of Calvary, trusting in the all-sufficient propitiation for sin. When he came back from the gates of death, it was to preach the gospel with greater fervor than ever before. The people themselves had come from attending the sick and the dying, and they felt, as never before, the value of the gospel.

Zwingli had arrived at a clearer understanding of its truths and had more fully experienced in himself its renewing power. "Christ," he said, " . . . has purchased for us a never-ending redemption. . . . His passion is . . . an eternal sacrifice, and everlastingly effectual to heal; it satisfies the divine justice forever in behalf of all those who rely upon it with firm and unshaken faith. . . . Wherever there is faith in God, there a zeal exists urging and impelling men to good works."[8]

Step by step the Reformation advanced in Zurich. In alarm its enemies aroused to active opposition. Repeated attacks were made upon Zwingli. The teacher of heresy must be silenced. The bishop of Constance dispatched three deputies to the Council of Zurich, accusing Zwingli of endangering the peace and order of society. If the authority of the church were to be set aside, he urged, universal anarchy would result.

The council declined to take action against

Zwingli, and Rome prepared for a fresh attack. The Reformer exclaimed: "Let them come on; I fear them as the beetling cliff fears the waves that thunder at its feet."[9] The efforts of the ecclesiastics only furthered the cause which they sought to overthrow. The truth continued to spread. In Germany its adherents, cast down by Luther's disappearance, took heart again as they saw the progress of the gospel in Switzerland. As the Reformation became established in Zurich, its fruits were more fully seen in the suppression of vice and the promotion of order.

Disputation With Romanists

Seeing how little had been accomplished by persecution in suppressing Luther's work in Germany, the Romanists decided they would hold a disputation with Zwingli. They would make sure of victory by choosing not only the place of combat but the judges that should decide between the disputants. And if they could once get Zwingli in their power, they would take care that he did not escape. This purpose, however, was carefully concealed.

The disputation was appointed to be held at Baden. But the Council of Zurich, suspecting the designs of the papists and warned by the burning piles kindled in the papal cantons for confessors of the gospel, forbade their pastor to expose himself to this peril. To go to Baden, where the blood of martyrs for the truth had just been shed, was to go to certain death. Oecolampadius and Haller were chosen to represent the Reformers, while the famous Dr. Eck, supported by a host of learned doctors and prelates, was the champion of Rome.

The secretaries were all chosen by the papists, and others were forbidden to take notes, on pain of death. Notwithstanding, a student in attendance at the disputation made a record each evening of the arguments that day presented. These papers two other students undertook to deliver, with the daily letters of

Oecolampadius, to Zwingli at Zurich. The Reformer answered, giving counsel. To elude the vigilance of the guard at the city gates, these messengers brought baskets of poultry on their heads and were permitted to pass without hindrance.

Zwingli "has labored more," said Myconius, "by his meditations, his sleepless nights, and the advice which he transmitted to Baden, than he would have done by discussing in person in the midst of his enemies."[10]

The Romanists had come to Baden in their richest robes and glittering with jewels. They fared luxuriously, their tables spread with costly delicacies and choice wines. In marked contrast appeared the Reformers, whose frugal fare kept them but short time at table. Oecolampadius's landlord, taking occasion to watch him in his room, found him always in study or at prayer, and reported that the heretic was at least "very pious."

At the conference, "Eck haughtily ascended a pulpit splendidly decorated, while the humble Oecolampadius, meanly clothed, was forced to take his seat in front of his opponent on a rudely carved stool." Eck's stentorian voice and unbounded assurance never failed him. The defender of the faith was to be rewarded by a handsome fee. When better arguments failed, he had resort to insults and even oaths.

Oecolampadius, modest and self-distrustful, had shrunk from the combat. Though gentle and courteous in demeanor, he proved himself able and unflinching. The Reformer adhered steadfastly to the Scriptures. "Custom," he said, "has no force in our Switzerland, unless it be according to the constitution; now, in matters of faith, the Bible is our constitution."[11]

The calm, clear reasoning of the Reformer, so gently and modestly presented, appealed to minds that turned in disgust from Eck's boastful assumptions.

The discussion continued eighteen days. The papists claimed the victory. Most of the deputies sided with

Rome, and the diet pronounced the Reformers vanquished and declared that they, together with Zwingli, were cut off from the church. But the contest resulted in a strong impetus to the Protestant cause. Not long afterward the important cities of Bern and Basel declared for the Reformation.

References
1. Wylie, bk. 8, ch. 5.
2. *Ibid.*, bk. 8, ch. 6.
3. D'Aubigne, bk. 8, ch. 9.
4. *Ibid.*, bk. 8, ch. 5.
5. *Ibid.*, bk. 8, ch. 5.
6. *Ibid.*, bk. 8, ch. 6.
7. *Ibid.*, bk. 8, ch. 6.
8. *Ibid.*, bk. 8, ch. 9.
9. Wylie, bk. 8, ch. 11.
10. D'Aubigne, bk. 11, ch. 13.
11. *Ibid.*, bk. 11, ch. 13.

10/ Progress in Germany

Luther's mysterious disappearance excited consternation throughout Germany. Wild rumors were circulated and many believed he had been murdered. There was great lamentation, and many bound themselves by solemn oath to avenge his death.

Though at first exultant at the supposed death of Luther, his enemies were filled with fear now that he had become a captive. "The only remaining way of saving ourselves," said one, "is to light torches, and hunt for Luther through the whole world, to restore him to the nation that is calling for him."[1] The tidings that he was safe, though a prisoner, calmed the people, while his writings were read with greater eagerness than ever before. Increasing numbers joined the cause of the heroic man who had defended the Word of God.

The seed Luther had sown sprang up everywhere. His absence accomplished a work his presence would have failed to do. Now that their great leader was removed, other laborers pressed forward so that the work nobly begun might not be hindered.

Satan now attempted to deceive and destroy the people by palming off upon them a counterfeit in place of the true work. As there were false christs in the first century, so there arose false prophets in the sixteenth.

A few men imagined themselves to receive special revelations from Heaven and to have been divinely commissioned to carry forward the Reformation which, they declared, had been but feebly begun by Luther. In truth, they were undoing the work which he had accomplished. They rejected the principle of the Reformation—that the Word of God is the all-sufficient rule of faith and practice. For that unerring guide they substituted the uncertain standard of their own feelings and impressions.

Others naturally inclined to fanaticism united with them. The proceedings of these enthusiasts created no little excitement. Luther had aroused the people to feel the necessity of reform, and now some really honest persons were misled by the pretensions of the new "prophets."

The leaders of the movement urged their claims upon Melanchthon: "We are sent by God to instruct the people. We have held familiar conversations with the Lord; we know what will happen; in a word, we are apostles and prophets, and appeal to Dr. Luther."

The Reformers were perplexed. Said Melanchthon: "There are indeed extraordinary spirits in these men; but what spirits? . . . On the one hand, let us beware of quenching the Spirit of God, and on the other, of being led astray by the spirit of Satan."[2]

The Fruit of the New Teaching Apparent

The people were led to neglect the Bible or to cast it wholly aside. Students, spurning all restraint, abandoned their studies and withdrew from the university. The men who thought themselves competent to revive and control the work of the Reformation succeeded only in bringing it to the verge of ruin. The Romanists now regained their confidence and exclaimed exultingly: "One last struggle, and all will be ours."

Luther at the Wartburg, hearing of what had occurred, said with deep concern: "I always expected that Satan would send us this plague."[3] He perceived the true character of those pretended "prophets." The opposition of pope and emperor had not caused so great perplexity and distress as now. From the professed "friends" of the Reformation had risen its worst enemies to stir up strife and create confusion.

Luther had been urged forward by the Spirit of God and had been carried beyond himself. Yet he often trembled for the result of his work: "If I knew that my doctrine injured one man, one single man, however lowly and obscure—which it cannot, for it is the gospel itself—I would rather die ten times than not retract it."[4]

Wittenberg itself was falling under the power of fanaticism and lawlessness. Throughout Germany Luther's enemies were charging it upon him. In bitterness of soul he asked, "Can such, then, be the end of this great work of the Reformation?" Again, as he wrestled with God in prayer, peace flowed into his heart. "The work is not mine, but Thine own," he said. But he determined to return to Wittenberg.

He was under the ban of the empire. Enemies were at liberty to take his life, friends forbidden to shelter him. But he saw that the work of the gospel was imperiled, and in the name of the Lord he went out fearlessly to battle for truth. In a letter to the elector Luther said: "I am going to Wittenberg under a protection far higher than that of princes and electors. I think not of soliciting your highness's support, and far from desiring your protection, I would rather protect you myself. . . . There is no sword that can further this cause. God alone must do everything." In a second letter, Luther added: "I am ready to incur the displeasure of your highness and the anger of the whole world. Are not the Wittenbergers my sheep? And ought I not, if necessary, to expose myself to death for their sakes?"[5]

The Power of the Word

It was soon noised through Wittenberg that Luther had returned and was to preach. The church was filled. With great wisdom and gentleness he instructed and reproved:

"The mass is a bad thing; God is opposed to it; it ought to be abolished. . . . But let no one be torn from it by force. . . . God's . . . word must act, and not we.

. . . We have a right to speak: we have not the right to act. Let us preach; the rest belongs unto God. Were I to employ force, what should I gain? God lays hold upon the heart; and when the heart is taken, all is won. . . .

"I will preach, discuss, and write; but I will constrain none, for faith is a voluntary act. . . . I stood up against the pope, indulgences, and papists, but without violence or tumult. I put forward God's word; I preached and wrote—this was all I did. And yet while I was asleep, . . . the word that I had preached overthrew popery, so that neither prince nor emperor has done it so much harm. And yet I did nothing; the word alone did all."[6] The Word of God broke the spell of fanatical excitement. The gospel brought back misguided people into the way of truth.

Several years later the fanaticism broke out with more terrible results. Said Luther: "To them the Holy Scriptures were but a dead letter, and they all began to cry, 'The Spirit! the Spirit!' But most assuredly I will not follow where their spirit leads them."[7]

Thomas Münzer, the most active of the fanatics, was a man of considerable ability, but he had not learned true religion. "He was possessed with a desire of reforming the world, and forgot, as all enthusiasts do, that the reformation should begin with himself."[8] He was unwilling to be second, even to Luther. He himself, he claimed, had been divinely commissioned to introduce the true reform: "He who possesses this spirit, possesses the true faith, although he should never see the Scriptures in his life."[9]

The fanatical teachers gave themselves up to be governed by impressions, regarding every thought and impulse as the voice of God. Some even burned their Bibles. Münzer's doctrines were received by thousands. He soon declared that to obey princes was to attempt to serve both God and Belial.

Münzer's revolutionary teachings led the people to break away from all control. Terrible scenes of strife followed, and the fields of Germany were drenched with blood.

Agony of Soul Now Pressed Upon Luther

The papist princes declared that the rebellion was the fruit of Luther's doctrines. This charge could not but cause the Reformer great distress—that the cause of truth should be disgraced by being ranked with the basest fanaticism. On the other hand, the leaders in the revolt hated Luther. He had not only denied their claims to divine inspiration, but had pronounced them rebels against the civil authority. In retaliation they denounced him as a base pretender.

The Romanists expected to witness the downfall of the Reformation. And they blamed Luther even for the errors which he had most earnestly endeavored to correct. The fanatical party, falsely claiming to have been treated with injustice, gained sympathy and came to be regarded as martyrs. Thus the ones in opposition to the Reformation were pitied and lauded. This was the work of the same spirit of rebellion first manifested in heaven.

Satan is constantly seeking to deceive men and lead them to call sin righteousness, and righteousness sin. Counterfeit holiness, spurious sanctification, still exhibits the same spirit as in the days of Luther, diverting minds from Scripture and leading men to follow feelings and impressions rather than the law of God.

Fearlessly did Luther defend the gospel from attack. With the Word of God he warred against the usurped authority of the pope, while he stood firm as a rock against the fanaticism that sought to ally itself with the Reformation.

Each of these opposing elements set aside the Holy Scriptures, exalting human wisdom as the source of truth. Rationalism idolizes reason and makes this the criterion for religion. Romanism, claiming an inspiration descended in unbroken line from the apostles, gives opportunity for extravagance and corruption to be concealed under the "apostolic" commission. The inspiration claimed by Münzer proceeded from the vagaries of the imagination. True Christianity receives the Word of God as the test of all inspiration.

Upon his return from Wartburg, Luther completed his translation of the New Testament, and the gospel soon afterward was given to the people of Germany in their own language. This translation was received with great joy by all who loved the truth.

The priests were alarmed at the thought that common people would now be able to discuss with them God's Word and that their own ignorance would thus be exposed. Rome summoned all her authority to prevent the circulation of the Scriptures. But the more she prohibited the Bible, the greater was the anxiety of the people to know what it really taught. All who could read carried it about with them and could not be satisfied until they had committed large portions to memory. Luther immediately began the translation of the Old Testament.

Luther's writings were welcomed alike in city and in hamlet. "What Luther and his friends composed, others circulated. Monks, convinced of the unlawfulness of monastic obligations, but too ignorant to proclaim the word of God, . . . sold the books of Luther and his friends. Germany soon swarmed with these bold colporteurs."[10]

Bible Study Everywhere

At night the teachers of the village schools read aloud to little groups gathered at the fireside. With every effort some souls would be convicted of the truth. "The entrance of thy words giveth light; it giveth understanding unto the simple." Psalm 119:130.

The papists who had left the study of the Scriptures to the priests and monks now called on them to refute the new teachings. But, ignorant of the Scriptures, priests and friars were totally defeated. "Unhappily," said a Catholic writer, "Luther had persuaded his followers to put no faith in any other oracle than the Holy Scriptures."[11] Crowds would gather to hear truth advocated by men of little education. The shameful ignorance of great men was made apparent as their arguments were met by the simple teachings of God's Word. Laborers, soldiers, women, and even children, were better acquainted with the Bible than priests and learned doctors.

Generous-minded youths were devoted to study, investigating Scripture and familiarizing themselves with the masterpieces of antiquity. Possessing active minds and intrepid hearts, these young men soon acquired such knowledge that for a long period none could compete with them. The people had found in the new teachings that which supplied the wants of their souls, and they turned away from those who had so long fed them with the worthless husks of superstitious rites and human traditions.

When persecution was kindled against the teachers of the truth, they gave heed to the words of Christ: "When they persecute you in this city, flee ye into another." Matthew 10:23. The fugitives would find somewhere a hospitable door opened to them, and they would preach Christ, sometimes in the church or in private houses or in the open air. The truth spread with irresistible power.

In vain ecclesiastical and civil authorities resorted to imprisonment, torture, fire, and sword. Thousands of believers sealed their faith with their blood, and yet persecution served only to extend the truth. The fanaticism which Satan endeavored to unite with it resulted in making more clear the contrast between the work of Satan and the work of God.

References
1. D'Aubigne, bk. 9, ch. 1.
2. *Ibid.*, bk. 9, ch. 7.
3. *Idem.*
4. *Idem.*

5. *Ibid.*, bk. 9, ch. 8.
6. *Idem.*
7. *Ibid.*, bk. 10, ch. 10.
8. *Ibid.*, bk. 9, ch. 8.
9. *Ibid.*, bk. 10, ch. 10.
10. *Ibid.*, bk. 9, ch. 11.
11. D'Aubigne, bk. 9, ch. 11.

11/ The Protest of the Princes

One of the noblest testimonies ever uttered for the Reformation was the Protest offered by the Christian princes of Germany at the Diet of Spires in 1529. The courage and firmness of those men of God gained for succeeding ages liberty of conscience, and gave to the reformed church the name of Protestant.

God's providence had held in check the forces that opposed the truth. Charles V was bent on crushing the Reformation, but as often as he raised his hand to strike he had been forced to turn aside the blow. Again and again at the critical moment the armies of the Turk appeared on the frontier, or the king of France or even the pope himself made war upon him. Thus amid the strife and tumult of nations, the Reformation had been left to strengthen and extend.

At last, however, the papal sovereigns made common cause against the Reformers. The emperor summoned a diet to convene at Spires in 1529 for the purpose of crushing heresy. If peaceable means failed, Charles was prepared to resort to the sword.

The papists at Spires openly manifested their hostility toward the Reformers. Said Melanchthon: "We are the execration and the sweepings of the world; but Christ will look down on His poor people, and will preserve them."[1] The people of Spires thirsted for the Word of God, and, notwithstanding prohibition, thousands flocked to services held in the chapel of the elector of Saxony. This hastened the crisis. Religious toleration had been legally established, and the evangelical states were resolved to oppose the infringement of their rights. Luther's place was supplied by his colaborers and the princes whom God had raised up to defend His cause. Frederick of Saxony had been removed by death, but Duke John, his successor, had joyfully welcomed the Reformation and displayed great courage.

The priests demanded that the states which had accepted the Reformation submit to Romish jurisdiction. The Reformers, on the other hand, could not consent that Rome should again bring under her control those states that had received the Word of God.

It was finally proposed that where the Reformation had not become established, the Edict of Worms should be enforced; and that "where the people could not conform to it without danger of revolt, they should at least effect no new reform, . . . they should not oppose the celebration of the mass, they should permit no Roman Catholic to embrace Lutheranism." This measure passed the diet, to the great satisfaction of the priests and prelates.

Mighty Issues at Stake

If this edict were enforced, "the Reformation could neither be extended . . . nor be established on solid foundations . . . where it already existed."[2] Liberty would be prohibited. No conversions would be allowed. The hopes of the world seemed about to be extinguished.

The evangelical party looked to one another in blank dismay: "What is to be done?" "Shall the chiefs of the Reformation submit, and accept the edict? . . . The Lutheran princes were guaranteed the free exercise of their religion. The same boon was extended to all those of their subjects who, prior to the passing of the measure, had embraced the reformed views. Ought not this to content them? . . .

"Happily they looked at the principle on which this arrangement was based, and they acted in faith. What was that principle? It was the right of Rome to coerce conscience and forbid free inquiry. But were not themselves and their Protestant subjects to enjoy religious freedom? Yes, as a favor specially stipulated for in the arrangement, but not as a right. . . . The acceptance of the proposed arrangement would have been a virtual admission that religious liberty ought to be confined to reformed Saxony; and as to all the rest of Christendom, free inquiry and the profession of the reformed faith were crimes and must be visited with the dungeon and the stake. Could they consent to localize religious liberty? . . . Could the Reformers have pleaded that they were innocent of the blood of those hundreds and thousands who, in pursuance of this arrangement, would have to yield up their lives in popish lands?"[3]

"Let us reject this decree," said the princes. "In matters of conscience the majority has no power." To protect liberty of conscience is the duty of the state, and this is the limit of its authority in matters of religion.

The papists determined to put down what they termed "daring obstinacy." The representatives of the free cities were required to declare whether they would accede to the terms of the proposition. They pleaded for delay, but in vain. Nearly one half sided with the Reformers, knowing that their position marked them for future condemnation and persecution. Said one, "We must either deny the word of God, or—be burnt."[4]

Noble Stand of the Princes

King Ferdinand, the emperor's representative, tried the art of persuasion. He "begged the princes to accept the decree, assuring them that the emperor would be exceedingly pleased with them." But these faithful men answered calmly: "We will obey the emperor in everything that may contribute to maintain peace and the honor of God."

The king at last announced that "their only remaining course was to submit to the majority." Having thus spoken, he withdrew, giving the Reformers no opportunity for reply. "They sent a deputation entreating the king to return." He answered only, "It is a settled affair; submission is all that remains."[5]

The imperial party flattered themselves that the cause of the emperor and the pope was strong, and that of the Reformers weak. Had the Reformers depended upon human aid alone, they would have been as powerless as the papists supposed. But they appealed "from the report of the Diet to the word of God, and from the emperor Charles to Jesus Christ, the King of kings and Lord of lords."

As Ferdinand had refused to regard their conscientious convictions, the princes decided not to heed his absence, but to bring their protest before the national council without delay. A solemn declaration was drawn up and presented to the diet:

"We protest by these presents . . . that we, for us and for our people, neither consent nor adhere in any manner whatsoever to the proposed decree, in anything that is contrary to God, to His holy word, to our right conscience, to the salvation of our souls. . . . For this reason we reject the yoke that is imposed on us. . . . At the same time we are in expectation that his imperial majesty will behave toward us like a Christian prince who loves God above all things; and we declare ourselves ready to pay unto him, as well as unto you, gracious lords, all the affection and obedience that are our just and legitimate duty."[6]

The majority were filled with amazement and alarm at the boldness of the protesters. Dissension, strife, and bloodshed seemed inevitable. But the Reformers, relying upon the arm of Omnipotence, were "full of courage and firmness."

"The principles contained in this celebrated protest . . . constitute the very essence of Protestantism. . . . Protestantism sets the power of conscience above the magistrate, and the authority of the word of God above the visible church. . . . It . . . says with the prophets and apostles, '*we must obey God rather than man.*' In presence of the crown of Charles the Fifth, it uplifts the crown of Jesus Christ.''[7] The Protest of Spires was a solemn witness against religious intolerance and an assertion of the right of all men to worship God according to their own consciences.

The experience of these noble Reformers contains a lesson for all succeeding ages. Satan is still opposed to the Scriptures being made the guide of life. In our time there is need of a return to the great Protestant principle—the Bible, and the Bible only, as the rule of faith and duty. Satan is still working to destroy religious liberty. The antichristian power which the protesters of Spires rejected is now seeking to reestablish its lost supremacy.

The Diet at Augsburg

The evangelical princes had been denied a hearing by King Ferdinand, but to quiet the dissensions which disturbed the empire, Charles V in the year following the Protest of Spires convoked a diet at Augsburg. He announced his intention to preside in person. The Protestant leaders were summoned.

The elector of Saxony was urged by his councilors not to appear at the diet: "Is it not risking everything to go and shut oneself up within the walls of a city with a powerful enemy?" But others nobly declared, "Let the princes only comport themselves with courage, and God's cause is saved." "God is faithful; He will not abandon us," said Luther.[8]

The elector set out for Augsburg. Many went forward with gloomy countenance and troubled heart. But Luther, who accompanied them as far as Coburg, revived their faith by singing the hymn written on that journey, "A Mighty Fortress Is Our God." Many a heavy heart lightened at the sound of the inspiring strains.

The reformed princes had determined upon having a

statement of their views, with the evidence from the Scriptures, to present before the diet. The task of its preparation was committed to Luther, Melanchthon, and their associates. This Confession was accepted by the Protestants, and they assembled to affix their names to the document.

The Reformers were solicitous that their cause should not be confounded with political questions. As the Christian princes advanced to sign the Confession, Melanchthon interposed, saying, "It is for the theologians and ministers to propose these things; let us reserve for other matters the authority of the mighty ones of the earth." "God forbid," replied John of Saxony, "that you should exclude me. I am resolved to do what is right, without troubling myself about my crown. I desire to confess the Lord. My electoral hat and my ermine are not so precious to me as the cross of Jesus Christ." Said another of the princes as he took the pen, "If the honor of my Lord Jesus Christ requires it, I am ready . . . to leave my goods and life behind." "I would rather renounce my subjects and my states, rather quit the country of my fathers staff in hand," he continued, "than receive any other doctrine than that which is contained in this Confession."[9]

The appointed time came. Charles V, surrounded by the electors and the princes, gave audience to the Protestant Reformers. In that august assembly the truths of the gospel were clearly set forth and the errors of the papal church pointed out. That day has been pronounced "the greatest day of the Reformation, and one of the most glorious in the history of Christianity and of mankind."[10]

The monk of Wittenberg had stood alone at Worms. Now in his stead were the most powerful princes of the empire. "I am overjoyed," Luther wrote, "that I have lived until this hour, in which Christ has been publicly exalted by such illustrious confessors, and in so glorious an assembly."

That which the emperor had forbidden to be

preached from the pulpit was proclaimed from the palace; what many had regarded as unfit even for servants to listen to was heard with wonder by the masters and lords of the empire. Crowned princes were the preachers, and the sermon was the royal truth of God. "Since the apostolic age there has never been a greater work or a more magnificent confession."[11]

One of the principles most firmly maintained by Luther was that there should be no resort to secular power in support of the Reformation. He rejoiced that the gospel was confessed by princes of the empire; but when they proposed to unite in a defensive league, he declared that "the doctrine of the gospel would be defended by God alone. . . . All the politic precautions suggested were, in his view, attributable to unworthy fear and sinful mistrust."[12]

At a later date, referring to the league contemplated by the reformed princes, Luther declared that the only weapon in this warfare should be "the sword of the Spirit." He wrote to the elector of Saxony: "We cannot on our conscience approve of the proposed alliance. The cross of Christ must be borne. Let your highness be without fear. We shall do more by our prayers than all our enemies by their boastings."[13]

From the secret place of prayer came the power that shook the world in the Reformation. At Augsburg Luther "did not pass a day without devoting three hours at least to prayer." In the privacy of his chamber he was heard to pour out his soul before God in words "full of adoration, fear, and hope." To Melanchthon he wrote: "If the cause is unjust, abandon it; if the cause is just, why should we belie the promises of Him who commands us to sleep without fear?"[14] The Protestant Reformers had built on Christ. The gates of hell could not prevail against them!

References
    1. D'Aubigne, bk. 13, ch. 5.
    2. *Idem.*

3. Wylie, bk. 9, ch. 15.
4. D'Aubigne, bk. 13, ch. 5.
5. *Idem.*
6. D'Aubigne, bk. 13, ch. 6.
7. *Idem.*
8. *Ibid.*, bk. 14, ch. 2.
9. *Ibid.*, bk. 14, ch. 6.
10. *Ibid.*, bk. 14, ch. 7.
11. *Idem.*
12. D'Aubigne, London ed., bk. 10, ch. 14.
13. *Ibid.*, bk. 14, ch. 1.
14. *Ibid.*, bk. 14, ch. 6.

12/ Daybreak in France

The Protest of Spires and the Confession at Augsburg were followed by years of conflict and darkness. Weakened by divisions, Protestantism seemed destined to be destroyed.

But in the moment of his apparent triumph, the emperor was smitten with defeat. He was forced at last to grant toleration to the doctrines which it had been the ambition of his life to destroy. He saw his armies wasted by battle, his treasuries drained, his many kingdoms threatened by revolt, while everywhere the faith he had endeavored to suppress was extending. Charles V had been battling against omnipotent power. God had said, "Let there be light," but the emperor had sought to keep the darkness unbroken. Worn out with the long struggle, he abdicated the throne and buried himself in a cloister.

In Switzerland, while many cantons accepted the reformed faith, others clung to the creed of Rome. Persecution gave rise to civil war. Zwingli and many who had united in reform fell on the bloody field of Cappel. Rome was triumphant and in many places seemed about to recover all that she had lost. But God had not forsaken His cause or His people. In other lands He raised up laborers to carry forward the reform.

In France, one of the first to catch the light was Lefevre, a professor in the University of Paris. In his researches into ancient literature, his attention was directed to the Bible, and he introduced its study among his students. He had undertaken to prepare a history of the saints and martyrs as given in the legends of the church, and had already made considerable progress in it, when, thinking that he might obtain assistance from the Bible, he began its study. Here indeed he found saints, but not such as figured in the Roman [Catholic Church] calendar. In disgust he turned away from his self-appointed task and devoted himself to the Word of God.

In 1512, before either Luther or Zwingli had begun the work of reform, Lefevre wrote, "It is God who gives us, by faith, that righteousness which by grace alone justifies to eternal life."[1] And while teaching that the glory of salvation belongs solely to God, he also declared that the duty of obedience belongs to man.

Some among Lefevre's students listened eagerly to his words and long after the teacher's voice was silenced, continued to declare the truth. Such was William Farel. The son of pious parents and a devoted Romanist, he burned with zeal to destroy all who should dare to oppose the church. "I would gnash my teeth like a furious wolf," he afterward said, "when I heard anyone speaking against the pope." But adoration of the saints, worshiping at the altars, and adorning with gifts the holy shrines could not bring peace of soul. Conviction of sin fastened upon him, which all acts of penance failed to banish. He listened to Lefevre's words: "Salvation is of grace." "It is the cross of Christ alone that openeth the gates of heaven, and shutteth the gates of hell."[2]

By a conversion like that of Paul, Farel turned from the bondage of tradition to the liberty of the sons of God. "Instead of the murderous heart of a ravening wolf," he came back, he says, "quietly like a meek and harmless lamb, having his heart entirely withdrawn from the pope, and given to Jesus Christ."[3]

While Lefevre spread the light among students, Farel went forth to declare the truth in public. A dignitary of the church, the bishop of Meaux, soon united with them. Other teachers joined in proclaiming the gospel, and it won adherents from the homes of artisans and peasants to the palace of the king. The sister of Francis I accepted the reformed faith. With high hopes the Reformers looked forward to the time when France should be won to the gospel.

French New Testament

But their hopes were not to be realized. Trial and persecution awaited the disciples of Christ. However, a time of peace intervened, that they might gain strength to meet the tempest; and the Reformation made rapid progress. Lefevre undertook the translation of the New Testament; and at the very time when Luther's German Bible issued from the press in Wittenberg, the French New Testament was published at Meaux. Soon the peasants of Meaux were in possession of the Holy Scriptures. The laborers in the field, the artisans in the workship, cheered their daily toil by talking of the precious truths of the Bible. Though belonging to the humblest class, an unlearned and hardworking peasantry, the reforming, uplifting power of divine grace was seen in their lives.

The light kindled at Meaux shed its beams afar. Every day the number of converts was increasing. The rage of the hierarchy was for a time held in check by the king, but the papal leaders finally prevailed. The stake was set up. Many witnessed for the truth amid the flames.

In the lordly halls of the castle and the palace there were kingly souls by whom truth was valued above wealth or rank or even life. Louis de Berquin was of noble birth, devoted to study, polished in manners, and of blameless morals. "He crowned all his other virtues by holding Lutheranism in special abhorrence." But, providentially guided to the Bible, he was amazed to find there "not the doctrines of Rome, but the doctrines of Luther." He gave himself to the cause of the gospel.

The Romanists of France thrust him into prison as a

heretic, but he was set at liberty by the king. For years, Francis wavered between Rome and the Reformation. Berquin was three times imprisoned by the papal authorities, only to be released by the monarch, who refused to sacrifice him to the malice of the hierarchy. Berquin was repeatedly warned of the danger that threatened him in France and urged to follow the steps of those who had found safety in voluntary exile.

Bold Berquin

But Berquin's zeal only waxed stronger. He determined upon bolder measures. He would not only stand in defense of the truth, he would attack error. The most active of his opponents were the learned monks of the theological department in the University of Paris, one of the highest ecclesiastical authorities in the nation. From the writings of these doctors, Berquin drew twelve propositions which he publicly declared to be "opposed to the Bible," and he appealed to the king to act as judge in the controversy.

The monarch, glad of an opportunity of humbling the pride of these haughty monks, bade the Romanists defend their cause by the Bible. This weapon would avail them little; torture and the stake were arms which they better understood how to wield. Now they saw themselves about to fall into the pit into which they had hoped to plunge Berquin. They looked about them for some way of escape.

"Just at that time an image of the virgin at the corner of one of the streets was mutilated." Crowds flocked to the place, with mourning and indignation. The king was deeply moved. "These are the fruits of the doctrines of Berquin," the monks cried. "All is about to be overthrown—religion, the laws, the throne itself—by this Lutheran conspiracy."[4]

The king withdrew from Paris, and the monks were left free to work their will. Berquin was tried and condemned to die, and lest Francis should interpose to save him, the sentence was executed on the very day it was pronounced. At noon an immense throng gathered to witness the event, and many saw with astonishment that the victim had been chosen from the best and bravest of the noble families of France. Amazement, indignation, scorn, and bitter hatred darkened the faces of that surging crowd, but upon one face no shadow rested. The martyr was conscious only of the presence of his Lord.

Berquin's countenance was radiant with the light of heaven. He wore "a cloak of velvet, a doublet of satin and damask, and golden hose."[5] He was about to testify to his faith in the presence of the King of kings, and no token of mourning should belie his joy.

As the procession moved slowly through the crowded streets, the people marked with wonder the joyous triumph of his bearing. "He is," they said, "like one who sits in a temple, and meditates on holy things."

Berquin at the Stake

At the stake, Berquin endeavored to address a few words to the people; but the monks began to shout and the soldiers to clash their arms, and their clamor drowned the martyr's voice. Thus in 1529 the highest ecclesiastical authority of cultured Paris "set the populace of 1793 the base example of stifling on the scaffold the sacred words of the dying."[6] Berquin was strangled, and his body was consumed in the flames.

Teachers of the reformed faith departed to other fields. Lefevre made his way to Germany. Farel returned to his native town in eastern France, to spread the light in the home of his childhood. The truth which he taught found listeners. Soon he was banished from the city. He traversed the villages, teaching in private dwellings and secluded meadows, finding shelter in the forests and among rocky caverns which had been his haunts in boyhood.

As in apostolic days, persecution had "fallen out rather unto the furtherance of the gospel." Philippians

1:12. Driven from Paris and Meaux, "they that were scattered abroad went everywhere preaching the word." Acts 8:4. And thus the light found its way into many remote provinces of France.

The Call of Calvin

In one of the schools of Paris was a thoughtful, quiet youth marked for the blamelessness of his life, for intellectual ardor, and for religious devotion. His genius and application made him the pride of the college, and it was confidently anticipated that John Calvin would become one of the ablest defenders of the church.

But a ray of divine light penetrated the walls of scholasticism and superstition by which Calvin was enclosed. Olivetan, a cousin of Calvin, had joined the Reformers. The two kinsmen discussed together the matters disturbing Christendom. "There are but two religions in the world," said Olivetan, the Protestant. "The one . . . which men have invented, in . . . which man saves himself by ceremonies and good works; the other is that one religion which is revealed in the Bible, and which teaches man to look for salvation solely from the free grace of God."

"I will have none of your new doctrines," exclaimed Calvin; "think you that I have lived in error all my days?"[7] But alone in his chamber he pondered his cousin's words. He saw himself without an intercessor in the presence of a holy and just Judge. Good works, the ceremonies of the church, all were powerless to atone for sin. Confession, penance, could not reconcile the soul with God.

Witness to a Burning

Chancing one day to visit one of the public squares, Calvin witnessed the burning of a heretic. Amid the tortures of that dreadful death and under the terrible condemnation of the church, the martyr manifested a faith and courage which the young student painfully contrasted with his own despair and darkness. Upon the Bible, he knew, the "heretics" rested their faith. He determined to study it and discover the secret of their joy.

In the Bible he found Christ. "O Father," he cried, "His sacrifice has appeased Thy wrath; His blood has washed away my impurities; His cross has borne my curse; His death has atoned for me. . . . Thou hast touched my heart, in order that I may hold in abomination all other merits save those of Jesus."[8]

Now he determined to devote his life to the gospel. But he was naturally timid and desired to devote himself to study. The earnest entreaties of his friends, however, at last won his consent to become a public teacher. His words were as dew falling to refresh the earth. He was now in a provincial town under the protection of the princess Margaret, who, loving the gospel, extended her protection to its disciples. Calvin's work began with the people at their homes. Those who heard the message carried the good news to others. He went forward, laying the foundation of churches that were to yield fearless witnesses for the truth.

Paris was to receive another invitation to accept the gospel. The call of Lefevre and Farel had been rejected, but again the message was to be heard by all classes in that great capital. The king had not yet fully sided with Rome against the Reformation. Margaret resolved that the reformed faith should be preached in Paris. She ordered a Protestant minister to preach in the churches. This being forbidden by the papal dignitaries, the princess threw open the palace. It was announced that every day a sermon would be preached, and the people were invited to attend. Thousands assembled every day.

The king ordered that two of the churches of Paris should be opened. Never had the city been so moved by the Word of God. Temperance, purity, order, and industry were taking the place of drunkenness, licentiousness, strife, and idleness. While many accepted the gospel, the majority of the people rejected it. The papists succeeded in regaining the ascendancy. Again the churches were closed, and the stake was set up.

Calvin was still in Paris. At last the authorities determined to bring him to the flames. He had no thought of danger when friends came hurrying to his room with the news that officers were on their way to arrest him. At that instant a loud knocking was heard at the outer entrance. There was not a moment to be lost. Friends detained the officers at the door, while others assisted the Reformer to let himself down from a window, and he rapidly made his way to the cottage of a laborer who was a friend to the reform. He disguised himself in the garments of his host, and, shouldering a hoe, started on his journey. Traveling southward, he again found refuge in the dominions of Margaret.

Calvin could not long remain inactive. As soon as the storm had somewhat abated, he sought a new field of labor in Poitiers, where already the new opinions had found favor. Persons of all classes gladly listened to the gospel. As the number of hearers increased, it was thought safer to assemble outside the city. A cave where trees and overhanging rocks made the seclusion complete was chosen as the place of meeting. In this retired spot the Bible was read and explained. Here the Lord's Supper was celebrated for the first time by the Protestants of France. From this little church several faithful evangelists were sent out.

Once more Calvin returned to Paris, but he found almost every door of labor closed. He at last determined to depart to Germany. Scarcely had he left France when a storm burst over the Protestants. The French Reformers determined to strike a bold blow against the superstitions of Rome that should arouse the whole nation. Placards attacking the mass were in one night posted all over France. This zealous but ill-judged movement gave the Romanists a pretext for demanding the destruction of the "heretics" as agitators dangerous to the throne and the peace of the nation.

One of the placards was attached to the door of the

king's private chamber. The unexampled boldness of obtruding these startling utterances into the royal presence aroused the wrath of the king. His rage found utterance in the terrible words: "Let all be seized without distinction who are suspected of Lutheresy. I will exterminate them all."[9] The king had determined to throw himself fully on the side of Rome.

A Reign of Terror

A poor adherent of the reformed faith who had been accustomed to summon the believers to their secret assemblies was seized. With the threat of instant death at the stake, he was commanded to conduct the papal emissary to the home of every Protestant in the city. Fear of the flames prevailed, and he consented to betray his brethren. Morin, the royal detective, with the traitor, slowly and silently passed through the streets of the city. On arriving opposite the house of a Lutheran, the betrayer made a sign, but no word was uttered. The procession halted, the house was entered, the family were dragged forth and chained, and the terrible company went forward in search of fresh victims. "Morin made all the city quake. . . . It was a reign of terror."[10]

The victims were put to death with cruel torture, it being specially ordered that the fire should be lowered in order to prolong their agony. But they died as conquerors, their constancy unshaken, their peace unclouded. Their persecutors felt themselves defeated. "All Paris was enabled to see what kind of men the new opinions could produce. There was no pulpit like the martyr's pile. The serene joy that lighted up the faces of these men as they passed along . . . to the place of execution . . . pleaded with resistless eloquence in behalf of the gospel."[11]

Protestants were charged with plotting to massacre the Catholics, to overthrow the government, and to murder the king. Not a shadow of evidence could be produced in support of the allegations. Yet the cruelties inflicted upon the innocent Protestants accumulated in a weight of retribution, and in after-centuries wrought the very doom they had predicted upon the king, his government, and his subjects. But it was brought about by infidels and by the papists themselves. The suppression of Protestantism was to bring upon France these dire calamities.

Suspicion, distrust, and terror now pervaded all classes of society. Hundreds fled from Paris, self-constituted exiles from their native land, in many cases thus giving the first intimation that they favored the reformed faith. The papists looked about them in amazement at thought of the unsuspected "heretics" that had been tolerated among them.

Printing Declared Abolished

Francis I had delighted to gather at his court men of letters from every country. But, inspired with zeal to stamp out heresy, this patron of learning issued an edict declaring printing abolished all over France! Francis I presents one among the many examples on record showing that intellectual culture is not a safeguard against religious intolerance and persecution.

The priests demanded that the affront offered to high Heaven in the condemnation of the mass be expiated in blood. January 21, 1535, was fixed upon for the awful ceremonial. Before every door was a lighted torch in honor of the "holy sacrament." Before daybreak the procession formed at the palace of the king.

"The host was carried by the bishop of Paris under a magnificent canopy, . . . supported by four princes of the blood. . . . After the host walked the king. . . . Francis I on that day wore no crown, nor robe of state."[12] At every altar he bowed in humiliation, not for the vices that defiled his soul, nor the innocent blood that stained his hands, but for the "deadly sin" of his subjects who had dared to condemn the mass.

In the great hall of the bishop's palace the monarch

appeared and in words of moving eloquence bewailed "the crime, the blasphemy, the day of sorrow and disgrace," that had come upon the nation. And he called upon every loyal subject to aid in the extirpation of the pestilent "heresy" that threatened France with ruin. Tears choked his utterance, and the whole assembly wept, with one accord exclaiming, "We will live and die for the Catholic religion!"[13]

"The grace that bringeth salvation" had appeared, but France, illuminated by its radiance, had turned away, choosing darkness rather than light. They had called evil good, and good evil, till they had fallen victims to their wilful self-deception. The light that would have saved them from deception, from staining their souls with blood-guiltiness, they had willfully rejected.

Again the procession formed. "At short distances scaffolds had been erected on which certain Protestant Christians were to be burned alive, and it was arranged that the fagots should be lighted at the moment the king approached, and that the procession should halt to witness the execution."[14] There was no wavering on the part of the victims. On being urged to recant, one answered: "I only believe in what the prophets and the apostles formerly preached, and what all the company of saints believed. My faith has a confidence in God which will resist all the powers of hell."[15]

Upon reaching the palace, the crowd dispersed and the king and the prelates withdrew, congratulating themselves that the work would be continued to the complete destruction of "heresy."

The gospel of peace which France rejected was to be too surely rooted out, and terrible would be the results. On January 21, 1793, another procession passed through the streets of Paris. "Again the king was the chief figure; again there were tumult and shouting; again there was heard the cry for more victims; again there were black scaffolds; and again the scenes of the day were closed by horrid executions; Louis XVI, struggling hand to hand with his jailers and execution-ers, was dragged forward to the block, and there held down by main force till the axe had fallen, and his dissevered head rolled on the scaffold."[16] Near the same spot 2800 human beings perished by the guillotine.

The Reformation had presented to the world an open Bible. Infinite Love had unfolded to men the principles of heaven. When France rejected the gift of heaven, she sowed seeds of ruin. The inevitable outworking of cause and effect resulted in the Revolution and the Reign of Terror.

The bold and ardent Farel had been forced to flee from the land of his birth to Switzerland. Yet he continued to exert a decided influence upon the reform in France. With the assistance of other exiles, the writings of the German Reformers were translated into French and together with the French Bible were printed in large quantities. By colporteurs these works were sold extensively in France.

Farel entered upon his work in Switzerland in the humble guise of a schoolmaster, cautiously introducing the truths of the Bible. Some believed, but the priests came forward to stop the work, and superstitious people were roused to oppose it. "That cannot be the gospel of Christ," urged the priests, "seeing the preaching of it does not bring peace, but war."[17]

From village to village he went, enduring hunger, cold, and weariness, and everywhere in peril of his life. He preached in the marketplace, in the churches, sometimes in the pulpits of the cathedrals. More than once he was beaten almost to death. Yet he pressed forward. One after another he saw towns and cities which had been strongholds of popery opening their gates to the gospel.

Farel had desired to plant the Protestant standard in Geneva. If this city could be won, it would be a center for the Reformation in France, Switzerland, and Italy. Many of the surrounding towns and hamlets had been gained.

With a single companion he entered Geneva. But

only two sermons was he permitted to preach. The priests summoned him before an ecclesiastical council, to which they came with arms concealed under their robes, determined to take his life. A furious mob was gathered to make sure of his death if he should escape the council. The presence of magistrates and an armed force, however, saved him. Early next morning he was conducted across the lake to a place of safety. Thus ended his first effort to evangelize Geneva.

For the next trial a lowlier instrument was chosen— a young man so humble in appearance that he was coldly treated even by the professed friends of reform. But what could such a one do where Farel had been rejected? "God hath chosen the weak things of the world to confound the things which are mighty." 1 Corinthians 1:27.

Froment, the Schoolmaster

Froment began his work as a schoolmaster. The truths which he taught the children at school they repeated at their homes. Soon the parents came to hear the Bible explained. New Testaments and tracts were freely distributed. After a time this laborer also was forced to flee, but the truths he taught had taken hold upon the minds of the people. The Reformation had been planted. The preachers returned, and Protestant worship was finally established in Geneva.

The city had already declared for the Reformation when Calvin entered its gates. He was on his way to Basel when forced to take the circuitous route by Geneva.

In this visit Farel recognized the hand of God. Though Geneva had accepted the reformed faith, yet the work of regeneration must be wrought in the heart by the power of the Holy Spirit, not by the decrees of councils. While the people of Geneva had cast off the authority of Rome, they were not so ready to renounce the vices that had flourished under her rule.

In the name of God Farel solemnly adjured the

young evangelist to remain and labor there. Calvin drew back in alarm. He shrank from contact with the bold and even violent spirit of the Genevese. He desired to find a quiet retreat for study, and there, through the press, instruct and build up the churches. But he dared not refuse. It seemed to him "that the hand of God was stretched down from heaven, that it lay hold of him, and fixed him irrevocably to the place he was so impatient to leave."[18]

The Thunder of Anathema

The anathemas of the pope thundered against Geneva. How was this little city to resist the powerful hierarchy that had forced kings and emperors to submission?

The first triumphs of the Reformation past, Rome summoned new forces to accomplish its destruction. The order of the Jesuits was created, the most cruel, unscrupulous, and powerful of all the champions of popery. Dead to the claims of natural affection, and conscience wholly silenced, they knew no rule, no tie, but that of their order. (See Appendix.)

The gospel of Christ had enabled its adherents to endure suffering, undismayed by cold, hunger, toil, and poverty, to uphold truth in face of the rack, the dungeon, and the stake. Jesuitism inspired its followers with a fanaticism that enabled them to endure like dangers, and to oppose to the power of truth all the weapons of deception. There was no crime too great to commit, no deception too base to practice, no disguise too difficult for them to assume. It was their studied aim to overthrow Protestantism and reestablish papal supremacy.

They wore a garb of sanctity, visiting prisons and hospitals, ministering to the sick and the poor, and bearing the sacred name of Jesus, who went about doing good. But under this blameless exterior, criminal and deadly purposes were often concealed.

It was a fundamental principle of the order that the

end justifies the means. Lying, theft, perjury, assassination, were commendable when they served the interests of the church. Under disguise the Jesuits worked their way into offices of state, climbing up to be the counselors of kings and shaping the policy of nations. They became servants to act as spies upon their masters. They established colleges for princes and nobles, and schools for the common people. The children of Protestant parents were drawn into an observance of popish rites. Thus the liberty for which the fathers had toiled and bled was betrayed by the sons. Wherever the Jesuits went, there followed a revival of popery.

To give them greater power, a bull was issued reestablishing the Inquisition. This terrible tribunal was again set up by popish rulers, and atrocities too terrible to bear the light of day were repeated in its secret dungeons. In many countries thousands upon thousands of the very flower of the nation, the most intellectual and highly educated, were slain or forced to flee to other lands. (See Appendix.)

Victories for the Reformation

Such were the means which Rome invoked to quench the light of the Reformation and to restore the ignorance and superstition of the Dark Ages. But under God's blessings and the labors of noble men whom He raised up to succeed Luther, Protestantism was not overthrown. Not to the arms of princes was it to owe its strength. The humblest and least powerful nations became its strongholds. It was little Geneva; it was Holland, wrestling against the tyranny of Spain; it was bleak, sterile Sweden, that gained victories for the Reformation.

For nearly thirty years Calvin labored at Geneva for the advancement of the Reformation throughout Europe. His course was not faultless, nor were his doctrines free from error. But he was instrumental in promulgating truths of special importance, in maintaining Protestantism against the fast-returning tide of popery, and in promoting in the reformed churches simplicity and purity of life.

From Geneva, publications and teachers went out to spread the reformed doctrines. To this point the persecuted of all lands looked for instruction and encouragement. The city of Calvin became a refuge for the hunted Reformers of all Western Europe. They were welcomed and tenderly cared for; and finding a home here, they blessed the city of their adoption by their skill, their learning, and their piety. John Knox, the brave Scottish Reformer, not a few of the English Puritans, Protestants of Holland and of Spain, and the Huguenots of France, carried from Geneva the torch of truth to lighten the darkness of their native lands.

References
1. Wylie, bk. 13, ch. 1.
2. *Ibid.*, bk. 13, ch. 2.
3. D'Aubigne, bk. 12, ch. 3.
4. *Idem.*
5. D'Aubigne, *History of the Reformation in Europe in the Time of Calvin*, bk. 2, ch. 16.
6. Wylie, bk. 13, ch. 9.
7. Wylie, bk. 13, ch. 7.
8. Martyn, vol. 3, ch. 13.
9. D'Aubigne, bk. 2, ch. 30.
10. *Ibid.*, bk. 4, ch. 10.
11. Wylie, bk. 13, ch. 20.
12. *Ibid.*, bk. 13, ch. 21.
13. D'Aubigne, bk. 4, ch. 12.
14. Wylie, bk. 13, ch. 21.
15. D'Aubigne, bk. 4, ch. 12.
16. Wylie, bk. 13, ch. 21.
17. Wylie, bk. 14, ch. 3.
18. D'Aubigne, bk. 9, ch. 17.

13/ The Netherlands and Scandinavia

In the Netherlands the papal tyranny very early called forth protest. Seven hundred years before Luther, the Roman pontiff was fearlessly impeached by two bishops, who, having been sent on an embassy to Rome, had learned the true character of the "holy see": "You set up yourself in the temple of God; instead of pastor, you are become a wolf to the sheep. . . . Whereas you ought to be a servant of servants, as you call yourself, you endeavor to become a lord of lords. . . . You bring the commands of God into contempt."[1]

Others arose from century to century to echo this protest. The Waldensian Bible they translated in verse into the Dutch language. They declared "that there was great advantage in it; no jests, no fables, no trifles, no deceits, but the words of truth." Thus wrote the friends of the ancient faith, in the twelfth century.[2]

Now began the Romish persecutions; but the believers continued to multiply, declaring that the Bible is the only infallible authority in religion and that "no man should be coerced to believe, but should be won by preaching."[3]

The teachings of Luther found in the Netherlands earnest and faithful men to preach the gospel. Menno Simons, educated a Roman Catholic and ordained to the priesthood, was wholly ignorant of the Bible and would not read it for fear of heresy. In dissipation he endeavored to silence the voice of conscience, but without avail. After a time he was led to the study of the New Testament; this, with Luther's writings, caused him to accept the reformed faith.

He soon after witnessed a man put to death for having been rebaptized. This led him to study the Bible in regard to infant baptism. He saw that repentance and faith are required as the condition of baptism.

Menno withdrew from the Roman Church and devoted his life to teaching the truths which he had received. In both Germany and the Netherlands a class of fanatics had risen, outraging order and decency, and proceeding to insurrection. Menno strenuously opposed the erroneous teachings and wild schemes of the fanatics. For twenty-five years he traversed the Netherlands and northern Germany, exerting a widespread influence, exemplifying in his own life the precepts which he taught. He was a man of integrity, humble and gentle, sincere and earnest. Great numbers were converted under his labors.

In Germany Charles V had banned the Reformation, but the princes stood as a barrier against his tyranny. In the Netherlands his power was greater. Persecuting edicts followed in quick succession. To read the Bible, to hear or preach it, to pray to God in secret, to refrain from bowing to an image, to sing a psalm was punishable with death. Thousands perished under Charles and Philip II.

At one time a whole family was brought before the inquisitors, charged with remaining away from mass and worshiping at home. The youngest son answered: "We fall on our knees, and pray that God may enlighten our minds and pardon our sins; we pray for our sovereign, that his reign may be prosperous and his life happy; we pray for our magistrates, that God may preserve them." The father and one of his sons were condemned to the stake.[4]

Not only men but women and maidens displayed unflinching courage. "Wives would take their stand by their husband's stake, and while he was enduring the fire they would whisper words of solace, or sing psalms to cheer him." "Young maidens would lie down in their living grave as if they were entering into their chamber of nightly sleep; or go forth to the scaffold and the fire, dressed in their best apparel, as if they were going to their marriage."[5]

Persecution increased the number of witnesses for truth. Year after year the monarch urged on his cruel work, but in vain. William of Orange at last brought to Holland freedom to worship God.

Reformation in Denmark

In the countries of the North the gospel found a peaceful entrance. Students at Wittenberg returning home carried the reformed faith to Scandinavia. Luther's writings also spread the light. The hardy people of the North turned from the corruption and superstitions of Rome to welcome the life-giving truths of the Bible.

Tausen, "the Reformer of Denmark," as a boy early gave evidence of vigorous intellect and entered a cloister. Examination showed him to possess talent that promised good service to the church. The young student was granted permission to choose a university of Germany or the Netherlands for himself, with one proviso: he must not go to Wittenberg to be endangered by heresy. So said the friars.

Tausen went to Cologne, one of the strongholds of Romanism. Here he soon became disgusted. About the same time he read Luther's writings with delight and greatly desired to enjoy the personal instruction of the Reformer. But to do so he must risk forfeiting his superior's support. His decision was soon made and erelong he was a student at Wittenberg.

On returning to Denmark, he did not reveal his secret, but endeavored to lead his companions to a purer faith. He opened the Bible and preached Christ to them as the sinner's only hope of salvation. Great was the wrath of the prior, who had built high hopes on him as a defender of Rome. He was at once removed from his own monastery to another and confined to his cell. Through the bars of his cell Tausen communicated to his companions a knowledge of the truth. Had those Danish fathers been skilled in the church's plan of dealing with heresy, Tausen's voice would never again have been heard; but instead of consigning him to some underground dungeon, they expelled him from the monastery.

A royal edict, just issued, offered protection to the teachers of the new doctrine. The churches were opened to him, and the people thronged to listen. The New Testament in Danish was widely circulated. Efforts to overthrow the work resulted in extending it, and erelong Denmark declared its acceptance of the reformed faith.

Progress in Sweden

In Sweden also, young men from Wittenberg carried the water of life to their countrymen. Two leaders in the Swedish Reformation, Olaf and Laurentius Petri, studied under Luther and Melanchthon. Like the great Reformer, Olaf aroused the people by his eloquence, while Laurentius, like Melanchthon, was thoughtful and calm. Both were of unflinching courage. The Catholic priests stirred up the ignorant and superstitious people. Upon several occasions, Olaf Petri barely escaped with his life. These Reformers were, however, protected by the king, who determined upon a reformation and welcomed these able assistants in the battle against Rome.

In the presence of the monarch and leading men of Sweden, Olaf Petri with great ability defended the reformed faith. He declared that the teachings of the Fathers are to be received only when in accord with Scripture; that the essential doctrines of the faith are presented in the Bible in a clear manner, so that all may understand them.

This contest serves to show us "the sort of men that formed the rank and file of the army of the Reformers.

They were not illiterate, sectarian, noisy controversialists—far from it. They were men who had studied the Word of God and knew well how to wield the weapons with which the armory of the Bible supplied them. [They were] scholars and theologians, men who have thoroughly mastered the whole system of gospel truth, and who win an easy victory over the sophists of the schools and the dignitaries of Rome."[6]

The king of Sweden accepted the Protestant faith, and the national assembly declared in its favor. At the desire of the king, the two brothers undertook the translation of the whole Bible. It was ordered by the diet that throughout the kingdom, ministers should explain the Scriptures, and that the children in the schools should be taught to read the Bible.

Freed from Romish oppression, the nation attained to a strength and greatness it had never before reached. A century later, this hitherto feeble nation—the only one in Europe that dared lend a helping hand—came to the deliverance of Germany in the terrible struggle of the Thirty Years' War. All Northern Europe seemed about to be brought again under the tyranny of Rome. The armies of Sweden enabled Germany to win toleration for Protestants and to restore liberty of conscience to those countries that had accepted the Reformation.

References
1. Gerard Brandt, *History of the Reformation in and About the Low Countries*, bk. 1, p. 6.
2. *Ibid.*, p. 14.
3. Martyn, vol. 2, p. 87.
4. Wylie, bk. 18, ch. 6.
5. *Ibid.*
6. *Ibid.*, bk. 10, ch. 4.

14/Truth Advances in Britain

While Luther was opening a closed Bible to the people of Germany, Tyndale was impelled by the Spirit of God to do the same for England. Wycliffe's Bible had been translated from the Latin text, which contained many errors. The cost of manuscript copies was so great that it had had a narrow circulation.

In 1516, for the first time the New Testament was printed in the original Greek tongue. Many errors of former versions were corrected, and the sense was more clearly rendered. It led many among the educated to a better knowledge of truth and gave a new impetus to the work of reform. But the common people were still, to a great extent, debarred from God's Word. Tyndale was to complete the work of Wycliffe in giving the Bible to his countrymen.

He fearlessly preached his convictions. To the papist claim that the church had given the Bible, and the church alone could explain it, Tyndale responded: "Far from having given us the Scriptures, it is you who have hidden them from us; it is you who burn those who teach them, and if you could, you would burn the Scriptures themselves."[1]

Tyndale's preaching excited great interest. But the priests endeavored to destroy his work. "What is to be done?" he exclaimed. "I cannot be everywhere. Oh! if Christians possessed the Holy Scriptures in their own tongue, they could of themselves withstand these sophists. Without the Bible it is impossible to establish the laity in the truth."[2]

A new purpose now took possession of his mind.

"Shall not the gospel speak the language of England among us? . . . Ought the church to have less light at noonday than at the dawn? . . . Christians must read the New Testament in their mother tongue."[3] Only by the Bible could men arrive at the truth.

A learned Catholic in controversy with him exclaimed, "We were better to be without God's laws than the pope's." Tyndale replied, "I defy the pope and all his laws; and if God spare my life, ere many years I will cause a boy that driveth the plow to know more of the Scripture than you do."[4]

Tyndale Translates the English New Testament

Driven from home by persecution, he went to London and there for a time labored undisturbed. But again the papists forced him to flee. All England seemed closed against him. In Germany he began the printing of the English New Testament. When forbidden to print in one city, he went to another. At last he made his way to Worms, where, a few years before, Luther had defended the gospel before the diet. In that city were many friends of the Reformation. Three thousand copies of the New Testament were soon finished, and another edition followed.

The Word of God was secretly conveyed to London and circulated throughout the country. The papists attempted to suppress the truth, but in vain. The bishop of Durham bought a bookseller's whole stock of Bibles for the purpose of destroying them, supposing that this would hinder the work. But the money thus furnished purchased material for a new and better edition. When Tyndale was afterward made a prisoner, his liberty was offered him on condition that he reveal the names of those who helped him meet the expense of printing his Bibles. He replied that the bishop of Durham had done more than any other person by paying a large price for the books left on hand.

Tyndale finally witnessed for his faith by a martyr's death; but the weapons he prepared enabled other soldiers to do battle through the centuries, even to our time.

Latimer maintained from the pulpit that the Bible ought to be read in the language of the people. "Let us not take any bywalks, but let God's word direct us: let us not walk after . . . our forefathers, nor seek not what they did, but what they should have done."[5]

Barnes and Frith, Ridley and Cranmer, leaders in the English Reformation, were men of learning, highly esteemed for zeal or piety in the Romish communion. Their opposition to the papacy was the result of their knowledge of the errors of the "holy see."

Infallible Authority of Scripture

The grand principle maintained by these Reformers—the same held by the Waldenses, Wycliffe, Huss, Luther, Zwingli, and those with them—was the infallible authority of Scripture. By its teaching they tested all doctrines and all claims. Faith in God's Word sustained these holy men as they yielded up their lives at the stake. "Be of good comfort," exclaimed Latimer to his fellow martyr as the flames were about to silence their voices, "we shall this day light such a candle, by God's grace, in England, as I trust shall never be put out."[6]

For hundreds of years after the churches of England submitted to Rome, those of Scotland maintained their freedom. In the twelfth century, however, popery became established, and in no country was the darkness deeper. Still rays of light came to pierce the gloom. The Lollards, coming from England with the Bible and the teachings of Wycliffe, did much to preserve the knowledge of the gospel. With the opening of the Reformation came the writings of Luther and Tyndale's English New Testament. These messengers silently traversed the mountains and valleys, kindling into new life the torch of truth so nearly extinguished and undoing the work which four centuries of oppression had done.

Then the papist leaders, suddenly awakening to danger, brought to the stake some of the noblest of the sons of Scotland. These dying witnesses throughout the land thrilled the souls of the people with an undying purpose to cast off the shackles of Rome.

John Knox

Hamilton and Wishart, with a long line of humbler disciples, yielded up their lives at the stake. But from the burning pile of Wishart there came one whom the flames were not to silence, one who under God was to strike the death knell of popery in Scotland.

John Knox turned away from the traditions of the church to feed upon the truths of God's Word. The teaching of Wishart confirmed his determination to forsake Rome and join himself to the persecuted Reformers.

Urged by his companions to preach, he shrank with trembling from its responsibility. It was only after days of painful conflict with himself that he consented. But having once accepted, he pressed forward with undaunted courage. This truehearted Reformer feared not the face of man. When brought face to face with the queen of Scotland, John Knox was not to be won by caresses; he quailed not before threats. He had taught the people to receive a religion prohibited by the state, she declared, and had thus transgressed God's command enjoining subjects to obey their princes. Knox answered firmly: "If all the seed of Abraham had been of the religion of Pharaoh, whose subjects they long were, I pray you, madam, what religion would there have been in the world? Or if all men in the days of the apostles had been of the religion of the Roman emperors, what religion would there have been upon the face of the earth?"

Said Mary: "Ye interpret the Scriptures in one manner, and they [Roman Catholics] interpret in another; whom shall I believe, and who shall be judge?"

"Ye shall believe God, that plainly speaketh in His word," answered the Reformer. . . . The word of God is plain in itself; and if there appear any obscurity in one place, the Holy Ghost, which is never contrary to Himself, explains the same more clearly in other places."[7]

With undaunted courage the fearless Reformer, at the peril of his life, kept to his purpose, until Scotland was free from popery.

In England the establishment of Protestantism as the national religion diminished, but did not wholly stop, persecution. Not a few of Rome's forms were retained. The supremacy of the pope was rejected, but in his place the monarch was enthroned as head of the church. There was still a wide departure from the purity of the gospel. Religious liberty was not yet understood. Though the horrible cruelties which Rome employed were resorted to but rarely by Protestant rulers, yet the right of every man to worship God according to his own conscience was not acknowledged. Dissenters suffered persecution for hundreds of years.

Thousands of Pastors Expelled

In the seventeenth century thousands of pastors were expelled and the people were forbidden to attend any religious meetings except such as were sanctioned by the church. In the sheltering depths of the forest, those persecuted children of the Lord assembled to pour out their souls in prayer and praise. Many suffered for their faith. The jails were crowded, families broken up. Yet persecution could not silence their testimony. Many were driven across the ocean to America and there laid the foundations of civil and religious liberty.

In a dungeon crowded with felons, John Bunyan breathed the atmosphere of heaven and wrote his wonderful allegory of the pilgrim's journey from the land of destruction to the celestial city. *Pilgrim's Progress* and *Grace Abounding to the Chief of Sinners* have guided many feet into the path of life.

In a day of spiritual darkness Whitefield and the

Wesleys appeared as light bearers for God. Under the established church the people had lapsed into a state hardly to be distinguished from heathenism. The higher classes sneered at piety; the lower classes were abandoned to vice. The church had no courage or faith to support the downfallen cause of truth.

Justification by Faith

The great doctrine of justification by faith, so clearly taught by Luther, had been almost wholly lost sight of; the Romish principle of trusting to good works for salvation had taken its place. Whitefield and the Wesleys were sincere seekers for the favor of God. This, they had been taught, was to be secured by virtue and observance of the ordinances of religion.

When Charles Wesley at one time fell ill and anticipated that death was approaching, he was asked upon what he rested his hope of eternal life. His answer: "I have used my best endeavors to serve God." The friend seemed not fully satisfied with this answer. Wesley thought: "What! . . . Would he rob me of my endeavors? I have nothing else to trust to."[8] Such was the darkness that had settled on the church, turning men from their only hope of salvation—the blood of the crucified Redeemer.

Wesley and his associates were led to see that God's law extends to the thoughts as well as to the words and actions. By diligent and prayerful efforts they endeavored to subdue the evils of the natural heart. They lived a life of self-denial and humiliation, observing with exactness every measure which they thought could be helpful in obtaining that holiness which could secure the favor of God. But in vain were their endeavors to free themselves from the condemnation of sin or to break its power.

The fires of divine truth, well-nigh extinguished upon the altars of Protestantism, were to be rekindled from the ancient torch handed down by the Bohemian Christians. Some of these, finding refuge in Saxony, maintained the ancient faith. From these Christians light came to Wesley.

John and Charles were sent on a mission to America. On board ship was a company of Moravians. Violent storms were encountered, and John, face to face with death, felt he had not the assurance of peace with God. The Germans manifested a calmness and trust to which he was a stranger. "I had long before," he says, "observed the great seriousness of their behavior. . . . There was now an opportunity of trying whether they were delivered from the spirit of fear, as well as from that of pride, anger, and revenge. In the midst of the psalm wherewith their service began, the sea broke over, split the mainsail in pieces, covered the ship, and poured in between the decks as if the great deep had already swallowed us up. A terrible screaming began among the English. The Germans calmly sang on. I asked one of them afterwards, 'Were you not afraid?' He answered, 'I thank God, no.' I asked, 'But were not your women and children afraid?' He replied mildly, 'No; our women and children are not afraid to die.' "[9]

Wesley's Heart "Strangely Warmed"

On his return to England, Wesley arrived at a clearer understanding of Bible faith under the instruction of a Moravian. At a meeting of the Moravian society in London a statement was read from Luther. As Wesley listened, faith was kindled in his soul. "I felt my heart strangely warmed," he says. "I felt I did trust in Christ, Christ alone, for salvation: and an assurance was given me, that He had taken away *my* sins, even *mine*, and saved *me* from the law of sin and death."[10]

Now he had found that the grace he had toiled to win by prayers and fasts and self-abnegation was a gift, "without money and without price." His whole soul burned with the desire to spread everywhere the glorious gospel of God's free grace. "I look upon all the world as my parish," he said; "in whatever part of it I am, I judge it meet, right, and my bounden duty, to declare unto all that are willing to hear, the glad tidings of salvation."[11]

He continued his strict and self-denying life, not now as the *ground*, but the *result* of faith; not the *root*, but the *fruit* of holiness. The grace of God in Christ will be manifest in obedience. Wesley's life was devoted to preaching the great truths he had received—justification through faith in the atoning blood of Christ, and the renewing power of the Holy Spirit upon the heart, bringing forth fruit in a life conformed to the example of Christ.

Whitefield and the Wesleys were contemptuously called "Methodists" by their ungodly fellow students—a name which is at the present time regarded as honorable. The Holy Spirit urged them to preach Christ and Him crucified. Thousands were truly converted. It was necessary that these sheep be protected from ravening wolves. Wesley had no thought of forming a new denomination, but he organized them under what was called the Methodist Connection.

Mysterious and trying was the opposition which these preachers encountered from the established church—yet the truth had entrance where doors would otherwise remain closed. Some of the clergy were roused from their moral stupor and became zealous preachers in their own parishes.

In Wesley's time, men of different gifts did not harmonize upon every point of doctrine. The differences between Whitefield and the Wesleys threatened at one time to create alienation, but as they learned meekness in the school of Christ, mutual forbearance and charity reconciled them. They had no time to dispute, while error and iniquity were teeming everywhere.

Wesley Escapes Death

Men of influence employed their powers against them. Many clergy manifested hostility, and the doors of the churches were closed against a pure faith. The clergy, denouncing them from the pulpit, aroused the elements of darkness and iniquity. Again and again John Wesley escaped death by a miracle of God's mercy. When there seemed no way of escape, an angel in human form came to his side, the mob fell back, and the servant of Christ passed in safety from danger.

Of his deliverance on one of these occasions, Wesley said: "Although many strove to lay hold on my collar or clothes, to pull me down, they could not fasten at all: only one got fast hold of the flap of my waistcoat, which was soon left in his hand; the other flap, in the pocket of which was a bank note, was torn but half off. . . . A lusty man just behind, struck at me several times, with a large oaken stick; with which if he had struck me once on the back part of my head, it would have saved him all further trouble. But every time, the blow was turned aside, I know not how; for I could not move to the right hand or left."[12]

The Methodists of those days endured ridicule and persecution, often violence. In some instances, public notices were posted, calling upon those who desired to break the windows and rob the houses of the Methodists to assemble at a given time and place. Systematic persecution was carried on against a people whose only fault was seeking to turn sinners to the path of holiness.

The spiritual declension in England just before the time of Wesley was in a great degree the result of teaching that Christ had abolished the moral law and that Christians are under no obligation to observe it. Others declared that it was unnecessary for ministers to exhort the people to obedience of its precepts, since those whom God had elected to salvation would "be led to the practice of piety and virtue" while those doomed to eternal reprobation "did not have power to obey the divine law."

Others, holding that "the elect cannot fall from grace nor forfeit the divine favor," arrived at the hideous conclusion that "the wicked actions they commit are not really sinful, . . . and that, consequently, they have no occasion either to confess their sins or to break them off by repentance."[13] Therefore, they declared, even one of the vilest of sins "considered universally an enormous violation of the divine law is not a sin in the sight of God" if committed by one of the elect. "They cannot do anything that is either displeasing to God or prohibited by the law."

These monstrous doctrines are essentially the same as the later teaching that there is no unchangeable divine law as the standard of right, but that morality is indicated by society itself and constantly subject to change. All these ideas are inspired by him who among the sinless inhabitants of heaven began his work to break down the righteous restraints of the law of God.

The doctrine of divine decrees, unalterably fixing the character of men, had led many to rejection of the law of God. Wesley steadfastly opposed this doctrine which led to antinomianism. "The grace of God that bringeth salvation hath appeared to *all men.*" "God our Saviour . . . will have *all men* to be saved, and to come unto the knowledge of the truth. For there is one God, and one mediator between God and men, the man Christ Jesus; who gave himself a ransom for *all.*" Christ, "the true Light, . . . lighteth *every man* that cometh into the world." Titus 2:11; 1 Timothy 2:3-6; John 1:9. Men fail of salvation through their own wilful refusal of the gift of life.

In Defense of the Law of God

In answer to the claim that at the death of Christ the Decalogue had been abolished with the ceremonial law, Wesley said: "The moral law, contained in the Ten Commandments and enforced by the prophets, He did not take away. This is a law which never can be broken, which 'stands fast as the faithful witness in heaven.' "

Wesley declared the perfect harmony of the law and the gospel. "On the one hand, the law continually makes way for, and points us to, the gospel; on the other, the gospel continually leads us to a more exact fulfilling of the law. The law, for instance, requires us to love God, to love our neighbor, to be meek, humble, or holy. We feel that we are not sufficient for these things; . . . but we see a promise of God to give us that love, and to make us humble, meek, and holy: we lay hold of this gospel, of these glad tidings; . . . 'the righteousness of the law is fulfilled in us,' through faith which is in Christ Jesus. . . .

"In the highest rank of the enemies of the gospel of Christ," said Wesley, "are they who . . . teach men to break . . . not one only, whether of the least or of the greatest, but all the commandments at a stroke. . . . They honor Him just as Judas did when he said, 'Hail, Master, and kissed Him.' . . . It is no other than betraying Him with a kiss, to talk of His blood, and take away His crown; to set light by any part of His law, under pretense of advancing His gospel."[14]

Harmony of Law and Gospel

To those who urged that "the preaching of the gospel answers all the ends of the law," Wesley replied: "It does not answer the very first end of the law, namely, the convincing men of sin, the awakening those who are still asleep on the brink of hell. . . . It is absurd, therefore, to offer a physician to them that are whole, or that at least imagine themselves so to be. You are first to convince them that they are sick; otherwise they will not thank you for your labor. It is equally absurd to offer Christ to them whose heart is whole having never been broken."[15]

While preaching the gospel of the grace of God, Wesley, like his Master, sought to "magnify the law, and make it honorable." Isaiah 42:21. Glorious were the results he was permitted to behold. At the close of above half a century spent in ministry, his adherents numbered more than half a million. But the multitude that through his labors had been lifted from the degradation of sin to a higher and purer life will never be known till the whole family of the redeemed gather in the kingdom of God. His life presents a lesson of priceless worth to every Christian.

Would that the faith, untiring zeal, self-sacrifice, and devotion of this servant of Christ might be reflected in the churches of today!

References

1. D'Aubigne, *History of the Reformation of the Sixteenth Century*, bk. 18, ch. 4.

2. *Ibid*.

3. *Idem*.

4. Anderson, *Annals of the English Bible* (rev. edition, 1862), p. 19.

5. Hugh Latimer, "First Sermon Preached Before King Edward VI."

6. *Works of Hugh Latimer*, vol. 1, p. xiii.

7. David Laing, *The Collected Works of John Knox*, vol. 2, pp. 281, 284.

8. John Whitehead, *Life of the Rev. Charles Wesley*, p. 102.

9. *Ibid*., p. 10.

10. *Ibid*., p. 52.

11. *Ibid*., p. 74.

12. John Wesley, *Works*, vol. 3, pp. 297, 298.

13. McClintock & Strong, *Cyclopedia*, art. "Antinomians."

14. Wesley, Sermon 25.

15. Wesley, Sermon 35.

15/ France's Reign of Terror: Its True Cause

Some nations welcomed the Reformation as a messenger of Heaven. In other lands the light of Bible knowledge was almost wholly excluded. In one country truth and error struggled for centuries for the mastery. At last the truth of Heaven was thrust out. The restraint of God's Spirit was removed from a people that had despised the gift of His grace. And all the world saw the fruit of wilful rejection of light.

The war against the Bible in France culminated in the Revolution, the legitimate result of Rome's suppression of the Scriptures. (See Appendix.) It presented the most striking illustration ever witnessed of the working out of the teaching of the Roman Church.

The Revelator points to the terrible results that were to accrue especially to France from the domination of the "man of sin":

"The holy city shall they tread under foot forty and two months. And I will give power unto my two witnesses, and they shall prophesy a thousand two hundred and threescore days, clothed in sackcloth. . . . And when they shall have finished their testimony, the beast that ascendeth out of the bottomless pit shall make war against them, and shall overcome them, and kill them. And their dead bodies shall lie in the street of the great city, which spiritually is called Sodom and Egypt, where also our Lord was crucified. . . . And they that dwell upon the earth shall rejoice over them, and make merry, and shall send gifts one to another; because these two prophets tormented them that dwelt on the earth. And after three days and a half the Spirit of life from God entered into them, and they stood upon their feet; and great fear fell upon them which saw them." Revelation 11:2-11.

The "forty and two months" and "a thousand two hundred and threescore days" are the same, the time in which the church of Christ was to suffer oppression from Rome. The 1260 years began in A.D. 538 and terminated in 1798. (See Appendix.) At that time a French army made the pope a prisoner, and he died in exile. The papal hierarchy has never since been able to wield the power before possessed.

The persecution of the church did not continue throughout the entire 1260 years. God in mercy to His people cut short the time of their fiery trial through the influence of the Reformation.

The "two witnesses" represent the Scriptures of the Old and the New Testament, important testimonies to the origin and perpetuity of the law of God, and also to the plan of salvation.

"They shall prophesy a thousand two hundred and threescore days, clothed in sackcloth." When the Bible was proscribed, its testimony perverted; when those who dared proclaim its truths were betrayed, tortured, martyred for their faith or compelled to flee— then the faithful "witnesses" prophesied "in sackcloth." In the darkest times faithful men were given wisdom and authority to declare God's truth. (See Appendix.)

"And if any man will hurt them, fire proceedeth out of their mouth, and devoureth their enemies: and if any man will hurt them, he must in this manner be killed." Revelation 11:5. Men cannot with impunity trample upon the Word of God!

"When they shall have finished [are finishing] their testimony." As the two witnesses were approaching the termination of their work in obscurity, war was to be made upon them by "the beast that ascendeth out of the bottomless pit." Here is brought to view a new manifestation of satanic power.

It had been Rome's policy, professing reverence for the Bible, to keep it locked up in an unknown tongue, hidden from the people. Under her rule the witnesses prophesied "clothed in sackcloth." But "the beast from the bottomless pit" was to make open, avowed war upon the Word of God.

"The great city" in whose streets the witnesses are slain, and where their dead bodies lie is "spiritually" Egypt. Of all nations in Bible history, Egypt most boldly denied the existence of the living God and resisted His commands. No monarch ever ventured upon more highhanded rebellion against Heaven than did the king of Egypt, Pharaoh: "I know not the Lord, neither will I let Israel go." Exodus 5:2, ARV. This is atheism; and the nation represented by Egypt would voice a similar denial of God and manifest a like spirit of defiance.

"The great city" is also compared, "spiritually," to Sodom. The corruption of Sodom was especially manifested in licentiousness. This sin was also to be a characteristic of the nation that should fulfill this scripture.

According to the prophet, then, a little before 1798 some power of satanic character would rise to war upon the Bible. And in the land where the testimony of God's "two witnesses" should thus be silenced, there would be manifest the atheism of Pharaoh and the licentiousness of Sodom.

A Striking Fulfillment of Prophecy

This prophecy received a striking fulfillment in the history of France during the Revolution, in 1793. "France stands apart in the world's history as the single state which, by the decree of her Legislative Assembly, pronounced that there was no God, and of which the entire population of the capital, and a vast majority elsewhere, women as well as men, danced and sang with joy in accepting the announcement."[1]

France presented also the characteristics which distinguished Sodom. The historian presents together the atheism and the licentiousness of France: "Intimately connected with these laws affecting religion, was that which reduced the union of marriage—the most sacred engagement which human beings can form, and the permanence of which leads most strongly to the consolidation of society—to the state of a mere civil contract of a transitory character, which any two persons might engage in and cast loose at pleasure. . . . Sophie Arnoult, an actress famous for the witty things she said, described the republican marriage as 'the sacrament of adultery.' "[2]

Enmity Against Christ

"Where also our Lord was crucified." This was also fulfilled by France. In no country had the truth encountered more cruel opposition. In the persecution visited upon the confessors of the gospel France had crucified Christ in the person of His disciples.

Century after century the blood of the saints had been shed. While the Waldenses laid down their lives on the mountains of Piedmont "for the testimony of Jesus Christ," similar witness had been borne by the Albigenses of France. The disciples of the Reformation had been put to death with horrible tortures. King and nobles, highborn women and delicate maidens had feasted their eyes on the agonies of the martyrs of Jesus. The brave Huguenots had poured out their blood on many a hard-fought field, hunted down like wild beasts.

The few descendants of the ancient Christians that still lingered in France in the eighteenth century, hiding away in the mountains of the south, cherished the faith of their fathers. They were dragged away to lifelong slavery in the galleys. The most refined and intelligent of the French were chained, in horrible torture, amidst robbers and assassins. Others were shot down in cold blood as they fell upon their knees in prayer. Their country, laid waste with the sword, the axe, the fagot, "was converted into one vast, gloomy wilderness."

"These atrocities were enacted . . . in no dark age, but in the brilliant era of Louis XIV. Science was then cultivated, letters flourished, the divines of the court and of the capital were learned and eloquent men, and greatly affected the graces of meekness and charity."[3]

The Most Horrible of Crimes

But most horrible among the fiendish deeds of the dreadful centuries was the St. Bartholomew Massacre. The king of France, urged on by priests and prelates, lent his sanction. A bell, tolling at dead of night, was a signal for the slaughter. Protestants by thousands, sleeping in their homes, trusting the honor of their king, were dragged forth and murdered.

For seven days the massacre continued in Paris. By order of the king it was extended to all towns where Protestants were found. Noble and peasant, old and young, mother and child, were cut down together. Throughout France 70,000 of the flower of the nation perished.

"When the news of the massacre reached Rome, the exultation among the clergy knew no bounds. The cardinal of Lorraine rewarded the messenger with a thousand crowns; the cannon of St. Angelo thundered forth a joyous salute; and bells rang out from every steeple; bonfires turned night into day; and Gregory XIII, attended by the cardinals and other ecclesiastical dignitaries, went in long procession to the church of St. Louis, where the cardinal of Lorraine chanted a *Te Deum*. . . . A medal was struck to commemorate the massacre. . . . A French priest . . . spoke of 'that day so full of happiness and joy, when the most holy father received the news, and went in solemn state to render thanks to God and St. Louis.' "[4]

The same master spirit that urged on the St. Bartholomew Massacre led in the scenes of the Revolution. Jesus Christ was declared an impostor, and the cry of the French infidels was "Crush the Wretch," meaning Christ. Blasphemy and wickedness went hand in hand. In all this, homage was paid to Satan, while Christ, in His characteristics of truth, purity, and unselfish love, was "crucified."

"The beast that ascendeth out of the bottomless pit shall make war against them, and shall overcome them, and kill them." Revelation 11:10. The atheistic power that ruled in France during the Revolution and the Reign of Terror did wage such war against God and His Word. The worship of the Deity was abolished by the National Assembly. Bibles were collected and publicly burned. The institutions of the Bible were abolished. The weekly rest day was set aside, and in its stead every tenth day was devoted to reveling. Baptism and the Communion were prohibited. Announcements posted over burial places declared death to be an eternal sleep.

All religious worship was prohibited, except that of "liberty" and the country. The "constitutional bishop of Paris was brought forward . . . to declare to the Convention that the religion which he had taught so many years was, in every respect, a piece of priestcraft, which had no foundation either in history or sacred truth. He disowned, in solemn and explicit terms, the existence of the Deity to whose worship he had been consecrated."[5]

"And they that dwell upon the earth shall rejoice over them, and make merry, and shall send gifts one to another; because these two prophets tormented them that dwelt on the earth." Revelation 11:10. Infidel France had silenced the reproving voice of God's two witnesses. The word of truth lay "dead" in her streets, and those who hated God's law were jubilant. Men publicly defied the King of heaven.

Blasphemous Boldness

One of the "priests" of the new order said: "God, if You exist, avenge Your injured name. I bid You defiance! You remain silent; You dare not launch Your thunders. Who after this will believe in Your existence?''[6] What an echo is this of Pharaoh's demand: "Who is Jehovah, that I should obey his voice?"

"The fool hath said in his heart, There is no God." And the Lord declares, "Their folly shall be manifest unto all." Psalm 14:1; 2 Timothy 3:9. After France had renounced the worship of the living God she descended to degrading idolatry by the worship of the Goddess of Reason, a profligate woman. And this in the representative assembly of the nation! "One of the ceremonies of this insane time stands unrivaled for absurdity combined with impiety. The doors of the Convention were thrown open. . . . The members of the municipal body entered in solemn procession, singing a hymn in praise of liberty, and escorting, as the object of their future worship, a veiled female, whom they termed the Goddess of Reason. Being brought within the bar, she was unveiled with great form, and placed on the right of the president, when she was generally recognized as a dancing girl of the opera."

The Goddess of Reason

"The installation of the Goddess of Reason was renewed and imitated throughout the nation, in such places where the inhabitants desired to show themselves equal to all the heights of the Revolution."[7]

When the "goddess" was brought into the Convention, the orator took her by the hand, and turning to the assembly said: " 'Mortals, cease to tremble before the powerless thunders of a God whom your fears have created. Henceforth acknowledge no divinity but Reason. I offer you its noblest and purest image; if you must have idols, sacrifice only to such as this. . . .'

"The goddess, after being embraced by the president, was mounted on a magnificent car, and conducted to the cathedral of Notre Dame, to take the place of the Deity. There she was elevated on a high altar, and received the adoration of all present."[8]

Popery began the work which atheism was completing, hurrying France on to ruin. Writers in referring to the horrors of the Revolution say that these excesses are to be charged upon the throne and the church. (See Appendix.) In strict justice they are to be charged upon the church. Popery had poisoned the minds of kings against the Reformation. The genius of Rome inspired the cruelty and oppression which proceeded from the throne.

Wherever the gospel was received, the minds of the people were awakened. They began to cast off the shackles that had held them bondslaves of ignorance and superstition. Monarchs saw it and trembled for their despotism.

Rome was not slow to inflame their jealous fears. Said the pope to the regent of France in 1525: "This mania [Protestantism] will not only confound and destroy religion, but all principalities, nobility, laws, orders, and ranks besides." A papal nuncio warned the king: "The Protestants will upset all civil as well as religious order. . . . The throne is in as much danger as the altar."[9] Rome succeeded in arraying France against the Reformation.

The teaching of the Bible would have implanted in the hearts of the people principles of justice, temperance, and truth, which are the cornerstone of a nation's prosperity. "Righteousness exalteth a nation." Thereby "the throne is established." Proverbs 14:34; 16:12. See Isaiah 32:17. He who obeys the divine law will most truly respect and obey the laws of the country. France prohibited the Bible. Century after century men of integrity, of intellectual and moral strength, who had the faith to suffer for truth, toiled as slaves in the galleys, perished at the stake, or rotted in dungeon cells. Thousands found safety in flight for 250 years after the opening of the Reformation.

"Scarcely was there a generation of Frenchmen during that long period that did not witness the disciples of the gospel fleeing before the insane fury of the persecutor, and carrying with them the intelligence, the arts, the industry, the order, in which, as a rule, they preeminently excelled, to enrich the lands in which they found an asylum. . . . If all that was now driven away had been retained in France, what a . . . great, prosperous, and happy country—a pattern to the nations—would she have been! But a blind and inexorable bigotry chased from her soil every teacher of virtue, every champion of order, every honest defender of the throne. . . . At last the ruin of the state was complete."[10] The Revolution with its horrors was the result.

What Might Have Been

"With the flight of the Huguenots a general decline settled upon France. Flourishing manufacturing cities fell into decay. . . . It is estimated that, at the breaking out of the Revolution, two hundred thousand paupers in Paris claimed charity from the hands of the king. The Jesuits alone flourished in the decaying nation."[11]

The gospel would have brought to France the solution of those problems that baffled her clergy, king, and legislators, and finally plunged the nation into ruin. But under Rome the people had lost the Saviour's lessons of self-sacrifice and unselfish love for the good of others. The rich had no rebuke for the oppression of the poor; the poor no help for their degradation. The selfishness of the wealthy and powerful grew more and more oppressive. For centuries, the rich wronged the poor, and the poor hated the rich.

In many provinces the laboring classes were at the mercy of landlords and were forced to submit to exhorbitant demands. The middle and lower classes were heavily taxed by the civil authorities and clergy. "The farmers and the peasants might starve, for aught their oppressors cared. . . . The lives of the agricultural laborers were lives of incessant work and unrelieved misery; their complaints . . . were treated with insolent contempt. . . . Bribes were notoriously accepted by the judges. . . . Of the taxes, . . . not half ever found its way into the royal or episcopal treasury;

the rest was squandered in profligate self-indulgence.
And the men who thus impoverished their fellow-sub-
jects were themselves exempt from taxation and entitled by law or custom to all the appointments of the
state. . . . For their gratification millions were condemned to hopeless and degrading lives." (See Appendix.)

For more than half a century before the Revolution
the throne was occupied by Louis XV, distinguished as
an indolent, frivolous, and sensual monarch. With the
state financially embarrassed and the people exasperated, it needed no prophet's eye to foresee a terrible
outbreak. In vain the necessity of reform was urged.
The doom awaiting France was pictured in the king's
selfish answer, "After me, the deluge!"

Rome had influenced the kings and ruling classes to
keep the people in bondage, purposing to fasten both
rulers and people in her shackles upon their souls. A
thousandfold more terrible than the physical suffering
which resulted from her policy was the moral degradation. Deprived of the Bible, and abandoned to selfishness, the people were shrouded in ignorance and
sunken in vice, wholly unfitted for self-government.

Results Reaped in Blood

Instead of holding the masses in blind submission to
her dogmas, Rome's work resulted in making them
infidels and revolutionists. Romanism they despised as
priestcraft. The only god they knew was the god of
Rome. They regarded her greed and cruelty as the fruit
of the Bible, and they would have none of it.

Rome had misrepresented the character of God, and
now men rejected both the Bible and its Author. In the
reaction, Voltaire and his associates cast aside God's
Word altogether and spread infidelity. Rome had
ground down the people under her iron heel; and now
the masses cast off all restraint. Enraged, they rejected
truth and falsehood together.

At the opening of the Revolution, by a concession of

the king, the people were granted representation exceeding that of nobles and clergy combined. Thus the balance of power was in their hands; but they were not prepared to use it with wisdom and moderation. An outraged populace resolved to revenge themselves. The oppressed wrought out the lesson they had learned under tyranny and became the oppressors of those who had oppressed them.

France reaped in blood the harvest of her submission to Rome. Where France, under Romanism, had set up the first stake at the opening of the Reformation, there the Revolution set up its first guillotine. On the spot where the first martyrs to the Protestant faith were burned in the sixteenth century, the first victims were guillotined in the eighteenth. When the restraints of God's law were cast aside, the nation swept on to revolt and anarchy. The war against the Bible stands in world history as the Reign of Terror. He who triumphed today was condemned tomorrow.

King, clergy, and nobles were compelled to submit to the atrocities of a maddened people. Those who decreed the death of the king soon followed him to the scaffold. A general slaughter of all suspected of hostility to the Revolution was determined. France became a vast field for contending masses, swayed by the fury of passions. "In Paris one tumult succeeded another, and the citizens were divided into a medley of factions, that seemed intent on nothing but mutual extermination. . . . The country was nearly bankrupt, the armies were clamoring for arrears of pay, the Parisians were starving, the provinces were laid waste by brigands, and civilization was almost extinguished in anarchy and license."

All too well the people had learned the lessons of cruelty and torture which Rome had so diligently taught. It was not now the disciples of Jesus that were dragged to the stake. Long ago these had perished or been driven into exile. "The scaffolds ran red with the blood of the priests. The galleys and the prisons, once crowded with Huguenots, were now filled with their persecutors. Chained to the bench and toiling at the oar, the Roman Catholic clergy experienced all those woes which their church had so freely inflicted on the gentle heretics." (See Appendix.)

"Then came those days . . . when spies lurked in every corner; when the guillotine was long and hard at work every morning; when the jails were filled as close as the holds of a slave ship; when the gutters ran foaming with blood into the Seine. . . . Long rows of captives were mowed down with grapeshot. Holes were made in the bottom of crowded barges. . . . The number of young lads and of girls of seventeen who were murdered by that execrable government, is to be reckoned by hundreds. Babies torn from the breast were tossed from pike to pike along the Jacobin ranks." (See Appendix.)

All this was as Satan would have it. His policy is deception and his purpose is to bring wretchedness upon men, to deface the workmanship of God, to mar the divine purpose of love, and thus cause grief in heaven. Then by his deceptive arts, he leads men to throw the blame on God, as if all this misery were the result of the Creator's plan. When the people found Romanism to be a deception, he urged them to regard all religion as a cheat and the Bible as a fable.

The Fatal Error

The fatal error which wrought such woe for France was the ignoring of this one great truth: true freedom lies within the proscriptions of the law of God. "O that thou hadst hearkened to my commandments! then had thy peace been as a river, and thy righteousness as the waves of the sea." Isaiah 48:18. Those who will not read the lesson from the Book of God are bidden to read it in history.

When Satan wrought through the Roman Church to lead men away from obedience, his work was disguised. By the working of the Spirit of God his purposes were prevented from reaching their full fruition. The people did not trace the effect to its cause and discover the source of their miseries. But in the Revolution the law of God was openly set aside by the National Council. And in the Reign of Terror which followed, the working of cause and effect could be seen by all.

The transgression of a just and righteous law must result in ruin. The restraining Spirit of God, which imposes a check upon the cruel power of Satan, was in a great measure removed, and he whose delight is the wretchedness of men was permitted to work his will. Those who had chosen rebellion were left to reap its fruits. The land was filled with crimes. From devastated provinces and ruined cities a terrible cry was heard of bitter anguish. France was shaken as if by an earthquake. Religion, law, social order, the family, the state, and the church—all were smitten down by the impious hand that had been lifted against the law of God.

God's faithful witnesses, slain by the blasphemous power that "ascendeth out of the bottomless pit," were not long to remain silent. "After three days and a half the Spirit of life from God entered into them, and they stood upon their feet; and great fear fell upon them which saw them." Revelation 11:11. In 1793 the decrees which set aside the Bible passed the French Assembly. Three years and a half later a resolution rescinding these decrees was adopted by the same body. Men recognized the necessity of faith in God and His Word as the foundation of virtue and morality.

Concerning the "two witnesses" [the Old and New Testaments] the prophet declares further: "And they heard a great voice from heaven saying unto them, Come up hither. And they ascended up to heaven in a cloud; and their enemies beheld them." Revelation 11:12. "God's two witnesses" have been honored as never before. In 1804 the British and Foreign Bible Society was organized, followed by similar organizations upon the continent of Europe. In 1816 the American Bible Society was founded. The Bible has since been translated into many hundreds of languages and dialects. (See Appendix.)

Preceding 1792, little attention was given to foreign missions. But toward the close of the eighteenth century a great change took place. Men became dissatisfied with rationalism and realized the necessity of divine revelation and experimental religion. From this time foreign missions attained unprecedented growth. (See Appendix.)

Improvements in printing have given impetus to circulating the Bible. The breaking down of ancient prejudice and national exclusiveness and the loss of secular power by the pontiff of Rome have opened the way for the entrance of the Word of God. The Bible has now been carried to every part of the globe.

The infidel Voltaire said: "I am weary of hearing people repeat that twelve men established the Christian religion. I will prove that one man may suffice to overthrow it." Millions have joined in the war upon the Bible. But it is far from being destroyed. Where there were a hundred in Voltaire's time, there are now a hundred thousand copies of the Book of God. In the words of an early Reformer, "The Bible is an anvil that has worn out many hammers."

Whatever is built upon the authority of man will be overthrown; but that which is founded upon the rock of God's Word shall stand forever.

References

1. *Blackwood Magazine*, November, 1870.
2. Sir Walter Scott, *Life of Napoleon*, vol. 1, ch. 17.
3. Wylie, bk. 22, ch. 7.
4. Henry White, *The Massacre of St. Bartholomew*, ch. 14, par. 34.
5. Scott, vol. 1, ch. 17.
6. Lacretelle, *History*, vol. 11, p. 309: in Sir Archibald Alison, *History of Europe*, vol. 1, ch. 10.
7. Scott, vol. 1, ch. 17.

8. M. A. Thiers, *History of the French Revolution*, vol. 2, pp. 370, 371.

9. D'Aubigne, *History of the Reformation in Europe in the Time of Calvin*, bk. 2, ch. 36.

10. Wylie, bk. 13, ch. 20.

11. *Ibid*.

16/ Seeking Freedom in a New World

Though the authority and creed of Rome were rejected, not a few of her ceremonies were incorporated into the worship of the Church of England. It was claimed that things not forbidden in Scripture were not intrinsically evil. Their observance tended to narrow the gulf which separated the reformed churches from Rome, and it was urged that they would promote acceptance of the Protestant faith by Romanists.

Another class did not so judge. They looked upon these customs as badges of the slavery from which they had been delivered. They reasoned that God has in His Word established the regulations governing His worship, and that men are not at liberty to add to these or to detract from them. Rome began by enjoining what God had not forbidden, and ended by forbidding what He had explicitly enjoined.

Many regarded the customs of the English Church as monuments of idolatry, and they could not unite in her worship. But the church, supported by civil authority, would permit no dissent. Unauthorized assemblies for worship were prohibited under penalty of imprisonment, exile, or death.

Hunted, persecuted, and imprisoned, Puritans could discern no promise of better days. Some, determined to seek refuge in Holland, were betrayed into the hands of their enemies. But steadfast perseverance finally conquered, and they found shelter on friendly shores.

They had left their houses and their means of livelihood. They were strangers in a strange land, forced to resort to untried occupations to earn their bread. But they lost no time in idleness or repining. They thanked God for the blessings granted them and found joy in unmolested spiritual communion.

God Overruled Events

When God's hand seemed pointing them across the sea to a land where they might found a state and leave their children the heritage of religious liberty, they went forward in the path of providence. Persecution and exile were opening the way to freedom.

When first constrained to separate from the English Church, the Puritans joined themselves by a covenant as the Lord's free people "to walk together in all His ways made known or to be made known to them."[1] Here was the vital principle of Protestantism. With this purpose the Pilgrims departed from Holland to find a home in the New World. John Robinson, their pastor, in his farewell address to the exiles said:

"I charge you before God and His blessed angels to follow me no farther than I have followed Christ. If God should reveal anything to you by any other instrument of His, be as ready to receive it as ever you were to receive any truth of my ministry; for I am very confident the Lord hath more truth and light yet to break forth out of His holy word."[2]

"For my part, I cannot sufficiently bewail the condition of the reformed churches, who . . . will go at present no farther than the instruments of their reformation. The Lutherans cannot be drawn to go beyond what Luther saw; . . . and the Calvinists, you see, stick fast where they were left by that great man of God, who yet saw not all things. . . . Though they were burning and shining lights in their time, yet they penetrated not into the whole counsel of God, but were they now living, would be as willing to embrace further light as that which they first received."[3]

"Remember your promise and covenant with God and with one another, to receive whatever light and truth shall be made known to you from His written word; but withal, take heed, I beseech you, what you receive for truth, and compare it and weigh it with other scriptures of truth before you accept it; for it is not possible the Christian world should come so lately out of such thick antichristian darkness, and that full perfection of knowledge would break forth at once.''[4]

The desire for liberty of conscience inspired the Pilgrims to cross the sea, endure the hardships of the wilderness, and lay the foundation of a mighty nation. Yet the Pilgrims did not yet comprehend the principle of religious liberty. The freedom which they sacrificed so much to secure for themselves, they were not ready to grant to others. The doctrine that God has committed to the church the right to control the conscience and to define and punish heresy is one of the most deeply rooted of papal errors. The Reformers were not entirely free from Rome's spirit of intolerance. The dense darkness in which popery had enveloped Christendom had not yet been wholly dissipated.

A kind of state church was formed by the colonists, the magistrates being authorized to suppress heresy. Thus secular power was in the hands of the church. These measures led to the inevitable result—persecution.

Roger Williams

Like the early Pilgrims, Roger Williams came to the New World to enjoy religious freedom. But, unlike them, he saw—what so few had yet seen—that this freedom was the inalienable right of all. He was an earnest seeker for truth. Williams ''was the first person in modern Christendom to establish civil government on the doctrine of the liberty of conscience.''[5] ''The public or the magistrates may decide,'' he said, ''what is due from man to man; but when they attempt to prescribe a man's duties to God, they are out of place, and there can be no safety; for it is clear that if the magistrate had the power, he may decree one set of opinions or beliefs today and another tomorrow; as has been done in England by different kings and queens, and by different popes and councils in the Roman Church."[6]

Attendance at the established church was required under penalty of fine or imprisonment. "To compel men to unite with those of a different creed, he [Williams] regarded as an open violation of their natural rights; to drag to public worship the irreligious and the unwilling, seemed only like requiring hypocrisy. . . . 'No one should be bound to worship, or,' he added, 'to maintain a worship, against his own consent.' "[7]

Roger Williams was respected, yet his demand for religious liberty could not be tolerated. To avoid arrest he was forced to flee amid the cold and storms of winter into the unbroken forest.

"For fourteen weeks," he says, "I was sorely tossed in a bitter season, not knowing what bread or bed did mean." But "the ravens fed me in the wilderness," and a hollow tree often served for a shelter.[8] He continued his painful flight through snow and trackless forest until he found refuge with an Indian tribe whose confidence and affection he had won.

He laid the foundation of the first state of modern times that recognized the right "that every man should have liberty to worship God according to the light of his own conscience."[9] His little state, Rhode Island, increased and prospered until its foundation principles—civil and religious liberty—became the cornerstones of the American Republic.

Document of Freedom

The American Declaration of Independence declared: "We hold these truths to be self-evident, that all men are created equal; that they are endowed by their Creator with certain unalienable rights; that among these are life, liberty, and the pursuit of happiness." The Constitution guarantees the inviolability of conscience: "Congress shall make no law respecting an establishment of religion, or prohibiting the free exercise thereof."

"The framers of the Constitution recognized the eternal principle that man's relation with his God is above human legislation, and his rights of conscience inalienable. . . . It is an inborn principle which nothing can eradicate."[10]

The tidings spread through Europe of a land where every man might enjoy the fruit of his own labor and obey his conscience. Thousands flocked to the shores of the New World. In twenty years from the first landing at Plymouth (1620), as many thousand Pilgrims were settled in New England.

"They asked nothing from the soil but the reasonable returns of their own labor. . . . They patiently endured the privations of the wilderness, watering the tree of liberty with their tears, and with the sweat of their brow, till it took deep root in the land."

Surest Safeguard of National Greatness

Bible principles were taught in the home, school, and church; its fruits were manifest in thrift, intelligence, purity, and temperance. One might for years "not see a drunkard, or hear an oath, or meet a beggar."[11] Bible principles are the surest safeguards of national greatness. The feeble colonies grew into powerful states, and the world marked the prosperity of "a church without a pope, and a state without a king."

But increasing numbers were attracted to America by motives different from those of the Pilgrims. The numbers increased of those who sought only worldly advantage.

The early colonists permitted only members of the church to vote or to hold office in the government. This measure had been accepted to preserve the purity of the state; it resulted in the corruption of the church. Many united with the church without a change of heart. Even in the ministry were those who were ignorant of the renewing power of the Holy Spirit. From the days of Constantine to the present, attempting to build up the church by the aid of the state, while it may appear to bring the world nearer to the church, in reality brings the church nearer to the world.

The Protestant churches of America, and those in Europe as well, failed to press forward in the path of reform. The majority, like the Jews in Christ's day or the papists in the time of Luther, were content to believe as their fathers had believed. Errors and superstitions were retained. The Reformation gradually died out, until there was almost as great need of reform in the Protestant churches as in the Roman Church in the time of Luther. There was the same reverence for the opinions of men and substitution of human theories for God's Word. Men neglected to search the Scriptures and thus continued to cherish doctrines which had no foundation in the Bible.

Pride and extravagance were fostered under the guise of religion, and the churches became corrupted. Traditions that were to ruin millions were taking deep root. The church was upholding these traditions instead of contending for "the faith which was once delivered unto the saints."

Thus were degraded the principles for which the Reformers had suffered so much.

References
1. J. Brown, *The Pilgrim Fathers*, p. 74.
2. Martyn, vol. 5, p. 70.
3. D. Neal, *History of Puritans*, vol. 1, p. 269.
4. Martyn, vol. 5, pp. 70, 71.
5. Bancroft, pt. 1, ch. 15, par. 16.
6. Martyn, vol. 5, p. 340.
7. Bancroft, pt. 1, ch. 15, par. 2.
8. Martyn, vol. 5, pp. 349, 350.
9. *Ibid.*, vol. 5, p. 354.
10. Congressional Documents (U.S.A.), serial No. 200, Document No. 271.
11. Bancroft, pt. 1, ch. 19, par. 25.

17/Promises of Christ's Return

The promise of Christ's second coming to complete the great work of redemption is the keynote of the Sacred Scriptures. From Eden, the children of faith have waited the coming of the Promised One to bring them again to the lost Paradise.

Enoch, the seventh in descent from them that dwelt in Eden, who for three centuries walked with God, declared, "Behold, the Lord cometh with ten thousands of his saints, to execute judgment upon all." Jude 14, 15. Job in the night of affliction exclaimed, "I know that my redeemer liveth, and that he shall stand at the latter day upon the earth: . . . in my flesh shall I see God: whom I shall see for myself, and mine eyes shall behold, and not another." Job 19:25-27. The poets and prophets of the Bible have dwelt on the coming of Christ in words glowing with fire. "Let the heavens rejoice, and let the earth be glad . . . before the Lord: for he cometh, for he cometh to judge the earth: he shall judge the world with righteousness, and the people with his truth." Psalm 96:11-13.

Said Isaiah: "It shall be said in that day, Lo, this is our God; we have waited for him, and he will save us: this is the Lord; we have waited for him, we will be glad and rejoice in his salvation." Isaiah 25:9.

The Saviour comforted His disciples with the assurance that He would come again: "In my father's house are many mansions. . . . I go to prepare a place for you. And if I go, . . . I will come again, and receive you unto myself." "The Son of man shall come in his glory, and all the holy angels with him, then shall he sit upon the throne of his glory: and before him shall be gathered all nations." John 14:2, 3; Matthew 25:31, 32.

Angels repeated to the disciples the promise of His return: "This *same* Jesus, which is taken up from you into heaven, shall *so* come in like manner as ye have seen him go into heaven." Acts 1:11. And Paul testified: "The Lord *himself* shall descend from heaven with a shout, with the voice of the archangel, and with the trump of God." 1 Thessalonians 4:16. Said the prophet of Patmos: "Behold he cometh with clouds; and every eye shall see him." Revelation 1:7.

Then the long-continued rule of evil shall be broken: "The kingdoms of this world" will become "the kingdoms of our Lord, and of his Christ; and he shall reign for ever and ever." Revelation 11:15. "The Lord God will cause righteousness and praise to spring forth before all the nations." Isaiah 61:11.

Then the peaceful kingdom of the Messiah shall be established: "The Lord shall comfort Zion: he will comfort all her waste places; and he will make her wilderness like Eden, and her desert like the garden of the Lord." Isaiah 51:3.

The coming of the Lord has been in all ages the hope of His true followers. Amid suffering and persecution, the "appearing of the great God and our Saviour Jesus Christ" was the "blessed hope." Titus 2:13. Paul pointed to the resurrection to take place at the Saviour's advent, when the dead in Christ should rise, and together with the living be caught up to meet the Lord in the air. "And so," he said, "shall we ever be with the Lord. Wherefore comfort one another with these words." 1 Thessalonians 4:17.

On Patmos the beloved disciple heard the promise, "Surely I come quickly," and his response voices the prayer of the church, "Even so, come, Lord Jesus." Revelation 22:20.

From the dungeon, the stake, the scaffold, where saints and martyrs witnessed for the truth, comes down the centuries the utterance of their faith and hope. Being "assured of His personal resurrection, and consequently of their own at His coming, for this cause," says one of these Christians, "they despised death, and were found to be above it."[1] The Waldenses cherished the same faith. Wycliffe, Luther, Calvin, Knox, Ridley, and Baxter looked in faith for the Lord's coming. Such was the hope of the apostolic church, of the "church in the wilderness," and of the Reformers.

Prophecy not only foretells the manner and object of Christ's second coming, but presents tokens by which men are to know when that day is near. "There shall be signs in the sun, and in the moon, and in the stars." Luke 21:25. "The sun shall be darkened, and the moon shall not give her light, and the stars of heaven shall fall, and the powers that are in heaven shall be shaken. And then shall they see the Son of man coming in the clouds with great power and glory." Mark 13:24-26. The revelator thus describes the first of the signs to precede the second advent: "There was a great earthquake; and the sun became black as sackcloth of hair, and the moon became as blood." Revelation 6:12.

The Earthquake That Shook the World

In fulfillment of this prophecy there occurred in 1755 the most terrible earthquake ever recorded. Known as the earthquake of Lisbon, it extended to Europe, Africa, and America. It was felt in Greenland, the West Indies, Madeira, Norway and Sweden, Great Britain and Ireland, an extent of not less than four million square miles. In Africa the shock was almost as severe as in Europe. A great part of Algiers was destroyed. A vast wave swept over the coast of Spain and Africa engulfing cities.

Mountains, "some of the largest in Portugal, were impetuously shaken, as it were, from their very foundations; and some of them opened at their summits, which were split and rent in a wonderful manner, huge masses of them being thrown down into the adjacent valleys. Flames are related to have issued from these mountains.''

At Lisbon ''a sound of thunder was heard underground, and immediately afterwards a violent shock threw down the greater part of that city. In the course of about six minutes, sixty thousand persons perished. The sea first retired, and laid the bar dry; it then rolled in, rising fifty feet or more above its ordinary level.''[2]

The earthquake happened on a holyday, when the churches and convents were full of people, very few of whom escaped.''[3] ''The terror of the people was beyond description. Nobody wept; it was beyond tears. They ran hither and thither, delirious with horror and astonishment, beating their faces and breasts, crying, 'Misericordia! the world's at an end!' Mothers forgot their children, and ran about loaded with crucifixed images. Unfortunately, many ran to the churches for protection; but in vain was the sacrament exposed; in vain did the poor creatures embrace the altars; images, priests, and people were buried in one common ruin.''

Darkening of the Sun and Moon

Twenty-five years later appeared the next sign mentioned in the prophecy—the darkening of the sun and moon. The time of its fulfillment had been definitely pointed out in the Saviour's conversation with His disciples upon Olivet. *''In those days, after* that tribulation, the sun shall be darkened, and the moon shall not give her light.''* Mark 13:24. The 1260 days, or years, terminated in 1798. A quarter of a century earlier, persecution had almost wholly ceased. Following this persecution, the sun was to be darkened. On May 19, 1780, this prophecy was fulfilled.

An eyewitness in Massachusetts described the event as follows: ''A heavy black cloud spread over the entire sky except a narrow rim at the horizon, and it was as dark as it usually is at nine o'clock on a summer evening. . . .

"Fear, anxiety, and awe gradually filled the minds of the people. Women stood at the door, looking out upon the dark landscape; men returned from their labor in the fields; the carpenter left his tools, the blacksmith his forge, the tradesman his counter. Schools were dismissed, and tremblingly the children fled homeward. Travelers put up at the nearest farmhouse. 'What is coming?' queried every lip and heart. It seemed as if a hurricane was about to dash across the land, or as if it was the day of the consummation of all things.

"Candles were used; and hearth fires shone as brightly as on a moonless evening in autumn. . . . Fowls retired to their roosts and went to sleep, cattle gathered at the pasture bars and lowed, frogs peeped, birds sang their evening songs, and bats flew about. But the human knew that night had not come. . . .

"Congregations came together in many . . . places. The texts for the extemporaneous sermons were invariably those that seemed to indicate that the darkness was consonant with Scriptural prophecy. . . . The darkness was most dense shortly after eleven o'clock."[4]

"In most parts of the country it was so great in the daytime, that the people could not tell the hour by either watch or clock, nor dine, nor manage their domestic business, without the light of candles."[5]

Moon as Blood

"Nor was the darkness of the night less uncommon and terrifying than that of the day; notwithstanding there was almost a full moon, no object was discernible but by the help of some artificial light, which, when seen from the neighboring houses and other places at a distance appeared through a kind of Egyptian darkness which seemed almost impervious to the rays."[6] "If every luminous body in the universe had been shrouded in impenetrable shades, or struck out of existence, the darkness could not have been more complete."[7] After midnight the darkness disappeared, and the moon, when first visible, had the appearance of blood.

May 19, 1780, stands in history as "The Dark Day." Since the time of Moses no darkness of equal density, extent, and duration has ever been recorded. The description given by eyewitnesses is an echo of the words recorded by Joel 2500 years previous: "The sun shall be turned into darkness, and the moon into blood, before the great and the terrible day of the Lord come." Joel 2:31.

"When these things begin to come to pass," Christ said, "then look up, and lift up your heads; for your redemption draweth nigh." He pointed His followers to the budding trees of spring: "When they now shoot forth, ye see and know of your own selves that summer is now nigh at hand. So likewise ye, when ye see these things come to pass, know ye that the kingdom of God is nigh at hand." Luke 21:28, 30, 31.

But in the church love for Christ and faith in His coming had grown cold. The professed people of God were blinded to the Saviour's instructions concerning the signs of His appearing. The doctrine of the second advent had been neglected, until it was, to a great extent, ignored and forgotten, especially in America. An absorbing devotion to money-making, the rush for popularity and power, led men to put far in the future that solemn day when the present order of things should pass away.

The Saviour foretold the state of backsliding that would exist just prior to His second advent. For those living at this time, Christ's admonition is: "Take heed to yourselves, lest at any time your hearts be overcharged with surfeiting, and drunkenness, and cares of this life, and so that day come upon you unawares." "Watch ye therefore, and pray always, that ye may be accounted worthy to escape all these things that shall come to pass, and to stand before the Son of man." Luke 21:34, 36.

It was needful that men be roused to prepare for the solemn events connected with the close of probation.

"The day of the Lord is great and very terrible; and who can abide it?" Who shall stand when He appeareth who is "of purer eyes than to behold evil," and cannot "look on iniquity"? "I will punish the world for their evil, and the wicked for their iniquity; and I will cause the arrogancy of the proud to cease, and will lay low the haughtiness of the terrible." "Neither their silver nor their gold shall be able to deliver them;" "their goods shall become a booty, and their houses a desolation." Joel 2:11; Habakkuk 1:13; Isaiah 13:11; Zephaniah 1:18, 13.

The Call to Arouse

In view of that great day the Word of God calls upon His people to seek His face with repentance:

"The day of the Lord cometh, for it is nigh at hand." " Sanctify a fast, call a solemn assembly: gather the people, sanctify the congregation, assemble the elders, gather the children: . . . Let the priests, the ministers of the Lord, weep between the porch and the altar." "Turn ye even to me with all your heart, and with fasting, and with weeping, and with mourning: And rend your heart, and not your garments, and turn unto the Lord your God: for he is gracious and merciful, slow to anger, and of great kindness." Joel 2:1, 15-17, 12, 13.

To prepare a people to stand in the day of God, a great work of reform was to be accomplished. In His mercy He was about to send a message to arouse His professed people and lead them to make ready for the coming of the Lord.

This warning is brought to view in Revelation 14. Here is a threefold message represented as proclaimed by heavenly beings and immediately followed by the coming of the Son of man to reap "the harvest of the earth." The prophet saw an angel flying "in the midst of heaven, having the everlasting gospel to preach unto them that dwell on the earth, and to every nation, and kindred, and tongue, and people. saying with a loud voice, Fear God, and give glory to him; for the hour of his judgment is come: and worship him that made heaven, and earth, and the sea, and the fountains of waters." Revelation 14:6, 7.

This message is a part of "the everlasting gospel." The work of preaching has been entrusted to men. Holy angels direct, but the actual proclamation of the gospel is performed by the servants of Christ on earth. Faithful men, obedient to the promptings of God's Spirit and the teachings of His Word, were to proclaim this warning. They had been seeking the knowledge of God, counting it "better than the merchandise of silver, and the gain thereof than fine gold." "The secret of the Lord is with them that fear him; and he will show them his covenant." Proverbs 3:14; Psalm 25:14.

A Message Given by Humble Men

Had scholarly theologians been faithful watchmen, diligently and prayerfully searching the Scriptures, they would have known the time. The prophecies would have opened to them the events about to take place. But the message was given by humbler men. Those who neglect to seek the light when it is within their reach are left in darkness. But the Saviour declares, "He that followeth me shall not walk in darkness, but shall have the light of life." John 8:12. To that soul some star of heavenly radiance will be sent to guide him into all truth.

At the time of Christ's first advent the priests and scribes of the Holy City might have discerned "the signs of the times" and proclaimed the coming of the Promised One. Micah designated His birthplace, Daniel, the time of His advent. Micah 5:2; Daniel 9:25. The Jewish leaders were without excuse if they did not know. Their ignorance was the result of sinful neglect.

With profound interest the elders of Israel should have been studying the place, the time, the circumstances, of the greatest event in the world's history—the coming of the Son of God. The people should have been watching that they might welcome the world's Redeemer. But at Bethlehem two weary travelers from Nazareth traversed the length of the narrow street to the eastern extremity of town, vainly seeking a shelter for the night. No doors were open to receive them. In a wretched hovel prepared for cattle, they at last found refuge, and there the Saviour of the world was born.

Angels were appointed to carry the glad tidings to those prepared to receive it and who would joyfully make it known. Christ had stooped to take upon Himself man's nature, to bear infinite woe as He should make His soul an offering for sin. Yet angels desired that even in His humiliation the Son of the Highest might appear before men with a dignity and glory befitting His character. Would the great men of earth assemble at Israel's capital to greet His coming? Would angels present Him to the expectant company?

An angel visited the earth to see who were prepared to welcome Jesus. But he heard no voice of praise that the period of Messiah's coming was at hand. The angel hovered over the chosen city and temple where the divine presence had been manifested for ages, but even there was the same indifference. The priests in pomp and pride offered polluted sacrifices. The Pharisees with loud voices addressed the people or made boastful prayers at the corners of the streets. Kings, philosophers, rabbis, all were unmindful of the wondrous fact that the Redeemer of men was about to appear.

In amazement the celestial messenger was about to return to heaven with the shameful tidings, when he discovered a group of shepherds watching their flocks. As they gazed into the starry heavens, they contemplated the prophecy of a Messiah to come and longed for the advent of the world's Redeemer. Here was a company prepared to receive the heavenly message. Suddenly celestial glory flooded all the plain, an innumerable company of angels was revealed; and as if the joy were too great for one messenger to bring from heaven, a multitude of voices broke forth in the anthem which all the nations of the saved shall one day sing: "Glory to God in the highest, and on earth peace, good will toward men." Luke 2:14.

What a lesson is this wonderful story of Bethlehem! How it rebukes our unbelief, our pride and self-sufficiency. How it warns us to beware, lest we also fail to discern the signs of the times and therefore know not the day of our visitation.

It was not alone among lowly shepherds that angels found watchers for Messiah's coming. In the land of the heathen also were those that looked for Him—rich, noble wise men—the philosophers of the East. From the Hebrew Scriptures they had learned of the Star to arise out of Jacob. With eager desire they awaited His coming who should be not only the "Consolation of Israel," but a "Light to lighten the Gentiles," and "for salvation unto the ends of the earth." Luke 2:25, 32; Acts 13:47. The Heaven-sent star guided Gentile strangers to the birthplace of the newborn King.

It is "unto them that look for him" that Christ is to "appear the second time without sin unto salvation." Hebrews 9:28. Like the tidings of the Saviour's birth, the message of the second advent was not committed to the religious leaders of the people. They had refused light from heaven; therefore they were not of the number described by the apostle Paul: "But ye, brethren, are not in darkness, that that day should overtake you as a thief. Ye are all the children of light and the children of the day: we are not of the night, nor of darkness." 1 Thessalonians 5:4, 5.

The watchmen upon the walls of Zion should have been the first to catch the tidings of the Saviour's advent, the first to proclaim Him near. But they were at ease, while the people were asleep in their sins. Jesus saw His church, like the barren fig tree, covered with pretentious leaves, yet destitute of precious fruit. The spirit of true humility, penitence, and faith was lacking. There were pride, formalism, selfishness, oppression. A backsliding church closed their eyes to the signs of the times. They departed from God and separated themselves from His love. As they refused to comply with the conditions, His promises were not fulfilled to them.

Many of the professed followers of Christ refused to receive the light from heaven. Like the Jews of old, they knew not the time of their visitation. The Lord passed them by and revealed His truth to those who, like the shepherds of Bethlehem and the Eastern Magi, had given heed to all the light they had received.

References
1. See Daniel T. Taylor, *The Reign of Christ on Earth:* or, *The Voice of the Church in All Ages*, p. 33.
2. Sir Charles Lyell, *Principles of Geology*, p. 495.
3. *Encyclopedia Americana*, art. "Lisbon," (ed. 1831).
4. *The Essex Antiquarian*, April 1899, vol. 3, no. 4, pp. 53, 54.
5. William Gordon, *History of the Rise, Progress and Establishment of the Independence of the U.S.A.*, vol. 3, p. 57.
6. Isaiah Thomas, *Massachusetts Spy;* or, *American Oracle of Liberty*, vol. 10, no. 472, (May 25, 1780).
7. Letter by Dr. Samuel Tenney, of Exeter, New Hampshire, December 1785, in *Massachusetts Historical Society Collections*, 1792, (1st series, vol. 1, p. 97).

18/ New Light in the New World

An upright, honest farmer, who sincerely desired to know the truth, was the man chosen of God to lead out in the proclamation of Christ's second coming. Like many other reformers, William Miller had battled with poverty and learned the lessons of self-denial.

Even in childhood he gave evidence of more than ordinary intellectual strength. As he grew older, his mind was active and well developed, and he had a keen thirst for knowledge. His love of study and a habit of careful thought and close criticism rendered him a man of sound judgment and comprehensive views. He possessed an irreproachable moral character and an enviable reputation. He filled civil and military offices with credit. Wealth and honor seemed wide open to him.

In childhood he had been subject to religious impressions. In early manhood, however, he was thrown into the society of deists,* whose influence was strong from the fact that they were mostly good citizens, humane and benevolent. Living in the midst of Christian institutions, their characters had been to some extent molded by their surroundings. For the excellencies which won them respect they were indebted to the Bible, and yet these good gifts were perverted to exert an influence against the Word of God. Miller was led to adopt their sentiments.

*Deism: the belief that God exists and created the world, but thereafter assumed no control over it nor concern for the lives of people; the belief that reason is sufficient for the knowledge of truth, thus rejecting revelation.—*Webster's New World Dictionary*.

Current interpretations of Scripture presented difficulties which seemed to him insurmountable; yet his new belief, while setting aside the Bible, offered nothing better, and he remained far from satisfied. But when Miller was thirty-four, the Holy Spirit impressed his heart with his condition as a sinner. He found no assurance of happiness beyond the grave. The future was dark and gloomy. Referring to his feelings at this time, he said:

"The heavens were as brass over my head, and the earth as iron under my feet. . . . The more I thought, the more scattered were my conclusions. I tried to stop thinking, but my thoughts would not be controlled. I was truly wretched, but did not understand the cause. I murmured and complained, but knew not of whom. I knew that there was a wrong, but knew not how or where to find the right."

Miller Finds a Friend

"Suddenly," he says, "the character of a Saviour was vividly impressed upon my mind. It seemed that there might be a being so good and compassionate as to himself atone for our transgressions, and thereby save us from suffering the penalty of sin. . . . But the question arose, How can it be proved that such a being does exist? Aside from the Bible, I found that I could get no evidence of the existence of such a Saviour, or even of a future state. . . .

"I saw that the Bible did bring to view just such a Saviour as I needed; and I was perplexed to find how an uninspired book should develop principles so perfectly adapted to the wants of a fallen world. I was constrained to admit that the Scriptures must be a revelation from God. They became my delight; and in Jesus I found a friend. The Saviour became to me the chiefest among ten thousand; and the Scriptures, which before were dark and contradictory, now became the lamp to my feet and light to my path. . . . I found the Lord God to be a Rock in the midst of the ocean of life. The Bible now became my chief study, and I can truly say, I searched it with great delight. . . . I wondered why I had not seen its beauty and glory before, and marveled that I could have ever rejected it. . . . I lost all taste for other reading, and applied my heart to get wisdom from God.''[1]

Miller publicly professed his faith. But his infidel associates brought forward all those arguments which he himself had often urged against the Scriptures. He reasoned that if the Bible is a revelation from God, it must be consistent with itself. He determined to study the Scriptures and ascertain if every apparent contradiction could be harmonized.

Dispensing with commentaries, he compared scripture with scripture by the aid of the marginal references and concordance. Beginning with Genesis, reading verse by verse, when he found anything obscure it was his custom to compare it with every other text which seemed to refer to the matter under consideration. Every word was permitted to have its bearing upon the text. Thus whenever he met with a passage hard to be understood he found an explanation in some other portion of the Scriptures. He studied with earnest prayer for divine enlightenment, and he experienced the truth of the psalmist's words: "The entrance of thy words giveth light; it giveth understanding unto the simple." Psalm 119:130.

With intense interest he studied Daniel and the Revelation and found that the prophetic symbols could be understood. He saw that all the various figures, metaphors, similitudes, etc., were either explained in their immediate connection or defined in other scriptures and were to be literally understood. Link after link of the chain of truth rewarded his efforts. Step by step he traced the great lines of prophecy. Angels of heaven were guiding his mind.

He became satisfied that the popular view of a temporal millennium before the end of the world was not sustained by the Word of God. This doctrine, pointing to a thousand years of peace before the coming of the Lord, is contrary to the teachings of Christ and His apostles, who declared that the wheat and the tares are to grow together until the harvest, the end of the world, and that "evil men and seducers shall wax worse and worse." 2 Timothy 3:13.

Personal Coming of Christ

The doctrine of the world's conversion and the spiritual reign of Christ was not held by the apostolic church. It was not generally accepted by Christians until about the beginning of the eighteenth century. It taught men to look far in the future for the coming of the Lord and prevented them from giving heed to the signs heralding His approach. It led many to neglect preparation to meet their Lord.

Miller found the literal, personal coming of Christ plainly taught in Scripture. "The Lord himself shall descend from heaven with a shout, with the voice of the Archangel, and with the trump of God." "They shall see the Son of man coming in the clouds of heaven with power and great glory." "As the lightning cometh out of the east, and shineth even unto the west; so shall also the coming of the Son of man be." "The Son of man shall come in his glory, and all the holy angels with him." "And he shall send his angels with a great sound of a trumpet, and they shall gather together his elect." 1 Thessalonians 4:16, 17; Matthew 24:30, 27; 25:31; 24:31.

At His coming the righteous dead will be raised and the righteous living changed. "We shall not all sleep, but we shall all be changed, in a moment, in the twinkling of an eye, at the last trump: for the trumpet shall sound, and the dead shall be raised incorruptible, and we shall be changed. For this corruptible must put on incorruption, and this mortal must put on immortality." "The dead in Christ shall rise first: then we which are alive and remain shall be caught up together with them in the clouds, to meet the Lord in the air: and so shall we ever be with the Lord." 1 Corinthians 15:51-53; 1 Thessalonians 4:16, 17.

Man in his present state is mortal, corruptible; but the kingdom of God will be incorruptible. Therefore man in his present state cannot enter into the kingdom of God. When Jesus comes, He confers immortality upon His people, and then calls them to inherit the kingdom of which they have hitherto been only heirs.

Scripture and Chronology

These and other scriptures clearly proved to Miller that the universal reign of peace and the setting up of the kingdom of God upon the earth were subsequent to the second advent. Furthermore, the condition of the world corresponded to the prophetic description of the last days. He was forced to the conclusion that the period allotted for the earth in its present state was about to close.

"Another kind of evidence that vitally affected my mind," he says, "was the chronology of the Scriptures. . . . I found that predicted events, which had been fulfilled in the past, often occurred within a given time. . . . Events . . . once only a matter of prophecy, . . . were fulfilled in accordance with the predictions."[2]

When he found chronological periods that extended to the second coming of Christ, he could not but regard them as the "times before appointed" which God had revealed unto His servants. "Those things which are revealed belong unto us and to our children forever." The Lord declares that He "will do nothing, but he revealeth his secret unto his servants the prophets." Deuteronomy 29:29; Amos 3:7. The students of God's Word may confidently expect to find the most stupendous event in human history clearly pointed out in the Scriptures.

"I was fully convinced," says Miller, "that all Scripture given by inspiration of God is profitable; that it . . . was written as holy men were moved by the

Holy Ghost, and was written 'for our learning, that we through patience and comfort of the Scriptures might have hope.' . . . I therefore felt that in endeavoring to comprehend what God had in His mercy seen fit to reveal to us, I had no right to pass over the prophetic periods.''[3]

The prophecy which seemed most clearly to reveal the *time* of the second advent was Daniel 8:14: "Unto two thousand and three hundred days; then shall the sanctuary be cleansed." Making Scripture its own interpreter, Miller learned that a day in symbolic prophecy represents a year. (See Appendix.) He saw that the 2300 prophetic days, or literal years, would extend far beyond the close of the Jewish dispensation, hence it could not refer to the sanctuary of that dispensation.

Miller accepted the general view that in the Christian age the earth is the "sanctuary," and therefore understood that the cleansing of the sanctuary foretold in Daniel 8:14 represented the purification of the earth by fire at the second coming of Christ. If the correct starting point could be found for the 2300 days, he concluded that the time of the second advent could be revealed.

Discovering the Prophetic Timetable

Miller continued the examination of the prophecies, whole nights as well as days being devoted to the study of what now appeared of such stupendous importance. In the eighth chapter of Daniel he could find no clue to the starting point of the 2300 days; the angel Gabriel, though commanded to make Daniel understand the vision, gave him only a partial explanation. As the terrible persecution to befall the church was unfolded to the prophet's vision, he could endure no more. Daniel "fainted, and was sick certain days." "I was astonished at the vision," he says, "but none understood it." Daniel 8:27.

Yet God had bidden His messenger, "Make this man

to understand the vision." In obedience, the angel returned to Daniel, saying: "I am now come forth to give thee skill and understanding. . . . therefore understand the matter, and consider the vision." One important point in chapter 8 had been left unexplained, namely, the 2300 days; therefore the angel, resuming his explanation, dwells chiefly upon the time:

"Seventy weeks are determined upon thy people and upon thy holy city. . . . Know therefore and understand, that from the going forth of the commandment to restore and to build Jerusalem unto the Messiah the Prince shall be seven weeks, and threescore and two weeks: the street shall be built again, and the wall, even in troublous times. And after threescore and two weeks shall Messiah be cut off, but not for himself: . . . And he shall confirm the covenant with many for one week: and in the midst of the week he shall cause the sacrifice and the oblation to cease." Daniel 8:16; 9:22, 23, 24-27.

The angel had been sent to Daniel to explain the point he had failed to understand—"unto two thousand and three hundred days; then shall the sanctuary be cleansed." The first words of the angel are, "Seventy weeks are determined upon thy people and upon thy holy city." The word *determined* literally signifies "cut off." Seventy weeks, 490 years, are to be cut off as specially pertaining to the Jews.

Two Time Periods Begin Together

But from what were they cut off? As the 2300 days was the only period of time mentioned in chapter 8, the seventy weeks must therefore be a part of the 2300 days. The two periods must begin together, the seventy weeks to date from "the going forth of the commandment" to restore and build Jerusalem. If the date of this commandment could be found, then the starting point for the 2300 days would be ascertained.

In the seventh chapter of Ezra the decree is found, issued by Artaxerxes, king of Persia, in 457 B.C. Three kings, in originating and completing the decree, brought it to the perfection required by the prophecy to mark the beginning of the 2300 years. Taking 457 B.C., when the decree was completed, as the date of the "commandment," every specification of the seventy weeks was seen to have been fulfilled. (See Appendix.)

"From the going forth of the commandment to restore and to build Jerusalem unto the Messiah the Prince shall be seven weeks, and threescore and two weeks"—sixty-nine weeks, or 483 years. The decree of Artaxerxes went into effect in the autumn of 457 B.C. From this date, 483 years extend to the autumn of A.D. 27. At that time this prophecy was fulfilled. In the autumn of A.D. 27 Christ was baptized by John and received the anointing of the Spirit. After His baptism He went into Galilee, "preaching the gospel of the kingdom of God, and saying, *The time* is fulfilled." Mark 1:14, 15.

The Gospel Given to the World

"And he shall confirm the covenant with many for one week"—the last seven years of the period allotted to the Jews. During this time, from A.D. 27 to A.D. 34, Christ and His disciples extended the gospel invitation especially to the Jews. The Saviour's direction was: "Go not into the way of the Gentiles, and into any city of the Samaritans enter ye not: but go rather to the lost sheep of the house of Israel." Matthew 10:5, 6.

"In the midst of the week he shall cause the sacrifice and the oblation to cease." In A.D. 31, three and a half years after His baptism, our Lord was crucified. With the great sacrifice offered upon Calvary, type had met antitype. All the sacrifices and oblations of the ceremonial system were to cease.

The 490 years allotted to the Jews ended in A.D. 34. At that time, through action of the Jewish Sanhedrin, the nation sealed its rejection of the gospel by the martyrdom of Stephen and the persecution of the followers of Christ. Then the message of salvation was given to the world. The disciples, forced by persecution to flee from Jerusalem, "went everywhere preaching the word." Acts 8:4.

Thus far every specification of the prophecies is strikingly fulfilled. The beginning of the seventy weeks is fixed beyond question at 457 B.C., and their expiration in A.D. 34. The seventy weeks (490 days) having been cut off from the 2300, there were 1810 days remaining. After the end of the 490 days, the 1810 days were still to be fulfilled. From A.D. 34, 1810 years extend to 1844. Consequently the 2300 days of Daniel 8:14 terminate in 1844. At the expiration of this great prophetic period, "the sanctuary shall be cleansed." Thus the time of the cleansing of the sanctuary—almost universally believed to take place at the second advent—was pointed out. (See chart, p. 220.)

Startling Conclusion

At the outset Miller had not the slightest expectation of reaching the conclusion at which he had now arrived. He himself could hardly credit the results of his investigation. But the Scripture evidence was too clear to be set aside.

In 1818 he reached the solemn conviction that in about twenty-five years Christ would appear for the redemption of His people. "I need not speak," says Miller, "of the joy that filled my heart in view of the delightful prospect, nor of the ardent longings of my soul for a participation in the joys of the redeemed. . . . Oh, how bright and glorious the truth appeared! . . .

"The question came home to me with mighty power regarding my duty to the world, in view of the evidence that had affected my own mind."[4] He could not but feel that it was his duty to impart to others the light which he had received. He expected opposition from the ungodly, but was confident that all Christians would rejoice in the hope of meeting the Saviour. He hesitated to present the prospect of glorious deliverance, so soon to be consumated, lest he should be in error and mislead others. He was thus led to review and to consider carefully every difficulty which presented itself to his mind. Five years spent thus left him convinced of the correctness of his position.

"Go and Tell It to the World"

"When I was about my business," he said, "it was continually ringing in my ears, 'Go and tell the world of their danger.' This text was constantly occurring to me: 'When I say unto the wicked, O wicked man, thou shalt surely die; if thou dost not speak to warn the wicked from his way, that wicked man shall die in his iniquity; but his blood will I require at thine hand.' I felt that if the wicked could be effectually warned, multitudes of them would repent; and that if they were not warned, their blood might be required at my hand."[5] The words were ever recurring to his mind: "Go and tell it to the world; their blood will I require at thy hand." For nine years he waited, the burden still pressing upon his soul, until in 1831 he for the first time publicly gave the reasons of his faith.

He was now fifty, unaccustomed to public speaking, but his labors were blessed. His first lecture was followed by a religious awakening. Thirteen entire families, with the exception of two persons, were converted. He was urged to speak in other places, and in nearly every place sinners were converted. Christians were roused to greater consecration, and deists and infidels were led to acknowledge the truth of the Bible. His preaching aroused the public mind and checked the growing worldliness and sensuality of the age.

In many places Protestant churches of nearly all denominations were thrown open to him, and invitations usually came from the ministers. It was his rule not to labor in any place to which he had not been invited, yet he soon found himself unable to comply with half the requests that poured in. Many were convinced of the certainty and nearness of Christ's coming and their need of preparation. In some of the large cities, liquor dealers turned their shops into meeting rooms; gambling dens were broken up; infidels and even the most abandoned profligates were reformed. Prayer meetings were established by the various denominations at almost every hour, businessmen assembling at midday for prayer and praise. There was no extravagant excitement. His work, like that of the early Reformers, tended rather to convince the understanding and arouse the conscience than merely to excite emotion.

In 1833 Miller received a license to preach from the Baptist Church. A large number of the ministers of his denomination approved his work; it was with their formal sanction that he continued his labors. He traveled and preached unceasingly, never receiving enough to meet the expense of travel to the places where he was invited. Thus his public labors were a heavy tax upon his property.

"The Stars Shall Fall"

In 1833 the last of the signs appeared which were promised by the Saviour as tokens of His second advent: "The stars shall fall from heaven." And John in the Revelation declared, "The stars of heaven fell unto the earth, even as a fig tree casteth her untimely figs, when she is shaken of a mighty wind." Matthew 24:29; Revelation 6:13. This prophecy received a striking fulfillment in the great meteoric shower of November 13, 1833, the most extensive and wonderful display of falling stars ever recorded. "Never did rain fall much thicker than the meteors fell toward the earth; east, west, north, and south, it was the same. In a word, the whole heavens seemed in motion. . . . From two o'clock until broad daylight, the sky being perfectly serene and cloudless, an incessant play of dazzlingly brilliant luminosities was kept up in the whole heavens."[6] "It seemed as if the whole starry heavens had congregated at one point near the zenith, and were simultaneously shooting forth, with the velocity of lightning, to every part of the horizon; and yet they were not exhausted—thousands swiftly followed in the tracks of thousands, as if created for the occasion."[7] "A more correct picture of a fig tree casting its figs when blown by a mighty wind, it was not possible to behold."[8]

In the New York *Journal of Commerce* of November 14, 1833, appeared a long article regarding this phenomenon: "No philosopher or scholar has told or recorded an event, I suppose, like that of yesterday morning. A prophet eighteen hundred years ago foretold it exactly, if we will be at the trouble of understanding stars falling to mean falling stars, . . . in the only sense in which it is possible to be literally true."

Thus was displayed the last of those signs of His coming, concerning which Jesus bade His disciples: "When ye shall see all these things, know that it is near, even at the doors." Matthew 24:33. Many who witnessed the falling of the stars looked upon it as a herald of the coming judgment.

In 1840 another remarkable fulfillment of prophecy excited widespread interest. Two years before, Josiah Litch published an exposition of Revelation 9, predicting the fall of the Ottoman Empire "in A.D. 1840, sometime in the month of August." Only a few days previous to its accomplishment he wrote: "It will end on the 11th of August, 1840, when the Ottoman power in Constantinople may be expected to be broken."[9]

Prediction Fulfilled

At the very time specified, Turkey accepted the protection of the allied powers of Europe and thus placed herself under the control of Christian nations. The event exactly fulfilled the prediction. (See Appendix.) Multitudes were convinced of the principles of prophetic interpretation adopted by Miller and his associates. Men of learning and position united with Miller in preaching and publishing his views. From 1840 to 1844 the work rapidly extended.

William Miller possessed strong mental powers, and

he added to these the wisdom of heaven by connecting himself with the Source of wisdom. He commanded respect wherever integrity and moral excellence were valued. With Christian humility, he was attentive and affable to all, ready to listen to others and weigh their arguments. He tested all theories by the Word of God, and his sound reasoning and knowledge of Scripture enabled him to refute error.

Yet, as with earlier Reformers, the truths he presented were not received by popular religious teachers. As these could not maintain their position by Scripture, they resorted to the doctrines of men, the traditions of the Fathers. But the Word of God was the only testimony accepted by the preachers of the advent truth. Ridicule and scoffing were employed on the part of opponents in maligning those who looked with joy for the return of their Lord and were striving to live holy lives and prepare others for His appearing. It was made to appear a sin to study the prophecies of the coming of Christ and the end of the world. Thus the popular ministry undermined faith in the Word of God. Their teaching made men infidels, and many took license to walk after ungodly lusts. Then the authors of the evil charged it all upon Adventists.

While drawing crowded houses of intelligent hearers, Miller's name was seldom mentioned by the religious press except by ridicule or denunciation. The ungodly, emboldened by religious teachers, resorted to blasphemous witticisms on him and his work. The gray-headed man who had left a comfortable home to travel at his own expense to bear to the world the solemn warning of the judgment near was denounced as a fanatic.

Interest and Unbelief

Interest continued to increase. From scores and hundreds, congregations had grown to as many thousands. But after a time, opposition was manifest against these converts, and the churches began to take disciplinary steps with those who had embraced Miller's views. This called forth a response from his pen: "If we are wrong, pray show us wherein consists our wrong. Show us from the word of God that we are in error; we have had ridicule enough; that can never convince us that we are in the wrong; the word of God alone can change our views. Our conclusions have been formed deliberately and prayerfully, as we have seen the evidence in the Scriptures."[10]

When the iniquity of the antediluvians moved God to bring a flood upon the earth, He first made known to them His purpose. For 120 years was sounded the warning to repent. But they believed it not. They mocked the messenger of God. If Noah's message were true, why did not all the world see and believe it? One man's assertions against the wisdom of thousands! They would not credit the warning nor seek shelter in the ark.

Scoffers pointed to the unvarying succession of the seasons, the blue skies that had never poured out rain. In contempt they declared the preacher of righteousness a wild enthusiast. They went on, more intent on their evil ways than before. But at the appointed time God's judgments were visited upon the rejecters of His mercy.

Skeptics and Unbelievers

Christ declared that as the people of Noah's day "knew not until the flood came, and took them all away; so shall also the coming of the Son of man be." Matthew 24:39. When the professed people of God are uniting with the world, when the luxury of the world becomes the luxury of the church, when all look forward to many years of worldly prosperity—then, suddenly as the lightning flashes, will come the end of their delusive hopes. As God sent His servant to warn the world of the coming Flood, so He sent chosen messengers to make known the nearness of the final judgment. And as Noah's contemporaries laughed to scorn the predictions of the preacher of righteousness, so in Miller's day many of the professed people of God scoffed at the words of warning.

There can be no more conclusive evidence that the churches have departed from God than the animosity excited by this Heaven-sent message.

Those who accepted the advent doctrine felt that it was time to take a stand. "The things of eternity assumed to them . . . reality. Heaven was brought near, and they felt themselves guilty before God."[11] Christians were made to feel that time was short, that what they had to do for their fellow men must be done quickly. Eternity seemed to open before them. The Spirit of God gave power to their appeals to prepare for the day of God. Their daily life was a rebuke to unconsecrated church members. These did not wish to be disturbed in their pleasure, money-making, and ambition for worldly honor. Hence the opposition against the advent faith.

Opposers endeavored to discourage investigation by teaching that the prophecies were sealed. Thus Protestants followed the steps of Romanists. Protestant churches claimed that an important part of the Word, that part specially applicable to our time, could not be understood. Ministers declared that Daniel and the Revelation were incomprehensible mysteries.

But Christ directed His disciples to the words of the prophet Daniel, "Whoso readeth, let him *understand*." Matthew 24:15. And the Revelation *is* to be understood. "The Revelation of Jesus Christ, which God gave unto him, to show unto his servants things which must shortly come to pass. . . . *Blessed* is he that *readeth*, and they that *hear* the words of this prophecy, and *keep* those things which are written therein: for the time is at hand." Revelation 1:1-3, italics supplied.

"Blessed is he that readeth"—there are those who will not read; "and they that hear"—there are some who refuse to hear anything concerning the prophecies; "and keep those things which are written therein"—many refuse to heed the instructions in the Revelation; none of these can claim the blessing promised.

How dare men teach that the Revelation is beyond human understanding? It is a mystery revealed, a book opened. Revelation directs the mind to Daniel. Both present important instruction concerning events at the close of world history.

John saw the dangers, conflicts, and final deliverance of the people of God. He records the closing messages which are to ripen the harvest of the earth, either for the heavenly garner or for the fires of destruction, that those who turn from error to truth might be instructed concerning the perils and conflicts before them.

Why, then, this widespread ignorance concerning an important part of Holy Writ? It is the result of a studied effort of the prince of darkness to conceal from men that which reveals his deceptions. For this reason, Christ the Revelator, foreseeing the warfare against the Revelation, pronounced a blessing upon all who should read, hear, and observe the prophecy.

References

1. S. Bliss, *Memories of William Miller*, pp. 65-67.
2. *Ibid.*, pp. 74, 75.
3. *Ibid.*
4. *Ibid.*, pp. 76, 77, 81.
5. Ezekiel 33:8, 9; Bliss, p. 92.
6. R. M. Devens, *American Progress: or, The Great Events of the Greatest Century,* ch. 28, pars. 1-5.
7. F. Reed, *Christian Advocate and Journal*, Dec. 13, 1833.
8. "The Old Countryman," *Portland* (Maine) *Evening Advertiser*, Nov. 26, 1833.
9. Josiah Litch, *Signs of the Times*, August 1, 1840.
10. Bliss, pp. 250, 252.
11. *Ibid.*, p. 146.

19/ Why the Great Disappointment?

The work of God presents, from age to age, a striking similarity in every great reformation or religious movement. The principles of God's dealing with men are ever the same. The important movements of the present have their parallel in those of the past, and the experience of the church in former ages has lessons for our own time.

God by His Holy Spirit especially directs His servants on earth in carrying forward the work of salvation. Men are instruments in the hand of God. To each is granted a measure of light sufficient to enable him to perform the work given him to do. But no man has ever attained to a full understanding of the divine purpose in the work for his own time. Men do not fully comprehend in all its bearing the message which they utter in His name. Even the prophets did not fully comprehend the revelations committed to them. The meaning was to be unfolded from age to age.

Peter says: Of this salvation "the prophets have inquired and searched diligently, who prophesied of the grace that should come unto you: searching *what,* or *what manner of time* the Spirit of Christ which was in them did signify, when it testified beforehand the sufferings of Christ, and the glory that should follow. Unto whom it was revealed, that not unto *themselves,* but unto *us* they did minister." 1 Peter 1:10-12, italics supplied. What a lesson to the people of God in the Christian age! Those holy men of God "inquired and searched diligently" concerning revelations given for generations yet unborn. What a rebuke to the world-loving indifference which is content to declare that the prophecies cannot be understood.

Not infrequently the minds of even God's servants are so blinded by tradition and false teaching that they only partially grasp the things revealed in His Word. The disciples of Christ, even when the Saviour was with them, had the popular conception of the Messiah as a temporal prince who was to exalt Israel to universal empire. They could not understand His words foretelling His suffering and death.

"The Time Is Fulfilled"

Christ had sent them forth with the message: "The time is fulfilled, and the kingdom of God is at hand: repent ye, and believe the gospel." Mark 1:15. That message was based on the prophecy of Daniel 9. The "sixty-nine weeks" were to extend to "the Messiah the Prince," and the disciples looked forward to the establishment of Messiah's kingdom at Jerusalem to rule over the whole earth.

They preached the message committed to them, though they misapprehended its meaning. While their announcement was founded on Daniel 9:25, they did not see in the next verse that Messiah was to be "cut off." Their hearts had been set upon the glory of an earthly empire; this blinded their understanding. At the very time when they expected to see their Lord ascend the throne of David, they beheld Him seized, scourged, derided, and condemned on the cross. What despair and anguish wrung the heart of those disciples!

Christ had come at the exact time foretold. Scripture had been fulfilled in every detail. The Word and the Spirit of God attested the divine commission of His Son. And yet the disciples' minds were shrouded in doubt. If Jesus had been the true Messiah, would they have been plunged into grief and disappointment? This was the question that tortured their souls during the hopeless hours of that Sabbath between His death and resurrection.

Yet they were not forsaken. "When I sit in darkness, the Lord shall be a light unto me. . . . He will bring me forth to the light, and I shall behold his righteousness." "Unto the upright there ariseth light in the darkness." "I will make darkness light before them, and crooked things straight. These things will I do unto them, and not forsake them." Micah 7:8, 9; Psalm 112:4; Isaiah 42:16.

The announcement made by the disciples was correct, "The time is fulfilled, the kingdom of God is at hand." At the expiration of "the time"—the sixty-nine weeks of Daniel 9 which were to extend to the Messiah, "the Anointed One"—Christ had received the anointing of the Spirit after His baptism by John. The "kingdom of God" was not, as they had been taught to believe, an earthly empire. Nor was it that future, immortal kingdom in which "all dominions shall serve and obey him." Daniel 7:27.

The expression "kingdom of God" designates both the kingdom of grace and the kingdom of glory. The apostle says: "Let us therefore come boldly unto *the throne of grace*, that we may obtain mercy, and find grace." Hebrews 4:16. The existence of a throne implies the existence of a kingdom. Christ uses the expression "the kingdom of heaven" to designate the work of grace upon the hearts of men. So the throne of glory represents the kingdom of glory. Matthew 25:31, 32. This kingdom is yet future. It is not to be set up until the second advent of Christ.

When the Saviour yielded up His life and cried out, "It is finished," the promise of salvation made to the sinful pair in Eden was ratified. The kingdom of grace, which had before existed by the promise of God, was then established.

Thus the death of Christ—the event which the disciples looked upon as the destruction of their hope—was that which made it forever sure. While it brought a cruel disappointment, it was the proof that their belief had been correct. The event that had filled them with despair opened the door of hope to all God's faithful ones in all ages.

Intermingled with the pure gold of the disciples' love for Jesus was the base alloy of selfish ambitions. Their vision was filled with the throne, the crown, and the glory. Their pride of heart, their thirst for worldly glory, had led them to pass unheeded the Saviour's words showing the true nature of His kingdom, and pointing forward to His death. These errors resulted in the trial which was permitted for their correction. To the disciples was to be entrusted the glorious gospel of their risen Lord. To prepare them for this work, the experience which seemed so bitter had been permitted.

After His resurrection Jesus appeared to His disciples on the way to Emmaus, and, "expounded unto them in all the Scriptures the things concerning himself." It was His purpose to fasten their faith upon the "sure word of prophecy" (Luke 24:27; 2 Peter 1:19); not merely by His personal testimony, but by the prophecies of the Old Testament. And as the very first step in imparting this knowledge, Jesus directed the disciples to "Moses and all the prophets" of the Old Testament Scriptures.

Despair to Assurance

In a more complete sense than ever before the disciples had "found him, of whom Moses in the law, and the prophets, did write." The uncertainty, the despair, gave place to assurance, to unclouded faith. They had passed through the deepest trial possible for them to experience and had seen how the word of God had been triumphantly accomplished. Henceforward what could daunt their faith? In the keenest sorrow they had "strong consolation," a hope which was as "an anchor of the soul, both sure and steadfast." Hebrews 6:18, 19.

Saith the Lord: "My people shall never be ashamed." "Weeping may endure for a night, but joy cometh in the morning." Joel 2:26; Psalm 30:5. On His resurrection day these disciples met the Saviour, and their hearts burned within them as they listened to His words. Before His ascension, Jesus bade them, "Go ye into all the world, and preach the gospel," adding, "Lo, I am with you alway." Mark 16:15; Matthew 28:20. On the Day of Pentecost the promised Comforter descended, and the souls of the believers thrilled with the conscious presence of their ascended Lord.

The Disciples' Message Compared to the 1844 Message

The experience of the disciples at the first advent of Christ had its counterpart in the experience of those who proclaimed His second advent. As the disciples preached, "The time is fulfilled, the kingdom of God is at hand," so Miller and his associates proclaimed that the last prophetic period in the Bible was about to expire, that the judgment was at hand, and that the everlasting kingdom was to be ushered in. The preaching of the disciples in regard to time was based on the seventy weeks of Daniel 9. The message given by Miller and his associates announced the termination of the 2300 days of Daniel 8:14, of which the seventy weeks form a part. The preaching of each was based upon the fulfillment of a different portion of the same prophetic period.

Like the first disciples, William Miller and his associates did not fully comprehend the message which they bore. Errors long established in the church prevented a correct interpretation of an important point in the prophecy. Therefore, though they proclaimed the message God had committed to them, yet through a misapprehension of its meaning they suffered disappointment.

Miller adopted the general view that the earth is the "sanctuary," and he believed that the "cleansing of the sanctuary" represented the purification of the earth by fire at the coming of the Lord. Therefore, the close of the 2300 days, he concluded, revealed the time of the second advent.

The cleansing of the sanctuary was the last service

performed by the high priest in the yearly round of ministration. It was the closing work of the atonement—a removal or putting away of sin from Israel. It prefigured the closing work of our High Priest in heaven in the removal or blotting out of the sins of His people which are registered in the heavenly records. This service involves investigation, a work of judgment, and it immediately precedes the coming of Christ in the clouds of heaven, for when He comes every case has been decided. Says Jesus: "My reward is with me, to give every man according as his work shall be." Revelation 22:12. It is this work of judgment that is announced in the first angel's message of Revelation 14:7: "Fear God, and give glory to him; for the hour of his judgment is come."

Those who proclaimed this warning gave the right message at the right time. As the disciples were mistaken in regard to the kingdom to be set up at the end of the "seventy weeks," so Adventists were mistaken in regard to the event to take place at the expiration of the "2300 days." In both cases popular errors blinded the mind to truth. Both fulfilled the will of God in delivering the message He desired to be given, and both through misapprehension of their message suffered disappointment.

Yet God accomplished His purpose in permitting the warning of judgment to be given as it was. In His providence the message was for the testing and purification of the church. Were their affections set upon this world or upon Christ and heaven? Were they ready to renounce their worldly ambitions and welcome the advent of their Lord?

The disappointment also would test the hearts of those who had professed to receive the warning. Would they rashly give up their experience and cast away their confidence in God's Word when called to endure the reproach of the world and the test of delay and disappointment? Because they did not immediately understand the dealings of God, would they cast aside truths sustained by the clear testimony of His Word?

This test would teach the danger of accepting the interpretations of men instead of making the Bible its own interpreter. The children of faith would be led to a closer study of the Word, to examine more carefully the foundation of their faith, and to reject everything, however widely accepted by the Christian world, that was not founded upon Scripture.

That which in the hour of trial seemed dark would afterward be made plain. Notwithstanding the trial resulting from their errors, they would learn by a blessed experience that the Lord is "very pitiful, and of tender mercy"; that all His paths "are mercy and truth unto such as keep his covenant and his testimonies." Psalm 25:10.

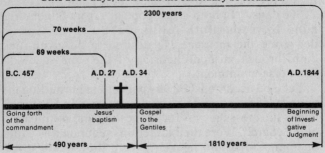

"Unto 2300 days; then shall the sanctuary be cleansed."

20/ Love for Christ's Coming

A great religious awakening is foretold in the first angel's message of Revelation 14. An angel is seen flying "in the midst of heaven, having the everlasting gospel to preach unto them that dwell on the earth, and to every nation, and kindred, and tongue, and people." "With a loud voice" he proclaims: "Fear God, and give glory to him; for the hour of his judgment is come: and worship him that made heaven, and earth, and the sea, and the fountains of waters." Revelation 14:6, 7.

An angel represents the exalted character of the work to be accomplished by the message and the power and glory that were to attend it. The angel's flight "in the midst of heaven," the "loud voice," and its promulgation "to every nation, and kindred, and tongue, and people" give evidence of the rapid, worldwide extent of the movement. As to the time when it is to take place, it announces the opening of the judgment.

This message is a part of the gospel which could be proclaimed only in the last days, for only then would it be true that the hour of judgment *had come*. That part of his prophecy which related to the last days, Daniel was bidden to close up and seal "to the time of the end." Daniel 12:4. Not till this time could a message concerning the judgment be proclaimed, based on a fulfillment of these prophecies.

Paul warned the church not to look for the coming of Christ in his day. Not till after the great apostasy and the long reign of the "man of sin" can we look for the advent of our Lord. See 2 Thessalonians 2:3. The "man of sin"—also "the mystery of iniquity," "the son of perdition," and "that wicked,"—represents the papacy, which was to maintain its supremacy for 1260 years. This period ended in 1798. The coming of Christ could not take place before that time. Paul covers with his caution the whole of the Christian dispensation down to the year 1798. This side of that time the message of Christ's second coming is to be proclaimed.

No such message has ever been given in past ages. Paul, as we have seen, did not preach it; he pointed into the then far-distant future for the coming of the Lord. The Reformers did not proclaim it. Martin Luther placed the judgment about 300 years into the future from his day. But since 1798 the book of Daniel has been unsealed, and many have proclaimed the message of the judgment near.

In Different Countries Simultaneously

Like the Reformation of the sixteenth century, the Advent Movement appeared in different countries at the same time. Men of faith were led to study the prophecies and saw convincing evidence that the end was at hand. Isolated bodies of Christians, solely by the study of the Scriptures, arrived at the belief that the Saviour's advent was near.

Three years after Miller had arrived at his exposition of the prophecies, Dr. Joseph Wolff, "the missionary to the world," began to proclaim the Lord's soon coming. Born in Germany of Hebrew parentage, he was, while very young, convinced of the truth of the Christian religion. He had been an eager listener to conversations in his father's house as devout Hebrews assembled to recount the hopes of their people, the glory of the coming Messiah, and the restoration of Israel. One day, hearing Jesus of Nazareth mentioned, the boy inquired who He was. "A Jew of the greatest talent," was the answer; "but as He pretended to be the Messiah, the Jewish tribunal sentenced Him to death."

"Why," rejoined the questioner, "is Jerusalem destroyed, and why are we in captivity?"

"Alas, alas!" answered his father, "because the Jews murdered the prophets." The thought was at once suggested to the child: "Perhaps Jesus was also a prophet, and the Jews killed Him when He was innocent." Though forbidden to enter a Christian church, he would often linger outside to listen to the preaching. When only seven years old, he was boasting to a Christian neighbor of the future triumph of Israel at the advent of the Messiah. The old man said kindly: "Dear boy, I will tell you who the real Messiah was: He was Jesus of Nazareth, . . . whom your ancestors have crucified. . . . Go home and read the fifty-third chapter of Isaiah, and you will be convinced that Jesus Christ is the Son of God."[1]

He went home and read the scripture. How perfectly it had been fulfilled in Jesus of Nazareth. Were the words of the Christian true? The boy asked of his father an explanation of the prophecy but was met with silence so stern that he never again dared to refer to the subject.

When only eleven years old, he went out into the world to gain an education, to choose his religion and his lifework. Alone and penniless, he had to make his own way. He studied diligently, maintaining himself by teaching Hebrew. He was led to accept the Romish faith and went to pursue his studies in the College of the Propaganda at Rome. Here he openly attacked the abuses of the church and urged reform. After a time, he was removed. It became evident that he could never be brought to submit to the bondage of Romanism. He was declared incorrigible and left to go where he pleased. He made his way to England and united with the English Church. After two years' study he set out in 1821 upon his mission.

Wolff saw that the prophecies bring to view Christ's second advent with power and glory. While he sought to lead his people to Jesus of Nazareth as the Promised

One, to point them to His first coming as a sacrifice for sin, he taught them also of His second coming.

Wolff believed the coming of the Lord to be at hand. His interpretation of the prophetic periods placed it within a few years of the time pointed out by Miller. "Did our Lord . . . not give us signs of the times, in order that we may know at least the approach of His coming, as one knows the approach of the summer by the fig tree putting forth its leaves? Enough . . . shall be known by the signs of the times, to induce us to prepare for His coming, as Noah prepared the ark."[2]

Against Popular Interpretations

Concerning the popular system of interpreting the Scriptures, Wolff wrote: "The greater part of the Christian church have swerved from the plain sense of Scripture, and . . . suppose that when they are reading *Jews*, they must understand *Gentiles;* and when they read *Jerusalem*, they must understand the *church;* and if it is said *earth*, it means *sky;* and for the coming of the *Lord* they must understand the progress of the *missionary societies;* and going up to the mountain of the Lord's house, signifies a grand *class meeting of Methodists.*"[3]

From 1821 to 1845, Wolff traveled in Egypt, Abyssinia, Palestine, Syria, Persia, Bokhara, India, and the United States.

Power in the Book

Dr. Wolff traveled in the most barbarous countries without protection, enduring hardships and surrounded with countless perils. He was starved, sold as a slave, three times condemned to death, beset by robbers, and sometimes nearly perished from thirst. Once he was stripped and left to travel hundreds of miles on foot through mountains, snow beating in his face and his naked feet benumbed by the frozen ground.

When warned against going unarmed among savage, hostile tribes, he declared himself "provided with arms"—"prayer, zeal for Christ, and confidence in His help." "I am also provided with the love of God and my neighbor in my heart, and the Bible is in my hand." "I felt my power was in the Book, and that its might would sustain me."[4]

He persevered until the message had been carried to a large part of the habitable globe. Among Jews, Turks, Parsees, Hindus, and other nationalities and races he distributed the Word of God in various tongues, and everywhere heralded the approach of the Messiah.

In Bokhara he found the doctrine of the Lord's soon coming held by an isolated people. The Arabs of Yemen, he says, "are in possession of a book called *Seera,* which gives notice of the second coming of Christ and His reign in glory; and they expect great events to take place in the year 1840." "I found children of Israel, of the tribe of Dan, . . . who expect, with the children of Rechab, the speedy arrival of the Messiah in the clouds of heaven."[5]

A similar belief was found by another missionary in Tatary. A Tatar priest put the question as to when Christ would come the second time. When the missionary answered that he knew nothing about it, the priest seemed surprised at such ignorance in a Bible teacher, and stated his own belief, founded on prophecy, that Christ would come about 1844.

The Advent Message in England

As early as 1826 the advent message began to be preached in England. The exact time of the advent was not generally taught, but the truth of Christ's soon coming in power and glory was extensively proclaimed. An English writer states that about 700 ministers of the Church of England were engaged in preaching "this gospel of the kingdom."

The message pointing to 1844 as the time of the Lord's coming was also given in Great Britain. Advent publications from the United States were widely circulated. In 1842 Robert Winter, an Englishman who had received the advent faith in America, returned to his native country to herald the coming of the Lord. Many united with him in the work in various parts of England.

In South America, Lacunza, a Spaniard and a Jesuit, received the truth of Christ's speedy return. Desiring to escape the censure of Rome, he published his version under the assumed name of Rabbi Ben-Ezra, representing himself as a converted Jew. About 1825 his book was translated into English. It served to deepen the interest already awakening in England.

Revelation Unfolds to Bengel

In Germany the doctrine had been taught by Bengel, a Lutheran minister and a biblical scholar. While preparing a sermon from Revelation 21, the light of Christ's second coming broke in upon his mind. The prophecies of the Revelation unfolded to his understanding. Overwhelmed with the importance and glory of the scenes presented by the prophet, he was forced to turn for a time from the subject. In the pulpit it again presented itself to him with vividness. From that time he devoted himself to the study of the prophecies and soon arrived at the belief that the coming of Christ was near. The date which he fixed as the time of the second advent was within a few years of that afterward held by Miller.

Bengel's writings spread in his own state of Würtemberg and to other parts of Germany. The advent message was heard in Germany at the same time that it was attracting attention in other lands.

At Geneva, Gaussen preached the second advent. When he entered the ministry he was inclined to skepticism. In his youth he had become interested in prophecy. After reading Rollin's *Ancient History*, his attention was called to the second chapter of Daniel. He was struck with the exactness with which the prophecy had been fulfilled. Here was testimony to the inspiration of the Scriptures. He could not rest satisfied with rationalism, and, in studying the Bible he was led to a positive faith.

He arrived at the belief that the coming of the Lord was at hand. Impressed with the importance of this truth, he desired to bring it before the people. But the popular belief that the prophecies of Daniel cannot be understood was a serious obstacle. He finally determined—as Farel had done before him in evangelizing Geneva—to begin with the children, through whom he hoped to interest the parents. He said, "I gather an audience of children; if the group enlarges, if it is seen that they listen, are pleased, interested, that they understand and explain the subject, I am sure to have a second circle soon, and in their turn, grown people will see that it is worth their while to sit down and study. When this is done, the cause is gained."[6]

As he addressed the children, older persons came to listen. The galleries of his church were filled with hearers, men of rank and learning, and strangers and foreigners visiting Geneva. Thus the message was carried to other parts.

Encouraged, Gaussen published his lessons with the hope of promoting the study of the prophetic books. He afterward became a teacher in a theological school, while on Sunday he continued his work as catechist, addressing the children and instructing them in the Scriptures. From the professor's chair, through the press, and as a teacher of children, he for many years was instrumental in calling the attention of many to the prophecies which showed that the coming of the Lord was near.

Child-Preachers of Scandinavia

In Scandinavia also the advent message was proclaimed. Many were roused to confess and forsake their sins and seek pardon in the name of Christ. But the clergy of the state church opposed the movement, and some who preached the message were thrown into prison.

In many places where the preachers of the Lord's soon coming were thus silenced, God was pleased to send the message through little children. As they were under age, the state could not restrain them, and they were permitted to speak unmolested.

In the humble dwellings of laborers the people assembled to hear the warning. Some of the child preachers were not more than six or eight years of age; and while their lives testified that they loved the Saviour, they ordinarily manifested only the intelligence and ability usually seen in children of that age. When standing before the people, however, they were moved by an influence beyond their natural gifts. Tone and manner changed, and with solemn power they gave the warning of the judgment, "Fear God, and give glory to him; for the hour of his judgment is come."

The people heard with trembling. The Spirit of God spoke to hearts. Many were led to search the Scriptures, the intemperate and immoral were reformed, and a work was done so marked that even ministers of the state church were forced to acknowledge that the hand of God was in the movement.

It was God's will that tidings of the Saviour's coming should be given in Scandinavia, and He put His Spirit upon the children that the work might be accomplished. When Jesus drew near to Jerusalem, the people, intimidated by the priests and rulers, ceased their joyful proclamation as they entered the gates of Jerusalem. But the children in the temple courts took up the refrain, and cried, "Hosanna to the Son of David!" Matthew 21:8-16. As God wrought through children at the time of Christ's first advent, so He wrought through them in giving the message of His second advent.

The Message Spreads

America became the center of the great advent movement. The writings of Miller and his associates were carried to distant lands, wherever missionaries had penetrated in all the world. Far and wide spread the message of the everlasting gospel: "Fear God, and give glory to him; for the hour of his judgment is come."

The prophecies which seemed to point to the coming of Christ in the spring of 1844 took deep hold of the minds of the people. Many were convinced that the arguments from the prophetic periods were correct, and sacrificing pride of opinion, they joyfully received the truth. Some ministers left their salaries and churches and united in proclaiming the coming of Jesus. Comparatively few ministers, however, would accept this message; therefore it was largely committed to humble laymen. Farmers left their fields; mechanics, their tools; traders, their merchandise; professional men, their positions. They willingly endured toil, privation, and suffering, that they might call men to repentance unto salvation. The advent truth was accepted by thousands.

Simple Scripture Brings Conviction

Like John the Baptist the preachers laid the axe at the root of the tree and urged all to bring forth "fruits meet for repentance." In marked contrast to assurances of peace and safety heard from popular pulpits, the simple testimony of Scripture brought conviction which few were able wholly to resist. Many sought the Lord with repentance. The affections that had so long clung to earthly things they now fixed on heaven. With hearts softened and subdued they joined to sound the cry: "Fear God, and give glory to him; for the hour of his judgment is come."

Sinners inquired with weeping: "What must I do to be saved?" Those who had been dishonest were anxious to make restitution. All who found peace in Christ longed to see others share the blessing. The hearts of parents were turned to their children, and the hearts of children to their parents. Malachi 4:5, 6. Barriers of pride and reserve were swept away. Heartfelt confessions were made. Everywhere were souls pleading with God. Many wrestled all night in prayer for the assurance that their sins were pardoned, or for the conversion of relatives or neighbors.

All classes, rich and poor, high and low, were anxious to hear the doctrine of the second advent. The Spirit of God gave power to His truth. The presence of holy angels was felt in these assemblies, and many were daily added to the believers. Vast crowds listened in silence to the solemn words. Heaven and earth seemed to approach each other. Men sought their homes with praises on their lips, and the glad sound rang out upon the still night air. None who attended those meetings could ever forget those scenes of deepest interest.

The Message Opposed

The proclamation of a definite time for Christ's coming called forth great opposition from many of all classes, from the minister in the pulpit to the most Heaven-daring sinner. Many declared that they had no opposition to the doctrine of the second advent; they merely objected to the definite time. But God's all-seeing eye read their hearts. They did not wish to hear of Christ's coming to judge the world in righteousness. Their works would not bear the inspection of the heart-searching God, and they feared to meet their Lord. Like the Jews at the time of Christ's first advent they were not prepared to welcome Jesus. They not only refused to listen to the plain arguments from the Bible but ridiculed those who were looking for the Lord. Satan flung the taunt in the face of Christ that His professed people had so little love for Him that they did not desire His appearing.

"No man knoweth the day nor the hour" was the argument most often brought forward by rejecters of the advent faith. The scripture is: "Of that day and hour knoweth no man, no, not the angels of heaven, but my Father only." Matthew 24:36. A clear explanation of this text was given by those who were looking for the Lord, and the wrong use of it by their opponents was clearly shown.

One saying of the Saviour must not be made to destroy another. Though no man knoweth the day nor the hour of His coming, we are required to know when it is near. To refuse or neglect to know when His advent is near will be as fatal for us as it was for those in the days of Noah not to know when the Flood was coming. Christ says,"If therefore thou shalt not watch, I will come on thee as a thief, and thou shalt not know what hour I will come upon thee." Revelation 3:3.

Paul speaks of those who have heeded the Saviour's warning: "Ye, brethren, are not in darkness, that that day should overtake you as a thief. Ye are all the children of light, and the children of the day." 1 Thessalonians 5:2-5.

But those who desired an excuse to reject truth closed their ears to this explanation, and the words "No man knoweth the day nor the hour" continued to be echoed by the scoffer and even the professed minister of Christ. As the people began to inquire the way of salvation, religious teachers stepped in between them and the truth by falsely interpreting the Word of God.

The most devoted in the churches were usually the first to receive the message. Wherever the people were not controlled by the clergy, wherever they would search the Word of God for themselves, the advent doctrine needed only to be compared with Scripture to establish its divine authority.

Many were misled by husbands, wives, parents, or children and were made to believe it a sin even to listen to such "heresies" as were taught by the Adventists. Angels were bidden to keep faithful watch over these souls, for another light was yet to shine upon them from the throne of God.

Those who had received the message watched for the coming of their Saviour. The time when they expected to meet Him was at hand. They approached this hour with a calm solemnity. None who experienced this can forget those precious hours of waiting. For some weeks preceding the time, worldly business was for the most part laid aside. Sincere believers carefully examined their hearts as if in a few hours to close their eyes upon earthly scenes. There was no making of "ascension robes" (see Appendix), but all felt the need of internal evidence that they were prepared to meet the Saviour. Their white robes were purity of soul—characters cleansed by the atoning blood of Christ. Would that there were still with the people of God the same heart searching, the same earnest faith.

God designed to prove His people. His hand covered a mistake in the reckoning of the prophetic periods. The time of expectation [that is, that Christ would come in the spring of 1844] passed, and Christ did not appear. Those who had looked for their Saviour experienced a bitter disappointment. Yet God was testing the hearts of those who professed to be waiting for His appearing. Many had been actuated by fear. These persons declared that they had never believed that Christ would come. They were among the first to ridicule the sorrow of the true believers.

But Jesus and all the heavenly host looked with love and sympathy upon the faithful yet disappointed ones. If the veil separating the visible from the invisible world could have been swept back, angels would have been seen drawing near to these steadfast souls and shielding them from the shafts of Satan.

References

1. *Travels and Adventures of the Rev. Joseph Wolff*, vol. 1, pp. 6, 7.

2. Joseph Wolff, *Researches and Missionary Labors*, pp. 404, 405.

3. *Journal of the Rev. Joseph Wolff*, p. 96.

4. W. H. D. Adams, *In Perils Oft*, pp. 192, 201.

5. *Journal of the Rev. Joseph Wolff*, pp. 377, 389.

6. L. Gaussen, *Daniel the Prophet*, vol. 2, preface.

21/Reaping the Whirlwind

William Miller and his associates had sought to awaken professors of religion to the true hope of the church and their need of a deeper Christian experience. They labored also to awaken the unconverted to repentance and conversion. "They made no attempt to convert men to a sect. They labored among all parties and sects." Said Miller, "I thought to benefit all. Supposing that all Christians would rejoice in the prospect of Christ's coming, and that those who could not see as I did would not love any less those who should embrace this doctrine, I did not conceive there would ever be any necessity for separate meetings. . . . The great majority of those who were converted under my labors united with the various existing churches."[1]

But as religious leaders decided against the advent doctrine, they denied their members the privilege of attending preaching upon the second advent or even speaking of their hope in the church. The believers loved their churches. But as they saw their right to investigate the prophecies denied, they felt that loyalty to God forbade them to submit. Hence they felt justified in separating. In the summer of 1844 about fifty thousand withdrew from the churches.

In most of the churches, there had been for years a gradual but steadily increasing conformity to worldly practices and a corresponding decline in spiritual life. But in that year there were evidences of a marked declension in nearly all the churches of the land. The fact was widely commented on by both the press and the pulpit.

Mr. Barnes, author of a commentary and pastor of one of the leading churches in Philadelphia, "stated that . . . now there are *no awakenings, no conversions*, not much apparent growth in grace in professors, and none come to his study to converse about the salvation of their souls. . . . There is an increase of worldly-mindedness. *Thus it is with all the denominations.*"[2]

In the month of February of the same year, Professor Finney of Oberlin College said: "In general, the Protestant churches of our country, as such, were either apathetic or hostile to nearly all the moral reforms of the age. . . . Spiritual apathy is almost all-pervading, and is fearfully deep; so the religious press of the whole land testifies. . . . Very extensively church members are becoming devotees of fashion, join hands with the ungodly in parties of pleasure, in dancing, in festivities, etc. . . . *The churches generally are becoming sadly degenerate.* They have gone very far from the Lord and He has withdrawn Himself from them."

Man's Rejection of Light

Spiritual darkness is due, not to arbitrary withdrawal of divine grace on the part of God, but to rejection of light on the part of men. The Jewish people, by devotion to the world and forgetfulness of God, were in ignorance concerning Messiah's advent. In their unbelief they rejected the Redeemer. God did not cut off the Jewish nation from the blessings of salvation. Those who rejected the truth had "put darkness for light, and light for darkness." Isaiah 5:20.

After their rejection of the gospel the Jews continued to maintain their ancient rites, while they admitted that the presence of God was no longer among them. The prophecy of Daniel pointed unmistakably to the time of Messiah's coming and directly foretold His death. So they discouraged its study, and finally the rabbis pronounced a curse on all who should attempt to compute the time. In blindness and impenitence the people of Israel during succeeding centuries have stood, indifferent to the gracious offers of salvation, unmindful of the blessings of the gospel, a solemn and fearful warning of the danger of rejecting light from heaven.

He who stifles conviction of duty because it interferes with his inclinations will finally lose the power to distinguish between truth and error. The soul is separated from God. Where divine truth is spurned, the church will be in darkness, faith and love grow cold, and dissension enters. Church members center their interests in worldly pursuits, and sinners become hardened in their impenitence.

The First Angel's Message

The first angel's message of Revelation 14 was designed to separate the professed people of God from corrupting influences. In this message, God sent to the church a warning which, had it been accepted, would have corrected the evils that were shutting them away from Him. Had they received the message, humbling their hearts and seeking a preparation to stand in His presence, the Spirit of God would have been manifested. The church would again have reached that unity, faith, and love of apostolic days, when the believers "were of one heart and of one soul," and when "the Lord added to the church daily such as should be saved." Acts 4:32; 2:47.

If God's people would receive light from His Word, they would reach that unity which the apostle describes, "the unity of the Spirit in the bond of peace." "There is," he says, "*one* body, and *one* Spirit, even as ye are called in *one* hope of your calling; one Lord, one faith, one baptism." Ephesians 4:3-5.

Those who accepted the advent message came from different denominations, and their denominational barriers were hurled to the ground. Conflicting creeds were shivered to atoms. False views of the second advent were corrected. Wrongs were made right, hearts united in sweet fellowship. Love reigned supreme. This doctrine would have done the same for all, if all had received it.

Ministers, who as watchmen should have been the first to discern the tokens of Jesus' coming, had failed to learn the truth from the prophets or from the signs of the times. Love for God and faith in His Word had grown cold, and the advent doctrine only aroused their unbelief. As of old the testimony of God's Word was met with the inquiry: "Have any of the rulers or of the Pharisees believed?" John 7:48. Many discouraged the study of the prophecies, teaching that the prophetic books were sealed and were not to be understood. Multitudes, trusting their pastors, refused to listen; and others, though convinced of the truth, dared not confess it lest they should be "put out of the syna-gogue." John 9:22. The message God sent for testing the church revealed how great was the number who had set their affections on this world rather than on Christ.

Refusing the warning of the first angel was the cause of that fearful condition of worldliness, backsliding, and spiritual death which existed in the churches in 1844.

The Second Angel's Message

In Revelation 14 the first angel is followed by a sec-ond, proclaiming "Babylon is fallen, is fallen, that great city, because she made all nations drink of the wine of the wrath of her fornication." Revelation 14:8. The term "Babylon" is derived from "Babel," and signifies confusion. In Scripture it designates various forms of false or apostate religion. In Revelation 17 Babylon is represented as a woman—a figure used in the Bible as the symbol of the church, a virtuous woman representing a pure church; a vile woman, an apostate church.

In the Bible the relation between Christ and His church is represented by marriage. The Lord declares:

"I will betroth thee unto me forever; yea, I will betroth thee unto me in righteousness." "I am married unto you." And Paul says: "I have espoused you to one husband that I may present you as a chaste virgin to Christ." Hosea 2:19; Jeremiah 3:14; 2 Corinthians 11:2.

Spiritual Adultery

Unfaithfulness of the church to Christ in allowing worldly things to occupy the soul is likened to violation of the marriage vow. The sin of Israel in departing from the Lord is presented under this figure. "As a wife treacherously departeth from her husband, so have ye dealt treacherously with me, O house of Israel, saith the Lord;" "as a wife that committeth adultery, which taketh strangers instead of her husband!" Jeremiah 3:20; Ezekiel 16:32.

Says the apostle James: "Ye adulterers and adulteresses, know ye not that the friendship of the world is enmity with God? whosoever therefore will be a friend of the world is the enemy of God." James 4:4.

The woman (Babylon) is "arrayed in purple and scarlet color, and decked with gold and precious stones, and pearls, having a golden cup in her hand full of abominations and filthiness: . . . and upon her forehead was a name written, Mystery, Babylon the Great, the mother of harlots." Says the prophet: "I saw the woman drunken with the blood of the saints, and with the blood of the martyrs of Jesus." Babylon is "that great city, which reigneth over the kings of the earth." Revelation 17:4-6, 18.

The power that for centuries maintained sway over the monarchs of Christendom is Rome. The purple, scarlet color, gold, precious stones, and pearls, picture the magnificence affected by the haughty see of Rome. No other power could be so truly declared "drunken with the blood of the saints" as that church which so cruelly persecuted the followers of Christ.

Babylon is also charged with unlawful connection

with the "kings of the earth." By departure from the Lord and alliance with the heathen the Jewish church became a harlot, and Rome, seeking the support of worldly powers, receives a like condemnation.

Babylon is "the *mother* of harlots." Her *daughters* must be churches that cling to her doctrines and follow her example of sacrificing truth in order to form an alliance with the world. The message announcing the *fall* of Babylon must apply to religious bodies that were once pure and have become corrupt. Since this message follows the warning of the judgment, it must be given in the last days. Therefore it cannot refer to the Roman Church alone, for that church has been in a fallen condition for centuries.

Furthermore, the people of God are called to come out of Babylon. According to this scripture, many of God's people must still be in Babylon. And in what religious bodies are the greater part of the followers of Christ now to be found? In churches professing the Protestant faith. At the time of their rise these churches took a noble stand for truth, and God's blessing was with them. But they fell by the same desire which was the ruin of Israel—imitating the practices and courting the friendship of the ungodly.

Union With the World

Many Protestant churches have followed Rome's example of connection with "the kings of the earth"— the state churches, by their relation to secular governments; and other denominations, by seeking favor of the world. The term "Babylon"—confusion—may be applied to these bodies professing to derive their doctrine from the Bible, yet divided into almost innumerable sects with conflicting creeds.

A Roman Catholic work argues that "if the Church of Rome were ever guilty of idolatry in relation to the saints, her daughter, the Church of England, stands guilty of the same, which has ten churches dedicated to Mary for one dedicated to Christ."[3]

And Dr. Hopkins declares: "There is no reason to consider the antichristian spirit and practices to be confined to that which is now called the Church of Rome. The Protestant churches have much of antichrist in them, and are far from being wholly reformed from . . . corruptions and wickedness."[4]

Concerning the separation of the Presbyterian Church from Rome, Dr. Guthrie writes: "Three hundred years ago, our church, with an open Bible on her banner, and this motto, 'Search the Scriptures,' on her scroll, marched out from the gates of Rome." Then he asks the significant question: "Did they come *clean* out of Babylon?"[5]

First Departures From The Gospel

How did the church first depart from the simplicity of the gospel? By conforming to paganism, to facilitate acceptance of Christianity by the heathen. "Toward the latter end of the second century most of the churches assumed a new form. . . . As the old disciples retired to their graves, their children, along with new converts, . . . came forward and new-modeled the cause." "A pagan flood, flowing into the church, carried with it its customs, practices, and idols."[6] The Christian religion secured the favor and support of secular rulers. It was nominally accepted by multitudes. But many "remained in substance pagans, especially worshiping in secret their idols."[7]

Has not the same process been repeated in nearly every church calling itself Protestant? As the founders who possessed the true spirit of reform pass away, their descendants "new-model the cause." Blindly refusing to accept any truth in advance of what their fathers saw, the children of the reformers depart from their example of self-denial and renunciation of the world.

Alas, how widely have popular churches departed from the Bible standard! Said John Wesley, speaking of money: "Do not waste any part of so precious a talent, . . . by superfluous or expensive apparel, or by needless ornaments. Waste no part of it in curiously adorning your houses; in superfluous or expensive furniture; in costly pictures, painting, gilding. . . . So long as thou art 'clothed in purple and fine linen,' and farest 'sumptuously every day,' no doubt many will applaud thy elegance of taste, thy generosity and hospitality. But rather be content with the honor that cometh from God.''[8]

Rulers, politicians, lawyers, doctors, merchants, join the church as a means of advancing their worldly interests. The religious bodies, reenforced by the wealth of these baptized worldlings, make a still higher bid for popularity. Splendid, extravagant churches are erected. A high salary is paid for a talented minister to entertain the people. His sermons must be smooth and pleasing for fashionable ears. Thus fashionable sins are concealed under a pretense of godliness.

A writer in the New York *Independent* speaks thus concerning Methodism as it is: "The line of separation between the godly and the irreligious fades out into a kind of penumbra, and zealous men on both sides are toiling to obliterate all difference between their modes of action and enjoyment.''

In this tide of pleasure-seeking, self-sacrifice for Christ's sake is almost wholly lost. "If funds are wanted now, . . . nobody must be called on to give. Oh, no! have a fair, tableau, mock trial, antiquarian supper, or something to eat—anything to amuse the people.''

Robert Atkins draws a picture of spiritual declension in England: "*Apostasy, apostasy, apostasy,* is engraven on the very front of every church; and did they know it, and did they feel it, there might be hope; but, alas! they cry, 'We are rich, and increased in goods, and stand in need of nothing.' ''[9]

The great sin charged against Babylon is that she "made all nations drink of the wine of the wrath of her fornication.'' This cup represents false doctrines that she has accepted as the result of her friendship with the world. In turn she exerts a corrupting influence upon the world by teaching doctrines opposed to the plain statements of the Bible.

Were it not that the world is intoxicated with the wine of Babylon, multitudes would be convicted and converted by the plain truths of the Word of God. But religious faith appears so confused and discordant that people know not what to believe. The sin of the world's impenitence lies at the door of the church.

The message of the second angel did not reach its complete fulfillment in 1844. The churches then experienced a moral fall in their refusal of the light of the advent message, but that fall was not complete. As they have continued to reject the special truths for this time they have fallen lower and lower. Not yet, however, can it be said that "Babylon is fallen, . . . because she made *all nations* drink of the wine of the wrath of her fornication." Protestant churches are included in the solemn denunciation of the second angel. But the work of apostasy has not yet reached its culmination.

Before the coming of the Lord, Satan will work "with *all* power and signs and lying wonders, and with all deceivableness of unrighteousness;" and they that "receive not the love of the truth, that they might be saved," will be left to receive "strong delusion, that they should believe a lie." 2 Thessalonians 2:9-11. Not until the union of the church with the world shall be fully accomplished will the fall of Babylon be complete. The change is progressive and the perfect fulfillment of Revelation 14:8 is yet future.

Notwithstanding the spiritual darkness in the churches which constitute Babylon, the great body of Christ's true followers are still to be found in their communion. Many have never seen the special truths for this time. Not a few long for clearer light. They look in vain for the image of Christ in the churches with which they are connected.

Revelation 18 points to the time when the people of

God still in Babylon will be called upon to separate from her communion. This message, the last ever given to the world, will accomplish its work. The light of truth will shine upon all whose hearts are open to receive it, and all the children of the Lord in Babylon will heed the call: "Come out of her, my people." Revelation 18:4.

References

1. Bliss, p. 328.

2. *Congregational Journal*, May 23, 1844.

3. Richard Challoner, *The Catholic Christian Instructed*, Preface, pp. 21, 22.

4. Samuel Hopkins, "A Treatise on the Millennium," *Works*, vol. 2, p. 328.

5. Thomas Guthrie, *The Gospel in Ezekiel*, p. 237.

6. Robert Robinson, *Ecclesiastical Researches* (ed. 1792), ch. 6, par. 17, p. 51.

7. Gavazzi, *Lectures* (ed. 1854), p. 278.

8. Wesley, *Works*, Sermon 50, "The Use of Money."

9. Second Advent Library, tract No. 39.

22/Prophecies Fulfilled

When the time passed at which the Lord's coming was first expected—the spring of 1844—those who had looked for His appearing were in doubt and uncertainty. Many continued to search the Scriptures, examining anew the evidence of their faith. The prophecies, clear and conclusive, pointed to the coming of Christ as near. The blessing of the Lord in conversion and revival among Christians had testified that the message was of Heaven. Interwoven with prophecies which they had regarded as applying to the time of the second advent was instruction encouraging them to wait patiently in the faith that what was now dark to their understanding would be made plain. Among these prophecies was Habakkuk 2:1-4. No one, however, noticed that an apparent delay—a tarrying time—is in the prophecy. After the disappointment, this scripture appeared very significant: "The vision is yet for an appointed time, but at the end it shall speak, and not lie: though it tarry, wait for it; because it will surely come, it will not tarry. . . . The just shall live by his faith."

Ezekiel's prophecy also was a comfort to believers: "Thus saith the Lord God, . . . The days are at hand, and the effect of every vision. . . . I will speak, and the word that I shall speak shall come to pass; it shall be no more prolonged." "The word which I have spoken shall be done." Ezekiel 12:23-25, 28.

The waiting ones rejoiced. He who knows the end from the beginning had given them hope. Had it not been for such portions of Scripture, their faith would have failed.

The parable of the ten virgins of Matthew 25 also illustrates the experience of the Adventist people. Here is brought to view the church in the last days. Their experience is illustrated by the incidents of an Eastern marriage:

"Then shall the kingdom of heaven be likened unto ten virgins, which took their lamps, and went forth to meet the bridegroom. And five of them were wise, and five were foolish. They that were foolish took their lamps, and took no oil with them: but the wise took oil in their vessels with their lamps. While the bridegroom tarried, they all slumbered and slept. And at midnight there was a cry made, Behold, the bridegroom cometh; go ye out to meet him." Matthew 25:1-6.

The coming of Christ, as announced by the first angel's message, was understood to be represented by the coming of the bridegroom. The widespread reformation under the proclamation of Christ's soon coming answered to the going forth of the virgins. In this parable, all had taken their lamps, the Bible, and had gone "forth to meet the bridegroom." But while the foolish "took no oil with them," "the wise took oil in their vessels with their lamps." The latter had studied the Scriptures to learn the truth and had a personal experience, a faith in God which could not be overthrown by disappointment and delay. Others moved from impulse, their fears excited by the message. But they had depended upon the faith of the brethren, satisfied with the flickering light of emotion, without a thorough understanding of truth or a genuine work of grace in the heart. These had gone forth "to meet" the Lord in the prospect of immediate reward but were not prepared for delay and disappointment. Their faith failed.

"While the bridegroom tarried, they all slumbered and slept." By the tarrying of the bridegroom is represented the passing of the time, the disappointment, the seeming delay. Those whose faith was based on a personal knowledge of the Bible had a rock beneath their feet which the waves of disappointment could not wash away. "They all slumbered and slept," one class in abandonment of their faith, the other patiently waiting till clearer light should be given. The superficial could no longer lean upon the faith of their brethren. Each must stand or fall for himself.

Fanaticism Appears

About this time, fanaticism began to appear. Some manifested a bigoted zeal. Their fanatical ideas met with no sympathy from the great body of Adventists, yet they brought reproach upon the cause of truth.

Satan was losing his subjects, and in order to bring reproach upon the cause of God, he sought to deceive some who professed the faith and drive them to extremes. Then his agents stood ready to seize upon every error, every unbecoming act, and hold it up in the most exaggerated light to render Adventists odious. The greater the number whom he could crowd in to profess faith in the second advent while his power controlled their hearts, the greater advantage would he gain.

Satan is "the accuser of the brethren." Revelation 12:10. His spirit inspires men to watch for the defects of the Lord's people and to hold them up to notice, while their good deeds are passed by without mention.

In all the history of the church no reformation has been carried forward without encountering serious obstacles. Wherever Paul raised up a church some who professed to receive the faith brought in heresies. Luther also suffered distress from fanatical persons who claimed that God had spoken directly through them, who set their own ideas above Scripture. Many were beguiled by the new teachers and joined Satan in tearing down what God had moved Luther to build up. The Wesleys encountered the wiles of Satan in pushing unbalanced, unsanctified ones into fanaticism.

William Miller had no sympathy with fanaticism. "The devil," said Miller, "has great power over the minds of some at the present day." "I have often obtained more evidence of inward piety from a kindling eye, a wet cheek, and a choked utterance, than from all the noise in Christendom."[1]

In the Reformation its enemies charged the evils of fanaticism upon the ones who were laboring most earnestly against it. A similar course was pursued by the opposers of the advent movement. Not content with exaggerating the errors of fanatics, they circulated reports that had not the slightest semblance of truth. Their peace was disturbed by the proclamation of Christ at the door. They feared it might be true, yet hoped it was not. This was the secret of their warfare against Adventists.

The preaching of the first angel's message tended directly to repress fanaticism. Those who participated in these solemn movements were in harmony; their hearts were filled with love for one another and for Jesus, whom they expected soon to see. The one faith, the one blessed hope, proved a shield against the assaults of Satan.

Mistake Corrected

"While the bridegroom tarried, they all slumbered and slept. And at midnight there was a cry made, Behold, the bridegroom cometh; go ye out to meet him." In the summer of 1844 the message was proclaimed in the very words of Scripture.

That which led to this movement was the discovery that the decree of Artaxerxes for the restoration of Jerusalem, which formed the starting point for the period of the 2300 days, went into effect in the autumn of 457 B.C., and not at the beginning of the year, as had been believed. Reckoning from the autumn of 457, the 2300 years terminate in the autumn of 1844. The Old Testament types also pointed to the autumn as the time when the "cleansing of the sanctuary" must take place.

The slaying of the Passover lamb was a shadow of the death of Christ, a type fulfilled, not only as to the event, but as to the time. On the fourteenth day of the first Jewish month, the very day and month on which for centuries the Passover lamb had been slain, Christ instituted that feast which was to commemorate His own death as "the Lamb of God." That same night He was taken to be crucified and slain.

In like manner the types which relate to the second advent must be fulfilled at the time pointed out in the symbolic service. The cleansing of the sanctuary, or the Day of Atonement, occurred on the tenth day of the seventh Jewish month when the high priest, having made an atonement for all Israel, and thus removed their sins from the sanctuary, came forth and blessed the people. So it was believed that Christ would appear to purify the earth by the destruction of sin and sinners, and to bless His waiting people with immortality. The tenth day of the seventh month, the great Day of Atonement, the time of the cleansing of the sanctuary, which in 1844 fell upon the twenty-second of October, was regarded as the time of the Lord's coming. The 2300 days would terminate in the autumn, and the conclusion seemed irresistible.

"Midnight Cry"

The arguments carried strong conviction, and the "midnight cry" was heralded by thousands of believers. Like a tidal wave the movement swept from city to city, from village to village. Fanaticism disappeared like early frost before the rising sun. The work was similar to those seasons of returning unto the Lord which among ancient Israel followed messages of reproof from His servants. There was little ecstatic joy, but rather deep searching of heart, confession of sin, and forsaking of the world. There was unreserved consecration to God.

Of all the great religious movements since the days of the apostles, none have been more free from human imperfection and the wiles of Satan than was that of the autumn of 1844.

At the call, "The bridegroom cometh," the waiting ones "arose and trimmed their lamps"; they studied the Word of God with an intensity of interest before unknown. It was not the most talented, but the most humble and devoted, who were the first to obey the call. Farmers left their crops in the fields, mechanics laid down their tools and with rejoicing went out to give the warning. The churches in general closed their doors against this message, and a large company of those who received it withdrew their connection. Unbelievers who flocked to the Adventist meetings felt convincing power attending the message, "Behold, the bridegroom cometh!" Faith brought answers to prayer. Like showers of rain upon the thirsty earth, the Spirit of grace descended upon the earnest seekers. Those who expected soon to stand face to face with their Redeemer felt a solemn joy. The Holy Spirit melted the heart.

Those who received the message came up to the time when they hoped to meet their Lord. They prayed much with one another. They often met in secluded places to commune with God, and the voice of intercession ascended to heaven from fields and groves. The assurance of the Saviour's approval was more necessary to them than their daily food, and if a cloud darkened their minds, they did not rest until they felt the witness of pardoning grace.

Disappointed Again

But again, the time of expectation passed, and their Saviour did not appear. Now they felt as did Mary when, coming to the Saviour's tomb and finding it empty, she exclaimed with weeping: "They have taken away my Lord, and I know not where they have laid him." John 20:13.

A fear that the message might be true had served as a restraint upon the unbelieving world. But as no tokens of God's wrath were seen, they recovered from their fears and resumed their reproach and ridicule. A large class who had professed to believe renounced their faith. The scoffers won the weak and cowardly to their ranks, and all these united in declaring that the world might remain the same for thousands of years.

The earnest, sincere believers had given up all for Christ and had, as they believed, given their last warning to the world. With intense desire they had prayed, "Come, Lord Jesus." But now to take up again the burden of life's perplexities and to endure the taunts of a scoffing world was a terrible trial.

When Jesus rode triumphantly into Jerusalem, His followers believed that He was about to ascend the throne of David and deliver Israel from her oppressors. With high hopes, many spread their outer garments as a carpet in His path or strewed before Him the leafy branches of the palm. The disciples were accomplishing the purpose of God, yet they were doomed to a bitter disappointment. But a few days passed ere they witnessed the Saviour's agonizing death and laid Him in the tomb. Their hopes died with Jesus. Not till their Lord had come forth from the grave could they perceive that all had been foretold by prophecy.

Messages Given at the Right Time

In like manner Miller and his associates fulfilled prophecy and gave a message which Inspiration had foretold should be given to the world. They could not have given it had they fully understood the prophecies pointing out their disappointment, and presenting another message to be preached to all nations before the Lord should come. The first and second angels' messages were given at the right time and accomplished the work which God designed to accomplish by them.

The world had been expecting that if Christ did not appear, Adventism would be given up. But while many yielded their faith there were some who stood firm. The fruits of the advent movement, the spirit of heart searching, of renouncing of the world and reformation of life, testified that it was of God. They dared not deny that the Holy Spirit had witnessed to the preaching of the second advent. They could detect no error in the prophetic periods. Their opponents had not succeeded in overthrowing their prophetic interpretation. They could not consent to renounce positions reached through earnest, prayerful study of the Scriptures, by minds enlightened by the Spirit of God and hearts burning with its living power, and which had stood firm against learning and eloquence.

Adventists believed that God had led them to give the warning of the judgment. "It has," they declared, "tested the hearts of all who heard it, . . . so that those who will examine their own hearts, may know on which side . . . they would have been found, had the Lord then come—whether they would have exclaimed, 'Lo! this is our God, we have waited for him, and he will save us;' or whether they would have called to the rocks and mountains to fall on them to hide them from the face of him that sitteth in the throne!"[2]

The feelings of those who still believed that God had led are expressed in the words of William Miller: "My hope in the coming of Christ is as strong as ever. I have done only what, after years of solemn consideration, I felt it my duty to do." "Many thousands, to all human appearance, have been made to study the Scriptures by the preaching of the time; and by that means, through faith and the sprinkling of the blood of Christ, have been reconciled to God."[3]

Belief Maintained

God's Spirit still abode with those who did not rashly deny the light they had received and denounce the advent movement. "Cast not away therefore your confidence, which hath great recompense of reward. For ye have need of patience, that, after ye have done the will of God, ye might receive the promise. For yet a little while, and he that shall come will come, and will not tarry. Now the just shall live by faith: but if any man draw back, my soul shall have no pleasure in him. But we are not of them who draw back unto perdition; but of them that believe to the saving of the soul." Hebrews 10:35-39.

This admonition is addressed to the church in the last days. It is plainly implied that the Lord would appear to tarry. The people here addressed had done the will of God in following the guidance of His Spirit and His Word; yet they could not understand His purpose in their experience. They were tempted to doubt whether God had indeed been leading them. At this time the words were applicable: "Now the just shall live by faith." Bowed down by disappointed hopes, they could stand only by faith in God and His Word. To renounce their faith and deny the power of the Holy Spirit which had attended the message would be drawing back toward perdition. Their only safe course was to cherish the light already received of God, continue to search the Scriptures, and patiently wait and watch to receive further light.

References
   1. Bliss, pp. 236, 237.
   2. *The Advent Herald and Signs of the Times Reporter*, vol. 8, no. 14 (Nov. 13, 1844).
   3. Bliss, pp. 256, 255, 277, 280, 281.

23/The Open Mystery of the Sanctuary

The scripture which above all others had been both the foundation and the central pillar of the advent faith was the declaration, "Unto two thousand and three hundred days; then shall the sanctuary be cleansed." Daniel 8:14. These had been familiar words to all believers in the Lord's soon coming. But the Lord had not appeared. The believers knew that God's Word could not fail; their interpretation of the prophecy must be at fault. But where was the mistake?

God had led His people in the great advent movement. He would not permit it to end in darkness and disappointment, reproached as false and fanatical. Though many abandoned their reckoning of the prophetic periods and denied the movement based thereon, others were unwilling to renounce points of faith and experience sustained by the Scriptures and the Spirit of God. It was their duty to hold fast the truths already gained. With earnest prayer they studied the Scriptures to discover their mistake. As they could see no error in their reckoning of the prophetic periods, they examined more closely the subject of the sanctuary.

They learned that there is no Scripture evidence sustaining the popular view that the earth is the sanctuary; but they found a full explanation of the sanctuary, its nature, location, and services:

"Then verily the first covenant had also ordinances of divine service and a worldly sanctuary. For there was a tabernacle made; the first, wherein was the candlestick, and the table, and the shewbread; which is called the sanctuary. And after the second veil, the tabernacle which is called the holiest of all; which had the golden censer, and the ark of the covenant overlaid round about with gold, wherein was the golden pot that had manna, and Aaron's rod that budded, and the tables of the covenant; and over it the cherubims of gold shadowing the mercy seat." Hebrews 9:1-5.

The "sanctuary" was the tabernacle built by Moses at the command of God as the earthly dwelling place of the Most High. "Let them make me a sanctuary; that I may dwell among them" (Exodus 25:8), was the direction given to Moses. The tabernacle was a structure of great magnificence. Besides the outer court, the tabernacle itself consisted of two apartments called the holy and the most holy place, separated by a beautiful curtain, or veil. A similar veil closed the entrance to the first apartment.

Holy and Most Holy Places

In the holy place was the candlestick on the south with its seven lamps giving light both day and night; on the north stood the table of shewbread. Before the veil separating the holy from the most holy was the golden altar of incense, from which the cloud of fragrance, with the prayers of Israel, was daily ascending before God.

In the most holy place stood the ark, a chest overlaid with gold, the depository of the Ten Commandments. Above the ark was the mercy seat surmounted by two cherubim wrought of solid gold. In this apartment the divine presence was manifested in the cloud of glory between the cherubim.

After the settlement of the Hebrews in Canaan, the tabernacle was replaced by the temple of Solomon, which, though a permanent structure and upon a larger scale, observed the same proportions and was similarly furnished. In this form the sanctuary existed—except while it lay in ruins in Daniel's time—until its destruction by the Romans in A.D. 70. This is the only sanctuary on earth of which the Bible gives any information, the sanctuary of the first covenant. But has the new covenant no sanctuary?

Turning again to the book of Hebrews, the seekers for truth found that a second or new covenant sanctuary was implied in the words already quoted: "Then verily the first covenant had *also* ordinances of divine service, and a worldly sanctuary." Turning back to the beginning of the previous chapter, they read: "Now of the things which we have spoken this is the sum: We have such an high priest, who is set on the right hand of the throne of the Majesty in the heavens; a minister of the sanctuary, and of the true tabernacle, which the Lord pitched, and not man." Hebrews 8:1, 2.

Here is revealed the sanctuary of the new covenant. The sanctuary of the first covenant was pitched by Moses; this is pitched by the Lord. In that sanctuary earthly priests performed their service; in this, Christ, our great High Priest, ministers at God's right hand. One sanctuary was on earth, the other is in heaven.

The tabernacle built by Moses was made after a pattern. The Lord directed: "According to all that I show thee, after the pattern of the tabernacle, and the pattern of all the instruments thereof, even so shall ye make it." "Look that thou make them after their pattern, which was showed thee in the mount." The first tabernacle "was a figure for the time then present, in which were offered both gifts and sacrifices"; its holy places "patterns of things in the heavens." The priests served "unto the example and shadow of heavenly things." "Christ is not entered into the holy places made with hands, which are the figures of the true; but into heaven itself, now to appear in the presence of God for us." Exodus 25:9, 40; Hebrews 9:23; 8:5; 9:24.

The sanctuary in heaven is the great original of which the sanctuary built by Moses was a copy. The splendor of the earthly tabernacle reflected the glories of that heavenly temple where Christ ministers for us before the throne of God. Important truths concerning the heavenly sanctuary and man's redemption were taught by the earthly sanctuary and its services.

The Two Apartments

The holy places of the sanctuary in heaven are represented by the two apartments in the sanctuary on earth. John was granted a view of the temple of God in heaven. He beheld there "seven lamps of fire burning before the throne." He saw an angel "having a golden censer; and there was given unto him much incense, that he should offer it with the prayers of all saints upon the golden altar which was before the throne." Revelation 4:5; 8:3. Here the prophet beheld the first apartment of the sanctuary in heaven; and he saw there the "seven lamps of fire" and the "golden altar," represented by the golden candlestick and the altar of incense in the sanctuary on earth.

Again, "The temple of God was opened," and he looked within the inner veil upon the holy of holies. Here he beheld "the ark of his testament," represented by the chest constructed by Moses to contain the law of God. Revelation 11:19.

Thus those studying the subject found proof of the existence of a sanctuary in heaven. John testifies that he saw it in heaven.

In the temple in heaven, in the most holy place, is God's law. The ark that enshrines the law is covered with the mercy seat, before which Christ pleads His blood in the sinner's behalf. Thus is represented the union of justice and mercy in the plan of redemption, a union that fills all heaven with wonder. This is the mystery of mercy into which angels desire to look—that God can be just while He justifies the repenting sinner, that Christ could stoop to raise multitudes from ruin and clothe them with the spotless garments of His own righteousness.

The work of Christ as man's intercessor is presented in Zechariah: "He shall build the temple of the Lord;

and he shall bear the glory, and shall sit and rule upon his [the Father's] throne; and he shall be a priest upon his throne: and the counsel of peace shall be between them both." Zechariah 6:12, 13.

"He shall build the temple of the Lord." By His sacrifice and mediation Christ is the foundation and builder of the church of God, "the chief corner stone; in whom all the building fitly framed together groweth into an holy temple in the Lord." Ephesians 2:20, 21. "He shall bear the glory." The song of the ransomed ones will be: "Unto him that loved us, and washed us from our sins in his own blood, . . . to him be glory and dominion for ever and ever." Revelation 1:5, 6.

He "shall sit and rule upon his throne; and he shall be a priest upon his throne." The kingdom of glory has not yet been ushered in. Not until His work as a mediator shall be ended will God give unto Him a kingdom of which "there shall be no end." Luke 1:33. As priest, Christ is now set down with the Father in His throne. Upon the throne is He who "hath borne our griefs, and carried our sorrows," "in all points tempted like as we are, yet without sin," that He might be "able to succor them that are tempted." Isaiah 53:4; Hebrews 4:15; 2:18. The wounded hands, the pierced side, the marred feet, plead for fallen man whose redemption was purchased at such cost.

"And the counsel of peace shall be between them both." The love of the Father is the fountain of salvation for the lost race. Said Jesus to His disciples, "The Father himself loveth you." God was "in Christ, reconciling the world unto himself." "God so loved the world, that he gave his only begotten Son." John 16:27; 2 Corinthians 5:19; John 3:16.

The Sanctuary Mystery Solved

The "true tabernacle" in heaven is the sanctuary of the new covenant. At the death of Christ the typical service ended. As Daniel 8:14 is fulfilled in this dispensation, the sanctuary to which it refers must be the sanctuary of the new covenant. Thus the prophecy, "Unto two thousand and three hundred days; then shall the sanctuary be cleansed," points to the sanctuary in heaven.

But what is the cleansing of the sanctuary? Can there be anything in heaven to be cleansed? In Hebrews 9 the cleansing of both the earthly and the heavenly sanctuary is plainly taught: "Almost all things are by the law purged with blood; and without shedding of blood is no remission. It was therefore necessary that the patterns of things in the heavens should be purified with these [the blood of animals]; but the heavenly things themselves with better sacrifices than these" (Hebrews 9:22, 23), even the precious blood of Christ.

The Cleansing of the Sanctuary

The cleansing in the real service must be accomplished with the blood of Christ. "Without shedding of blood is no remission." Remission, or putting away of sin, is the work to be accomplished.

But how could there be sin connected with the sanctuary in heaven? This may be learned by reference to the symbolic service, for the priests on earth served "unto the example and shadow of heavenly things." Hebrews 8:5.

The ministry of the earthly sanctuary consisted of two divisions. The priests ministered daily in the holy place, while once a year the high priest performed a special work of atonement in the most holy, for the cleansing of the sanctuary. Day by day the repentant sinner brought his offering and, placing his hand upon the victim's head, confessed his sins, in figure transferring them from himself to the innocent sacrifice. The animal was then slain. "The life of the flesh is in the blood." Leviticus 17:11. The broken law of God demanded the life of the transgressor. The blood, representing the life of the sinner whose guilt the victim bore, was carried by the priest into the holy place and sprinkled before the veil, behind which was the law that the sinner had transgressed. By this ceremony the sin was transferred in figure to the sanctuary. In some cases the blood was not taken into the holy place, but the flesh was then eaten by the priest. Both ceremonies symbolized the transfer of sin from the penitent to the sanctuary.

Such was the work that went on throughout the year. The sins of Israel were thus transferred to the sanctuary, and a special work became necessary for their removal.

The Great Day of Atonement

Once a year, on the great Day of Atonement, the priest entered the most holy place for the cleansing of the sanctuary. Two kids of the goats were brought and lots were cast, "one lot for the Lord, and the other lot for the scapegoat." Verse 8. The goat for the Lord was slain as a sin offering for the people, and the priest was to bring his blood within the veil and sprinkle it before the mercy seat and also upon the altar of incense before the veil.

"And Aaron shall lay both his hands upon the head of the live goat, and confess over him all the iniquities of the children of Israel, and all their transgressions in all their sins, putting them upon the head of the goat, and shall send him away by the hand of a fit man into the wilderness: and the goat shall bear upon him all their iniquities unto a land not inhabited." Leviticus 16:21, 22. The scapegoat came no more into the camp of Israel.

The ceremony was designed to impress the Israelites with the holiness of God and His abhorrence of sin. Every man was required to afflict his soul while this work of atonement was going forward. All business was laid aside, and Israel were to spend the day in prayer, fasting, and searching of heart.

A substitute was accepted in the sinner's stead, but the sin was not canceled by the blood of the victim; it was transferred to the sanctuary. By the offering of blood the sinner acknowledged the authority of the law, confessed his transgression, and expressed his faith in a Redeemer to come; but he was not yet entirely released from the condemnation of the law. On the Day of Atonement the high priest, having taken an offering from the congregation, went into the most holy place. He sprinkled the blood of this offering upon the mercy seat, directly over the law, to make satisfaction for its claims. Then, as mediator, he took the sins upon himself and bore them from the sanctuary. Placing his hands upon the head of the scapegoat, he in figure transferred all these sins from himself to the goat. The goat then bore them away, and they were regarded as forever separated from the people.

Heavenly Reality

What was done in type in the ministration of the earthly sanctuary, is done in reality in the heavenly sanctuary. After His ascension our Saviour began His work as our high priest: "Christ is not entered into the holy places made with hands, which are the figures of the true; but into heaven itself, now to appear in the presence of God for us." Hebrews 9:24.

The ministration of the priest in the first apartment, "within the veil" which separated the holy place from the outer court, represents the work on which Christ entered at His ascension. The priest in the daily ministration presented before God the blood of the sin offering, also the incense which ascended with the prayers of Israel. So did Christ plead His blood before the Father in behalf of sinners and present before Him, with the fragrance of His own righteousness, the prayers of penitent believers. Such was the ministry in the first apartment of the sanctuary in heaven.

Thither the faith of Christ's disciples followed Him as He ascended. Here their hopes centered, "which hope we have as an anchor of the soul, both sure and steadfast, and which entereth into that within the veil; whither the forerunner is for us entered, even Jesus, made an high priest for ever." "By his own blood he entered in once into the holy place, having obtained eternal redemption for us." Hebrews 6:19, 20; 9:12.

For eighteen centuries this work continued in the first apartment of the sanctuary. The blood of Christ secured pardon and acceptance with the Father in behalf of penitent believers, yet their sins still remained upon the books of record. As in the typical service there was a work of atonement at the close of the year, so before Christ's work for men is completed there is a work of atonement for the removal of sin from the sanctuary. This began when the 2300 days ended. At that time our High Priest entered the most holy to cleanse the sanctuary.

A Work of Judgment

In the new covenant the sins of the repentant are by faith placed upon Christ and transferred in fact to the heavenly sanctuary. And as the typical cleansing of the earthly sanctuary was accomplished by the removal of the sins by which it had been polluted, so the actual cleansing of the heavenly is accomplished by the removal, or blotting out, of the sins there recorded. But before this can be accomplished there must be an examination of the books of record to determine who, through repentance and faith in Christ, are entitled to the benefits of His atonement. The cleansing of the sanctuary therefore involves a work of investigation—a work of judgment—prior to the coming of Christ, for when He comes, His reward is with Him to give to every man according to his works. Revelation 22:12.

Thus those who followed the light of the prophetic word saw that, instead of coming to the earth at the termination of the 2300 days in 1844, Christ entered the most holy place of the heavenly sanctuary to perform the closing work of atonement preparatory to His coming.

When Christ by virtue of His blood removes the sins of His people from the heavenly sanctuary at the close of His ministry, He will place them upon Satan, who must bear the final penalty. The scapegoat was sent away into a land not inhabited, never to come again into the congregation of Israel. So will Satan be forever banished from the presence of God and His people, and he will be blotted from existence in the final destruction of sin and sinners.

24/What Is Christ Doing Now?

The subject of the sanctuary unlocked the mystery of the disappointment. It opened to view a complete system of truth, connected and harmonious, showing that God's hand had directed the great advent movement. Those who had looked in faith for His second coming expected Him to appear in glory, but as their hopes were disappointed, they had lost sight of Jesus. Now in the holy of holies they again beheld their High Priest, soon to appear as king and deliverer. Light from the sanctuary illumined the past, the present, and the future. Though they had failed to understand the message which they bore, yet it had been correct.

The mistake had not been in the reckoning of the prophetic periods, but in the *event* to take place at the end of the 2300 days. Yet all that was foretold by the prophecy had been accomplished.

Christ had come, not to the earth, but to the most holy place of the temple in heaven: "I saw in the night visions, and behold, one like the Son of man came with the clouds of heaven, and came"—not to the earth, but—"to the Ancient of Days, and they brought him near before him." Daniel 7:13.

This coming was foretold also by Malachi: "The Lord, whom ye seek, shall suddenly come to his temple, even the messenger of the covenant, whom ye delight in: behold, he shall come, saith the Lord of hosts." Malachi 3:1. The coming of the Lord to His temple was "sudden," unexpected, to His people. They were not looking for Him there.

The people were not yet ready to meet their Lord. There was still a work of preparation to be accomplished for them. As they should by faith follow their High Priest in His ministration, new duties would be revealed. Another message was to be given to the church.

Who Shall Stand?

Says the prophet: "Who may abide the day of his coming? and who shall stand when he appeareth? . . . He shall sit as a refiner and purifier of silver: and he shall purify the sons of Levi, and purge them as gold and silver, that they may offer unto the Lord an offering in righteousness." Malachi 3:2, 3. Those living on earth when the intercession of Christ shall cease are to stand in the sight of God without a mediator. Their robes must be spotless, their characters purified from sin by the blood of sprinkling. Through the grace of God and their own diligent effort they must be conquerors in the battle with evil. While the investigative judgment is going forward in heaven, while the sins of penitent believers are being removed from the sanctuary, there is to be a special work of putting away sin among God's people on earth. This work is presented in the message of Revelation 14. When this work shall have been accomplished, the followers of Christ will be ready for His appearing. Then the church which our Lord at His coming is to receive will be "a glorious church, not having spot, or wrinkle, or any such thing." Ephesians 5:27.

"Behold, the Bridegroom Cometh"

The coming of Christ as High Priest to the most holy place for the cleansing of the sanctuary (Daniel 8:14), the coming of the Son of man to the Ancient of Days (Daniel 7:13), and the coming of the Lord to His temple (Malachi 3:11) are the same event. This is also represented by the coming of the bridegroom to the marriage in the parable of the ten virgins of Matthew 25.

In the parable, when the bridegroom came, "they that were ready went in with him to the marriage." This coming of the bridegroom takes place before the marriage. The marriage represents the reception by Christ of His kingdom. The Holy City, the New Jerusalem, the capital and representative of the kingdom, is called "the bride, the Lamb's wife." Said the angel to John: "Come hither, I will show thee the bride, the Lamb's wife." "He carried me away in the spirit," says the prophet, "and showed me that great city, the holy Jerusalem, descending out of heaven from God." Revelation 21:9, 10.

The bride represents the Holy City, and the virgins that go out to meet the bridegroom are a symbol of the church. In the Revelation the people of God are said to be guests at the marriage supper. If *guests,* they cannot be the *bride.* Christ will receive from the Ancient of Days in heaven "dominion, and glory, and a kingdom," the New Jerusalem, the capital of His kingdom, "prepared as a bride adorned for her husband." Having received the kingdom, He will come as King of kings and Lord of lords for the redemption of His people who are to partake of the marriage supper of the Lamb. Daniel 7:14; Revelation 21:2.

Waiting for Their Lord

The proclamation "Behold, the bridegroom cometh" led thousands to expect the immediate advent of the Lord. At the appointed time the Bridegroom came, not to the earth, but to the Ancient of Days in heaven, to the marriage, the reception of His kingdom. "They that were ready went in with him to the marriage." They were not to be present in person, for they are on the earth. The followers of Christ are to "wait for their Lord, when he will *return from* the wedding." Luke 12:36. But they are to understand His work and follow Him by faith. In this sense they are said to go in to the marriage.

In the parable, those that had oil in their lamps went

in to the marriage. Those who, in the night of their bitter trial, had patiently waited, searching the Bible for clearer light—these saw the truth concerning the sanctuary in heaven and the Saviour's change of ministration. By faith they followed Him in His work in the sanctuary above. And all who accept the same truths, following Christ by faith as He performs the last work of mediation, go in to the marriage.

Closing Work in the Sanctuary

In the parable of Matthew 22 the judgment takes place before the marriage. Previous to the wedding the king comes in to see if all the guests are attired in the wedding garment, the spotless robe of character washed in the blood of the Lamb. Revelation 7:14. All who upon examination are seen to have the wedding garment on are accepted and accounted worthy of a share in God's kingdom and a seat upon His throne. This work of examination of character is the investigative judgment, the closing work in the sanctuary above.

When the cases of those who in all ages have professed Christ have been examined and decided, then probation will close and the door of mercy will be shut. Thus in one short sentence, "They that were ready went in with him to the marriage: and the door was shut," we are carried down to the time when the great work for man's salvation shall be completed.

In the earthly sanctuary, when the high priest on the Day of Atonement entered the most holy place, the ministration in the first apartment ceased. So when Christ entered the holy of holies to perform the closing work of the atonement, He ceased His ministry in the first apartment. Then the ministry in the second apartment began. Christ had completed only one part of His work as our intercessor, to enter upon another portion of the work. He still pleaded His blood before the Father in behalf of sinners.

While it is true that that door of hope and mercy by

which men had for 1800 years found access to God was closed, another door was opened. Forgiveness of sins was offered through the intercession of Christ in the most holy. There was still an "open door" to the heavenly sanctuary, where Christ was ministering in the sinner's behalf.

Now was seen the application of those words of Christ in the Revelation, addressed to this very time: "These things saith he that is holy, he that is true, he that hath the key of David, he that openeth, and no man shutteth; and shutteth, and no man openeth; . . . behold, I have set before thee an open door, and no man can shut it." Revelation 3:7, 8.

Those who by faith follow Jesus in the great work of the atonement receive the benefits of His mediation, while those who reject the light are not benefited thereby. The Jews who refused to believe on Christ as Saviour could not receive pardon through Him. When Jesus at His ascension entered the heavenly sanctuary to shed upon His disciples the blessings of His mediation, the Jews were left in total darkness to continue their useless sacrifices and offerings. The door by which men had formerly found access to God was no longer open. The Jews had refused to seek Him in the only way He could then be found, through the sanctuary in heaven.

The unbelieving Jews illustrate the careless and unbelieving among professed Christians who are willingly ignorant of the work of our High Priest. In the typical service, when the high priest entered the most holy place, all Israel were required to gather about the sanctuary and humble their souls before God, that they might receive pardon of sins and not be "cut off" from the congregation. How much more essential in this antitypical Day of Atonement that we understand the work of our High Priest and know what duties are required of us.

A message was sent from heaven to the world in Noah's day, and their salvation depended on how they treated that message. Genesis 6:6-9; Hebrews 11:7. In the time of Sodom, all but Lot with his wife and two daughters were consumed by fire sent down from heaven. Genesis 19. So in the days of Christ. The Son of God declared to the unbelieving Jews: "Your house is left unto you desolate." Matthew 23:38. Looking down to the last days, the same Infinite Power declares, concerning those who "received not the love of the truth, that they might be saved": "For this cause God shall send them strong delusion, that they should believe a lie." 2 Thessalonians 2:10, 11. As they reject the teachings of His Word, God withdraws His Spirit and leaves them to the deceptions which they love. But Christ still intercedes in man's behalf, and light will be given those who seek it.

The passing of the time in 1844 was followed by great trial to those who held the advent faith. Their only relief was the light which directed their minds to the sanctuary above. As they waited and prayed they saw that their great High Priest had entered upon another work of ministration. Following Him by faith, they were led to see also the closing work of the church. They had a clearer understanding of the first and second angels' messages, and were prepared to receive and give to the world the solemn warning of the third angel of Revelation 14.

25/God's Law Immutable

"The temple of God was opened in heaven, and there was seen in his temple the ark of his testament." Revelation 11:19. The ark of God's testament is in the holy of holies, the second apartment of the sanctuary. In the ministration of the earthly tabernacle, which served "unto the example and shadow of heavenly things," this apartment was opened only upon the great Day of Atonement for the cleansing of the sanctuary. Therefore the announcement that the temple of God was opened in heaven and the ark of His testament was seen points to the opening of the most holy place of the heavenly sanctuary in 1844 as Christ entered there to perform the closing work of the atonement. Those who by faith followed their great High Priest as He entered upon His ministry in the most holy place, beheld the ark of His testament. As they had studied the subject of the sanctuary they had come to understand the Saviour's change of ministration, and they saw that He was now officiating before the ark of God.

The ark in the tabernacle on earth contained the two tables of stone, upon which were inscribed the law of God. When the temple of God was opened in heaven, the ark of His testament was seen. Within the holy of holies in heaven, the divine law is enshrined—the law that was spoken by God and written with His finger on the tables of stone.

Those who arrived at an understanding of this point saw, as never before, the force of the Saviour's words:

"Till heaven and earth pass, one jot or one tittle shall in no wise pass from the law." Matthew 5:18. The law of God, being a revelation of His will, a transcript of His character, must forever endure.

In the bosom of the Decalogue is the Sabbath commandment. The Spirit of God impressed those students of His Word that they had ignorantly transgressed this precept by disregarding the Creator's rest day. They began to examine the reasons for observing the first day of the week. They could find no evidence that the fourth commandment had been abolished or that the Sabbath had been changed. They had been honestly seeking to know and to do God's will; now they manifested their loyalty to God by keeping His Sabbath holy.

Many were the efforts made to overthrow the faith of Adventist believers. None could fail to see that acceptance of the truth concerning the heavenly sanctuary involved the claims of God's law and the Sabbath of the fourth commandment. Here was the secret of the determined opposition to the harmonious exposition of Scriptures that revealed the ministry of Christ in the heavenly sanctuary. Men sought to close the door which God had opened, and to open the door which He had closed. But Christ had opened the door of ministration of the most holy place. The fourth commandment was included in the law there enshrined.

Those who accepted the light concerning the mediation of Christ and the law of God found that these were the truths of Revelation 14, a threefold warning to prepare the inhabitants of earth for the Lord's second coming. (See Appendix.) The announcement "The hour of his judgment is come" heralds a truth which must be proclaimed until the Saviour's intercession shall cease and He shall return to take His people to Himself. The judgment which began in 1844 must continue until the cases of all are decided, both of the living and the dead; hence it will extend to the close of human probation.

That men may be prepared to stand in the judgment, the message commands them to "fear God, and give glory to him," "and worship him that made heaven, and earth, and the sea and the fountains of waters." The result of acceptance of these messages is given: "Here are they that keep the commandments of God, and the faith of Jesus." Revelation 14:7, 12.

To be prepared for the judgment, men should keep the law of God, the standard of character in the judgment. Paul declares: "As many as have sinned in the law shall be judged by the law, . . . in the day when God shall judge the secrets of men by Jesus Christ." "The doers of the law shall be justified." Faith is essential in order to keep the law of God; for "without faith it is impossible to please him." "Whatsoever is not of faith is sin." Romans 2:12-16; Hebrews 11:6; Romans 14:23.

The first angel called upon men to "fear God, and give glory to him" and to worship Him as the Creator of heaven and earth. To do this, they must obey His law. Without obedience no worship can be pleasing to God. "This is the love of God, that we keep his commandments." 1 John 5:3; See Proverbs 28:9.

A Call to Worship the Creator

The duty to worship God is based upon the fact that He is the Creator. "O come, let us worship and bow down: let us kneel before the Lord our maker." Psalm 95:6; See Psalm 96:5; Psalm 100:3; Isaiah 40:25, 26; 45:18.

In Revelation 14, men are called to worship the Creator and keep the commandments of God. One of these commandments points to God as the Creator: "The seventh day is the Sabbath of the Lord thy God: . . . for in six days the Lord made heaven and earth, the sea, and all that in them is, and rested the seventh day: wherefore the Lord blessed the Sabbath day, and hallowed it." Exodus 20:10, 11. The Sabbath, the Lord says, is a "sign, . . . that ye may know that I am the

Lord your God." Ezekiel 20:20. Had the Sabbath been universally kept, man would have been led to the Creator as the object of worship. There would never have been an idolater, atheist, or infidel. Keeping the Sabbath is a sign of loyalty to "him that made heaven, and earth, and the sea, and the fountains of waters." The message which commands men to worship God and keep His commandments will especially call them to keep the fourth commandment.

In contrast to those who keep the commandments of God and the faith of Jesus, the third angel points to another class: "If any man worship the beast and his image, and receive his mark in his forehead, or in his hand, the same shall drink of the wine of the wrath of God." Revelation 14:9, 10. What is represented by the beast, the image, the mark?

The Identity of the Dragon

The prophecy in which these symbols are found begins with Revelation 12. The dragon that sought to destroy Christ at His birth is said to be Satan (Revelation 12:9); he moved upon Herod to put the Saviour to death. But the agent of Satan in making war upon Christ and His people during the first centuries was the Roman Empire, in which paganism was the prevailing religion. Thus the dragon is, in a secondary sense, a symbol of pagan Rome.

In Revelation 13 is another beast, "like unto a leopard," to which the dragon gave "his power, and his seat, and great authority." This symbol, as most Protestants have believed, represents the papacy, which succeeded to the power and seat and authority once held by the Roman empire. Of the leopardlike beast it is declared: "There was given unto him a mouth speaking great things and blasphemies. . . . And he opened his mouth in blasphemy against God, to blaspheme his name, and his tabernacle, and them that dwell in heaven. And it was given unto him to make war with the saints, and to overcome them: and power was given him over all kindreds, and tongues, and nations.'' Revelation 13:2:5-7. This prophecy, nearly identical with the description of the little horn of Daniel 7, unquestionably points to the papacy.

''Power was given unto him to continue forty and two months''—the three years and a half, or 1260 days, of Daniel 7—during which the papal power was to oppress God's people. This period, as stated in preceding chapters, began with the supremacy of the papacy, A.D. 538, and terminated in 1798. At that time the papal power received its ''deadly wound,'' and the prediction was fulfilled, ''He that leadeth into captivity shall go into captivity.''

The Rise of a New Power

At this point another symbol is introduced: ''I beheld another beast coming up out of the earth; and he had two horns like a lamb.'' Revelation 13:11. This nation is unlike those presented under the preceding symbols. The great kingdoms that have ruled the world were presented to the prophet Daniel as beasts of prey, rising when ''the four winds of heaven strove upon the great sea.'' Daniel 7:2.

But the beast with lamblike horns was seen ''coming up out of the earth.'' Instead of overthrowing other powers to establish itself, the nation thus represented must arise in territory previously unoccupied and grow up peacefully. It must be sought in the Western Continent.

What nation of the New World was in 1798 rising into power, giving promise of strength, and attracting the attention of the world? One nation, and only one, meets this prophecy—the United States of America. Almost the exact words of the sacred writer have been unconsciously employed by the historian in describing the rise of this nation. A prominent writer speaks of *''the mystery of her coming forth from vacancy,''* and says, ''Like a *silent seed* we grew into empire.''[1] A European journal in 1850 spoke of the United States "emerging" and "amid the silence of the earth daily adding to its power and pride."[2]

"And he had two horns like a lamb." The lamblike horns indicate youth, innocence, and gentleness. Among the Christian exiles who first fled to America from royal oppression and priestly intolerance were many who determined to establish civil and religious liberty. The Declaration of Independence sets forth the truth that "all men are created equal" and endowed with the inalienable right to "life, liberty, and the pursuit of happiness." The Constitution guarantees to the people the right of self-government, providing that representatives elected by popular vote shall enact and administer the laws. Freedom of religious faith was also granted. Republicanism and Protestantism became the fundamental principles of the nation, the secret of its power and prosperity. Millions have sought its shores, and the United States has risen to a place among the most powerful nations of the earth.

A Striking Contradiction

But the beast with lamblike horns "spake as a dragon. And he exerciseth all the power of the first beast before him, and causeth the earth and them which dwell therein to worship the first beast, whose deadly wound was healed; . . . saying to them that dwell on the earth, that they should make an image to the beast, which had the wound by a sword, and did live." Revelation 13:11-14.

The lamblike horns and dragon voice point to a contradiction. The prediction that it will speak "as a dragon" and exercise "all the power of the first beast" foretells a spirit of intolerance and persecution manifested by the dragon and the leopardlike beast. And the statement that the beast with two horns "causeth the earth and them which dwell therein to worship the first beast" indicates that the authority of this nation is to enforce homage to the papacy.

Such action would be contrary to the genius of its

free institutions, to the solemn avowals of the Declaration of Independence, and to the Constitution. The Constitution provides that "Congress shall make no law respecting an establishment of religion, or prohibiting the free exercise thereof," and that "no religious test shall ever be required as a qualification to any office of public trust under the United States." Flagrant violation of these safeguards to liberty is represented in the symbol. The beast with lamblike horns—in profession pure, gentle, and harmless—speaks as a dragon.

"Saying to them that dwell on the earth, that *they* should make an image to the beast." Here is presented a form of government in which the legislative power rests with the people, a most striking evidence that the United States is the nation denoted.

But what is the "image to the beast"? How is it to be formed?

When the early church became corrupted, she sought the support of secular power. The result: the papacy, a church that controlled the state, especially for the punishment of "heresy." In order for the United States to form an "image of the beast," the religious power must so control the civil government that the state will also be employed by the church to accomplish her own ends.

Protestant churches that have followed in the steps of Rome have manifested a similar desire to restrict liberty of conscience. An example is the long-continued persecution of dissenters by the Church of England. During the sixteenth and seventeenth centuries, nonconformist pastors and people were subjected to fine, imprisonment, torture, and martyrdom.

Apostasy led the early church to seek the aid of civil government, and this prepared the way for the papacy—the beast. Said Paul: "There" shall "come a falling away, . . . and that man of sin be revealed." 2 Thessalonians 2:3.

The Bible declares: "In the last days perilous times

shall come. For men shall be *lovers of their own selves*, covetous, boasters, proud, blasphemers, disobedient to parents, unthankful, unholy, without natural affection, trucebreakers, false accusers, incontinent, fierce, *despisers of those that are good*, traitors, heady, highminded, *lovers of pleasures more than lovers of God; having a form of godliness*, but denying the power thereof." 2 Timothy 3:1-5. "Now the Spirit speaketh expressly, that in the latter times some shall depart from the faith, giving heed to seducing spirits and doctrines of devils." 1 Timothy 4:1.

All that "received not the love of the truth, that they might be saved," will accept "strong delusion, that they should believe a lie." 2 Thessalonians 2:10, 11. When this state shall be reached, the same results will follow as in the first centuries.

The wide diversity of belief in Protestant churches is regarded by many as proof that no forced uniformity can ever be made. But there has been for years in Protestant churches a growing sentiment in favor of union. To secure such union, discussion of subjects upon which all were not agreed must be waived. In the effort to secure complete uniformity, it will be only a step to the resort to force.

When the leading churches of the United States, uniting upon such points of doctrine as are held by them in common, shall influence the state to enforce their decrees and to sustain their institutions, then Protestant America will have formed an image of the Roman hierarchy, and the infliction of civil penalties upon dissenters will inevitably result.

The Beast and His Image

The beast with two horns "causeth [commands] all, both small and great, rich and poor, free and bond, to receive a mark in their right hand, or in their foreheads: and that no man might buy or sell, save he that had the mark, or the name of the beast, or the number of his name." Revelation 13:16, 17. The third angel warns:

"If any man worship the beast and his image, and receive his mark in his forehead, or in his hand, the same shall drink of the wine of the wrath of God."

"The beast" whose worship is enforced is the first, or leopardlike, beast of Revelation 13—the papacy. The "image to the beast" represents that form of apostate Protestantism which will be developed when the Protestant churches seek the aid of civil power for the enforcement of their dogmas. The "mark of the beast" still remains to be defined.

Those who keep God's commandments are in contrast with those that worship the beast and his image and receive his mark. The keeping of God's law, on the one hand, and its violation, on the other, will make the distinction between the worshipers of God and the worshipers of the beast.

The special characteristic of the beast and of his image is the breaking of God's commandments. Says Daniel, of the little horn, the papacy: "He shall think to change the times and the law." Daniel 7:25, R.V. Paul styled the same power the "man of sin" (2 Thessalonians 2:3), who was to exalt himself above God. Only by changing God's law could the papacy exalt itself above God. Whoever should understandingly keep the law as thus changed would be giving supreme honor to papal laws, a mark of allegiance to the pope in place of God.

The papacy has attempted to change the law of God. The fourth commandment has been so changed as to authorize the observance of the first instead of the seventh day as the Sabbath. An intentional, deliberate change is presented: "He shall *think* to change the times and the law." The change in the fourth commandment exactly fulfills the prophecy. Here the papal power openly sets itself above God.

The worshipers of God will be especially distinguished by their regard for the fourth commandment, the sign of His creative power. The worshipers of the beast will be distinguished by their efforts to tear down the Creator's memorial, to exalt the institution of Rome. It was in behalf of Sunday as "the Lord's day" that popery first asserted its arrogant claims. (See Appendix.) But the Bible points to the seventh day as the Lord's day. Said Christ: "The Son of man is Lord also of the sabbath." Mark 2:28. See also Isaiah 58:13; Matthew 5:17-19. The claim so often put forth that Christ changed the Sabbath is disproved by His own words.

Complete Silence of New Testament

Protestants acknowledge "the complete silence of the New Testament so far as any explicit command for the Sabbath [Sunday, the first day of the week] or definite rules for its observance are concerned."[3]

"Up to the time of Christ's death, no change had been made in the day"; and, "so far as the record shows, they [the apostles] did not . . . give any explicit command enjoining the abandonment of the seventh day Sabbath, and its observance on the first day of the week."[4]

Roman Catholics acknowledge that the change of the Sabbath was made by their church, and declare that Protestants, by observing Sunday, recognize her power. The statement is made: "During the old law, Saturday was the day sanctified; but *the Church*, instructed by Jesus Christ, and directed by the Spirit of God, has substituted Sunday for Saturday; so now we sanctify the first, not the seventh day. Sunday means, and now is, the day of the Lord."[5]

As the sign of the authority of the Catholic Church, papist writers cite "the very act of changing the Sabbath into Sunday, which Protestants allow of; . . . because by keeping Sunday, they acknowledge the church's power to ordain feasts, and to command them under sin."[6]

What then is the change of the Sabbath, but the sign, or mark, of the authority of the Roman Church—"the mark of the beast"?

The Roman Church has not relinquished her claim to supremacy. When the world and the Protestant churches accept a sabbath of her creating, while they reject the Bible Sabbath, they virtually admit this assumption. In so doing they ignore the principle which separates them from Rome—that "the Bible, and the Bible only, is the religion of Protestants." As the movement for Sunday enforcement gains favor, it will eventually bring the whole Protestant world under the banner of Rome.

Romanists declare that "the observance of Sunday by the Protestants is an homage they pay, in spite of themselves, to the authority of the [Catholic] Church."[7] Enforcing a religious duty by secular power would form an image to the beast; hence the enforcement of Sundaykeeping in the United States would be an enforcement of the worship of the beast and his image.

Christians of past generations observed Sunday supposing they were keeping the Bible Sabbath, and there are now true Christians in every church who honestly believe that Sunday is of divine appointment. God accepts their sincerity and integrity. But when Sunday observance shall be enforced by law and the world shall be enlightened concerning the true Sabbath, then whoever shall transgress the command of God to obey a precept of Rome will thereby honor popery above God. He is paying homage to Rome. He is worshiping the beast and his image. Men will thereby accept the sign of allegiance to Rome—"the mark of the beast." It is not until the issue is thus plainly set before the people and they are brought to choose between the commandments of God and the commandments of men, that those who continue in transgression will receive "the mark of the beast."

The Warning of the Third Angel

The most fearful threatening ever addressed to mortals is contained in the third angel's message. Men are not to be left in darkness concerning this important matter; the warning is to be given the world before the visitation of God's judgments, that all may have opportunity to escape them. The first angel makes his announcement to "every nation, and kindred, and tongue, and people." The warning of the third angel is to be no less widespread. It is proclaimed with a loud voice and will command the attention of the world.

All will be divided into two great classes—those who keep the commandments of God and the faith of Jesus, and those who worship the beast and his image and receive his mark. Church and state will unite to compel "all" to receive "the mark of the beast," yet the people of God will not receive it. The prophet beholds "them that had gotten the victory over the beast, and over his image, and over his mark, and over the number of his name, stand on the sea of glass, having the harps of God." Revelation 15:2.

References
1. G. A. Townsend, *The New World Compared With the Old*, p. 462.
2. *Dublin Nation*.
3. George Elliott, *The Abiding Sabbath*, p. 184.
4. A. E. Waffle, *The Lord's Day*, pp. 186-188.
5. *Catholic Catechism of Christian Religion*.
6. Henry Tuberville, *An Abridgement of the Christian Doctrine*, p. 58.
7. Mgr. Segur, *Plain Talk About the Protestantism of Today*, p. 213.

26/ Champions for Truth

Sabbath reform in the last days is foretold in Isaiah: "Thus saith the Lord, Keep ye judgment, and do justice: for my salvation is near to come, and my righteousness to be revealed. Blessed is the man that doeth this, and the son of man that layeth hold on it; that keepeth the sabbath from polluting it, and keepeth his hand from doing any evil. . . . The sons of the stranger, that join themselves to the Lord, to serve him, and to love the name of the Lord, to be his servants, everyone that keepeth the sabbath from polluting it, and taketh hold of my covenant; even them will I bring to my holy mountain, and make them joyful in my house of prayer." Isaiah 56:1, 2, 6, 7.

These words apply in the Christian age, as shown by the context (verse 8). Here is foreshadowed the gathering in of the Gentiles by the gospel, when His servants preach to all nations the glad tidings.

The Lord commands, "Seal the law among my disciples." Isaiah 8:16. The seal of God's law is found in the fourth commandment. This only, of all the ten, brings to view both the name and the title of the Lawgiver. When the Sabbath was changed by the papal power, the seal was taken from the law. The disciples of Jesus are called upon to restore it by exalting the Sabbath as the Creator's memorial and sign of His authority.

The command is given: "Cry aloud, spare not, lift up thy voice like a trumpet, and show my people their transgression." Those whom the Lord designates as "my people" are to be reproved for their transgressions, a class who think themselves righteous in the service of God. But the solemn rebuke of the Searcher of hearts proves them to be trampling upon the divine precepts. Isaiah 58:1, 2.

The prophet thus points out the ordinance which has been forsaken: "Thou shalt raise up the foundations of many generations; and thou shalt be called, The repairer of the breach, The restorer of paths to dwell in. If thou turn away thy foot from the Sabbath, from doing thy pleasure on my holy day; and call the Sabbath a delight, the holy of the Lord, honourable; and shalt honour him, not doing thine own ways, nor finding thine own pleasure, nor speaking thine own words: then shalt thou delight thyself in the Lord." Isaiah 58:12-14.

The "breach" was made in the law of God when the Sabbath was changed by the Roman power. But the time has come for the breach to be repaired.

The Sabbath was kept by Adam in his innocence in Eden; by Adam, fallen yet repentant, when driven from his estate. It was kept by all the patriarchs from Abel to Noah, to Abraham, to Jacob. When the Lord delivered Israel, He proclaimed His law to the multitude.

True Sabbath Always Kept

From that day to the present the Sabbath has been kept. Though the "man of sin" succeeded in trampling underfoot God's holy day, yet hidden in secret places faithful souls paid it honor. Since the Reformation, some in every generation have maintained its observance.

These truths in connection with "the everlasting gospel" will distinguish the church of Christ at the time of His appearing. "Here are they that keep the commandments of God, and the faith of Jesus." Revelation 14:12.

Those who received the light concerning the sanctuary and the law of God were filled with joy as they saw the harmony of truth. They desired the light to be imparted to all Christians. But truths at variance with the world were not welcome to many who claimed to follow Christ.

As the claims of the Sabbath were presented, many said: "We have always kept Sunday, our fathers kept it, and many good men have died happy while keeping it. The keeping of a new Sabbath would throw us out of harmony with the world. What can a little company keeping the seventh day accomplish against all the world who are keeping Sunday?" By similar arguments the Jews justified their rejection of Christ. So, in the time of Luther, papists reasoned that true Christians had died in the Catholic faith; therefore that religion was sufficient. Such reasoning would prove a barrier to all advancement in faith.

Many urged that Sundaykeeping had been a widespread custom of the church for centuries. Against this argument it was shown that the Sabbath and its observance were more ancient, even as old as the world itself—established by the Ancient of Days.

In the absence of Bible testimony, many urged: "Why do not our great men understand this Sabbath question? Few believe as you do. It cannot be that you are right and all the men of learning are wrong."

To refute such arguments it was needful only to cite the Scriptures and the Lord's dealings with His people in all ages. The reason why He does not more often choose men of learning and position to lead out in reform is that they trust to their creeds and theological systems and feel no need to be taught of God. Men who have little of the learning of the schools are sometimes called to declare the truth, not because they are unlearned, but because they are not too self-sufficient to be taught of God. Their humility and obedience make them great.

The history of ancient Israel is a striking illustration of the past experience of the Adventist body. God led His people in the advent movement, even as He led the children of Israel from Egypt. If all who had labored unitedly in the work in 1844 had received the third angel's message and proclaimed it in the power of the Holy Spirit, years ago the earth would have been warned and Christ would have come for the redemption of His people.

Not God's Will

It was not the will of God that Israel should wander forty years in the wilderness; He desired to lead them directly to Canaan and establish them there, a holy, happy people. But "they could not enter in because of unbelief." Hebrews 3:19. In like manner, it was not the will of God that the coming of Christ should be so long delayed and His people remain so many years in this world of sin and sorrow. Unbelief separated them from God. In mercy to the world, Jesus delays His coming, that sinners may hear the warning and find shelter before the wrath of God shall be poured out.

Now as in former ages, the presentation of truth will excite opposition. Many with malice assail the character and motives of those who stand in defense of unpopular truth. Elijah was declared a troubler in Israel, Jeremiah a traitor, Paul a polluter of the temple. From that day to this, those who would be loyal to truth have been denounced as seditious, heretical, or schismatic.

The confession of faith made by saints and martyrs, those examples of holiness and steadfast integrity, inspires courage in those who are now called to stand as witnesses for God. To the servant of God at this time is the command addressed: "Lift up thy voice like a trumpet, and show my people their transgression, and the house of Jacob their sins." "I have set thee a watchman unto the house of Israel; therefore thou shalt hear the word at my mouth, and warn them from me." Isaiah 58:1; Ezekiel 33:7.

The great obstacle to the acceptance of truth is the fact that it involves inconvenience and reproach. This is the only argument against the truth which its advocates have never been able to refute. But true followers of Christ do not wait for truth to become popular. They accept the cross, with Paul counting that "our light affliction, which is but for a moment, worketh for us a far more exceeding and eternal weight of glory"; with one of old, "esteeming the reproach of Christ greater riches than the treasures in Egypt." 2 Corinthians 4:17; Hebrews 11:26.

We should choose the right because it is right, and leave consequences with God. To men of principle, faith, and daring, the world is indebted for its great reforms. By such men the work of reform for this time must be carried forward.

27/ How Successful Are Modern Revivals?

Wherever the Word of God has been faithfully preached, results have followed that attested its divine origin. Sinners felt their consciences quickened. Deep conviction took hold upon their minds and hearts. They had a sense of the righteousness of God, and cried out: "Who shall deliver me from the body of this death?" Romans 7:24. As the cross was revealed, they saw that nothing but the merits of Christ could atone for their transgressions. Through the blood of Jesus they had "remission of sins that are past." Romans 3:25.

These souls believed and were baptized and rose to walk in newness of life, by the faith of the Son of God to follow in His steps, to reflect His character, and to purify themselves even as He is pure. Things they once hated they now loved, and things they once loved they hated. The proud became meek, the vain and supercilious became serious and unobtrusive. The drunken became sober, the profligate pure. Christians sought not the "outward adorning of plaiting the hair, and of wearing of gold, or of putting on of apparel; but . . . that which is not corruptible, even the ornament of a meek and quiet spirit, which is in the sight of God of great price." 1 Peter 3:3, 4.

Revivals were characterized by solemn appeals to the sinner. The fruits were seen in souls who shrank not at self-denial but rejoiced that they were counted worthy to suffer for the sake of Christ. Men beheld a transformation in those who professed the name of Jesus. Such were the effects that in former years followed seasons of religious awakening.

But many revivals of modern times present a marked contrast. It is true that many profess conversion, and there are large accessions to the churches. Nevertheless the results are not such as to warrant the belief that there has been a corresponding increase of real spiritual life. The light which flames up for a time soon dies out.

Popular revivals too often excite the emotions, gratifying the love for what is new and startling. Converts thus gained have little desire to listen to Bible truth. Unless a religious service has something of a sensational character, it has no attraction for them.

With every truly converted soul the relation to God and to eternal things will be the great topic of life. Where in the popular churches of today is the spirit of consecration to God? Converts do not renounce pride and love of the world. They are no more willing to deny self and follow the meek and lowly Jesus than before their conversion. Godliness has well-nigh departed from many of the churches.

Notwithstanding the widespread declension of faith, there are true followers of Christ in these churches. Before the final visitation of God's judgments, there will be among the people of the Lord a revival of primitive godliness not witnessed since apostolic times. The Spirit of God will be poured out. Many will separate from those churches in which love of this world has supplanted love for God and His Word. Many ministers and people will gladly accept those great truths which prepare a people for the Lord's second coming.

The enemy of souls desires to hinder this work, and before the time for such a movement shall come, he will endeavor to prevent it by introducing a counterfeit. In those churches which he can bring under his power he will make it appear that God's special blessing is poured out. Multitudes will exult, "God is working marvelously," when the work is that of another spirit. Under a religious guise, Satan will seek to extend his influence over the Christian world. There is an emotional excitement, a mingling of the true with the false, well adapted to mislead.

Yet in the light of God's Word it is not difficult to determine the nature of these movements. Wherever men neglect the testimony of the Bible, turning away from these plain, soul-testing truths which require self-denial and renunciation of the world, there we may be sure that God's blessing is not bestowed. And by the rule, "Ye shall know them by their fruits," (Matthew 7:16) it is evident that these movements are not the work of the Spirit of God.

The truths of God's Word are a shield against the deceptions of Satan. Neglect of these truths has opened the door to the evils now widespread in the world. The importance of the law of God has been to a great extent lost sight of. A wrong conception of the divine law has led to errors in conversion and sanctification, lowering the standard of piety. Here is to be found the secret of the lack of the Spirit of God in the revivals of our time.

The Law of Liberty

Many religious teachers assert that Christ by His death abolished the law. Some represent it as a grievous yoke, and in contrast to the "bondage" of the law they present the "liberty" to be enjoyed under the gospel.

But not so did prophets and apostles regard the holy law of God. Said David: "I will walk at liberty: for I seek thy precepts." Psalm 119:45. The apostle James refers to the Decalogue as "the perfect law of liberty." James 1:25. The Revelator pronounces a blessing upon them "that do his commandments, that they may have right to the tree of life, and may enter in through the gates into the city." Revelation 22:14.

Had it been possible for the law to be changed or set aside, Christ need not have died to save man from the penalty of sin. The Son of God came to "magnify the law, and make it honorable." Isaiah 42:21. He said: "Think not that I am come to destroy the law"; "till heaven and earth pass, one jot or one tittle shall in no wise pass from the law." Concerning Himself He declared: "I delight to do thy will, O my God; yea, thy law is within my heart." Matthew 5:17, 18; Psalm 40:8.

The law of God is unchangeable, a revelation of the character of its Author. God is love, and His law is love. "Love is the fulfilling of the law." Says the psalmist: "Thy law is the truth"; "all thy commandments are righteousness." Paul declares: "The law is holy, and the commandment holy, and just, and good." Romans 13:10; Psalm 119:142, 172; Romans 7:12. Such a law must be as enduring as its Author.

It is the work of conversion and sanctification to reconcile men to God by bringing them into accord with the principles of His law. In the beginning, man was in perfect harmony with the law of God. But sin alienated him from his Maker. His heart was at war with God's law. "The carnal mind is enmity against God: for it is not subject to the law of God, neither indeed can be." Romans 8:7. But "God so loved the world, that he gave his only begotten Son," that man might be reconciled to God, restored to harmony with his Maker. This change is the new birth, without which "he cannot see the kingdom of God." John 3:16, 3.

Conviction of Sin

The first step in reconciliation to God is the conviction of sin. "Sin is the transgression of the law." "By the law is the knowledge of sin." 1 John 3:4; Romans 3:20. In order to see his guilt, the sinner must test his character by God's mirror which shows the perfection of a righteous character and enables him to discern the defects in his own.

The law reveals to man his sin, but provides no remedy. It declares that death is the portion of the transgressor. The gospel of Christ alone can free him from the condemnation or the defilement of sin. He must exercise repentance toward God, whose law has been transgressed, and faith in Christ, his atoning sacrifice. Thus he obtains "remission of sins that are past" (Romans 3:25) and becomes a child of God.

Is he now free to transgress God's law? Says Paul: "Do we then make void the law through faith? God forbid: yea, we establish the law." "How shall we, that are dead to sin, live any longer therein?" John declares: "This is the love of God, that we keep his commandments: and his commandments are not grievous." In the new birth the heart is brought into harmony with God, into accord with His law. When this change has taken place in the sinner he has passed from death unto life, from transgression and rebellion to obedience and loyalty. The old life has ended; the new life of reconciliation, faith, and love has begun. Then "the righteousness of the law" will "be fulfilled in us, who walk not after the flesh, but after the Spirit." The language of the soul will be: "O how love I thy law! it is my meditation all the day." Romans 3:31; 6:2; 1 John 5:3; Romans 8:4; Psalm 119:97.

Without the law, men have no true conviction of sin and feel no need of repentance. They do not realize their need of the atoning blood of Christ. The hope of salvation is accepted without a radical change of heart or reformation of life. Thus superficial conversions abound, and multitudes join the church who have never been united to Christ.

What Is Sanctification?

Erroneous theories of sanctification also spring from neglect or rejection of the divine law. These theories, false in doctrine and dangerous in practical results, are generally finding favor.

Paul declares, "This is the will of God, even your sanctification." The Bible clearly teaches what sanctification is and how it is to be attained. The Saviour prayed for His disciples: "Sanctify them through thy truth: thy word is truth." And Paul teaches that believers are to be "sanctified by the Holy Ghost." 1 Thessalonians 4:3; John 17:17; Romans 15:16.

What is the work of the Holy Spirit? Jesus told His disciples: "When he, the Spirit of truth, is come, he will guide you into all truth." John 16:13. And the psalmist says: "Thy law is the truth." Since the law of God is "holy and just and good," a character formed by obedience to that law will be holy. Christ is a perfect example of such a character. He says: "I have kept my Father's commandments." "I do always those things that please him." John 15:10; 8:29. The followers of Christ are to become like Him—by the grace of God to form characters in harmony with the principles of His holy law. This is Bible sanctification.

Only Through Faith

This work can be accomplished only through faith in Christ, by the power of the indwelling Spirit of God. The Christian will feel the promptings of sin, but he will maintain a constant warfare against it. Here is where Christ's help is needed. Human weakness becomes united to divine strength, and faith exclaims: "Thanks be to God, which giveth us the victory through our Lord Jesus Christ." 1 Corinthians 15:57.

The work of sanctification is progressive. When in conversion the sinner finds peace with God the Christian life has just begun. Now he is to "go on unto perfection," to grow up "unto the measure of the stature of the fulness of Christ." "I press toward the mark for the prize of the high calling of God in Christ Jesus." Hebrews 6:1; Ephesians 4:13; Philippians 3:14.

Those who experience Bible sanctification will manifest humility. They see their own unworthiness in contrast with the perfection of the Infinite One. The prophet Daniel was an example of true sanctification. Instead of claiming to be pure and holy, this honored prophet identified himself with the really sinful of Israel as he pleaded before God in behalf of his people. Daniel 10:11; 9:15, 18, 20; 10:8, 11.

There can be no self-exaltation, no boastful claim to freedom from sin on the part of those who walk in the shadow of Calvary's cross. They feel that it was their sin which caused the agony that broke the heart of the Son of God, and this thought will lead to self-abasement. Those who live nearest to Jesus discern most clearly the frailty and sinfulness of humanity, and their only hope is in the merit of a crucified and risen Saviour.

The sanctification now gaining prominence in the religious world carries a spirit of self-exaltation and disregard for the law of God that mark it as foreign to the Bible. Its advocates teach that sanctification is an instantaneous work, by which, through "faith alone," they attain perfect holiness. "Only believe," say they, "and the blessing is yours." No further effort on the part of the receiver is supposed to be required. At the same time they deny the authority of the law of God, urging that they are released from obligation to keep the commandments. But is it possible to be holy without coming into harmony with the principles which express God's nature and will?

The testimony of the Word of God is against this ensnaring doctrine of faith without works. It is not faith that claims the favor of Heaven without complying with the conditions upon which mercy is to be granted. It is presumption. See James 2:14-24.

Let none deceive themselves that they can become holy while willfully violating one of God's requirements. Known sin silences the witnessing voice of the Spirit and separates the soul from God. Though John dwells so fully upon love, he does not hesitate to reveal the true character of that class who claim to be sanctified while living in transgression of the law of God. "He that saith, I know him, and keepeth not his commandments, is a liar, and the truth is not in him. But whoso keepeth his word, in him verily is the love of God perfected." 1 John 2:4, 5. Here is the test of every man's profession. If men belittle and make light of

God's precepts, if they "break one of the least of these commandments and teach men so" (Matthew 5:18, 19), we may know that their claims are without foundation.

The claim to be without sin is evidence that he who makes this claim is far from holy. He has no true conception of the infinite purity and holiness of God, and the malignity and evil of sin. The greater the distance between himself and Christ, the more righteous he appears in his own eyes.

Biblical Sanctification

Sanctification embraces the entire being—spirit, soul, and body. See 1 Thessalonians 5:23. Christians are bidden to present their bodies, "a living sacrifice, holy, acceptable unto God." Romans 12:1. Every practice that weakens physical or mental strength unfits man for the service of his Creator. Those who love God with all their heart will constantly seek to bring every power of their being into harmony with the laws that promote their ability to do His will. They will not by indulgence of appetite or passion enfeeble or defile the offering they present to their heavenly Father.

Every sinful gratification tends to benumb and deaden the mental and spiritual perceptions; the Word or Spirit of God can make but a feeble impression on the heart. "Let us cleanse ourselves from all filthiness of the flesh and spirit, perfecting holiness in the fear of God." 2 Corinthians 7:1.

How many professed Christians are debasing their godlike manhood by gluttony, by wine drinking, by forbidden pleasure. And the church too often encourages the evil, to replenish her treasury which love for Christ is too feeble to supply. Were Jesus to enter the churches of today and behold the feasting there conducted in the name of religion, would He not drive out those desecrators, as He banished the moneychangers from the temple?

"Know ye not that your body is the temple of the

Holy Ghost which is in you, which ye have of God, and ye are not your own? for ye are bought with a price: therefore glorify God in your body, and in your spirit, which are God's." 1 Corinthians 6:19, 20. He whose body is the temple of the Holy Spirit will not be enslaved by a pernicious habit. His powers belong to Christ. His property is the Lord's. How could he squander this entrusted capital?

Professed Christians yearly expend an immense sum on pernicious indulgences. God is robbed in tithes and offerings, while they consume on the altar of destroying lust more than they give to relieve the poor or support the gospel. If all who profess Christ were truly sanctified, their means, instead of being spent for needless and hurtful indulgences, would be turned into the Lord's treasury. Christians would set an example of temperance and self-sacrifice. Then they would be the light of the world.

"The lust of the flesh, the lust of the eyes, and the pride of life" (1 John 2:16) control the masses. But Christ's followers have a holier calling. "Come out from among them, and be ye separate, saith the Lord, and touch not the unclean." To those who comply with the conditions, God's promise is, "I will receive you, and will be a Father unto you, and ye shall be my sons and daughters, saith the Lord Almighty." 2 Corinthians 6:17, 18.

Every step of faith and obedience brings the soul into closer connection with the Light of the World. The bright beams of the Sun of Righteousness shine upon the servants of God, and they are to reflect His rays. The stars tell us that there is a light in heaven with whose glory they are made bright; so Christians make it manifest that there is a God on the throne whose character is worthy of praise and imitation. The holiness of His character will be manifest in His witnesses.

Through the merits of Christ we have access to the throne of Infinite Power. "He that spared not his own Son, but delivered him up for us all, how shall he not with him also freely give us all things?'' Jesus says: ''If ye then, being evil, know how to give good gifts unto your children: how much more shall your heavenly Father give the Holy Spirit to them that ask him?'' ''If ye shall ask anything in my name, I will do it.'' ''Ask, and ye shall receive, that your joy may be full.'' Romans 8:32; Luke 11:13; John 14:14; 16:24.

It is the privilege of everyone so to live that God will approve and bless him. It is not the will of our heavenly Father that we should be ever under condemnation and darkness. There is no evidence of true humility in going with the head bowed down and the heart filled with thoughts of self. We may go to Jesus and be cleansed and stand before the law without shame and remorse.

Through Jesus the fallen sons of Adam become ''sons of God.'' ''He is not ashamed to call them brethren.'' The Christian's life should be one of faith, victory, and joy in God. ''The *joy* of the Lord is your strength.'' ''Rejoice evermore. Pray without ceasing. In everything give thanks: for this is the will of God in Christ Jesus concerning you.'' Hebrews 2:11; Nehemiah 8:10; 1 Thessalonians 5:16-18.

Such are the fruits of Bible conversion and sanctification; and it is because the great principles of righteousness set forth in the law are so indifferently regarded that these fruits are so rarely witnessed. This is why there is manifest so little of that deep, abiding work of the Spirit which marked former revivals.

It is by beholding that we become changed. As those sacred precepts in which God has opened to men the perfection and holiness of His character are neglected, and the minds of the people are attracted to human teachings and theories, there has followed a decline of piety in the church. It is only as the law of God is restored to its rightful position that there can be a revival of primitive faith and godliness among His professed people.

28/Facing Our Life Record

"I beheld till thrones were placed, and One that was ancient of days did sit: his raiment was white as snow, and the hair of his head like pure wool; his throne was fiery flames, and the wheels thereof burning fire. A fiery stream issued and came forth from before him: thousands of thousands ministered unto him, and ten thousand times ten thousand stood before him: the judgment was set, and the books were opened." Daniel 7:9, 10, R.V.

Thus was presented to Daniel's vision the great day when the lives of men pass in review before the Judge of all the earth. The Ancient of Days is God the Father. He, the source of all being, the fountain of all law, is to preside in the judgment. And holy angels as ministers and witnesses, attend.

"And, behold, one like the Son of man came with the clouds of heaven, and came to the Ancient of Days, and they brought him near before him. And there was given him dominion, and glory, and a kingdom, that all people, nations, and languages, should serve him: his dominion is an everlasting dominion, which shall not pass away." Daniel 7:13, 14.

The coming of Christ here described is not His second coming to the earth. He comes to the Ancient of Days in heaven to receive a kingdom which will be given Him at the close of His work as mediator. It is this coming, and not His second advent to the earth, that was to take place at the termination of the 2300 days in 1844. Our great High Priest enters the holy of holies to engage in His last ministration in behalf of man.

In the typical service only those whose sins were transferred to the sanctuary had a part in the Day of Atonement. So in the great final atonement and investigative judgment the only cases considered are those of the professed people of God. The judgment of the wicked is a separate work at a later period. "Judgment must begin at the house of God." 1 Peter 4:17.

The books of record in heaven are to determine the decisions of the judgment. The book of life contains the names of all who have ever entered the service of God. Jesus bade His disciples: "Rejoice, because your names are written in heaven." Paul speaks of his fellow workers, "whose names are in the book of life." Daniel declares that God's people shall be delivered, "every one that shall be found written in the book." And the revelator says that those only shall enter the City of God whose names "are written in the Lamb's book of life." Luke 10:20; Philippians 4:3; Daniel 12:1; Revelation 21:27.

In "a book of remembrance" are recorded the good deeds of "them that feared the Lord, and that thought upon his name." Every temptation resisted, every evil overcome, every word of pity expressed, every act of sacrifice, every sorrow endured for Christ's sake is recorded. "Thou tellest my wanderings: put thou my tears into thy bottle: are they not in thy book?" Malachi 3:16; Psalm 56:8.

Secret Motives

There is a record also of the sins of men. "God shall bring every work into judgment, with every secret thing, whether it be good, or whether it be evil." "Every idle word that men shall speak, they shall give account thereof in the day of judgment." "By thy words thou shalt be justified, and by thy words thou shalt be condemned." Secret motives appear in the register, for God "will bring to light the hidden things of darkness, and will make manifest the counsels of the hearts." Ecclesiastes 12:14; Matthew 12:36, 37; 1 Corinthians 4:5. Opposite each name in the books of heaven is entered every wrong word, every selfish act, every unfulfilled duty, and every secret sin. Heaven-sent warnings or reproofs neglected, wasted moments, the influence exerted for good or for evil with its far-reaching results, all are chronicled by the recording angel.

The Standard of Judgment

The law of God is the standard in the judgment. "Fear God, and keep his commandments: for this is the whole duty of man. For God shall bring every work into judgment." "So speak ye, and so do, as they that shall be judged by the law of liberty." Ecclesiastes 12:13, 14; James 2:12.

Those "accounted worthy" will have part in the resurrection of the just. Jesus said: "They which shall be accounted worthy to obtain that world, and the resurrection from the dead, . . . are the children of God, being the children of the resurrection." "They that have done good" shall come forth "unto the resurrection of life." Luke 20:35, 36; John 5:29. The righteous dead will not be raised until after the judgment at which they are accounted worthy of "the resurrection of life." Hence they will not be present in person when their records are examined and their cases decided.

Jesus will appear as their advocate, to plead in their behalf before God. "If any man sin, we have an advocate with the Father, Jesus Christ the righteous." "For Christ is not entered into the holy places made with hands, which are the figures of the true; but into heaven itself, now to appear in the presence of God for us." "Wherefore he is able also to save them to the uttermost that come unto God by him, seeing he ever liveth to make intercession for them." 1 John 2:1; Hebrews 7:25; 9:24.

As the books of record are opened in the judgment,

the lives of all who have believed on Jesus come in review before God. Beginning with those who first lived upon the earth, our Advocate presents the cases of each successive generation. Every name is mentioned, every case investigated. Names are accepted, names rejected. When any have sins remaining upon the books of record, unrepented of and unforgiven, their names will be blotted out of the book of life. The Lord declared to Moses: ''Whosoever hath sinned against me, him will I blot out of my book.'' Exodus 32:33.

All who have truly repented and by faith claimed the blood of Christ as their atoning sacrifice have had pardon entered in the books of heaven. As they have become partakers of the righteousness of Christ and their characters are found to be in harmony with the law of God, their sins will be blotted out, and they will be accounted worthy of eternal life. The Lord declares: ''I, even I, am he that blotteth out thy transgressions for mine own sake, and will not remember thy sins.'' ''He that overcometh, the same shall be clothed in white raiment; and I will . . . confess his name before my Father, and before his angels.'' ''Whosoever therefore shall confess me before men, him will I confess also before my Father which is in heaven. But whosoever shall deny me before men, him will I also deny before my Father which is in heaven.'' Isaiah 43:25; Revelation 3:5; Matthew 10:32, 33.

The divine Intercessor presents the plea that all who have overcome through faith in His blood be restored to their Eden home and crowned as joint heirs with Himself to ''the first dominion.'' Micah 4:8. Christ now asks that the divine plan in man's creation be carried into effect as if man had never fallen. He asks for His people not only pardon and justification, but a share in His glory and a seat upon His throne.

While Jesus is pleading for the subjects of His grace, Satan accuses them before God. He points to the record of their lives, the defects of character, the unlikeness to Christ, to all the sins he has tempted them to commit. Because of these he claims them as his subjects.

Jesus does not excuse their sins, but shows their penitence and faith. Claiming for them forgiveness, He lifts His wounded hands before the Father, saying: I have graven them on the palms of My hands. "The sacrifices of God are a broken spirit: a broken and a contrite heart, O God, thou wilt not despise." Psalm 51:17.

The Lord Rebukes Satan

And to the accuser He declares: "The Lord rebuke thee, O Satan; even the Lord that hath chosen Jerusalem rebuke thee: is not this a brand plucked out of the fire?" Zechariah 3:2. Christ will clothe His faithful ones with His own righteousness, that He may present them to His Father "a glorious church, not having spot, or wrinkle, or any such thing." Ephesians 5:27.

Thus will be realized the complete fulfillment of the new-covenant promise: "I will forgive their iniquity, and I will remember their sin no more." "In those days, and in that time, saith the Lord, the iniquity of Israel shall be sought for, and there shall be none; and the sins of Judah, and they shall not be found." "And it shall come to pass, that he that is left in Zion, and he that remaineth in Jerusalem, shall be called holy, even every one that is written among the living in Jerusalem." Jeremiah 31:34; 50:20; Isaiah 4:3.

The Blotting Out of Sins

The work of investigative judgment and blotting out of sins is to be accomplished before the second advent of the Lord. In the typical service the high priest came forth and blessed the congregation. So Christ, at the close of His work as mediator, will appear "without sin unto salvation." Hebrews 9:28.

The priest, in removing the sins from the sanctuary, confessed them upon the head of the scapegoat. Christ will place all these sins upon Satan, the instigator of sin. The scapegoat was sent away "unto a land not inhabited.'' Leviticus 16:22. Satan, bearing the guilt of sins he has caused God's people to commit, will for a thousand years be confined to the desolate earth and will at last suffer the penalty of fire that shall destroy the wicked. Thus the plan of redemption will reach its accomplishment in the final eradication of sin.

At the Time Appointed

At the time appointed—the close of the 2300 days in 1844—began the work of investigation and blotting out of sins. Sins not repented of and forsaken will not be blotted out of the books of record. Angels of God witnessed each sin and registered it. Sin may be denied, covered up from father, mother, wife, children, and associates; but it is laid bare before heaven. God is not deceived by appearances. He makes no mistakes. Men may be deceived by those corrupt in heart, but God reads the inner life.

How solemn is the thought! The mightiest conquerer on earth cannot call back the record of a single day. Our acts, our words, even our secret motives, though forgotten by us, will bear their testimony to justify or condemn.

In the judgment the use made of every talent will be scrutinized. How have we used our time, our pen, our voice, our money, our influence? What have we done for Christ in the person of the poor, the afflicted, the orphan, or the widow? What have we done with the light and truth given us? Only the love shown by works is counted genuine. Love alone in the sight of Heaven makes any act of value.

Hidden Selfishness Revealed

Hidden selfishness stands revealed in the books of heaven. How often were given to Satan the time, thought, and strength that belonged to Christ. Professed followers of Christ are absorbed in the acquirement of worldly possessions or the enjoyment of earthly pleasures. Money, time, and strength are sacrificed for display and self-indulgence; few are the moments devoted to prayer, to the searching of Scripture, to confession of sin.

Satan invents unnumbered schemes to occupy our minds. The archdeceiver hates the great truths that bring to view an atoning sacrifice and an all-powerful Mediator. With him everything depends on diverting minds from Jesus.

Those who would share the benefits of the Saviour's mediation should permit nothing to interfere with their duty to perfect holiness in the fear of God. The precious hours, instead of being given to pleasure or to gain-seeking, should be devoted to prayerful study of the Word of Truth. The sanctuary and the investigative judgment should be clearly understood. All need a knowledge of the position and work of their great High Priest. Otherwise it will be impossible to exercise the faith essential at this time.

The sanctuary in heaven is the center of Christ's work in behalf of men. It concerns every soul living on earth. It opens to view the plan of redemption, bringing us down to the close of the contest between righteousness and sin.

The Intercession of Christ

The intercession of Christ in man's behalf in the sanctuary above is as essential to the plan of salvation as was His death on the cross. By His death He began that work which He ascended to complete in heaven. We must by faith enter within the veil, "whither the forerunner is for us entered." Hebrews 6:20. There the light from the cross is reflected. There we gain a clearer insight into the mysteries of redemption.

"He that covereth his sins shall not prosper: but whoso confesseth and forsaketh them shall have mercy." Proverbs 28:13. If those who excuse their faults could see how Satan taunts Christ with their course, they would confess their sins and put them away. Satan works to gain control of the whole mind, and he knows that if defects are cherished, he will succeed. Therefore he constantly seeks to deceive the followers of Christ with his fatal sophistry that it is impossible for them to overcome. But Jesus declared to all who would follow Him: "My grace is sufficient for thee." "My yoke is easy, and my burden is light." 2 Corinthians 12:9; Matthew 11:30. Let none regard their defects as incurable. God will give faith and grace to overcome.

We are now living in the great day of atonement. While the high priest was making atonement for Israel, all were required to afflict their souls by repentance of sin. In like manner, all who would have their names retained in the book of life should now afflict their souls before God by true repentance. There must be deep, faithful searching of heart. The frivolous spirit indulged by so many must be put away. There is earnest warfare before all who would subdue the evil tendencies that strive for mastery. Every one must be found without "spot, or wrinkle, or any such thing." Ephesians 5:27.

At this time above all others it behooves every soul to heed the Saviour's admonition: "Watch and pray: for ye know not when the time is." Mark 13:33.

The Destiny of All Decided

Probation is ended a short time before the appearing of the Lord in the clouds of heaven. Christ, looking forward to that time, declares: "He that is unjust, let him be unjust still: and he which is filthy, let him be filthy still: and he that is righteous, let him be righteous still: and he that is holy, let him be holy still. And, behold, I come quickly; and my reward is with me, to give every man according as his work shall be." Revelation 22:11, 12.

Men will be planting and building, eating and drinking, all unconscious that the final decision has been pronounced in the sanctuary above. Before the Flood, after Noah entered the ark, God shut him in and shut the ungodly out; but for seven days the people continued their pleasure-loving life and mocked the warnings of judgment. "So," says the Saviour, "shall also the coming of the Son of man be." Silently, unnoticed as the midnight thief, will come the hour which marks the fixing of every man's destiny. "Watch ye therefore: . . . lest coming suddenly he find you sleeping." Matthew 24:39; Mark 13:35, 36.

Perilous is the condition of those who, growing weary of their watch, turn to the attractions of the world. While the man of business is absorbed in the pursuit of gain, while the pleasure-lover is seeking indulgence, while the daughter of fashion is arranging her adornments—it may be in that hour the Judge of all the earth will pronounce the sentence, "Thou art weighed in the balances, and art found wanting." Daniel 5:27.

29/ Why Was Sin Permitted?

Many see the work of evil, with its woe and desolation, and question how this can exist under the sovereignty of One who is infinite in wisdom, power, and love. Those who are disposed to doubt seize upon this as an excuse for rejecting the words of Holy Writ. Tradition and misinterpretation have obscured the teaching of the Bible concerning the character of God, the nature of His government, and the principles of His dealing with sin.

It is impossible to explain the origin of sin so as to give a reason for its existence. Yet enough may be understood concerning the origin and final disposition of sin to make fully manifest the justice and benevolence of God. God was in no wise responsible for sin; there was no arbitrary withdrawal of divine grace, no deficiency in the divine government, that gave occasion for rebellion. Sin is an intruder for whose presence no reason can be given. To excuse it is to defend it. Could excuse for it be found, it would cease to be sin. Sin is the outworking of a principle at war with the law of love, which is the foundation of the divine government.

Before the entrance of evil there was peace and joy throughout the universe. Love for God was supreme, love for one another impartial. Christ the Only Begotten of God was one with the eternal Father in nature, in character, and in purpose—the only being that could enter into all the counsels and purposes of God. "By him were all things created, that are in heaven, . . . whether they be thrones, or dominions, or principalities, or powers." Colossians 1:16.

The law of love being the foundation of the government of God, the happiness of all created beings depended on their accord with its principles of righteousness. God takes no pleasure in forced allegiance, and to all He grants freedom of will, that they may render Him voluntary service.

But there was one that chose to pervert this freedom. Sin originated with him, who, next to Christ, had been most honored by God. Before his fall, Lucifer was first of the covering cherubs, holy and undefiled. "Thus saith the Lord God; Thou sealest up the sum, full of wisdom, and perfect in beauty. Thou hast been in Eden the garden of God; every precious stone was thy covering. . . . Thou art the anointed cherub that covereth; and I have set thee so: thou wast upon the holy mountain of God; thou hast walked up and down in the midst of the stones of fire. Thou wast perfect in thy ways from the day that thou wast created, till iniquity was found in thee. . . . Thine heart was lifted up because of thy beauty, thou hast corrupted thy wisdom by reason of thy brightness." "Thou hast set thine heart as the heart of God." "Thou hast said, . . . I will exalt my throne above the stars of God. I will sit also upon the mount of the congregation. . . . I will ascend above the heights of the clouds; I will be like the most High." Ezekiel 28:12-17; 28:6; Isaiah 14:13, 14.

Coveting the honor which the Father had bestowed upon His Son, this prince of angels aspired to power which it was the prerogative of Christ alone to wield. A note of discord now marred the celestial harmonies. The exaltation of self awakened forebodings of evil in minds to whom God's glory was supreme. The heavenly councils pleaded with Lucifer. The Son of God presented before him the goodness and justice of the Creator and the sacred nature of His law. In departing from it, Lucifer would dishonor his Maker and bring ruin on himself. But the warning only aroused resistance. Lucifer allowed jealousy of Christ to prevail.

Pride nourished the desire for supremacy. The high

honors conferred on Lucifer called forth no gratitude to the Creator. He aspired to be equal with God. Yet the Son of God was the acknowledged Sovereign of heaven, one in power and authority with the Father. In all the counsels of God, Christ was a participant, but Lucifer was not permitted to enter into the divine purposes. "Why," questioned this mighty angel, "should Christ have the supremacy? Why is He thus honored above Lucifer?"

Discontent Among the Angels

Leaving his place in the presence of God, Lucifer went forth to diffuse discontent among the angels. With mysterious secrecy, concealing his real purpose under an appearance of reverence for God, he endeavored to excite dissatisfaction concerning the laws that governed heavenly beings, intimating that they imposed unnecessary restraint. Since their natures were holy, he urged that angels should obey the dictates of their own will. God had dealt unjustly with him in bestowing supreme honor upon Christ. He claimed he was not aiming at self-exaltation but was seeking to secure liberty for all the inhabitants of heaven, that they might attain a higher existence.

God bore long with Lucifer. He was not degraded from his exalted station even when he began to present false claims before the angels. Again and again he was offered pardon on condition of repentance and submission. Such efforts as only infinite love could devise were made to convince him of his error. Discontent had never before been known in heaven. Lucifer himself did not at first understand the real nature of his feelings. As his dissatisfaction was proved to be without cause, Lucifer was convinced that the divine claims were just and that he ought to acknowledge them before all heaven. Had he done this, he might have saved himself and many angels. If he had been willing to return to God, satisfied to fill the place appointed him, he would have been reinstated in his office. But pride forbade him to submit. He maintained that he had no need of repentance, and fully committed himself in the great controversy against his Maker.

All the powers of his master mind were now bent to deception, to secure the sympathy of the angels. Satan represented that he was wrongly judged and that his liberty was abridged. From misrepresentation of the words of Christ he passed to direct falsehood, accusing the Son of God of a design to humiliate him before the inhabitants of heaven.

All whom he could not subvert to his side he accused of indifference to the interests of heavenly beings. He resorted to misrepresentation of the Creator. It was his policy to perplex the angels with subtle arguments concerning the purposes of God. Everything simple he shrouded in mystery, and by artful perversion cast doubt upon the plainest statements of God. His high position gave greater force to his representations. Many were induced to unite with him in rebellion.

Disaffection Ripens Into Active Revolt

God in His wisdom permitted Satan to carry forward his work, until the spirit of disaffection ripened into revolt. It was necessary for his plans to be fully developed, that their true nature might be seen by all. Lucifer was greatly loved by the heavenly beings, and his influence over them was strong. God's government included not only the inhabitants of heaven, but of all the worlds He had created; and Satan thought that if he could carry the angels with him in rebellion, he could carry also the other worlds. Employing sophistry and fraud, his power to deceive was very great. Even the loyal angels could not fully discern his character or see to what his work was leading.

Satan had been so highly honored, and all his acts were so clothed with mystery, that it was difficult to disclose to the angels the true nature of his work. Until fully developed, sin would not appear the evil thing it was. Holy beings could not discern the consequences of setting aside the divine law. Satan at first claimed to be seeking to promote the honor of God and the good of all the inhabitants of heaven.

In His dealing with sin, God could employ only righteousness and truth. Satan could use what God could not—flattery and deceit. The true character of the usurper must be understood by all. He must have time to manifest himself by his wicked works.

The discord which his own course had caused in heaven, Satan charged upon God. All evil he declared to be the result of the divine administration. Therefore it was necessary that he demonstrate the working out of his proposed changes in the divine law. His own work must condemn him. The whole universe must see the deceiver unmasked.

Even when it was decided that he could no longer remain in heaven, Infinite Wisdom did not destroy Satan. The allegiance of God's creatures must rest upon a conviction of His justice. The inhabitants of heaven and of other worlds, being unprepared to comprehend the consequences of sin, could not then have seen the justice and mercy of God in the destruction of Satan. Had he been immediately blotted from existence, they would have served God from fear rather than from love. The influence of the deceiver would not have been fully destroyed, nor the spirit of rebellion eradicated. For the good of the universe through ceaseless ages Satan must more fully develop his principles, that his charges against the divine government might be seen in their true light by all created beings.

Satan's rebellion was to be to the universe a testimony to the terrible results of sin. His rule would show the fruit of setting aside the divine authority. The history of this terrible experiment of rebellion was to be a perpetual safeguard to all holy intelligences to save them from sin and its punishment.

When it was announced that with all his sympathizers the great usurper must be expelled from the abodes of bliss, the rebel leader boldly avowed contempt for the Creator's law. He denounced the divine statutes as a restriction of liberty and declared his purpose to secure the abolition of law. Freed from this restraint, the hosts of heaven might enter upon a more exalted state of existence.

Banished From Heaven

Satan and his host threw the blame of their rebellion upon Christ; if they had not been reproved, they would never have rebelled. Stubborn and defiant, yet blasphemously claiming to be innocent victims of oppressive power, the archrebel and his sympathizers were banished from heaven. See Revelation 12:7-9.

Satan's spirit still inspires rebellion on earth in the children of disobedience. Like him they promise men liberty through transgression of the law of God. Reproof of sin still arouses hatred. Satan leads men to justify themselves and seek the sympathy of others in their sin. Instead of correcting their errors, they excite indignation against the reprover, as if he were the cause of difficulty.

By the same misrepresentation of the character of God as he had practiced in heaven, causing Him to be regarded as severe and tyrannical, Satan induced man to sin. He declared that God's unjust restrictions had led to man's fall, as they had led to his own rebellion.

In the banishment of Satan from heaven, God declared His justice and honor. But when man sinned, God gave evidence of His love by yielding up His Son to die for the fallen race. In the atonement the character of God is revealed. The mighty argument of the cross demonstrates that sin was in no wise chargeable upon the government of God. During the Saviour's earthly ministry, the great deceiver was unmasked. The daring blasphemy of his demand that Christ pay him homage, the unsleeping malice that hunted Him from place to place, inspiring the hearts of priests and people to reject His love and to cry, "Crucify him! crucify him!"—all this excited the amazement and indignation of the universe. The prince of evil exerted all his power and cunning to destroy Jesus. Satan employed men as his agents to fill the Saviour's life with suffering and sorrow. The pent-up fires of envy and malice, hatred and revenge, burst forth on Calvary against the Son of God.

Now the guilt of Satan stood forth without excuse. He had revealed his true character. Satan's lying charges against the divine character appeared in their true light. He had accused God of seeking the exaltation of Himself in requiring obedience from His creatures and had declared that while the Creator exacted self-denial from all others, He Himself practiced no self-denial and made no sacrifice. Now it was seen that the Ruler of the universe had made the greatest sacrifice which love could make, for "God was in Christ, reconciling the world unto himself." 2 Corinthians 5:19. In order to destroy sin Christ had humbled Himself and become obedient unto death.

An Argument in Man's Behalf

All heaven saw God's justice revealed. Lucifer had claimed that the sinful race were beyond redemption. But the penalty of the law fell upon Him who was equal with God, and man was free to accept the righteousness of Christ and by penitence and humiliation to triumph over the power of Satan.

But it was not merely to redeem man that Christ came to earth to die. He came to demonstrate to all the worlds that God's law is unchangeable. The death of Christ proves it immutable and demonstrates that justice and mercy are the foundation of the government of God. In the final judgment it will be seen that no cause for sin exists. When the Judge of all the earth shall demand of Satan, "Why hast thou rebelled against Me?" the originator of evil can render no excuse.

In the Saviour's expiring cry, "It is finished," the death knell of Satan was rung. The great controversy was then decided, the final eradication of evil made certain. When "the day cometh, that shall burn as an oven; . . . all the proud, yea, and all that do wickedly, shall be stubble, and the day that cometh shall burn them up, saith the Lord of hosts, that it shall leave them neither root nor branch." Malachi 4:1.

Never will evil again be manifest. The law of God will be honored as the law of liberty. A tested and proved creation will never again turn from allegiance to Him whose character has been manifested as fathomless love and infinite wisdom.

30/ Satan and Man at War

"I will put enmity between thee and the woman, and between thy seed and her seed; it shall bruise thy head and thou shalt bruise his heel." Genesis 3:15. This enmity is not natural. When man transgressed the divine law, his nature became evil, in harmony with Satan. Fallen angels and wicked men united in desperate companionship. Had not God interposed, Satan and man would have entered into an alliance against Heaven, and the whole human family would have been united in opposition to God.

When Satan heard that enmity should exist between himself and the woman, and between his seed and her seed, he knew that by some means man was to be enabled to resist his power.

Christ implants in man enmity against Satan. Without this converting grace and renewing power, man would continue a servant ever ready to do Satan's bidding. But the new principle in the soul creates conflict; the power which Christ imparts enables man to resist the tyrant. To abhor sin instead of loving it displays a principle wholly from above.

The antagonism between Christ and Satan was strikingly displayed in the world's reception of Jesus. The purity and holiness of Christ called forth against Him the hatred of the ungodly. His self-denial was a perpetual reproof to a proud, sensual people. Satan and evil angels joined with evil men against the Champion of truth. The same enmity is manifested toward Christ's followers. Whoever resists temptation will arouse the wrath of Satan. Christ and Satan cannot harmonize. "All that will live godly in Christ Jesus shall suffer persecution." 2 Timothy 3:12.

Satan's agents seek to deceive Christ's followers and allure them from their allegiance. They pervert Scripture to accomplish their object. The spirit which put Christ to death moves the wicked to destroy His followers. All this is foreshadowed in that first prophecy: "I will put enmity between thee and the woman, and between thy seed and her seed."

Why is it that Satan meets no greater resistance? Because the soldiers of Christ have so little real connection with Christ. Sin is not to them repulsive as it was to their Master. They do not meet it with determined resistance. They are blinded to the character of the prince of darkness. Multitudes do not know that their enemy is a mighty general warring against Christ. Even ministers of the gospel overlook the evidences of his activity. They seem to ignore his very existence.

A Vigilant Foe

This vigilant foe is intruding his presence in every household, in every street, in the churches, in national councils, in courts of justice. Perplexing, deceiving, seducing, everywhere ruining the souls and bodies of men, women, and children. He breaks up families, sowing hatred, strife, sedition, and murder. And the world seems to regard these things as though God had appointed them and they must exist. All who are not decided followers of Christ are servants of Satan. When Christians choose the society of the ungodly, they expose themselves to temptation. Satan conceals himself from view and draws his deceptive covering over their eyes.

Conformity to worldly customs converts the church to the world, never the world to Christ. Familiarity with sin will cause it to appear less repulsive. When in the way of duty we are brought into trial, we may be sure God will protect us; but if we place ourselves under temptation we shall fall sooner or later.

The tempter often works most successfully through those least suspected of being under his control. Talent and culture are gifts of God; but when these lead away from Him, they become a snare. Many a man of cultured intellect and pleasant manners is a polished instrument in the hands of Satan.

Never forget the inspired warning sounding down the centuries to our time: "Be sober, be vigilant; because your adversary the devil, as a roaring lion, walketh about, seeking whom he may devour." "Put on the whole armour of God, that ye may be able to stand against the wiles of the devil." 1 Peter 5:8; Ephesians 6:11. Our great enemy is preparing for his last campaign. All who follow Jesus will be in conflict with this foe. The more nearly the Christian imitates the divine Pattern, the more surely will he make himself a mark for the attacks of Satan.

Satan assailed Christ with fierce and subtle temptations; but he was repulsed in every conflict. Those victories make it possible for us to conquer. Christ will give strength to all who seek it. No man without his own consent can be overcome by Satan. The tempter has no power to control the will or force the soul to sin. He can cause distress, but not defilement. The fact that Christ conquered should inspire His followers with courage to fight the battle against sin and Satan.

31/ Evil Spirits

Angels of God and evil spirits are plainly revealed in Scripture and interwoven with human history. Holy angels that "minister for them who shall be heirs of salvation" (Hebrews 1:14) are regarded by many as spirits of the dead. But the Scriptures present proof that these are not disembodied spirits of the dead.

Before the creation of man, angels were in existence, for when the foundations of the earth were laid, "the morning stars sang together, and all the sons of God shouted for joy." Job 38:7. After the fall of man, angels were sent to guard the tree of life before a human being had died. Angels are superior to men, for man was made "a little lower than the angels." Psalm 8:5.

Says the prophet, "I heard the voice of many angels round about the throne." In the presence of the King of kings they wait—"ministers of his, that do his pleasure," "hearkening unto the voice of his word," "an innumerable company." Revelation 5:11; Psalm 103:20, 21; Hebrews 12:22. As God's messengers they go forth, like "the appearance of a flash of lightning," so swift their flight. The angel that appeared at the Saviour's tomb, his countenance "like lightning," caused the keepers for fear of him to quake, and they "became as dead men." When Sennacherib blasphemed God and threatened Israel, "the angel of the Lord went out, and smote in the camp of the Assyrians an hundred fourscore and five thousand." Ezekiel 1:14; Matthew 28:3, 4; 2 Kings 19:35.

Angels are sent on missions of mercy to the children of God. To Abraham, with promises of blessing; to Sodom, to rescue Lot from doom; to Elijah, about to perish in the desert; to Elisha, with chariots and horses of fire when he was shut in by his foes; to Daniel, while abandoned to become the lion's prey; to Peter, doomed to death in Herod's dungeon; to the prisoners at Philippi; to Paul in the night of tempest on the sea; to open the mind of Cornelius to receive the gospel; to dispatch Peter with the message of salvation to the Gentile stranger—thus holy angels have ministered to God's people.

Guardian Angels

A guardian angel is appointed to every follower of Christ. "The angel of the Lord encampeth round about them that fear him, and delivereth them." Said the Saviour, speaking of those that believe in Him: "In heaven their angels do always behold the face of my Father." Psalm 34:7; Matthew 18:10. God's people, exposed to the unsleeping malice of the prince of darkness, are assured of the unceasing guardianship of angels. Such assurance is given because there are mighty agencies of evil to be met—agencies numerous, determined, and untiring.

Evil spirits, in the beginning created sinless, were equal in nature, power, and glory with the holy beings that are now God's messengers. But fallen through sin, they are leagued together for the dishonor of God and the destruction of men. United with Satan in rebellion, they cooperate in warfare against divine authority.

Old Testament history mentions their existence, but during the time when Christ was on earth evil spirits manifested their power in the most striking manner. Christ had come for man's redemption, and Satan determined to control the world. He had succeeded in establishing idolatry in every part of the earth except Palestine. To the only land not fully yielded to the tempter, Christ came, stretching out His arms of love, inviting all to find pardon and peace in Him. The hosts of darkness understood that if Christ's mission should be successful, their rule was soon to end.

That men have been possessed with demons is clearly stated in the New Testament. Persons thus afflicted were not merely suffering with disease from natural causes; Christ recognized the direct presence and agency of evil spirits. The demoniacs at Gadara, wretched maniacs, writhing, foaming, raging, were doing violence to themselves and endangering all who should approach them. Their bleeding, disfigured bodies and distracted minds presented a spectacle well pleasing to the prince of darkness. One of the demons controlling the sufferers declared, "My name is Legion: for we are many." Mark 5:9. In the Roman army a legion consisted of from three to five thousand men. At the command of Jesus the evil spirits departed from their victims, leaving them subdued, intelligent, and gentle. But the demons swept a herd of swine into the sea, and to the dwellers of Gadara the loss outweighed the blessing Christ had bestowed; the divine Healer was intreated to depart. See Matthew 8:22-34. By casting the blame of their loss upon Jesus, Satan aroused the selfish fears of the people and prevented them from listening to His words.

Christ allowed the evil spirits to destroy the swine as a rebuke to Jews who were raising unclean beasts for gain. Had not Christ restrained the demons, they would have plunged not only the swine, but also their keepers and owners into the sea.

Furthermore, this event was permitted that the disciples might witness the cruel power of Satan upon both man and beast, that they might not be deceived by His devices. It was also His will that the people should behold His power to break the bondage of Satan and release his captives. Though Jesus Himself departed, the men so marvelously delivered remained to declare the mercy of their Benefactor.

Other instances are recorded: The daughter of the

Syrophoenician woman, grievously vexed with a devil, whom Jesus cast out by His word (Mark 7:26-30); a youth who had a spirit that ofttimes "cast him into the fire, and into the waters, to destroy him" (Mark 9: 17-27); the maniac, tormented by a spirit of an unclean devil who disturbed the Sabbath quiet at Capernaum (Luke 4:33-36)—all were healed by the Saviour. In nearly every instance, Christ addressed the demon as an intelligent entity, commanding him to torment his victim no more. The worshipers at Capernaum "were all amazed, and spake among themselves, saying, What a word is this! for with authority and power he commandeth the unclean spirits, and they come out." Luke 4:36.

For the sake of obtaining supernatural power, some welcomed the satanic influence. These of course had no conflict with the demons. Of this class were those who possessed the spirit of divination—Simon Magus, Elymas the sorcerer, and the damsel who followed Paul and Silas at Philippi. See Acts 8:9, 18; 13:8; 16:16-18.

None are in greater danger than those who deny the existence of the devil and his angels. Many heed their suggestions while they suppose themselves to be following their own wisdom. As we approach the close of time, when Satan is to work with greatest power to deceive, he spreads everywhere the belief that he does not exist. It is his policy to conceal himself and his manner of working.

The great deceiver fears that we shall become acquainted with his devices. To disguise his real character he has caused himself to be so represented as to excite ridicule or contempt. He is pleased to be painted as ludicrous, misshapen, half animal and half human. He is pleased to hear his name used in sport and mockery. Because he has masked himself with consummate skill, the question is widely asked: "Does such a being really exist?" It is because Satan can readily control the minds of those who are unconscious of his influence that the Word of God unveils before us his secret forces, thus placing us on guard.

We may find shelter and deliverance in the superior power of our Redeemer. We carefully secure our houses with bolts and locks to protect our property and lives from evil men, but seldom think of the evil angels against whose attacks we have, in our own strength, no defense. If permitted, they can distract our minds, torment our bodies, destroy our possessions and our lives. But those who follow Christ are safe under His watchcare. Angels that excel in strength are sent to protect them. The wicked one cannot break through the guard which God has stationed about His people.

32/ How to Defeat Satan

The great controversy between Christ and Satan is soon to close, and the wicked one redoubles his efforts to defeat the work of Christ in man's behalf. To hold people in darkness and impenitence till the Saviour's mediation is ended is the object he seeks to accomplish. When indifference prevails in the church, Satan is not concerned. But when souls inquire, ''What must I do to be saved?'' he is on the ground to match his power against Christ and to counteract the influence of the Holy Spirit.

On one occasion, when the angels came to present themselves before the Lord, Satan came also among them, not to bow before the Eternal King, but to further his malicious designs against the righteous. See Job 1:6. He is in attendance when men assemble for worship, working with diligence to control the minds of the worshipers. As he sees the messenger of God searching the Scriptures, he takes note of the subject to be presented. Then he employs his cunning and shrewdness so that the message may not reach those whom he is deceiving on that very point. The one who most needs the warning will be urged into some business transaction or will by some other means be prevented from hearing the word.

Satan sees the Lord's servants burdened because of the darkness that enshrouds the people. He hears their prayers for divine grace and power to break the spell of indifference and indolence. Then with renewed zeal he tempts men to the indulgence of appetite or self-gratification, and thus benumbs their sensibilities so that they fail to hear the very things they most need to learn.

Satan knows that all who neglect prayer and the Scriptures will be overcome by his attacks. Therefore he invents every possible device to engross the mind. His right-hand helpers are always active when God is at work. They will present the most earnest, self-denying servants of Christ as deceived or deceivers. It is their work to misrepresent the motives of every noble deed, to circulate insinuations, and arouse suspicion in the minds of the inexperienced. But it may be readily seen whose children they are, whose example they follow, and whose work they do. "Ye shall know them by their fruits." Matthew 7:16; also see Revelation 12:10.

The Truth Sanctifies

The great deceiver has many heresies prepared to suit the varied tastes of those whom he would ruin. It is his plan to bring into the church insincere, unregenerate elements that will encourage doubt and unbelief. Many who have no real faith in God assent to some principles of truth and pass as Christians, and thus are enabled to introduce error as scriptural doctrine. Satan knows that the truth, received in love, sanctifies the soul. Therefore he seeks to substitute false theories, fables, another gospel. From the beginning, servants of God have contended against false teachers, not merely as vicious men, but as inculcators of falsehoods fatal to the soul. Elijah, Jeremiah, Paul, firmly opposed those who were turning men from the Word of God. That liberality which regards a correct faith as unimportant found no favor with these holy defenders of truth.

The vague and fanciful interpretations of Scripture and conflicting theories in the Christian world are the work of our great adversary to confuse minds. The discord and division among the churches are in a great measure due to wresting the Scriptures to support a favorite theory.

In order to sustain erroneous doctrines, some seize upon passages of Scripture separated from the context, quoting half a verse as proving their point, when the remaining portion shows the meaning to be the opposite. With the cunning of the serpent they entrench themselves behind disconnected utterances construed to suit carnal desires. Others seize upon figures and symbols, interpret them to suit their fancy, with little regard to the testimony of Scripture as its own interpreter, and then present their vagaries as the teachings of the Bible.

The Whole Bible a Guide

Whenever the study of the Scriptures is entered upon without a prayerful, teachable spirit, the plainest passages will be wrested from their true meaning. The whole Bible should be given to the people just as it reads.

God gave the sure word of prophecy; angels and even Christ Himself came to make known to Daniel and John things that "must shortly come to pass." Revelation 1:1. Important matters that concern our salvation were not revealed in a way to perplex and mislead the honest seeker after truth. The Word of God is plain to all who study it with prayerful heart.

By the cry, Liberality, men are blinded to the devices of their adversary. He succeeds in supplanting the Bible by human speculations; the law of God is set aside; and the churches are under the bondage of sin while they claim to be free.

God has permitted a flood of light to be poured upon the world in discoveries in science. But even the greatest minds, if not guided by the Word of God, become bewildered in their attempts to investigate the relations of science and revelation.

Human knowledge is partial and imperfect; therefore many are unable to harmonize their views of science with Scripture. Many accept mere theories as scientific facts, and they think that God's Word is to be tested by "science falsely so called." 1 Timothy 6:20. Because they cannot explain the Creator and His works by natural laws, Bible history is regarded as unreliable. Those who doubt the Old and New Testaments too often go a step further and doubt the existence of God. Having let go their anchor, they beat about on the rocks of infidelity.

It is a masterpiece of Satan's deceptions to keep men conjecturing in regard to that which God has not made known. Lucifer became dissatisfied because all the secrets of God's purposes were not confided to him, and he disregarded that which was revealed. Now he seeks to imbue men with the same spirit and lead them also to disregard the direct commands of God.

Truth Rejected Because It Involves a Cross

The less spiritual and self-denying the doctrines presented, the greater the favor with which they are received. Satan is ready to supply the heart's desire, and he palms off deception in the place of truth. It was thus that the papacy gained its power over the minds of men. And by rejection of the truth because it involves a cross, Protestants are following the same path. All who study convenience and policy, that they may not be at variance with the world, will be left to receive "damnable heresy" for truth. 2 Peter 2:1. He who looks with horror upon one deception will readily receive another. "For this cause God shall send them strong delusion, that they should believe a lie: that they all might be damned who believe not the truth, but had pleasure in unrighteousness." 2 Thessalonians 2:11, 12.

Dangerous Errors

Among the most successful agencies of the great deceiver are the lying wonders of spiritualism. As men reject the truth they fall a prey to deception.

Another error is the doctrine that denies the deity of Christ, claiming that He had no existence before His advent to this world. This theory contradicts the statements of our Saviour concerning His relationship with the Father and His pre-existence. It undermines faith in the Bible as a revelation from God. If men reject the testimony of Scripture concerning the deity of Christ, it is vain to argue with them; no argument, however conclusive, could convince them. None who hold this error can have a true conception of Christ or of the plan of God for man's redemption.

Still another error is the belief that Satan has no existence as a personal being, that the name is used in Scripture merely to represent men's evil thoughts and desires.

The teaching that the second advent of Christ is His coming to each individual at death is a device to divert minds from His personal coming in the clouds of heaven. Satan has thus been saying, "Behold, he is in the secret chambers" (See Matthew 24:23-26), and many have been lost by accepting this deception.

Again men of science claim that there can be no real answer to prayer; this would be a violation of law—a miracle, and miracles have no existence. The universe, say they, is governed by fixed laws, and God Himself does nothing contrary to these laws. Thus they represent God as bound by His own laws—as if divine laws could exclude divine freedom.

Were not miracles wrought by Christ and His apostles? The same Saviour is as willing to listen to the prayer of faith as when He walked visibly among men. The natural cooperates with the supernatural. It is a part of God's plan to grant us, in answer to the prayer of faith, that which He would not bestow did we not thus ask.

The Landmarks of the Word

Erroneous doctrines among the churches remove landmarks fixed by the Word of God. Few stop with the rejection of a single truth. The majority set aside one after another of the principles of truth, until they become infidels.

The errors of popular theology have driven many a soul to skepticism. It is impossible for him to accept doctrines which outrage one's sense of justice, mercy, and benevolence. Since these are represented as the teaching of the Bible, he refuses to receive it as the Word of God.

The Word of God is looked upon with distrust because it reproves and condemns sin. Those unwilling to obey endeavor to overthrow its authority. Not a few become infidels in order to justify neglect of duty. Others, too ease-loving to accomplish anything which requires self-denial, secure a reputation for superior wisdom by criticizing the Bible.

Many feel it is a virtue to stand on the side of unbelief, skepticism, and infidelity. But underneath an appearance of candor will be found self-confidence and pride. Many delight in finding something in the Scriptures to puzzle the minds of others. Some at first reason on the wrong side from a mere love of controversy. But having openly expressed unbelief, they unite with the ungodly.

Sufficient Evidence

God has given in His Word sufficient evidence of its divine character. Yet finite minds are inadequate fully to comprehend the purposes of the Infinite One. "How unsearchable are his judgments, and his ways past finding out!" Romans 11:33. We can discern boundless love and mercy united to infinite power. Our Father in heaven will reveal to us as much as it is for our good to know; beyond that we must trust the Hand that is omnipotent, the Heart that is full of love.

God will never remove all excuse for unbelief. All who look for hooks to hang their doubts upon will find them. And those who refuse to obey until every objection has been removed will never come to the light. The unrenewed heart is at enmity with God. But faith is inspired by the Holy Spirit and will flourish as it is cherished. No man can become strong in faith without determined effort. If men permit themselves to cavil, they will find doubt becoming more confirmed.

But those who doubt and distrust the assurance of His grace dishonor Christ. They are unproductive trees that shut away the sunlight from other plants, causing them to droop and die under the chilling shadow. The lifework of these persons will appear as a never-ceasing witness against them.

There is but one cause for those to pursue who honestly desire to be freed from doubts. Instead of questioning that which they do not understand, let them give heed to the light which already shines upon them, and they will receive greater light.

Satan can present a counterfeit so closely resembling the truth that it deceives those willing to be deceived, who desire to shun the sacrifice demanded by the truth. But it is impossible for him to hold under his power one soul who honesty desires, at whatever cost, to know the truth. Christ is the truth, the "Light, which lighteth every man that cometh into the world." "If any man will do his will, he shall know of the doctrine." John 1:9; 7:17.

The Lord permits His people to be subjected to the fiery ordeal of temptation, not because He takes pleasure in their distress, but because this is essential to their final victory. He could not, consistently with His own glory, shield them from temptation, for the object of the trial is to prepare them to resist all the allurements of evil. Neither wicked men nor devils can shut out God's presence from His people if they will confess and put away their sins and claim His promises. Every temptation, open or secret, may be successfully resisted, "not by might, nor by power, but by my spirit, saith the Lord of hosts." Zechariah 4:6.

"Who is he that will harm you, if ye be followers of that which is good?" 1 Peter 3:13. Satan is well aware that the weakest soul who abides in Christ is more than a match for the hosts of darkness. Therefore he seeks to draw away the soldiers of the cross from their strong fortification, while he lies in ambush, ready to destroy all who venture upon his ground. Only in reliance upon God and obedience to all His commandments can we be secure.

No man is safe for a day or an hour without prayer. Entreat the Lord for wisdom to understand His Word. Satan is an expert in quoting Scripture, placing his own interpretation on passages by which he hopes to cause us to stumble. We should study with humility of heart. While we must constantly guard against the devices of Satan, we should pray in faith continually: "Lead us not into temptation." Matthew 6:13.

33/ What Lies Beyond the Grave?

Satan, who had incited rebellion in heaven, desired to bring the inhabitants of the earth to unite in his warfare against God. Adam and Eve had been perfectly happy in obedience to the law of God—a constant testimony against the claim Satan had urged in heaven that God's law was oppressive. Satan determined to cause their fall, that he might possess the earth and here establish his kingdom in opposition to the Most High.

Adam and Eve had been warned against this dangerous foe, but he worked in the dark, concealing his purpose. Employing as his medium the serpent, then a creature of fascinating appearance, he addressed Eve: "Hath God said, Ye shall not eat of every tree of the garden?" Eve ventured to parley with him and fell victim to his wiles: "The woman said unto the serpent, We may eat of the fruit of the trees of the garden: but of the fruit of the tree which is in the midst of the garden, God hath said, Ye shall not eat of it, neither shall ye touch it, lest ye die. And the serpent said unto the woman, Ye shall not surely die: for God doth know that in the day ye eat thereof, then your eyes shall be opened, and ye shall be as gods, knowing good and evil." Genesis 3:1-5.

Eve yielded, and through her influence Adam was led into sin. They accepted the words of the serpent; they distrusted their Creator and imagined that He was restricting their liberty.

But what did Adam find to be the meaning of the words, "In the day that thou eatest thereof thou shalt surely die''? Was he to be ushered into a more exalted existence? Adam did not find this to be the meaning of the divine sentence. God declared that as a penalty for his sin, man should return to the ground: ''Dust thou art, and unto dust shalt thou return.'' Genesis 3:19. The words of Satan, ''Your eyes shall be opened,'' proved to be true in this sense only: their eyes were opened to discern their folly. They did know evil and tasted the bitter fruit of transgression.

The tree of life had the power of perpetuating life. Adam would have continued to enjoy free access to this tree and have lived forever, but when he sinned he was cut off from the tree of life and became subject to death. Immortality had been forfeited by transgression. There could have been no hope for the fallen race had not God, by the sacrifice of His Son, brought immortality within their reach. While ''death passed upon all men, for that all have sinned,'' Christ ''hath brought life and immortality to light through the gospel.'' Only through Christ can immortality be obtained. ''He that believeth on the Son hath everlasting life: and he that believeth not the Son shall not see life.'' Romans 5:12; 2 Timothy 1:10; John 3:36.

The Great Lie

The one who promised life in disobedience was the great deceiver. And the declaration of the serpent in Eden—''Ye shall not surely die''—was the first sermon ever preached on the immortality of the soul. Yet this declaration, resting solely upon the authority of Satan, is echoed from pulpits and received by the majority of mankind as readily as by our first parents. The divine sentence, ''The soul that sinneth, it shall die'' (Ezekiel 18:20) is made to mean, The soul that sinneth, it shall *not* die, but live eternally. Had man after his fall been allowed free access to the tree of life, sin would have been immortalized. But not one of the family of Adam has been permitted to partake of the life-giving fruit. Therefore there is no immortal sinner.

After the Fall, Satan bade his angels to inculcate the belief in man's natural immortality. Having induced the people to receive this error, they were to lead them to conclude that the sinner would live in eternal misery. Now the prince of darkness represents God as a revengeful tyrant, declaring that He plunges into hell all who do not please Him, that while they writhe in eternal flames, their Creator looks down on them with satisfaction. Thus the archfiend clothes with his attributes the Benefactor of mankind. Cruelty is satanic. God is love. Satan is the enemy who tempts man to sin and then destroys him if he can. How repugnant to love, mercy, and justice, is the doctrine that the wicked dead are tormented in an eternally burning hell, that for the sins of a brief earthly life they suffer torture as long as God shall live!

Where in God's Word is such teaching to be found? Are feelings of common humanity to be exchanged for the cruelty of the savage? No, such is not the teaching of the Book of God. "As I live, saith the Lord God, I have no pleasure in the death of the wicked; but that the wicked turn from his way and live: turn ye, turn ye from your evil ways; for why will ye die?" Ezekiel 33:11.

Does God delight in witnessing unceasing tortures? Is He regaled with the groans and shrieks of suffering creatures whom He holds in the flames? Can these horrid sounds be music in the ear of Infinite Love? Oh, dreadful blasphemy! God's glory is not enhanced by perpetuating sin through ceaseless ages.

The Heresy of Eternal Torment

Evil has been wrought by the heresy of eternal torment. The religion of the Bible, full of love and goodness, is darkened by superstition and clothed with terror. Satan has painted the character of God in false colors. Our merciful Creator is feared, dreaded, even hated. The appalling views of God which have spread over the world from the teaching of the pulpit have made millions of skeptics and infidels.

Eternal torment is one of the false doctrines, the wine of abominations (Revelation 14:8; 17:21), which Babylon makes all nations drink. Ministers of Christ accepted this heresy from Rome as they received the false sabbath. If we turn from God's Word and accept false doctrines because our fathers taught them, we fall under the condemnation pronounced on Babylon; we are drinking of the wine of her abominations.

A large class are driven to the opposite error. They see that Scripture represents God as a being of love and compassion and cannot believe that He will consign His creatures to an eternally burning hell. Holding that the soul is naturally immortal, they conclude that all mankind will be saved. Thus the sinner can live in selfish pleasure, disregarding the requirements of God, and yet be received into His favor. Such doctrine, presuming on God's mercy but ignoring His justice, pleases the carnal heart.

Universal Salvation Unscriptural

Believers in universal salvation wrest the Scriptures. The professed minister of Christ reiterates the falsehood uttered by the serpent in Eden, "Ye shall not surely die." "In the day ye eat thereof, then your eyes shall be opened, and ye shall be as gods." He declares that the vilest of sinners—the murderer, the thief, the adulterer—will after death enter into immortal bliss. A pleasing fable indeed, suited to gratify the carnal heart!

If it were true that all men passed directly to heaven at the hour of dissolution, we might well covet death rather than life. Many have been led by this belief to put an end to their existence. Overwhelmed with trouble and disappointment, it seems easy to break the thread of life and soar into the bliss of the eternal world.

God has given in His Word decisive evidence that He will punish the transgressors of His law. Is He too merciful to execute justice upon the sinner? Look to the cross of Calvary. The death of the Son of God testifies that "the wages of sin is death" (Romans 6:23), that every violation of God's law must receive retribution. Christ the sinless became sin for man. He bore the guilt of transgression and the hiding of His Father's face until His heart was broken and His life crushed out—all this that sinners might be redeemed. And every soul that refuses to partake of the atonement provided at such a cost must bear in his own person the guilt and punishment of transgression.

Conditions Are Specified

"I will give unto him that is athirst of the fountain of the water of life freely." This promise is only to those that thirst. "He that overcometh shall inherit all things; and I will be his God, and he shall be my son." Revelation 21:6, 7. Conditions are specified. To inherit all things, we must overcome sin.

"It shall not be well with the wicked." Ecclesiastes 8:13. The sinner is treasuring up unto himself "wrath against the day of wrath and revelation of the righteous judgment of God; who will render to every man according to his deeds," "tribulation and anguish upon every soul of man that doeth evil." Romans 2:5, 6, 9.

"No fornicator, nor unclean person, nor covetous man, who is an idolator, hath any inheritance in the kingdom of Christ and God." "Blessed are they that do his commandments, that they may have right to the tree of life, and may enter in through the gates into the city. For without are dogs, and sorcerers, and whoremongers, and murderers, and idolaters, and whosoever loveth and maketh a lie." Ephesians 5:5, ARV; Revelation 22:14, 15.

God has given to men a declaration of His method of dealing with sin. "All the wicked will he destroy." "The transgressors shall be destroyed together: the end of the wicked shall be cut off." Psalms 145:20; 37:38. The authority of the divine government will put down rebellion, yet retributive justice will be consistent with the character of God as a merciful, benevolent being.

God does not force the will. He takes no pleasure in slavish obedience. He desires that the creatures of His hands shall love Him because He is worthy of love. He would have them obey Him because they have an intelligent appreciation of His wisdom, justice, and benevolence.

The principles of the divine government are in harmony with the Saviour's precept, "Love your enemies." Matthew 5:44. God executes justice on the wicked for the good of the universe and even for the good of those on whom His judgments are visited. He would make them happy if He could. He surrounds them with tokens of His love and follows them with offers of mercy; but they despise His love, make void His law, and reject His mercy. Constantly receiving His gifts, they dishonor the Giver. The Lord bears long with their perversity; but will He chain these rebels to His side, force them to do His will?

Not Prepared to Enter Heaven

Those who have chosen Satan as their leader are not prepared to enter the presence of God. Pride, deception, licentiousness, cruelty, have become fixed in their characters. Can they enter heaven to dwell forever with those whom they hated on earth? Truth will never be agreeable to a liar; meekness will not satisfy self-esteem; purity is not acceptable to the corrupt; disinterested love does not appear attractive to the selfish. What enjoyment could heaven offer those who are absorbed in selfish interests?

Could those whose hearts are filled with hatred of God, of truth and holiness, mingle with the heavenly throng and join their songs of praise? Years of probation were granted them, but they never trained the mind to love purity. They never learned the language of heaven. Now it is too late.

A life of rebellion against God has unfitted them for

heaven. Its purity and peace would be torture to them; the glory of God would be a consuming fire. They would long to flee from that holy place and would welcome destruction, that they might be hidden from the face of Him who died to redeem them. The destiny of the wicked is fixed by their own choice. Their exclusion from heaven is voluntary with themselves, and just and merciful on the part of God. Like the waters of the Flood the fires of the great day declare God's verdict that the wicked are incurable. Their will has been exercised in revolt. When life is ended, it is too late to turn their thoughts from transgression to obedience, from hatred to love.

The Wages of Sin

"The wages of sin is death; but the gift of God is eternal life through Jesus Christ our Lord." While life is the inheritance of the righteous, death is the portion of the wicked. "The second death" is placed in contrast with everlasting life. Romans 6:23; see Revelation 20:14.

In consequence of Adam's sin, death passed upon the whole human race. All alike go down into the grave. And through the plan of salvation, all are to be brought forth from their graves: "There shall be a resurrection of the dead, both of the just and unjust," "for as in Adam all die, even so in Christ shall all be made alive." But a distinction is made between the two classes brought forth: "All that are in the graves shall hear his voice, and shall come forth; they that have done good, unto the resurrection of life; and they that have done evil, unto the resurrection of damnation." Acts 24:15; 1 Corinthians 15:22; John 5:28, 29.

The First Resurrection

They who have been "accounted worthy" of the resurrection of life are "blessed and holy." "On such the second death hath no power." Luke 20:35; Revelation 20:6. But those who have not secured pardon through repentance and faith must receive "the wages of sin," punishment "according to their works," ending in the "second death."

Since it is impossible for God to save the sinner in his sins, He deprives him of the existence which his transgressions have forfeited and of which he has proved himself unworthy. "Yet a little while, and the wicked shall not be: yea, thou shalt diligently consider his place, and it shall not be." "They shall be as though they had not been." Psalm 37:10; Obadiah 16. They sink into hopeless, eternal oblivion.

Thus will be made an end of sin. "Thou hast destroyed the wicked, thou hast put out their name forever and ever. O thou enemy, destructions are come to a perpetual end." Psalm 9:5, 6. John, in the Revelation hears a universal anthem of praise undisturbed by one note of discord. No lost souls blaspheme God as they writhe in never-ending torment. No wretched beings in hell will mingle their shrieks with the songs of the saved.

Upon the error of natural immortality rests the doctrine of consciousness in death. Like eternal torment, it is opposed to Scripture, to reason, and to our feelings of humanity.

According to popular belief, the redeemed in heaven are acquainted with all that takes place on earth. But how could it be happiness to the dead to know the troubles of the living, to see them enduring the sorrows, disappointments, and anguish of life? And how revolting the belief that as soon as the breath leaves the body the soul of the impenitent is consigned to the flames of hell!

What say the Scriptures? Man is not conscious in death: "His breath goeth forth, he returneth to his earth; in that very day his thoughts perish." "The living know that they shall die: but the dead know not anything. . . . Their love, and their hatred, and their envy, is now perished; neither have they any more a portion forever in anything that is done under the sun." "The grave cannot praise thee, death cannot celebrate thee: they that go down into the pit cannot hope for thy truth. The living, the living, he shall praise thee, as I do this day." "In death there is no remembrance of thee: in the grave who shall give thee thanks?" Psalm 146:4; Ecclesiastes 9:5, 6; Isaiah 38:18, 19; Psalm 6:5.

Peter on the day of Pentecost declared that David "is both dead and buried, and his sepulcher is with us unto this day." "For David is not ascended into the heavens." Acts 2:29, 34. The fact that David remains in the grave until the resurrection proves that the righteous do not go to heaven at death.

Said Paul: "If the dead rise not, then is not Christ raised: and if Christ be not raised, your faith is vain; ye are yet in your sins. Then they also which are fallen asleep in Christ are perished." 1 Corinthians 15:16-18. If for 4000 years the righteous had gone directly to heaven at death, how could Paul have said that if there is no resurrection, "they also which are fallen asleep in Christ are perished"?

When about to leave His disciples, Jesus did not tell them that they would soon come to Him: "I go to prepare a place for you," He said. "And if I go and prepare a place for you, I will come again, and receive you unto myself." John 14:2, 3. Paul tells us further, that "the Lord himself shall descend from heaven with a shout, with the voice of the Archangel, and with the trump of God: and the dead in Christ shall rise first: then we which are alive and remain shall be caught up together with them in the clouds, to meet the Lord in the air: and so shall we ever be with the Lord. And he adds: "Comfort one another with these words." 1 Thessalonians 4:16-18. At the coming of the Lord, the fetters of the tomb shall be broken and the "dead in Christ" shall be raised to eternal life.

All are to be judged according to the things written in the books and rewarded as their works have been. This judgment does not take place at death. "He hath appointed a day, in the which he will judge the world in righteousness." "Behold, the Lord cometh with ten thousands of his saints, to execute judgment upon all." Acts 17:31; Jude 15.

But if the dead already enjoy heaven or writhe in the flames of hell, what need of a future judgment? God's Word may be understood by common minds. But what candid mind can see either wisdom or justice in the current theory? Will the righteous receive the commendation, "Well done, thou good and faithful servant, . . . enter thou into the joy of thy Lord," when they have been dwelling in His presence for long ages? Are the wicked summoned from torment to receive sentence from the Judge, "Depart from me, ye cursed, into everlasting fire"? Matthew 25:21, 41.

The theory of the immortality of the soul was one of those false doctrines that Rome borrowed from paganism. Luther classed it with the "monstrous fables that form part of the Roman dunghill of decretals."[1] The Bible teaches that the dead sleep until the resurrection.

Blessed rest for the weary righteous! Time, be it long or short, is but a moment to them. They sleep; they are awakened by the trump of God to a glorious immortality. "For the trumpet shall sound, and the dead shall be raised incorruptible. . . . So when this corruptible shall have put on incorruption, and this mortal shall have put on immortality, then shall be brought to pass the saying that is written, Death is swallowed up in victory." 1 Corinthians 15:52-54.

Called forth from their slumber, they begin to think just where they ceased. The last sensation was the pang of death; the last thought, that they were falling beneath the power of the grave. When they arise from the tomb, their first glad thought will be echoed in the triumphal shout: "O death, where is thy sting? O grave, where is thy victory?" 1 Corinthians 15:55.

Reference
1. E. Petavel, *The Problem of Immortality,* p. 255.

34/Who Are the "Spirits" in Spiritualism?

The doctrine of natural immortality, first borrowed from pagan philosophy and in the darkness of the great apostasy incorporated into the Christian faith, has supplanted the truth that "the dead know not anything." Ecclesiastes 9:5. Multitudes believe that the spirits of the dead are the "ministering spirits sent forth to minister for them who shall be heirs of salvation." Hebrews 1:14.

The belief that spirits of the dead return to minister to the living has prepared the way for modern spiritualism. If the dead are privileged with knowledge far exceeding what they before possessed, why not return to earth and instruct the living? If spirits of the dead hover about their friends on earth, why not communicate with them? How can those who believe in man's consciousness in death reject "divine light" communicated by glorified spirits? Here is a channel regarded as sacred through which Satan works. Fallen angels appear as messengers from the spirit world.

The prince of evil has power to bring before men the appearance of departed friends. The counterfeit is perfect, reproduced with marvelous distinctness. Many are comforted with the assurance that their loved ones are enjoying heaven. Without suspicion of danger, they give ear "to seducing spirits, and doctrines of devils." 1 Timothy 4:1.

Those who went into the grave unprepared claim to be happy and to occupy exalted positions in heaven. Pretended visitants from the world of spirits sometimes utter warnings which prove to be correct. Then, as confidence is gained, they present doctrines that undermine the Scriptures. The fact that they state some truths and at times foretell future events gives an appearance of reliability, and their false teachings are accepted. The law of God is set aside, the Spirit of grace despised. The spirits deny the deity of Christ and place the Creator on a level with themselves.

While it is true that the results of trickery have often been palmed off as genuine manifestations, there have been, also, marked exhibitions of supernatural power, the direct work of evil angels. Many believe that spiritualism is merely human imposture. When brought face to face with manifestations which they cannot but regard as supernatural, they will be deceived and accept them as the great power of God.

By satanic aid Pharaoh's magicians counterfeited the work of God. See Exodus 7:10-12. Paul testifies that the coming of the Lord is to be preceded by "the working of Satan with all power and signs and lying wonders, and with all deceivableness of unrighteousness." 2 Thessalonians 2:9, 10. And John declares: "He doeth great wonders, so that he maketh fire come down from heaven on the earth in the sight of men, and deceiveth them that dwell on the earth by means of those miracles which he had power to do." Revelation 13:13, 14. No mere impostures are here foretold. Men are deceived by the miracles which Satan's agents do, not which they pretend to do.

Satan's Appeal to Intellectuals

To persons of culture and refinement the prince of darkness presents spiritualism in its more refined and intellectual aspects. He delights the fancy with enrapturing scenes and eloquent portrayals of love and charity. He leads men to take so great pride in their own wisdom that in their hearts they despise the Eternal One.

Satan beguiles men now as he beguiled Eve in Eden,

by exciting ambition for self-exaltation. "Ye shall be as gods," he declares, "knowing good and evil." Genesis 3:5. Spiritualism teaches "that man is the creature of progression . . . toward the Godhead." And again: "The judgment will be right, because it is the judgment of self. . . . The throne is within you." And another declares: "Any just and perfect being is Christ."

Thus Satan has substituted the sinful nature of man himself as the only rule of judgment. This is progress, not upward, but downward. Man will never rise higher than his standard of purity or goodness. If self is his loftiest ideal, he will never attain to anything more exalted. The grace of God alone has power to exalt man. Left to himself, his course must be downward.

Appeal to the Pleasure-loving

To the self-indulgent, the pleasure-loving, the sensual, spiritualism presents a less subtle disguise. In its grosser forms they find what is in harmony with their inclinations. Satan marks the sins each individual is inclined to commit and then takes care that opportunities shall not be wanting to gratify the tendency. He tempts men through intemperance to weaken physical, mental, and moral power. He destroys thousands through indulgence of passion, brutalizing the entire nature. And to complete his work, the spirits declare that "true knowledge places man above all law"; that "whatever is, is right"; that "God doth not condemn"; and that "all sins . . . are innocent." When people thus believe that desire is the highest law, that liberty is license, that man is accountable only to himself, who can wonder that corruption teems on every hand? Multitudes eagerly accept the promptings of lust. Satan sweeps into his net thousands who profess to follow Christ.

But God has given sufficient light to discover the snare. The very foundation of spiritualism is at war with Scripture. The Bible declares that the dead know not anything, that their thoughts have perished; they have no part in the joys or sorrows of those on earth.

Furthermore, God has forbidden pretended communication with departed spirits. The "familiar spirits," as these visitants from other worlds were called, are declared by the Bible to be "the spirits of devils." See Numbers 25:1-3; Psalm 106:28; 1 Corinthians 10:20; Revelation 16:14. Dealing with them was forbidden under penalty of death. Leviticus 19:31; 20:27. But spiritualism has made its way into scientific circles, invaded churches, and found favor in legislative bodies, even in the courts of kings. This mammoth deception is a revival in a new disguise of the witchcraft condemned of old.

By representing the basest of men as in heaven, Satan says to the world: "No matter whether you believe or disbelieve God and the Bible, live as you please; heaven is your home." Saith the Word of God: "Woe unto them that call evil good, and good evil; that put darkness for light, and light for darkness." Isaiah 5:20.

Bible Represented as Fiction

The apostles, personated by lying spirits, are made to contradict what they wrote when on earth. Satan is making the world believe that the Bible is fiction, a book suited to the infancy of the race, but now to be regarded as obsolete. The Book that is to judge him and his followers he puts in the shade; the Saviour of the world he makes to be no more than a common man. And believers in spiritual manifestations try to make it appear that there is nothing miraculous in our Saviour's life. Their own miracles, they declare, far exceed the works of Christ.

Spiritualism is now assuming a Christian guise. But its teachings cannot be denied or hidden. In its present form it is a more dangerous, more subtle, deception. It now professes to accept Christ and the Bible. But the Bible is interpreted in a manner pleasing to the unrenewed heart. Love is dwelt upon as the chief attribute of God, but is degraded to a weak sentimentalism. God's denunciations of sin, the requirements of His holy law, are kept out of sight. Fables lead men to reject the Bible as the foundation of their faith. Christ is as verily denied as before, but the deception is not discerned.

Few have a just conception of the deceptive power of spiritualism. Many tamper with it merely to gratify curiosity. They would be filled with horror at the thought of yielding to the spirits' control. But they venture on forbidden ground, and the destroyer exercises his power on them against their will. Let them once be induced to submit their minds to his direction, and he holds them captive. Nothing but the power of God, in answer to earnest prayer, can deliver these souls.

All who willfully cherish known sin are inviting the temptations of Satan. They separate themselves from God and the watchcare of His angels, and are without defense.

"When they shall say unto you, Seek unto them that have familiar spirits, and unto wizards that peep, and that mutter; should not a people seek unto their God? for the living to the dead? To the law and to the testimony: if they speak not according to this word, it is because there is no light in them." Isaiah 8:19, 20.

If men had been willing to receive the truth concerning the nature of man and the state of the dead, they would see in spiritualism Satan's power and lying wonders. But multitudes close their eyes to the light, and Satan weaves his snares about them. "Because they received not the love of the truth, that they might be saved," therefore "God shall send them strong delusion, that they should believe a lie." 2 Thessalonians 2:10, 11.

Those who oppose spiritualism assail Satan and his angels. Satan will not yield one inch of ground except as driven back by heavenly messengers. He can quote Scripture and will pervert its teachings. Those who would stand in this time of peril must understand for themselves the testimony of the Scriptures.

Spirits of devils personating relatives or friends will appeal to our tender sympathies and will work miracles. We must withstand them with the Bible truth that the dead know not anything and that they who thus appear are the spirits of devils.

All whose faith is not established on the Word of God will be deceived and overcome. Satan "works with all deceivableness of unrighteousness," and his deceptions will increase. But those who seek a knowledge of the truth and purify their souls through obedience will find in the God of truth a sure defense. The Saviour would sooner send every angel out of heaven to protect His people than leave one soul that trusts in Him to be overcome by Satan. Those who comfort themselves with the assurance that there is no punishment for the sinner, who renounce the truths which Heaven has provided as a defense for the day of trouble, will accept the lies offered by Satan, the delusive pretensions of spiritualism.

Scoffers hold up to ridicule the declarations of Scripture concerning the plan of salvation and the retribution to be visited upon the rejecters of truth. They affect great pity for minds so narrow, weak, and superstitious as to obey the requirements of God's law. So fully have they yielded to the tempter, so closely are they united with him and imbued with his spirit, that they have no inclination to break away from his snare.

The foundation of Satan's work was laid by the assurance given to Eve in Eden: "Ye shall not surely die." "In the day ye eat thereof, then your eyes shall be opened, and ye shall be as gods, knowing good and evil." Genesis 3:4, 5. His masterpiece of deception will be reached in the last remnant of time. Says the prophet: "I saw three unclean spirits like frogs; ...they are the spirits of devils, working miracles, which go forth unto the kings of the earth and of the whole world, to gather them to the battle of that great day of God Almighty." Revelation 16:13, 14.

Except those who are kept by the power of God through faith in His Word, the whole world will be swept into the ranks of this delusion. The people are fast being lulled to a fatal security, to be awakened only by the outpouring of the wrath of God.

35/Liberty of Conscience Threatened

Romanism is now regarded by Protestants with far greater favor than in former years. In those countries where Catholicism takes a conciliatory course to gain influence, the opinion is gaining ground that we do not differ so widely upon vital points as has been supposed and that a little concession on our part will bring us into better understanding with Rome. The time was when Protestants taught their children that to seek harmony with Rome would be disloyalty to God. But how widely different are the sentiments now expressed!

Defenders of the papacy declare that the church has been maligned, that it is unjust to judge the church of today by her reign during the centuries of ignorance and darkness. They excuse her horrible cruelty as the barbarism of the times.

Have these persons forgotten the claim of infallibility put forth by this power? Rome asserts that the "church *never erred;* nor will it, according to the Scriptures, *ever err.*"[1]

The papal church will never relinquish her claim to infallibility. Let the restraints now imposed by secular governments be removed and Rome be reinstated in her former power, and there would speedily be a revival of her tyranny and persecution.

It is true that there are real Christians in the Roman Catholic communion. Thousands in that church are serving God according to the best light they have. God looks with pitying tenderness upon these souls, educated in a faith that is delusive and unsatisfying. He will cause rays of light to penetrate the darkness, and many will yet take their position with His people.

But Romanism as a system is no more in harmony with the gospel of Christ now than at any former period. The Roman Church is employing every device to regain control of the world, to re-establish persecution, and to undo all that Protestantism has done. Catholicism is gaining ground on every side. See the increasing number of her churches. Look at the popularity of her colleges and seminaries, so widely patronized by Protestants. Look at the growth of ritualism in England and the frequent defections to the ranks of the Catholics.

Compromises and Concessions

Protestants have patronized popery; they have made compromises and concessions which papists themselves are surprised to see. Men are closing their eyes to the real character of Romanism. The people need to resist the advances of this dangerous foe to civil and religious liberty.

While Romanism is based upon deception, it is not coarse and clumsy. The religious service of the Roman Church is a most impressive ceremonial. Its gorgeous display and solemn rites fascinate the people and silence the voice of reason and conscience. The eye is charmed. Magnificent churches, imposing processions, golden altars, jeweled shrines, choice paintings, and exquisite sculpture appeal to the love of beauty. The music is unsurpassed. The rich notes of the deep-toned organ blending with the melody of many voices as it swells through the lofty domes and pillared aisles of her grand cathedrals, impress the mind with awe and reverence.

This outward splendor and ceremony mock the longings of the sin-sick soul. The religion of Christ needs no such attractions. The light shining from the cross appears so pure and lovely that no external decorations can enhance its true worth.

High conceptions of art, delicate refinement of taste, are often employed by Satan to lead men to forget the necessities of the soul and to live for this world alone.

The pomp and ceremony of Catholic worship has a seductive, bewitching power by which many are deceived. They come to look upon the Roman Church as the gate of heaven. None but those who plant their feet firmly on the foundation of truth, whose hearts are renewed by the Spirit of God, are proof against her influence. The form of godliness without the power is what the multitudes desire.

The church's claim to the right to pardon leads the Romanist to feel at liberty to sin, and the ordinance of confession tends also to give license to evil. He who kneels before fallen man and opens in confession the secret imaginations of his heart is degrading his soul. In unfolding the sins of his life to a priest—an erring mortal—his standard of character is lowered, and he is defiled in consequence. His thought of God is degraded to the likeness of fallen humanity, for the priest stands as a representative of God. This degrading confession of man to man is the secret spring from which has flowed much of the evil that is defiling the world. Yet to him who loves self-indulgence, it is more pleasing to confess to a fellow mortal than to open the soul to God. It is more palatable to human nature to do penance than to renounce sin; it is easier to mortify the flesh by sackcloth than to crucify fleshly lusts.

A Striking Similarity

While the Jews at Christ's first advent secretly trampled upon the law of God, they were outwardly rigorous in observance of its precepts, loading it down with exactions that made obedience burdensome. As the Jews professed to revere the law, so do Romanists claim to reverence the cross.

They place crosses on their churches, their altars, and their garments. Everywhere the insignia of the cross is outwardly honored and exalted. But the teachings of Christ are buried beneath senseless traditions and rigorous exactions. Conscientious souls are kept in fear of the wrath of an offended God, while many dignitaries of the church live in luxury and sensual pleasure.

It is Satan's constant effort to misrepresent the character of God, the nature of sin, and the real issues at stake in the great controversy. His sophistry gives men license to sin. At the same time he causes false conceptions of God so that they regard Him with fear and hate rather than with love. By perverted conceptions of the divine attributes, heathen nations were led to believe human sacrifices necessary to secure the favor of Deity. Horrible cruelties have been perpetrated under the various forms of idolatry.

Union of Paganism and Christianity

The Roman Catholic Church, uniting paganism and Christianity, and, like paganism, misrepresenting the character of God, has resorted to practices no less cruel. Instruments of torture compelled assent to her doctrines. Dignitaries of the church studied to invent means to cause the greatest possible torture and not end the life of those who would not concede to her claims. In many cases the sufferer hailed death as a sweet release.

For Rome's adherents she had the discipline of the scourge, of hunger, of bodily austerities. To secure the favor of Heaven, penitents were taught to sunder the ties which God has formed to bless and gladden man's earthly sojourn. The churchyard contains millions of victims who spent their lives in vain endeavors to repress, as offensive to God, every thought and feeling of sympathy with their fellow creatures.

God lays upon men none of these heavy burdens. Christ gives no example for men and women to shut themselves in monasteries in order to become fitted for heaven. He has never taught that love must be repressed.

The pope claims to be the vicar of Christ. But was Christ ever known to consign men to prison because they did not pay Him homage as the King of heaven? Was His voice heard condemning to death those who did not accept Him?

The Roman Church now presents a fair front to the world, covering with apologies her record of horrible cruelties. She has clothed herself in Christlike garments, but she is unchanged. Every principle of the papacy in past ages exists today. The doctrines devised in the dark ages are still held. The papacy that Protestants now honor is the same that ruled in the days of the Reformation, when men of God stood up at the peril of their lives to expose her iniquity.

The papacy is just what prophecy declared that she would be, the apostasy of the latter times. See 2 Thessalonians 2:3, 4. Beneath the variable appearance of the chameleon she conceals the invariable venom of the serpent. Shall this power, whose record for a thousand years is written in the blood of the saints, be now acknowledged as a part of the church of Christ?

A Change in Protestantism

The claim has been put forth in Protestant countries that Catholicism differs less from Protestantism than in former times. There has been a change; but the change is not in the papacy. Catholicism indeed resembles much Protestantism that now exists because Protestantism has so greatly degenerated since the days of Reformers.

The Protestant churches, seeking the favor of the world, believe good of all evil, and as the result they will finally believe evil of all good. They are now, as it were, apologizing to Rome for their uncharitable opinion of her, begging pardon for their "bigotry." Many urge that the intellectual and moral darkness prevailing during the Middle Ages favored the spread of Rome's superstitions and oppression; and that the greater intelligence of modern times and the increasing liberality in matters of religion forbid a revival of intolerance. The thought that such a state of things will exist in this enlightened age is ridiculed. But it should be remembered that the greater the light bestowed, the greater the darkness of those who pervert and reject it.

A day of great intellectual darkness has been favorable to the success of the papacy. A day of great intellectual light is equally favorable. In past ages when men were without the knowledge of the truth, thousands were ensnared, not seeing the net spread for their feet. In this generation many discern not the net and walk into it as readily as if blindfolded. When men exalt their own theories above the Word of God, intelligence can accomplish greater harm than ignorance. Thus the false science of the present day will prove successful in preparing the way for acceptance of the papacy, as did the withholding of knowledge in the Dark Ages.

Sunday Observance

Sunday observance is a custom which originated with Rome, which she claims as the sign of her authority. The spirit of the papacy—of conformity to worldly customs, the veneration for human traditions above the commandments of God—is permeating the Protestant churches and leading them to the same work of Sunday exaltation which the papacy has done before them.

Royal edicts, general councils and church ordinances sustained by secular power were the steps by which the pagan festival attained its position of honor in the Christian world. The first public measure enforcing Sunday observance was the law enacted by Constantine. Though virtually a heathen statute, it was enforced by the emperor after his nominal acceptance of Christianity.

Eusebius, a bishop who sought the favor of princes, and who was the special friend of Constantine, advanced the claim that Christ had transferred the Sabbath to Sunday. No testimony of Scripture was produced in proof. Eusebius himself unwittingly acknowledges its falsity. "All things," he says, "whatever that it was duty to do on the Sabbath, these we have transferred to the Lord's Day."[2]

As the papacy became established, Sunday exaltation was continued. For a time the seventh day was still regarded as the Sabbath, but steadily a change was effected. Later the pope gave directions that the parish priest should admonish violators of Sunday lest they bring some great calamity on themselves and neighbors.

The decrees of councils proving insufficient, the secular authorities were besought to issue an edict that would strike terror to the hearts of the people and force them to refrain from labor on Sunday. At a synod held in Rome, all previous decisions were reaffirmed and incorporated into ecclesiastical law and enforced by civil authorities.[3]

Still the absence of scriptural authority for Sundaykeeping occasioned embarrassment. The people questioned the right of their teachers to set aside the declaration, "The seventh day is the Sabbath of the Lord thy God," in order to honor the day of the sun. To supply the lack of Bible testimony, other expedients were necessary.

A zealous advocate of Sunday, who about the close of the twelfth century visited the churches of England, was resisted by faithful witnesses for the truth; and so fruitless were his efforts that he departed from the country for a season. When he returned, he brought with him a roll purporting to be from God Himself, which contained the needed command for Sunday observance, with awful threats to terrify the disobedient. This precious document was said to have fallen from heaven and to have been found in Jerusalem upon the altar of St. Simeon, in Golgotha. But, in fact, the pontifical palace at Rome was the source. Frauds and forgeries have in all ages been esteemed lawful by the papal hierarchy. (See Appendix, note for page 37.)

But notwithstanding all efforts to establish Sunday sacredness, papists themselves publicly confessed the divine authority of the Sabbath. In the sixteenth century a papal council declared: "Let all Christians remember that the seventh day was consecrated by God, and hath been received and observed, not only by the Jews, but by all others who pretend to worship God; though we Christians have changed their Sabbath into the Lord's Day."[4] Those who were tampering with the divine law were not ignorant of the character of their work.

Severe Penalties

A striking illustration of Rome's policy was given in the long and bloody persecution of the Waldenses, some of whom were observers of the Sabbath. (See Appendix.) The history of the churches of Ethiopia and Abyssinia is especially significant. Amid the gloom of the Dark Ages, the Christians of Central Africa were lost sight of and forgotten by the world and for many centuries enjoyed freedom in their faith. At last Rome learned of their existence, and the emperor of Abyssinia was beguiled into an acknowledgment of the pope as the vicar of Christ. An edict was issued forbidding the observance of the Sabbath under severe penalties.[5] But papal tyranny soon became a yoke so galling that the Abyssinians determined to break it. The Romanists were banished from their dominions and the ancient faith was restored.

While the churches of Africa kept the seventh day in obedience to the commandment of God, they abstained from labor on Sunday in conformity to the custom of the church. Rome trampled on the Sabbath of God to exalt her own, but the churches of Africa, hidden for nearly a thousand years, did not share this apostasy. When brought under Rome, they were forced to set aside the true and exalt the false sabbath. But no sooner had they regained their independence than they returned to obedience to the fourth commandment. (See Appendix.)

These records clearly reveal the enmity of Rome toward the true Sabbath and its defenders. The Word of God teaches that these scenes are to be repeated as Catholics and Protestants unite for the exaltation of Sunday.

The Beast With Lamblike Horns

The prophecy of Revelation 13 declares that the beast with lamblike horns shall cause "the earth and them which dwell therein" to worship the papacy—symbolized by the beast "like unto a leopard." The beast with two horns is also to say "to them that dwell on the earth, that they should make an image to the beast." Furthermore, it is to command all, "both small and great, rich and poor, free and bond," to receive the mark of the beast. Revelation 13:11-16. The United States is the power represented by the beast with lamblike horns. This prophecy will be fulfilled when the United States shall enforce Sunday observance, which Rome claims as the acknowledgment of her supremacy.

"I saw one of his heads as it were wounded to death; and his deadly wound was healed: and all the world wondered after the beast." Revelation 13:3. The deadly wound points to the downfall of the papacy in 1798. *After* this, says the prophet, "his deadly wound was healed: and all the world wondered after the beast." Paul states that the "man of sin" will carry forward his work of deception to the very close of time. 2 Thessalonians 2:3-8. And "all that dwell upon the earth shall worship him, whose names are not written in the book of life." Revelation 13:8. In both the Old and the New World, the papacy will receive homage in the honor paid to Sunday.

Since the middle of the nineteenth century, students of prophecy have presented this testimony to the world. Now is seen a rapid advance toward the fulfillment of the prediction. With Protestant teachers there is the same claim of divine authority for Sundaykeeping, and the same lack of scriptural evidence, as with papal leaders. The assertion that God's judgments are visited upon men for violation of the Sunday-sabbath will be repeated; already it is beginning to be urged.

Marvelous in shrewdness is the Roman Church. She can read what is to be—that Protestant churches are paying her homage in their acceptance of the false sabbath and that they are preparing to enforce it by the means she herself employed in bygone days. How readily she will come to the help of Protestants in this work is not difficult to conjecture.

The Roman Catholic Church forms one vast organization under the control of the papal see, its millions of communicants in every country bound in allegiance to the pope, whatever their nationality or their government. Though they may take the oath pledging loyalty to the state, yet back of this lies the vow of obedience to Rome.

History testifies of her artful and persistent efforts to insinuate herself into the affairs of nations, and having gained a foothold, to further her own aims, even at the ruin of princes and people.[6]

It is the boast of Rome that she never changes. Protestants little know what they are doing when they propose to accept the aid of Rome in the work of Sunday exaltation. While they are bent upon their purpose, Rome is aiming to re-establish her power, to recover her lost supremacy. Let the principle once be established that the church may control the power of the state; that religious observances may be enforced by secular laws; in short, that the authority of church and state is to dominate the conscience—and the triumph of Rome is assured.

The Protestant world will learn what the purposes of Rome are, only when it is too late to escape the snare. She is silently growing into power. Her doctrines are exerting their influence in legislative halls, in the churches, and in the hearts of men. She is strengthening her forces to further her own ends when the time shall come to strike. All that she desires is vantage ground. Whoever shall believe and obey the Word of God will incur reproach and persecution.

References

1. John L. von Mosheim, *Institutes of Ecclesiastical History,* book 3, century 11, part 2, chapter 2, section 9, note 17.

2. Robert Cox, *Sabbath Laws and Sabbath Duties,* p. 538.

3. See Heylyn, *History of the Sabbath,* pt. 2, ch. 5, sec. 7.

4. Thomas Morer, *Discourse in Six Dialogues on the Name, Notion, and Observation of the Lord's Day,* pp. 281, 282.

5. See Michael Geddes, *Church History of Ethiopia,* pp. 311, 312.

6. See, for example, John Dowling, *The History of Romanism,* bk. 5, ch. 6, sec. 55; and Mosheim, bk. 3, cent. 11, pt. 2, ch. 2, sec. 9, note 17.

36/The Impending Conflict

From the very beginning of the great controversy in heaven, it has been Satan's purpose to overthrow the law of God. Whether this be accomplished by casting aside the law altogether, or by rejecting one of its precepts, the result will be the same. He that offends "in one point" manifests contempt for the whole law; his influence and example are on the side of transgression; he becomes "guilty of all." James 2:10.

Satan has perverted the doctrines of the Bible, and errors have thus become incorporated into the faith of thousands. The last great conflict between truth and error is concerning the law of God, between the Bible and the religion of fable and tradition. The Bible is within the reach of all, but few accept it as the guide of life. In the church many deny the pillars of the Christian faith. Creation, the fall of man, the atonement, and the law of God are rejected either wholly or in part. Thousands regard it as an evidence of weakness to place implicit confidence in the Bible.

It is as easy to make an idol of false theories as to fashion an idol of wood or stone. By misrepresenting God, Satan leads men to conceive of Him in a false character. A philosophical idol is enthroned in the place of the living God as He is revealed in His Word, in Christ, and in the works of creation. The god of many philosophers, poets, politicians, journalists—of many universities, even of some theological institutions—is little better than Baal, the sun-god of Phoenicia in the days of Elijah.

No error strikes more boldly against the authority of Heaven, none is more pernicious in its results, than the doctrine that God's law is no longer binding. Suppose that prominent ministers were publicly to teach that the statutes which govern their land were not obligatory, that they restricted the liberties of the people and ought not to be obeyed; how long would such men be tolerated in the pulpit?

It would be more consistent for nations to abolish their statutes than for the Ruler of the universe to annul His law. The experiment of making void the law of God was tried in France when atheism became the controlling power. It was demonstrated that to throw off the restraints which God has imposed is to accept the rule of the prince of evil.

Setting Aside the Law of God

Those who teach the people to regard lightly the commandments of God sow disobedience to reap disobedience. Let the restraint imposed by the divine law be wholly cast aside, and human laws would soon be disregarded. The results of banishing God's precepts would be such as they do not anticipate. Property would no longer be safe. Men would obtain their neighbors' possessions by violence, and the strongest would become richest. Life itself would not be respected. The marriage vow would no longer stand as a bulwark to protect the family. He who had the power would take his neighbor's wife by violence. The fifth commandment would be set aside with the fourth. Children would not shrink from taking the life of their parents if by so doing they could obtain the desire of their corrupt hearts. The civilized world would become a horde of robbers and assassins, and peace and happiness would be banished from the earth.

Already this doctrine has opened the floodgates of iniquity on the world. Lawlessness and corruption sweep in like an overwhelming tide. Even in professedly Christian households there is hypocrisy, estrangement, betrayal of sacred trusts, indulgence of lust. Religious principle, the foundation of social life, seems a tottering mass ready to fall. Vile criminals are often made the recipients of attentions as if they had attained an enviable distinction. Great publicity is given to their crimes. The press publishes revolting details of vice, initiating others into fraud, robbery, and murder. The infatuation of vice, the terrible intemperance and iniquity of every degree should arouse all. What can be done to stay the tide of evil?

Intemperance Has Beclouded Many

Courts are corrupt, rulers are actuated by desire for gain and love of sensual pleasure. Intemperance has beclouded many so that Satan has almost complete control of them. Jurists are perverted, bribed, deluded. Drunkenness and revelry, dishonesty of every sort, are represented among those who administer the laws. Now that Satan can no longer keep the world under control by withholding the Scriptures, he resorts to other means to accomplish the same object. To destroy faith in the Bible serves as well as to destroy the Bible itself.

As in former ages, he has worked through the churches to further his designs. In combating unpopular truths in the Scriptures, they adopt interpretations which sow broadcast the seeds of skepticism. Clinging to the papal error of natural immortality and man's consciousness in death, they reject the only defense against the delusions of spiritualism. The doctrine of eternal torment has led many to disbelieve the Bible. As the claims of the fourth commandment are urged, it is found that the observance of the seventh-day Sabbath is enjoined; and as the only way to free themselves from a duty they are unwilling to perform, popular teachers cast away the law of God and the Sabbath together. As Sabbath reform extends, this rejection of the divine law to avoid the fourth commandment will become well-nigh universal. Religious leaders open the door to infidelity, spiritualism, and contempt for God's holy law—a fearful responsibility for the iniquity that exists in the Christian world.

Yet this very class claim that the enforcement of Sunday observance would improve the morals of society. It is one of Satan's devices to combine with falsehood just enough truth to give it plausibility. The leaders of the Sunday movement may advocate reforms which the people need, principles in harmony with the Bible; yet while there is with these a requirement contrary to God's law, His servants cannot unite with them. Nothing can justify setting aside the commandments of God for the precepts of men.

Through the two great errors, the immortality of the soul and Sunday sacredness, Satan will bring the people under his deceptions. While the former lays the foundation of spiritualism, the latter creates a bond of sympathy with Rome. The Protestants of the United States will be foremost in stretching their hands across the gulf to grasp the hand of spiritualism; they will reach over the abyss to clasp hands with the Roman power; and under the influence of this threefold union, this country will follow in the steps of Rome in trampling on the rights of conscience.

As spiritualism imitates the Christianity of the day, it has great power to deceive. Satan himself is "converted." He will appear as an angel of light. Through spiritualism, miracles will be wrought, the sick will be healed, and many undeniable wonders will be performed.

Papists who boast of miracles as a sign of the true church will be readily deceived by this wonderworking power; and Protestants, having cast away the shield of truth, will also be deluded. Papists, Protestants, and worldlings will alike see in this union a grand movement for the conversion of the world.

Through spiritualism, Satan appears as a benefactor of the race, healing diseases and presenting a new system of religious faith, but at the same time he leads multitudes to ruin. Intemperance dethrones reason; sensual indulgence, strife, and bloodshed follow. War excites the worst passions of the soul and sweeps into eternity its victims steeped in vice and blood. It is Satan's object to incite the nations to war, for he can thus divert the people from preparation to stand in the day of God.

Satan has studied the secrets of nature, and he uses all his power to control the elements as far as God allows. It is God that shields His creatures from the destroyer. But the Christian world has shown contempt for His law, and the Lord will do what He declared that He would—remove His protecting care from those who rebel against His law and force others to do the same. Satan has control of all whom God does not especially guard. He will favor and prosper some, in order to further his own designs; and he will bring trouble upon others, and lead men to believe that it is God who is afflicting them.

While appearing as a great physician who can heal all their maladies, Satan will bring disease and disaster until populous cities are reduced to ruin. In accidents by sea and land, in great conflagrations, in fierce tornadoes and hailstorms, in tempests, floods, cyclones, tidal waves, and earthquakes, in a thousand forms, Satan is exercising his power. He sweeps away the ripening harvest, and famine and distress follow. He imparts to the air a deadly taint, and thousands perish.

And then the great deceiver will persuade men to charge all their troubles on those whose obedience to God's commandments is a perpetual reproof to transgressors. It will be declared that men offend God by the violation of Sunday, that this sin has brought calamities which will not cease until Sunday observance shall be strictly enforced. "Those who destroy reverence for Sunday are preventing restoration of divine favour and prosperity." Thus the accusation urged of old against the servant of God will be repeated. "When Ahab saw Elijah, . . . Ahab said unto him, art thou he that troubleth Israel?" 1 Kings 18: 17, 18.

Miracle-working power will exert its influence against those who obey God rather than men. The "spirits" will declare that God has sent them to convince the rejecters of Sunday of their error. They will lament the great wickedness in the world and second the testimony of religious teachers that the degraded state of morals is caused by the desecration of Sunday.

Under the rule of Rome, those who suffered for the gospel were denounced as evildoers in league with Satan. So it will be now. Satan will cause those who honor God's law to be accused as men who bring judgments on the world. Through fear he endeavors to rule the conscience, moving religious and secular authorities to enforce human laws in defiance of the law of God.

Those who honor the Bible Sabbath will be denounced as enemies of law and order, breaking down the moral restraints of society, causing anarchy and corruption, and calling down the judgments of God on the earth. They will be accused of disaffection toward the government. Ministers who deny the obligation of the divine law will present from the pulpit the duty of obedience to civil authorities. In legislative halls and courts of justice, commandment-keepers will be condemned. A false coloring will be given their words; the worst construction will be put on their motives.

Dignitaries of church and state will unite to persuade or compel all to honor Sunday. Even in free America rulers and legislators will yield to the popular demand for a law enforcing Sunday observance. Liberty of conscience which has cost so great a sacrifice will no longer be respected. In the soon-coming conflict we shall see exemplified the prophet's words, "The dragon was wroth with the woman, and went to make war with the remnant of her seed, which keep the commandments of God, and have the testimony of Jesus Christ." Revelation 12:17.

37/Our Only Safeguard

The people of God are directed to the Scriptures as their safeguard against the delusive power of spirits of darkness. Satan employs every possible device to prevent men from obtaining a knowledge of the Bible. At every revival of God's work, he arouses to more intense activity. A final struggle against Christ and His followers is soon to open before us. So closely will the counterfeit resemble the true that it will be impossible to distinguish between them except by the Scriptures.

Those who endeavor to obey all the commandments of God will be opposed and derided. To endure the trial, they must understand the will of God as revealed in His Word. They can honor Him only as they have a right conception of His character, government, and purposes, and act in accordance with them. None but those who have fortified the mind with the truths of the Bible will stand through the last great conflict.

Before His crucifixion the Saviour explained to His disciples that He was to be put to death and rise again. Angels were present to impress His words on minds and hearts. But the words were banished from the disciples' minds. When the trial came, the death of Jesus as fully destroyed their hopes as if He had not forewarned them. So in the prophecies the future is opened before us as plainly as it was opened to the disciples by Christ.

When God sends warnings, He requires every person endowed with reason to heed the message. The fearful judgments against the worship of the beast and his image (Revelation 14:9-11) should lead all to learn what the mark of the beast is and how to avoid receiving it. But the masses of the people do not want Bible truth, because it interferes with the desires of the sinful heart. Satan supplies the deceptions they love.

But God will have a people to maintain the Bible, and the Bible only, as the standard of all doctrines and the basis of all reforms. The opinions of learned men, the deductions of science, the decisions of ecclesiastical councils, the voice of the majority—not one of these should be regarded as evidence for or against any doctrine. We should demand a plain "Thus saith the Lord." Satan leads the people to look to pastors, to professors of theology as their guides, instead of searching the Scriptures for themselves. By controlling these leaders, he can influence the multitudes.

When Christ came, the common people heard Him gladly. But the chief of the priesthood and leading men incased themselves in prejudice; they rejected the evidence of His Messiahship. "How is it," the people asked, "that our rulers and learned scribes do not believe on Jesus?" Such teachers led the Jewish nation to reject their Redeemer.

Exalting Human Authority

Christ had a prophetic view of the work of exalting human authority to rule the conscience, which has been so terrible a curse in all ages. His warnings not to follow blind leaders were placed on record as an admonition to future generations.

The Roman Church reserves to the clergy the right to interpret the Scriptures. Though the Reformation gave the Scriptures to all, yet the same principle which was maintained by Rome prevents multitudes in Protestant churches from searching the Bible for themselves. They are taught to accept its teachings *as interpreted by the church*. Thousands dare receive nothing, however plain in Scripture, that is contrary to their creed.

Many are ready to commit their souls to the clergy. They pass by the Saviour's teachings almost unnoticed. But are ministers infallible? How can we trust their guidance unless we know from God's Word that they are lightbearers? A lack of moral courage leads many to follow learned men, and they become hopelessly fastened in error. They see the truth for this time in the Bible and feel the power of the Holy Spirit attend its proclamation, yet they allow the clergy to turn them from the light.

Satan secures multitudes by attaching them by silken cords of affection to those who are enemies of the cross of Christ. This attachment may be parental, filial, conjugal, or social. Souls under their sway have not courage to obey their convictions of duty.

Many claim that it matters not what one believes, if his life is only right. But the life is molded by the faith. If truth is within reach and we neglect it, we virtually reject it, choosing darkness rather than light.

Ignorance is no excuse for error or sin, when there is every opportunity to know the will of God. A man traveling comes to a place where there are several roads and a signpost indicating where each one leads. If he disregards the sign and takes whichever road seems to be right, he may be sincere, but will in all probability find himself on the wrong road.

The First and Highest Duty

It is not enough to have good intentions, to do what a man thinks is right or what the minister tells him is right. He should search the Scriptures for himself. He has a chart pointing out every waymark on the heavenward journey, and he ought not to guess at anything.

It is the first and highest duty of every rational being to learn from the Scriptures what is truth, and then to walk in the light and encourage others to follow his example. We are to form our opinions for ourselves as we are to answer for ourselves before God.

Learned men, with a pretence of great wisdom,

teach that the Scriptures have a secret, spiritual meaning not apparent in the language employed. These men are false teachers. The language of the Bible should be explained according to its obvious meaning, unless a symbol or figure is employed. If men would but take the Bible as it reads, a work would be accomplished that would bring into the fold of Christ thousands now wandering in error.

Many a Scripture which learned men pass over as unimportant is full of comfort to him who has been taught in the school of Christ. An understanding of Bible truth depends not so much on the power of intellect brought to the search as on the singleness of purpose, the earnest longing after righteousness.

Results of Neglect of Prayer and Bible Study

The Bible should never be studied without prayer. The Holy Spirit alone can cause us to feel the importance of things easy to be understood, or prevent us from wresting difficult truths. Heavenly angels prepare the heart to comprehend God's Word. We shall be charmed with its beauty, strengthened by its promises. Temptations often appear irresistible because the tempted one cannot readily remember God's promises and meet Satan with the Scripture weapons. But angels are round about those willing to be taught, and they will bring to their remembrance the truths which are needed.

"He shall teach you all things, and bring all things to your remembrance, whatsoever I have said unto you." John 14:26. But the teachings of Christ must previously have been stored in the mind in order for the Spirit of God to bring them to our remembrance in the time of peril.

The destiny of earth's teeming multitudes is about to be decided. Every follower of Christ should earnestly inquire: "Lord what wilt thou have me to do?" Acts 9:6. We should now seek a deep and living experience in the things of God. We have not a moment to lose.

We are on Satan's enchanted ground. Sleep not, sentinels of God!

Many congratulate themselves on the wrong acts which they do not commit. It is not enough that they are trees in the garden of God. They are to bear fruit. In the books of heaven they are registered as cumberers of the ground. Yet with those who have slighted God's mercy and abused His grace, the heart of long-suffering love yet pleads.

In the summer there is no noticeable difference between evergreens and other trees; but when the blasts of winter come, the evergreens remain unchanged while other trees are stripped of their foliage. Let opposition arise, let intolerance again bear sway, let persecution be kindled, and the halfhearted and hypocritical will yield the faith; but the true Christian will stand firm, his faith stronger, his hope brighter, than in days of prosperity.

"He shall be as a tree planted by the waters, and that spreadeth out her roots by the river, and shall not see when heat cometh, but her leaf shall be green; and shall not be careful in the year of drought, neither shall cease from yielding fruit." Jeremiah 17:8.

38/God's Final Message

"I saw another angel come down from heaven, having great power; and the earth was lightened with his glory. And he cried mightily with a strong voice, saying, Babylon the great is fallen, is fallen, and is become the habitation of devils, and the hold of every foul spirit, and a cage of every unclean and hateful bird. . . . And I heard another voice from heaven, saying, Come out of her, my people, that ye be not partakers of her sins, and that ye receive not of her plagues." Revelation 18:1, 2, 4.

The announcement made by the second angel of Revelation 14 (verse 8) is to be repeated, with the additional mention of the corruptions which have been entering Babylon since that message was first given.

A terrible condition is here described. With every rejection of truth the minds of people will become darker, their hearts more stubborn. They will continue to trample upon one of the precepts of the Decalogue until they persecute those who hold it sacred. Christ is set at nought in the contempt placed upon His Word and His people.

The profession of religion will become a cloak to conceal the basest iniquity. A belief in spiritualism opens the door to doctrines of devils, and thus the influence of evil angels will be felt in the churches. Babylon has filled up the measure of her guilt, and destruction is about to fall.

But God still has a people in Babylon, and these faithful ones must be called out that they partake not of her sins and "receive not of her plagues." The angel comes down from heaven, lightening the earth with his glory and announcing the sins of Babylon. The call is heard: "Come out of her, my people." These announcements constitute the final warning to be given to the inhabitants of the earth.

The powers of earth, uniting to war against the commandments of God, will decree that "all, both small and great, rich and poor, free and bond" (Revelation 13:16) shall conform to the customs of the church by observance of the false sabbath. All who refuse will finally be declared deserving of death. On the other hand, the law of God enjoining the Creator's rest day threatens wrath against all who transgress its precepts.

With the issue thus clearly brought before him, whoever shall trample upon God's law to obey a human enactment receives the mark of the beast, the sign of allegiance to the power he chooses to obey instead of God. "If any man worship the beast and his image, and receive his mark in his forehead, or in his hand, the same shall drink of the wine of the wrath of God, which is poured out without mixture into the cup of his indignation." Revelation 14:9, 10.

Not one suffers the wrath of God until the truth has been brought home to his mind and conscience and has been rejected. Many have never had opportunity to hear the special truths for this time. He who reads every heart will leave none who desire the truth to be deceived as to the issues of the controversy. Everyone is to have sufficient light to make his decision intelligently.

The Great Test of Loyalty

The Sabbath, the great test of loyalty, is the truth especially controverted. While the observance of the false sabbath will be an avowal of allegiance to a power in opposition to God, the keeping of the true Sabbath is an evidence of loyalty to the Creator. While one class receive the mark of the beast, the other receive the seal of God.

Predictions that religious intolerance would gain control, that church and state would persecute those who keep the commandments of God, have been pronounced groundless and absurd. But as Sunday observance is widely agitated, the event so long doubted is seen to be approaching, and the message will produce an effect it could not have had before.

In every generation God has sent His servants to rebuke sin in the world and in the church. Many reformers, in entering upon their work, determined to exercise great prudence in attacking the sins of the church and the nation. They hoped, by the example of a pure Christian life, to lead the people back to the Bible. But the Spirit of God came upon them; fearless of consequences, they could not refrain from preaching the plain doctrines of the Bible.

Thus the message will be proclaimed. The Lord will work through humble instruments who consecrate themselves to His service. The laborers will be qualified rather by the unction of His Spirit than by the training of literary institutions. Men will be constrained to go forth with holy zeal, declaring the words which God gives. The sins of Babylon will be laid open. The people will be stirred. Thousands have never heard words like these. Babylon is the church, fallen because of her sins, because of her rejection of truth. As the people go to their teachers with the inquiry "Are these things so?" the ministers present fables to quiet the awakened conscience. But since many demand a plain "Thus saith the Lord," the popular ministry will stir up the sin-loving multitudes to revile and persecute those who proclaim it.

The clergy will put forth almost superhuman efforts to shut away the light, to suppress discussion of these vital questions. The church appeals to the strong arm of civil power, and, in this work, the papists and Protestants unite. As the movement for Sunday enforcement becomes more bold, commandment-keepers will be threatened with fines and imprisonment. Some will be offered positions of influence and other rewards to renounce their faith. But their answer is "Show us from the Word of God our error." Those arraigned before courts make a strong vindication of truth, and some who hear them are led to take their stand to keep all the commandments of God. Thousands otherwise would know nothing of these truths.

Obedience to God will be treated as rebellion. The parent will exercise severity toward the believing child. Children will be disinherited and driven from home. "All that will live godly in Christ Jesus shall suffer persecution." 2 Timothy 3:12. As the defenders of truth refuse to honor Sunday, some will be thrust into prison, some will be exiled, some will be treated as slaves. As the Spirit of God shall be withdrawn from men there will be strange developments. The heart can be very cruel when God's fear and love are removed.

The Storm Approaches

As the storm approaches, a large class who have professed faith in the third angel's message, but have not been sanctified through obedience to the truth, abandon their position and join the opposition. By uniting with the world they have come to view matters in nearly the same light, and they choose the popular side. Men who once rejoiced in the truth employ their talent and pleasing address to mislead souls. They become bitter enemies of their former brethren. These apostates are efficient agents of Satan to misrepresent and accuse Sabbathkeepers and stir up the rulers against them.

The Lord's servants have given the warning. God's Spirit has constrained them. They have not consulted their temporal interests, nor sought to preserve their reputation or their lives. The work seems far beyond their ability to accomplish. Yet they cannot turn back. Feeling their helplessness, they flee to the Mighty One for strength.

Different periods in history have been marked by the

development of some special truth, adapted to the necessities of God's people at that time. Every new truth has made its way against opposition. Christ's ambassadors must perform their duty and leave results with God.

Opposition Rises to New Heights

The opposition rises to a fierce height; the servants of God are again perplexed, for it seems to them that they have brought the crisis. But conscience and the Word of God assure them that their course is right. Their faith and courage rise with the emergency. Their testimony is "Christ has conquered the powers of earth, and shall we be afraid of a world already conquered?"

No man can serve God without enlisting against himself the opposition of the hosts of darkness. Evil angels will assail him, alarmed that his influence is taking the prey from their hands. Evil men will seek to separate him from God by alluring temptations. When these do not succeed, power is employed to force the conscience.

But so long as Jesus remains man's intercessor in the sanctuary above, the restraining influence of the Holy Spirit is felt by rulers and people. While many of our rulers are active agents of Satan, God also has His agents among the leading men of the nation. A few men will hold in check a powerful current of evil. The opposition of the enemies of truth will be restrained that the third angel's message may do its work. The final warning will arrest the attention of these leading men, and some will accept it and stand with the people of God during the time of trouble.

The Latter Rain and the Loud Cry

The angel who unites with the third angel is to lighten the whole earth with his glory. The first angel's message was carried to every mission station in the world, and in some countries there was the greatest religious interest witnessed since the Reformation. But these are to be exceeded by the last warning of the third angel.

The work will be similar to that of the Day of Pentecost. The "former rain" was given at the opening of the gospel to cause the upspringing of the precious seed; so the "latter rain" will be given at its close for the ripening of the harvest. Hosea 6:3; Joel 2:23. The great work of the gospel is not to close with less manifestation of the power of God than marked its opening. The prophecies which were fulfilled in the outpouring of the former rain at the opening of the gospel are again to be fulfilled in the latter rain at its close. Here are "the times of refreshing" to which the apostle Peter looked forward. Acts 3:19, 20.

Servants of God, their faces shining with holy consecration, will hasten from place to place to proclaim the message from heaven. Miracles will be wrought, the sick will be healed. Satan also works with lying wonders, even bringing down fire from heaven. Revelation 13:13. Thus the inhabitants of the earth will be brought to take their stand.

The message will be carried not so much by argument as by the deep conviction of the Spirit of God. The arguments have been presented, publications have exerted their influence, yet many have been prevented from fully comprehending the truth. Now the truth is seen in its clearness. Family connections, church relations are powerless to stay the honest children of God now. Notwithstanding the agencies combined against the truth, a large number take their stand upon the Lord's side.

39/The Time of Trouble

"At that time shall Michael stand up, the great Prince which standeth for the children of thy people: and there shall be a time of trouble, such as never was since there was a nation even to that same time: and at that time thy people shall be delivered, every one that shall be found written in the book." Daniel 12:1.

When the third angel's message closes, the people of God have accomplished their work. They have received "the latter rain" and are prepared for the trying hour before them. The final test has been brought upon the world, and all who have proved loyal to the divine precepts have received "the seal of the living God." Then Jesus ceases His intercession in the sanctuary above and with a loud voice says, "It is done." "He that is unjust, let him be unjust still: and he which is filthy, let him by filthy still: and he that is righteous, let him be righteous still: and he that is holy, let him be holy still." Revelation 22:11. Christ has made the atonement for His people and blotted out their sins. "The kingdom and dominion, and the greatness of the kingdom under the whole heaven" (Daniel 7:27) is about to be given to the heirs of salvation, and Jesus is to reign as King of kings and Lord of lords.

When He leaves the sanctuary, darkness covers the inhabitants of the earth. The righteous must live in the sight of a holy God without an intercessor. The restraint upon the wicked is removed, and Satan has entire control of the impenitent. The Spirit of God has been at last withdrawn. Satan will then plunge the inhabitants of the earth into one great, final trouble. Angels of God cease to hold in check the fierce winds of human passion. The whole world will be involved in ruin more terrible than that which came upon Jerusalem of old. There are forces now ready, only waiting the divine permission, to spread desolation everywhere.

Those who honor the law of God will be regarded as the cause of the fearful strife and bloodshed that fill the earth with woe. The power attending the last warning has enraged the wicked, and Satan will excite the spirit of hatred and persecution against all who have received the message.

When God's presence was withdrawn from the Jewish nation, priests and people still regarded themselves as the chosen of God. The ministration in the temple continued; daily the divine blessing was invoked upon a people guilty of the blood of God's Son. So when the irrevocable decision of the sanctuary has been pronounced and the destiny of the world has been forever fixed, the inhabitants of the earth will know it not. The forms of religion will be continued by a people from whom the Spirit of God has been withdrawn; the prince of evil will inspire them for the accomplishment of his malignant designs.

As the Sabbath becomes the special point of controversy throughout Christendom, it will be urged that the few who stand in opposition to the church and the state ought not to be tolerated, that it is better for them to suffer than for whole nations to be thrown into confusion and lawlessness. The same argument was brought against Christ. "It is expedient for us," said Caiaphas, that one man should die for the people, and that the whole nation perish not." John 11:50. This argument will appear conclusive; a decree will finally be issued against those who hallow the Sabbath of the fourth commandment, denouncing them and giving the people liberty after a certain time to put them to death. Romanism in the Old World and apostate Protestantism in the New will pursue a similar course. The people of God will then be plunged into those scenes of distress described as "the time of Jacob's trouble." Jeremiah 30:5-7; Genesis 32:24-30.

The Time of Jacob's Trouble

Because of the deception practiced to secure his father's blessing intended for Esau, Jacob had fled, alarmed by his brother's deadly threats. After remaining many years an exile, he had set out to return to his native country. On reaching the border he was filled with terror by the tidings of Esau's approach, doubtless bent on revenge. Jacob's only hope was in the mercy of God; his only defense must be prayer.

Alone with God, he confessed his sin with deep humiliation. The crisis in his life had come. In the darkness he continued praying. Suddenly a hand was laid upon his shoulder. He thought an enemy was seeking his life. With all the energy of despair he wrestled with his assailant. As the day began to break, the stranger put forth his superhuman power. Jacob seemed paralyzed and fell, a helpless, weeping suppliant, upon the neck of his mysterious antagonist. He knew then that it was the Angel of the covenant with whom he had been in conflict. Long had he endured remorse for his sin; now he must have the assurance that it was pardoned. The Angel urged, "Let me go, for the day breaketh," but the patriarch exclaimed, "I will not let thee go, except thou bless me." Jacob confessed his weakness and unworthiness, yet trusted the mercy of a covenant-keeping God. Through repentance and self-surrender, this sinful mortal prevailed with the Majesty of heaven.

Satan had accused Jacob before God because of his sin; he had moved Esau to march against him. During the patriarch's night of wrestling, Satan endeavored to discourage him and break his hold on God. He was driven almost to despair; but he had sincerely repented of his sin and held fast the Angel and urged his petition with earnest cries until he prevailed.

As Satan accused Jacob, he will urge his accusations against the people of God, but the company who keep the commandments of God resists his supremacy. He sees that holy angels are guarding them, and he infers that their sins have been pardoned. He has an accurate knowledge of the sins he has tempted them to commit and declares that the Lord cannot in justice forgive their sins and yet destroy him and his angels. He demands that they be given into his hands to destroy.

The Lord permits him to try them to the uttermost. Their confidence in God, their faith, will be severely tested. Satan endeavors to terrify them. He hopes so to destroy their faith that they will yield to temptation and turn from their allegiance to God.

Anguish That God Will Be Reproached

Yet the anguish which God's people suffer is not a dread of persecution. They fear that through some fault in themselves they will fail to realize the fulfillment of the Saviour's promise: I "will keep thee from the hour of temptation, which shall come upon all the world." Revelation 3:10. Should they prove unworthy because of their own defects of character, then God's holy name would be reproached.

They point to their past repentance of their many sins and plead the Saviour's promise: "Let him take hold of my strength, that he may make peace with me; and he shall make peace with me." Isaiah 27:5. Though suffering anxiety and distress, they do not cease their intercessions. They lay hold of God as Jacob laid hold of the Angel; and the language of their souls is "I will not let thee go, except thou bless me."

Sins Blotted Out

In the time of trouble, if the people of God had unconfessed sins to appear before them while tortured with fear and anguish, they would be overwhelmed. Despair would cut off their faith, and they could not plead with God for deliverance. But they have no concealed wrongs to reveal. Their sins have gone beforehand to judgment and have been blotted out, and they cannot bring them to remembrance.

The Lord shows in His dealings with Jacob that He will in no wise tolerate evil. All who excuse or conceal their sins and permit them to remain on the books of heaven unconfessed and unforgiven will be overcome by Satan. The more honorable the position they hold, the more sure the triumph of their adversary. Those who delay preparation cannot obtain it in the time of trouble, or at any subsequent time. The case of all such is hopeless.

Jacob's history is also an assurance that God will not cast off those who, betrayed into sin, have returned to Him with true repentance. God will send angels to comfort them in peril. The Lord's eye is upon His people. The flames of the furnace seem about to consume them, but the Refiner will bring them forth as gold tried in the fire.

A Faith That Endures

The season of distress and anguish before us will require a faith that can endure weariness, delay, and hunger, a faith that will not faint though severely tried. Jacob's victory is an evidence of the power of importunate prayer. All who will lay hold of God's promises, as he did, will succeed as he succeeded. Wrestling with God—how few know what it is! When waves of despair sweep over the suppliant, how few cling with faith to the promises of God.

Those who exercise but little faith now are in the greatest danger of falling under the power of satanic delusions. And even if they endure the test they will be plunged into deeper distress because they have never made it a habit to trust in God. We should now prove His promises.

Often trouble is greater in anticipation than in reality, but this is not true of the crisis before us. The most vivid presentation cannot reach the magnitude of the ordeal. In that time of trial every soul must stand for himself before God.

Now, while our High Priest is making the atonement for us, we should seek to become perfect in Christ. Not even by a thought could our Saviour be brought to yield to the power of temptation. Satan finds in human hearts some point where he can gain a foothold; some sinful desire is cherished, by means of which his temptations assert their power. But Christ declared of Himself: "The prince of this world cometh, and hath nothing in me." John 14:30. Satan could find nothing in the Son of God that would enable him to gain the victory. There was no sin in Him that Satan could use to his advantage. This is the condition in which those must be found who shall stand in the time of trouble.

It is in this life that we are to separate sin from us, through faith in the atoning blood of Christ. Our precious Saviour invites us to join ourselves to Him, to unite our weakness to His strength, our unworthiness to His merits. It rests with us to cooperate with Heaven in the work of conforming our characters to the divine model.

Fearful sights of a supernatural character will soon be revealed in the heavens, in token of the power of miracle-working demons. Spirits of devils will go forth to the "kings of the earth" and to the whole world, to urge them to unite with Satan in his last struggle against the government of heaven. Persons will arise pretending to be Christ Himself. They will perform miracles of healing and profess to have revelations from heaven contradicting the Scriptures.

The Crowning Act

As the crowning act in the great drama of deception, Satan himself will personate Christ. The church has long looked to the Saviour's advent as the consummation of her hopes. Now the great deceiver will make it appear that Christ has come. Satan will manifest himself as a majestic being of dazzling brightness, resembling the description of the Son of God in the Revelation. Revelation 1:13-15.

The glory that surrounds him is unsurpassed by anything that mortal eyes have yet beheld. The shout of triumph rings out, "Christ has come!" The people prostrate themselves before him. He lifts up his hands and blesses them. His voice is soft, yet full of melody. In compassionate tones he presents some of the same heavenly truths the Saviour uttered. He heals diseases, and then, in his assumed character of Christ, claims to have changed the Sabbath to Sunday. He declares that those who keep holy the seventh day are blaspheming his name. This is the strong, almost overmastering delusion. Multitudes give heed to sorceries, saying, This is "the great power of God." Acts 8:10.

God's People Not Misled

But the people of God will not be misled. The teachings of this false christ are not in accordance with the Scriptures. His blessing is pronounced upon the worshipers of the beast and his image, the very class on whom the Bible declares that God's unmingled wrath shall be poured out.

Furthermore, Satan is not permitted to counterfeit the manner of Christ's advent. The Saviour has warned His people against deception on this point. "There shall arise false christs, and false prophets, and shall show great signs and wonders; insomuch that, if it were possible, they shall deceive the very elect. . . . Wherefore if they shall say unto you, Behold, he is in the desert; go not forth: behold, he is in the secret chambers; believe it not. For as the lightning cometh out of the east, and shineth even unto the west; so shall also the coming of the Son of man be." Matthew 24:24-27. See also Matthew 25:31; Revelation 1:7; 1 Thessalonians 4:16, 17. This coming, there is no possibility of counterfeiting. It will be witnessed by the whole world.

Only diligent students of the Scriptures who have received the love of the truth will be shielded from the powerful delusion that takes the world captive. By the Bible testimony these will detect the deceiver in his disguise. Are the people of God now so firmly established upon His Word that they would not yield to the evidence of their senses? Would they, in such a crisis, cling to the Bible, and the Bible only?

As the decree issued by the various rulers of Christendom against commandment keepers shall withdraw the protection of government and abandon them to those who desire their destruction, the people of God will flee from the cities and villages and associate together in companies, dwelling in the most desolate and solitary places. Many will find refuge in the strongholds of the mountains, like the Christians of the Piedmont valleys. (See chapter four.) But many of all nations and of all classes, high and low, rich and poor, black and white, will be cast into the most unjust and cruel bondage. The beloved of God pass weary days shut in by prison bars, sentenced to be slain, apparently left to die in dark, loathsome dungeons.

Will the Lord forget His people in this trying hour? Did He forget faithful Noah, Lot, Joseph, Elijah, Jeremiah, or Daniel? Though enemies may thrust them into prison, yet dungeon walls cannot cut off communication between their souls and Christ. Angels will come to them in lonely cells. The prison will be as a palace, and the gloomy walls will be lighted up as when Paul and Silas sang at midnight in the Philippian dungeon.

God's judgments will be visited upon those who are seeking to destroy His people. To God, punishment is a "strange act." Isaiah 28:21; see also Ezekiel 33:11. The Lord is "merciful and gracious, longsuffering, and abundant in goodness and truth, . . . forgiving iniquity and transgression and sin." Yet He will "by no means clear the guilty." Exodus 34:6, 7; Nahum 1:3. The nation with which He bears long, and which has filled up the measure of its iniquity, will finally drink the cup of wrath unmixed with mercy.

When Christ ceases His intercession in the sanctuary, the unmingled wrath threatened against those who worship the beast will be poured out. The plagues on Egypt were similar to those more extensive judgments which are to fall upon the world just before the final deliverance of God's people. Says the revelator: "There fell a noisome and grievous sore upon the men which had the mark of the beast, and upon them which worshiped his image." The sea "became as the blood of a dead man." And "the rivers and fountains of waters . . . became blood." The angel declares: "Thou art righteous, O Lord, . . . because thou hast judged thus. For they have shed the blood of saints and prophets, and thou hast given them blood to drink; for they are worthy." Revelation 16:2-6, 8, 9. By condemning the people of God to death, they have as truly incurred the guilt of their blood as if it had been shed by their hands. Christ declared the Jews of His time guilty of all the blood of holy men shed since the days of Abel (Matthew 23:34-36), for they possessed the same spirit as these murderers of the prophets.

In the plague that follows, power is given to the sun "to scorch men with fire." The prophets describe this fearful time: "The harvest of the field is perished. . . . All the trees of the field are withered: because joy is withered away from the sons of men." "How do the beasts groan! the herds of cattle are perplexed, because they have no pasture. . . . The rivers of waters are dried up, and the fire hath devoured the pastures of the wilderness." Joel 1:11, 12, 18-20.

These plagues are not universal, yet they will be the most awful scourges ever known. All judgments prior to the close of probation have been mingled with mercy. The blood of Christ has shielded the sinner from the full measure of his guilt; but in the final judgment, wrath is unmixed with mercy. Multitudes will desire the shelter of God's mercy which they have despised.

While persecuted and distressed, while they suffer for want of food, the people of God will not be left to perish. Angels will supply their wants. "Bread shall be given him; his waters shall be sure." "I the Lord will hear them, I the God of Israel will not forsake them." Isaiah 33:16; 41:17.

Yet to human sight it will appear that the people of God must soon seal their testimony with their blood, as did the martyrs before them. It is a time of fearful agony. The wicked exult, "Where now is your faith? Why does not God deliver you out of our hands if you are indeed His people?" But the waiting ones remember Jesus dying on Calvary's cross. Like Jacob, all are wrestling with God.

Companies of Angels Watch

Angels are stationed about those who have kept the word of Christ's patience. They have witnessed their distress and heard their prayers. They wait the word of their Commander to snatch them from their peril. But they must wait a little longer. The people of God must drink of the cup and be baptized with the baptism. Matthew 20:20-23. Yet for the elect's sake the time of trouble will be shortened. The end will come more quickly than men expect.

Though a general decree has fixed the time when commandment-keepers may be put to death, their enemies will in some cases anticipate the decree and endeavor to take their lives. But none can pass the guardians stationed about every faithful soul. Some are assailed in their flight from the cities, but the swords raised against them break as a straw. Others are defended by angels in the form of men of war.

In all ages celestial beings have taken an active part in the affairs of men. They have accepted the hospitalities of human homes, acted as guides to benighted travelers, opened prison doors and set free the servants of the Lord. They came to roll away the stone from the Saviour's tomb.

Angels visit the assemblies of the wicked, as they went to Sodom, to determine whether they have passed the boundary of God's forbearance. The Lord, for the sake of a few who really serve Him, restrains calamities and prolongs the tranquillity of multitudes. Little do sinners realize that they are indebted for their lives to the faithful few whom they delight to oppress.

Often in the councils of this world, angels have been spokesmen. Human ears have listened to their appeals, human lips have ridiculed their counsels. These heavenly messengers have proved themselves better able to plead the cause of the oppressed than their most eloquent defenders. They have defeated and arrested evils that would have caused great suffering to God's people.

With earnest longing, God's people await the tokens of their coming King. As the wrestling ones urge their petitions before God, the heavens glow with the dawn of eternal day. Like the melody of angel songs the words fall upon the ear: "Help is coming." Christ's voice comes from the gates ajar: "Lo, I am with you. Be not afraid. I have fought the battle in your behalf, and in my name you are more than conquerors."

The precious Saviour will send help just when we need it. The time of trouble is a fearful ordeal for God's people, but every true believer may see by faith the bow of promise encircling him. "The redeemed of the Lord shall return, and come with singing unto Zion; and everlasting joy shall be upon their head: they shall obtain gladness and joy; and sorrow and mourning shall flee away." Isaiah 51:11.

If the blood of Christ's witnesses were shed at this time, their fidelity would not be a testimony to convince others of the truth, for the obdurate heart has beaten back the waves of mercy until they return no more. If the righteous were now to fall a prey to their enemies, it would be a triumph for the prince of darkness. Christ has spoken: "Come, my people, enter thou into thy chambers, and shut thy doors about thee: hide thyself as it were for a little moment until the indignation be overpast. For, behold, the Lord cometh out of his place to punish the inhabitants of the earth for their iniquity.'' Isaiah 26:20, 21.

Glorious will be the deliverance of those who have patiently waited for His coming and whose names are written in the book of life.

40/God's People Delivered

When the protection of human laws shall be withdrawn from those who honor the law of God, there will be in different lands a simultaneous movement for their destruction. As the time appointed in the decree draws near, the people will conspire to strike in one night a decisive blow which shall silence dissent and reproof.

The people of God—some in prison cells, some in forests and mountains—plead for divine protection. Armed men, urged on by evil angels, are preparing for the work of death. Now, in the hour of utmost extremity, God will interpose: "Ye shall have a song, as in the night when a holy solemnity is kept; and gladness of heart, as when one goeth . . . to come into the mountain of the Lord, to the mighty One of Israel. And the Lord shall cause his glorious voice to be heard, and shall shew the lighting down of his arm, with the indignation of his anger, and with the flame of a devouring fire, with scattering, and tempest, and hailstones." Isaiah 30:29, 30.

Throngs of evil men are about to rush upon their prey, when a dense blackness, deeper than night, falls on the earth. Then a rainbow spans the heavens and seems to encircle each praying company. The angry multitudes are arrested. The objects of their rage are forgotten. They gaze upon the symbol of God's covenant and long to be shielded from its brightness.

By the people of God a voice is heard, saying, "Look up." Like Stephen they look up and see the glory of God and the Son of man on His throne. See Acts 7:55, 56. They discern the marks of His humiliation, and hear the request, "I will that they also,

whom thou hast given me, be with me where I am."
John 17:24. A voice is heard saying, "They come,
holy, harmless, and undefiled! They have kept the
word of my patience."

At midnight God manifests His power for the deliverance of His people. The sun appears shining in its
strength. Signs and wonders follow. The wicked look
with terror on the scene, while the righteous behold the
tokens of their deliverance. In the midst of the angry
heavens is one clear space of indescribable glory
whence comes the voice of God like the sound of many
waters, saying, "It is done!" Revelation 16:17.

That voice shakes the heavens and the earth. There
is a mighty earthquake, "such as was not since men
were upon the earth, so mighty an earthquake, and so
great." Revelation 16:18. Ragged rocks are scattered
on every side. The sea is lashed into fury. There is
heard the shriek of a hurricane like the voice of demons. The earth's surface is breaking up. Its very
foundations seem to be giving way. Seaports that have
become like Sodom for wickedness are swallowed up
by the angry waters. "Babylon the great" has come in
remembrance before God, "to give unto her the cup of
the wine of the fierceness of his wrath." Revelation
16:19. Great hailstones do their work of destruction.
Proud cities are laid low. Lordly palaces on which men
have lavished their wealth crumble before their eyes.
Prison walls are rent asunder, and God's people are set
free.

Graves are opened, and "many of them that sleep in
the dust of the earth . . . awake, some to everlasting
life, and some to shame and everlasting contempt."
"They also which pierced him," those that derided
Christ's dying agonies, and the most violent opposers
of His truth, are raised to see the honor placed on the
loyal and obedient. Daniel 12:2; Revelation 1:7.

Fierce lightnings envelop the earth in a sheet of
flame. Above the thunder, voices, mysterious and awful, declare the doom of the wicked. Those who were

boastful and defiant, cruel to God's commandment-keeping people, now shudder in fear. Demons tremble while men are supplicating for mercy.

The Day of the Lord

Said the prophet Isaiah: "In that day a man shall cast the idols of his silver, and the idols of his gold, which they made each one for himself to worship, to the moles and to the bats; to go into the clefts of the rocks, and into the tops of the ragged rocks, for fear of the Lord, and for the glory of his majesty, when he ariseth to shake terribly the earth." Isaiah 2:20, 21.

Those who have sacrificed all for Christ are now secure. Before the world and in the face of death they have evinced their fidelity to Him who died for them. Their faces, so lately pale and haggard, are now aglow with wonder. Their voices rise in triumphant song: "God is our refuge and strength, a very present help in trouble. Therefore will not we fear, though the earth be removed, and though the mountains be carried into the midst of the sea; though the waters thereof roar and be troubled, though the mountains shake with the swelling thereof." Psalm 46:1-3.

While these words of holy trust ascend to God, the glory of the celestial city streams from the gates ajar. Then there appears against the sky a hand holding two tables of stone. That holy law, proclaimed from Sinai, is now revealed as the rule of judgment. The words are so plain that all can read them. Memory is aroused. The darkness of superstition and heresy is swept from every mind.

It is impossible to describe the horror and despair of those who have trampled upon God's law. To secure the favor of the world, they set aside its precepts and taught others to transgress. Now they are condemned by that law which they have despised. They see that they are without excuse. The enemies of God's law have a new conception of truth and duty. Too late they see that the Sabbath is the seal of the living God. Too late they see the sandy foundation upon which they have been building. They have been fighting against God. Religious teachers have led souls to perdition while professing to guide them to Paradise. How great is the responsibility of men in holy office, how terrible the results of their unfaithfulness!

The King of Kings Appears

The voice of God is heard declaring the day and hour of Jesus' coming. The Israel of God stand listening, their countenances lighted up with His glory. Soon there appears in the east a small black cloud. It is the cloud which surrounds the Saviour. In solemn silence the people of God gaze upon it as it draws nearer, until it is a great white cloud, its base a glory like consuming fire, and above it the rainbow of the covenant. Not now a "Man of sorrows," Jesus rides forth as a mighty conqueror. Holy angels, a vast, unnumbered throng, attend Him, "ten thousand times ten thousand, and thousands of thousands." Every eye beholds the Prince of life. A diadem of glory rests on His brow. His countenance outshines the noonday sun. "And he hath on his vesture and on his thigh a name written, King of kings, and Lord of lords." Revelation 19:16.

The King of kings descends upon the cloud, wrapped in flaming fire. The earth trembles before Him: "Our God shall come, and shall not keep silence: a fire shall devour before him, and it shall be very tempestuous round about him. He shall call to the heavens from above, and to the earth, that he may judge his people." Psalm 50:3, 4.

"And the kings of the earth, and the great men, and the rich men, and every bondman, and every freeman, hid themselves in the dens and in the rocks of the mountains; and said to the mountains and rocks, Fall on us, and hide us from the face of him that sitteth on the throne, and from the wrath of the Lamb: for the great day of his wrath is come; and who shall be able to stand?" Revelation 6:15-17.

Derisive jests have ceased, lying lips hushed. Nought is heard but the voice of prayer and the sound of weeping. The wicked pray to be buried beneath the rocks rather than meet the face of Him whom they have despised. That voice which penetrates the ear of the dead, they know. How often have its tender tones called them to repentance. How often has it been heard in the entreaties of a friend, a brother, a Redeemer. That voice awakens memories of warnings despised and invitations refused.

There are those who mocked Christ in His humiliation. He declared: "Hereafter shall ye see the Son of man sitting on the right hand of power, and coming in the clouds of heaven." Matthew 26:64. Now they behold Him in His glory; they are yet to see Him sitting on the right hand of power. There is the haughty Herod who jeered at His royal title. There are the men who placed upon His brow the thorny crown and in His hand the mimic scepter—those who bowed before Him in blasphemous mockery, who spat upon the Prince of life. They seek to flee from His presence. Those who drove the nails through His hands and feet behold these marks with terror and remorse.

With awful distinctness priests and rulers recall the events of Calvary, how, wagging their heads in satanic exultation, they exclaimed, "He saved others; himself he cannot save." Matthew 27:42. Louder than the shout, "Crucify him, crucify him!" which rang through Jerusalem, swells the despairing wail, "He is the Son of God!" They seek to flee from the presence of the King of kings.

In the lives of all who reject truth there are moments when conscience awakens, when the soul is harassed with vain regrets. But what are these compared with the remorse of that day! In the midst of their terror they hear the voices of the saints exclaiming: "Lo, this is our God; we have waited for him, and he will save us." Isaiah 25:9.

The voice of the Son of God calls forth the sleeping

saints. Throughout the earth the dead shall hear that voice, and they that hear shall live, a great army of every nation, kindred, tongue, and people. From the prison house of death they come, clothed with immortal glory, crying: "O death, where is thy sting? O grave, where is thy victory?" 1 Corinthians 15:55.

All come forth from their graves the same in stature as when they entered the tomb. But all arise with the freshness and vigor of eternal youth. Christ came to restore that which had been lost. He will change our vile bodies and fashion them like unto His glorious body. The mortal, corruptible form, once polluted with sin, becomes perfect, beautiful and immortal. Blemishes and deformities are left in the grave. The redeemed will "grow up" (Malachi 4:2) to the full stature of the race in its primeval glory, the last lingering traces of the curse of sin removed. Christ's faithful ones will in mind and soul and body reflect the perfect image of their Lord.

The living righteous are changed "in a moment, in the twinkling of an eye." At the voice of God they are made immortal and with the risen saints are caught up to meet their Lord in the air. Angels "gather together his elect from the four winds, from one end of heaven to the other." Matthew 24:31. Little children are borne to their mothers' arms. Friends long separated by death are united, nevermore to part, and with songs of gladness ascend together to the city of God.

Into the Holy City

Throughout the unnumbered host of the redeemed every glance is fixed upon Jesus. Every eye beholds His glory whose "visage was so marred more than any man, and his form more than the sons of men." Isaiah 52:14. Upon the heads of the overcomers Jesus places the crown of glory. For each there is a crown bearing his own "new name" (Revelation 2:17) and the inscription, "Holiness to the Lord." In every hand are placed the victor's palm and the shining harp. Then, as the commanding angels strike the note, every hand sweeps the strings with skillful touch in rich, melodious strains. Each voice is raised in grateful praise: "Unto him that loved us, and washed us from our sins in his own blood, and hath made us kings and priests unto God and his Father; to him be glory and dominion for ever and ever." Revelation 1:5, 6.

Before the ransomed throng is the Holy City. Jesus opens the gates, and the nations that have kept the truth enter in. Then His voice is heard, "Come, ye blessed of my Father, inherit the kingdom prepared for you from the foundation of the world." Matthew 25:34. Christ presents to the Father the purchase of His blood, declaring: "Here am I, and the children whom thou hast given me." "Those that thou gavest me I have kept." Hebrews 2:13; John 17:12. Oh, the rapture of that hour when the infinite Father, looking upon the ransomed, shall behold His image, sin's blight removed, and the human once more in harmony with the divine!

The Saviour's joy is in seeing, in the kingdom of glory, the souls saved by His agony and humiliation. The redeemed will be sharers in His joy; they behold those won through their prayers, labors, and loving sacrifice. Gladness will fill their hearts when they see that one has gained others, and these still others.

The Two Adams Meet

As the ransomed are welcomed to the city of God, there rings out an exultant cry. The two Adams are about to meet. The Son of God is to receive the father of our race—whom He created, who sinned, and for whose sin the marks of the crucifixion are on the Saviour's form. As Adam discerns the prints of the nails, in humiliation he casts himself at Christ's feet. The Saviour lifts him up and bids him look once more upon the Eden home from which he has so long been exiled.

Adam's life was filled with sorrow. Every dying leaf, every victim of sacrifice, every stain upon man's purity, was a reminder of his sin. Terrible was the agony of remorse as he met the reproaches cast upon himself as the cause of sin. Faithfully did he repent of his sin, and he died in the hope of a resurrection. Now, through the atonement, Adam is reinstated.

Transported with joy, he beholds the trees that were once his delight, whose fruit he himself had gathered in the days of his innocence. He sees the vines his own hands trained, the very flowers he once loved to care for. This is indeed Eden restored!

The Saviour leads him to the tree of life and bids him eat. He beholds a multitude of his family redeemed. Then he casts his crown at the feet of Jesus and embraces the Redeemer. He touches the harp, and the vaults of heaven echo the triumphant song: "Worthy, worthy, is the Lamb that was slain." Revelation 5:12. The family of Adam cast their crowns at the Saviour's feet as they bow in adoration. Angels wept at the fall of Adam and rejoiced when Jesus opened the grave for all who should believe on His name. Now they behold the work of redemption accomplished and unite their voices in praise.

Upon the "sea of glass as it were mingled with fire" are gathered the company that have "gotten the victory over the beast, and over his image, and over his mark, and over the number of his name." The hundred and forty and four thousand were redeemed from among men, and they sing "a new song," the song of Moses and the Lamb. Revelation 15:2, 3. None but the hundred and forty-four thousand can learn that song, for it is the song of an experience such as no other company ever had. "These are they which follow the Lamb whithersoever he goeth." These, having been translated from among the living, are "the firstfruits unto God and to the Lamb." Revelation 14:4, 5. They passed through the time of trouble such as never was since there was a nation; they endured the anguish of the time of Jacob's trouble; they stood without an intercessor through the final outpouring of God's judg-

ments. They "washed their robes, and made them
white in the blood of the Lamb." "In their mouth was
found no guile: for they are without fault" before God.
"They shall hunger no more, neither thirst any more;
neither shall the sun light on them, nor any heat. For
the Lamb which is in the midst of the throne shall feed
them, and shall lead them unto living fountains of waters: and God shall wipe away all tears from their
eyes." Revelation 7:14; 14:5; 7:16, 17.

The Redeemed in Glory

In all ages the Saviour's chosen have walked in narrow paths. They were purified in the furnace of affliction. For Jesus' sake they endured hatred, calumny,
self-denial, and bitter disappointments. They learned
the evil of sin, its power, its guilt, its woe; they look on
it with abhorrence. A sense of the infinite sacrifice
made for its cure humbles them and fills their hearts
with gratitude. They love much because they have
been forgiven much. See Luke 7:47. Partakers of
Christ's sufferings, they are fitted to be partakers of
His glory.

The heirs of God come from garrets, hovels, dungeons, scaffolds, mountains, deserts, caves. They
were "destitute, afflicted, tormented." Millions went
to the grave loaded with infamy because they refused
to yield to Satan. But now they are no longer afflicted,
scattered, and oppressed. Henceforth they stand clad
in richer robes than the most honored of the earth have
worn, crowned with diadems more glorious than were
ever placed on the brow of earthly monarchs. The King
of glory has wiped the tears from all faces. They pour
forth a song of praise, clear, sweet, and harmonious.
The anthem swells through the vaults of heaven: "Salvation to our God which sitteth upon the throne, and
unto the Lamb." And all respond, "Amen: Blessing,
and glory, and wisdom, and thanksgiving, and honor,
and power, and might, be unto our God for ever and
ever." Revelation 7:10, 12.

In this life we can only begin to understand the wonderful theme of redemption. With our finite comprehension we may consider most earnestly the shame and the glory, the life and the death, the justice and the mercy, that meet in the cross; yet with the utmost stretch of our mental powers we fail to grasp its full significance. The length and the breadth, the depth and the height, of redeeming love are but dimly comprehended. The plan of redemption will not be fully understood, even when the ransomed see as they are seen and know as they are known; but through the eternal ages new truth will continually unfold to the wondering and delighted mind. Though the griefs and pains and temptations of earth are ended and the cause removed, the people of God will ever have a distinct, intelligent knowledge of what their salvation has cost.

The cross will be the song of the redeemed through all eternity. In Christ glorified they behold Christ crucified. Never will it be forgotten that the Majesty of heaven humbled Himself to uplift fallen man, that He bore the guilt and shame of sin and the hiding of His Father's face till the woes of a lost world broke His heart and crushed out His life. The Maker of all worlds laid aside His glory from love to man—this will ever excite the wonder of the universe. As the nations of the saved look upon their Redeemer and know that His kingdom is to have no end, they break forth in song: "Worthy is the Lamb that was slain, and hath redeemed us to God by his own most precious blood!"

The mystery of the cross explains all mysteries. It will be seen that He who is infinite in wisdom could devise no plan for our salvation except the sacrifice of His Son. The compensation for this sacrifice is the joy of peopling the earth with ransomed beings, holy, happy, and immortal. Such is the value of the soul that the Father is satisfied with the price paid. And Christ Himself, beholding the fruits of His great sacrifice, is satisfied.

41/The Earth in Ruins

When the voice of God turns the captivity of His people, there is a terrible awakening of those who have lost all in the great conflict of life. Blinded by Satan's deceptions the rich prided themselves on their superiority to those less favored. But they had neglected to feed the hungry, clothe the naked, deal justly, and love mercy. Now they are stripped of all that made them great and are left destitute. They look with terror upon the destruction of their idols. They have sold their souls for earthly enjoyments and have not become rich toward God. Their lives are a failure, their pleasures turned to gall. The gain of a lifetime is swept away in a moment. The rich bemoan the destruction of their grand houses, the scattering of their gold and silver, and the fear that they themselves are to perish with their idols. The wicked lament that the result is what it is, but they do not repent of their wickedness.

The minister who has sacrificed truth to gain the favor of men now discerns the influence of his teachings. Every line written, every word uttered that led men to rest in a refuge of falsehood has been scattering seed; and now he beholds the harvest. Saith the Lord: "Woe be unto the pastors that destroy and scatter the sheep of my pasture! . . . Behold, I will visit upon you the evil of your doings." "With lies ye have made the heart of the righteous sad, whom I have not made sad; and strengthened the hands of the wicked, that he should not return from his wicked way, by promising him life." Jeremiah 23:1, 2; Ezekiel 13:22.

Ministers and people see that they have rebelled against the Author of all righteous law. Setting aside the divine precepts gave rise to thousands of springs of iniquity, until the earth became one vast sink of corruption. No language can express the longing which the disloyal feel for that which they have lost forever—eternal life.

The people accuse one another of having led them to destruction, but all unite in heaping their bitterest condemnation upon the unfaithful pastors who prophesied "smooth things" (Isaiah 30:10), who led their hearers to make void the law of God and persecute those who would keep it holy. "We are lost!" they cry, "and you are the cause." The hands that once crowned them with laurels will be raised for their destruction. Everywhere there is strife and bloodshed.

The Son of God and heavenly messengers have been in conflict with the evil one to warn, enlighten, and save the children of men. Now all have made their decisions; the wicked have fully united with Satan in his warfare against God. The controversy is not alone with Satan, but with men. "The Lord hath a controversy with the nations." Jeremiah 25:31.

The Angel of Death

Now the angel of death goes forth, represented in Ezekiel's vision by the men with the slaughtering weapons, to whom the command is given: "Slay utterly old and young, both maids, and little children, and women: but come not near any man upon whom is the mark; and begin at my sanctuary." "They began at the ancient men which were before the house," those who professed to be the spiritual guardians of the people. Ezekiel 9:6.

False watchmen are the first to fall. "The Lord cometh out of his place to punish the inhabitants of the earth for their iniquity: the earth also shall disclose her blood, and shall no more cover her slain." "A great tumult from the Lord shall be among them; and they shall lay hold every one on the hand of his neighbor, and his hand shall rise up against the hand of his neighbor." Isaiah 26:21; Zechariah 14:12, 13.

In the mad strife of their own fierce passions and by the outpouring of God's unmingled wrath, fall wicked priests, rulers, and people. "And the slain of the Lord shall be at that day from one end of the earth even unto the other." Jeremiah 25:33.

At the coming of Christ the wicked are destroyed by the brightness of His glory. Christ takes His people to the city of God, and the earth is emptied of its inhabitants. "Behold, the Lord maketh the earth empty, and maketh it waste, and turneth it upside down, and scattereth abroad the inhabitants thereof. . . . The land shall be utterly emptied and utterly spoiled: for the Lord hath spoken this word . . . because they have transgressed the laws, changed the ordinance, broken the everlasting covenant. Therefore hath the curse devoured the earth, and they that dwell therein are desolate: therefore the inhabitants of the earth are burned." Isaiah 24:1, 3, 5, 6.

The earth appears like a desolate wilderness. Cities destroyed by the earthquake, uprooted trees, ragged rocks torn out of the earth are scattered over its surface. Vast caverns mark the spot where the mountains have been rent from their foundations.

The Banishment of Satan

Now the event takes place foreshadowed in the last solemn service of the Day of Atonement. When the sins of Israel had been removed from the sanctuary by virtue of the blood of the sin offering, the scapegoat was presented alive before the Lord. The high priest confessed over him "all the iniquities of the children of Israel, . . . putting them upon the head of the goat." Leviticus 16:21. In like manner, when the work of atonement in the heavenly sanctuary has been completed, then, in the presence of God and heavenly angels and the host of the redeemed, the sins of God's people will be placed on Satan; he will be declared guilty of all the evil which he has caused them to commit. As the scapegoat was sent away into a land not inhabited, so Satan will be banished to the desolate earth.

After presenting scenes of the Lord's coming, the revelator continues: "I saw an angel come down from heaven, having the key of the bottomless pit and a great chain in his hand. And he laid hold on the dragon, that old serpent, which is the devil, and Satan, and bound him a thousand years, and cast him into the bottomless pit, and shut him up, and set a seal upon him, that he should deceive the nations no more, till the thousand years should be fulfilled: and after that he must be loosed a little season." Revelation 20:1-3.

The "bottomless pit" represents the earth in confusion and darkness. Looking forward to the great day of God, Jeremiah declares: "I beheld the earth, and, lo, it was without form, and void:* and the heavens, and they had no light. I beheld the mountains, and, lo, they trembled, and all the hills moved lightly. I beheld, and, lo, there was no man, and all the birds of the heavens were fled. I beheld, and, lo, the fruitful place was a wilderness, and all the cities thereof were broken down." Jeremiah 4:23-26.

Here is to be the home of Satan with his evil angels for a 1000 years. Limited to the earth, he will not have access to other worlds to tempt and annoy those who have never fallen. In this sense he is "bound." None remain on whom he can exercise his power. He is cut off from the work of deception and ruin which has been his sole delight.

Isaiah, looking forward to Satan's overthrow, exclaims: "How art thou fallen from heaven, O Lucifer, son of the morning! how art thou cut down to the

---

*The word for "deep" in Genesis 1:2 in the Greek translation of the Old Testament is *abyssos*, which also appears here in Jeremiah. This same word is found in the Greek text of Revelation 20:1, rendered in the King James Version "bottomless pit."

ground, which didst weaken the nations! . . . Thou hast said in thine heart, I will ascend into heaven, I will exalt my throne above the stars of God: . . . I will be like the Most High. Yet thou shalt be brought down to hell, to the sides of the pit. They that see thee shall narrowly look upon thee, and consider thee, saying, Is this the man that made the earth to tremble, that did shake kingdoms; that made the world as a wilderness, and destroyed the cities thereof; that *opened not the house of his prisoners?*" Isaiah 14:12-17.

For 6000 years Satan's prison-house has received God's people, but Christ has broken his bonds and set the prisoners free. Alone with his evil angels he realizes the effect of sin: "The kings of the nations, even all of them, lie in glory, every one in his own house [the grave]. But thou art cast out of thy grave like an abominable branch. . . . Thou shalt not be joined with them in burial, because thou hast destroyed thy land, and slain thy people." Isaiah 14:18-20.

For 1000 years, Satan will behold the results of his rebellion against the law of God. His sufferings are intense. He is now left to contemplate the part he has acted since he rebelled and to look forward with terror to the dreadful future when he must be punished.

During the 1000 years between the first and second resurrections, the judgment of the wicked takes place. Paul points to this as an event that follows the second advent. 1 Corinthians 4:5. The righteous reign as kings and priests. John says: "I saw thrones, and they sat upon them, and judgement was given unto them. . . . They shall be priests of God and of Christ and shall reign with him a thousand years." Revelation 20:4-6.

At this time "the saints shall judge the world." 1 Corinthians 6:12. In union with Christ they judge the wicked, deciding every case according to the deeds done in the body. Then the portion the wicked must suffer is meted out, according to their works, and it is recorded against their names in the book of death.

Satan and evil angels are judged by Christ and His

people. Says Paul: "Know ye not that we shall judge angels?" 1 Corinthians 6:3. Jude declares: "The angels which kept not their first estate, but left their own habitation, he hath reserved in everlasting chains under darkness unto the judgment of the great day." Jude 6.

At the close of the 1000 years, the second resurrection will take place. Then the wicked will be raised from the dead and appear before God for the execution of "the judgment written." Psalm 149:9. Thus the Revelator says: "The rest of the dead lived not again until the thousand years were finished." Revelation 20:5. And Isaiah declares, concerning the wicked: "They shall be gathered together as prisoners are gathered in the pit, and shall be shut up in the prison, and *after many days shall they be visited*." Isaiah 24:22.

42/Eternal Peace:
The Controversy Ended

At the close of the 1000 years, Christ returns to the earth accompanied by the redeemed and a retinue of angels. He bids the wicked dead arise to receive their doom. They come forth, numberless as the sands of the sea, bearing the traces of disease and death. What a contrast to those raised in the first resurrection!

Every eye is turned to behold the glory of the Son of God. With one voice the wicked hosts exclaim: "Blessed is he that cometh in the name of the Lord!" Matthew 23:39. It is not love that inspires this utterance. The force of truth urges the words from unwilling lips. As the wicked went in to the graves, so they come forth with the same enmity to Christ and the same spirit of rebellion. They are to have no new probation in which to remedy their past lives.

Says the prophet: "His feet shall stand in that day upon the Mount of Olives, . . . and the Mount of Olives shall cleave in the midst thereof." Zechariah 14:4. As the New Jerusalem comes down out of heaven, it rests upon the place made ready, and Christ, with His people and the angels, enters the holy city.

While cut off from his work of deception, the prince of evil was miserable and dejected, but as the wicked dead are raised and he sees the vast multitudes upon his side, his hopes revive. He determines not to yield the great controversy. He will marshal the lost under his banner. In rejecting Christ they have accepted the rule of the rebel leader, ready to do his bidding. Yet, true to his early cunning, he does not acknowledge himself to be Satan. He claims to be the rightful owner of the world whose inheritance has been unlawfully wrested from him. He represents himself as a redeemer, assuring his deluded subjects that his power has brought them from their graves. Satan makes the weak strong, and inspires all with his own energy to lead them to take possession of the city of God. He points to the unnumbered millions who have been raised from the dead, and declares that as their leader he is able to regain his throne and kingdom.

In the vast throng are the long-lived race that existed before the Flood, men of lofty stature and giant intellect; men whose wonderful works led the world to idolize their genius, but whose cruelty and evil inventions caused God to blot them from His creation. There are kings and generals who never lost a battle. In death these experienced no change. As they come up from the grave, they are actuated by the same desire to conquer that ruled them when they fell.

The Final Assault Against God

Satan consults with these mighty men. They declare that the army within the city is small in comparison with theirs and can be overcome. Skillful artisans construct implements of war. Military leaders marshal warlike men into companies and divisions.

At last the order to advance is given, and the countless host moves on, an army such as the combined forces of all ages could never equal. Satan leads the van, kings and warriors in his train. With military precision the serried ranks advance over the earth's broken surface to the City of God. By command of Jesus, the gates of the New Jerusalem are closed, and the armies of Satan make ready for the onset.

Now Christ appears to the view of His enemies. Far above the city, upon a foundation of burnished gold, is a throne. Upon this throne sits the Son of God, and around Him are the subjects of His kingdom. The glory of the Eternal Father is enshrouding His Son. The brightness of His presence flows out beyond the gates, flooding the earth with radiance.

Nearest the throne are those who were once zealous in the cause of Satan, but who, plucked as brands from the burning, have followed their Saviour with intense devotion. Next are those who perfected character in the midst of falsehood and infidelity, who honored the law of God when the world declared it void, and the millions, of all ages, who were martyred for their faith. Beyond is the "great multitude, which no man could number, of all nations, and kindreds, and people, and tongues, . . . clothed with white robes, and palms in their hands." Revelation 7:9. Their warfare is ended, their victory won. The palm branch is a symbol of triumph, the white robe an emblem of the righteousness of Christ which now is theirs.

In all that throng there are none to ascribe salvation to themselves by their own goodness. Nothing is said of what they have suffered; the keynote of every anthem is, Salvation to our God and to the Lamb.

Sentence Pronounced Against the Rebels

In the presence of the assembled inhabitants of earth and heaven the coronation of the Son of God takes place. And now, invested with supreme majesty and power, the King of kings pronounces sentence on the rebels who have transgressed His law and oppressed His people. "I saw a great white throne, and him that sat on it, from whose face the earth and the heaven fled away; and there was found no place for them. And I saw the dead, small and great, stand before God; and the books were opened: and another book was opened, which is the book of life: and the dead were judged out of those things which were written in the books, according to their works." Revelation 20:11, 12.

As the eye of Jesus looks upon the wicked, they are conscious of every sin they have ever committed. They see where their feet diverged from the path of holiness. The seductive temptations which they encouraged by indulgence in sin, the messengers of God despised, the warnings rejected, the waves of mercy beaten back by the stubborn, unrepentant heart—all appear as if written in letters of fire.

Above the throne is revealed the cross. Like a panoramic view appear the scenes of Adam's fall and the successive steps in the plan of redemption. The Saviour's lowly birth; His life of simplicity; His baptism in Jordan; the fast and temptation in the wilderness; His ministry unfolding to men heaven's blessings; the days crowded with deeds of mercy, the nights of prayer in the mountains; the plottings of envy and malice which repaid His benefits; the mysterious agony in Gethsemane beneath the weight of the sins of the world; His betrayal to the murderous mob; the events of that night of horror—the unresisting prisoner forsaken by His disciples, arraigned in the high priest's palace, in the judgment hall of Pilate, before the cowardly Herod, mocked, insulted, tortured, and condemned to die—all are vividly portrayed.

And now before the swaying multitude are revealed the final scenes: the patient Sufferer treading the path to Calvary; the Prince of heaven hanging on the cross; the priests and rabbis deriding His expiring agony; the supernatural darkness marking the moment when the world's Redeemer yielded up His life.

The awful spectacle appears just as it was. Satan and his subjects have no power to turn from the picture. Each actor recalls the part he performed. Herod, who slew the innocent children of Bethlehem; the base Herodias, upon whose soul rests the blood of John the Baptist; the weak, time-serving Pilate; the mocking soldiers; the maddened throng who cried, "His blood be on us, and on our children!"—all vainly seek to hide from the divine majesty of His countenance, while the redeemed cast their crowns at the Saviour's feet, exclaiming, "He died for me!"

There is Nero, monster of cruelty and vice, beholding the exaltation of those in whose anguish he found satanic delight. His mother witnesses her own work, how the passions encouraged by her influence and example have borne fruit in crimes that caused the world to shudder.

There are papist priests and prelates who claimed to be Christ's ambassadors, yet employed the rack, the dungeon, and the stake to control His people. There are the proud pontiffs who exalted themselves above God and presumed to change the law of the Most High. Those pretended fathers have an account to render to God. Too late they are made to see that the Omniscient One is jealous of His law. They learn now that Christ identifies His interests with His suffering people.

The whole wicked world stand arraigned on the charge of high treason against the government of heaven. They have none to plead their cause; they are without excuse; and the sentence of eternal death is pronounced against them.

The wicked see what they have forfeited by their rebellion. "All this," cries the lost soul, "I might have had. Oh, strange infatuation! I have exchanged peace, happiness, and honor for wretchedness, infamy, and despair." All see that their exclusion from heaven is just. By their lives they have declared: "We will not have this man [Jesus] to reign over us."

Satan Defeated

As if entranced, the wicked look upon the coronation of the Son of God. They see in His hands the tables of the divine law they have despised. They witness the outburst of adoration from the saved; and as the wave of melody sweeps over the multitudes without the city, all exclaim, "Just and true are thy ways, thou King of saints." Falling prostrate, they worship the Prince of life. Revelation 15:3.

Satan seems paralyzed. Once a covering cherub, he remembers whence he has fallen. From the council where once he was honored he is forever excluded. He sees another now standing near to the Father, an angel of majestic presence. He knows that the exalted position of this angel might have been his.

Memory recalls the home of his innocence, the peace and content that were his until his rebellion. He reviews his work among men and its results—the enmity of man toward his fellow men, the terrible destruction of life, the overturning of thrones, the tumults, conflicts, and revolutions. He recalls his constant efforts to oppose the work of Christ. As he looks upon the fruit of his toil he sees only failure. Again and again in the progress of the great controversy he has been defeated and compelled to yield.

The aim of the great rebel has ever been to prove the divine government responsible for the rebellion. He has led vast multitudes to accept his version. For thousands of years this chief of conspiracy has palmed off falsehood for truth. But the time has now come when the history and character of Satan are to be disclosed. In his last effort to dethrone Christ, destroy His people, and take possession of the City of God, the archdeceiver has been fully unmasked. Those united with him see the total failure of his cause.

Satan sees that his voluntary rebellion has unfitted him for heaven. He has trained his powers to war against God; the purity and harmony of heaven would be to him supreme torture. He bows down and confesses the justice of his sentence.

Every question of truth and error in the long-standing controversy has now been made plain. The results of setting aside the divine statutes have been laid open to the view of the whole universe. The history of sin will stand to all eternity as a witness that with the existence of God's law is bound up the happiness of all the beings He has created. The whole universe, loyal and rebellious, with one accord declare, "Just and true are thy ways, thou King of saints."

The hour has come when Christ is glorified above

every name that is named. For the joy set before Him—that He might bring many sons unto glory—He endured the cross. He looks upon the redeemed, renewed in His own image. He beholds in them the result of the travail of His soul, and He is satisfied. Isaiah 53:11. In a voice that reaches the multitudes, righteous and wicked, He declares: "Behold the purchase of my blood! For these I suffered, for these I died."

Violent End of the Wicked

Satan's character remains unchanged. Rebellion like a mighty torrent again bursts forth. He determines not to yield the last desperate struggle against the King of heaven. But of all the countless millions whom he has allured into rebellion, none now acknowledge his supremacy. The wicked are filled with the same hatred of God that inspires Satan, but they see that their case is hopeless. "Because thou hast set thine heart as the heart of God; behold, therefore I will bring strangers upon thee, the terrible of the nations: and they shall draw their swords against the beauty of thy wisdom, and they shall defile thy brightness. They shall bring thee down to the pit. . . . I will destroy thee, O covering cherub, from the midst of the stones of fire. . . . I will cast thee to the ground, I will lay thee before kings, that they may behold thee. . . . I will bring thee to ashes upon the earth in the sight of all them that behold thee. . . . Thou shalt be a terror, and never shalt thou be any more." Ezekiel 28:6-8, 16-19.

"The indignation of the Lord is upon all nations." "Upon the wicked he shall rain quick burning coals, fire and brimstone and an horrible tempest: this shall be the portion of their cup." Isaiah 34:2; Psalm 11:6. Fire comes down from God out of heaven. The earth is broken up. Devouring flames burst from every yawning chasm. The very rocks are on fire. The elements melt with fervent heat, the earth also, and the works that are therein are burned up. 2 Peter 3:10. The earth's surface seems one molten mass—a vast, seething lake of fire. It is "the day of the Lord's vengeance, and the year of recompenses for the controversy of Zion." Isaiah 34:8.

The wicked are punished "according to their deeds." Satan is made to suffer not only for his own rebellion, but for all the sins which he has caused God's people to commit. In the flames the wicked are at last destroyed, root and branch—Satan the root, his followers the branches. The full penalty of the law has been visited; the demands of justice have been met. Satan's work of ruin is forever ended. Now God's creatures are forever delivered from his temptations.

While the earth is wrapped in fire, the righteous abide safely in the Holy City. While God is to the wicked a consuming fire, He is to His people a shield. See Revelation 20:6; Psalm 84:11.

"I saw a new heaven and a new earth: for the first heaven and the first earth were passed away." Revelation 21:1. The fire that consumes the wicked purifies the earth. Every trace of the curse is swept away. No eternally burning hell will keep before the ransomed the fearful consequences of sin.

Reminders of the Crucifixion

One reminder alone remains: our Redeemer will ever bear the marks of His crucifixion, the only traces of the cruel work that sin has wrought. Through eternal ages the wounds of Calvary will show forth His praise and declare His power.

Christ assured His disciples that He went to prepare mansions for them in the Father's house. Human language is inadequate to describe the reward of the righteous. It will be known only to those who behold it. No finite mind can comprehend the glory of the Paradise of God!

In the Bible the inheritance of the saved is called "a country." Hebrews 11:14-16. There the heavenly Shepherd leads His flock to fountains of living waters. There are everflowing streams, clear as crystal, and beside them waving trees cast their shadows upon the paths prepared for the ransomed of the Lord. Wide-spreading plains swell into hills of beauty, and the mountains of God rear their lofty summits. On those peaceful plains, beside those living streams, God's people, so long pilgrims and wanderers, shall find a home.

"They shall build houses, and inhabit them; and they shall plant vineyards, and eat the fruit of them. They shall not build and another inhabit; they shall not plant, and another eat: . . . Mine elect shall long enjoy the work of their hands." "The wilderness and the solitary place shall be glad for them; and the desert shall rejoice, and blossom as the rose." "The wolf also shall dwell with the lamb, and the leopard shall lie down with the kid; . . . and a little child shall lead them. . . . They shall not hurt nor destroy in all my holy mountain." Isaiah 65:21, 22; 35:1; 11:6, 9.

Pain cannot exist in heaven. There will be no more tears, no funeral trains. "There shall be no more death, neither sorrow, nor crying: . . . for the former things are passed away." "The inhabitant shall not say, I am sick: the people that dwell therein shall be forgiven their iniquity." Revelation 21:4; Isaiah 33:24.

There is the New Jerusalem, the metropolis of the glorified new earth. "Her light was like unto a stone most precious, even like a jasper stone, clear as crystal." "The nations of them which are saved shall walk in the light of it: and the kings of the earth do bring their glory and honor into it." "The tabernacle of God is with men, and he will dwell with them, and they shall be his people, and God himself shall be with them, and be their God." Revelation 21:11, 24, 3.

In the City of God "there shall be no night." Revelation 22:5. There will be no weariness. We shall ever feel the freshness of the morning and ever be far from its close. The light of the sun will be superseded by a radiance which is not painfully dazzling, yet which immeasurably surpasses the brightness of our noontide.

The redeemed walk in the glory of perpetual day.

"I saw no temple therein: for the Lord God Almighty and the Lamb are the temple of it." Revelation 21:22. The people of God are privileged to hold open communion with the Father and the Son. Now we behold the image of God as in a mirror, but then we shall see Him face to face, without a dimming veil between.

The Triumph of God's Love

There the loves and sympathies which God Himself has planted in the soul shall find truest and sweetest exercise. The pure communion with holy beings and the faithful of all ages, the sacred ties that bind together "the whole family in heaven and earth"—these help to constitute the happiness of the redeemed. Ephesians 3:15.

There, immortal minds will contemplate with never-failing delight the wonders of creative power, the mysteries of redeeming love. Every faculty will be developed, every capacity increased. The acquirement of knowledge will not exhaust the energies. The grandest enterprises may be carried forward, the loftiest aspirations reached, the highest ambitions realized. And still there will arise new heights to surmount, new wonders to admire, new truths to comprehend, fresh objects to call forth the powers of mind and soul and body.

All the treasures of the universe will be open to God's redeemed. Unfettered by mortality, they wing their tireless flight to worlds afar. The children of earth enter into the joy and wisdom of unfallen beings and share treasures of knowledge gained through ages upon ages. With undimmed vision they gaze upon the glory of creation—suns and stars and systems, all in their appointed order circling the throne of Deity.

And the years of eternity, as they roll, will bring still more glorious revelations of God and of Christ. The more men learn of God, the greater will be their admiration of His character. As Jesus opens before them the riches of redemption and the amazing achievements in the great controversy with Satan, the hearts of the ransomed thrill with devotion, and ten thousand times ten thousand voices unite to swell the mighty chorus of praise.

''And every creature which is in heaven, and on the earth, and under the earth, and such as are in the sea, and all that are in them, heard I saying, Blessing, and honor, and glory, and power, be unto him that sitteth upon the throne, and unto the Lamb for ever and ever.'' Revelation 5:13.

The great controversy is ended. Sin and sinners are no more. The entire universe is clean. One pulse of harmony and gladness beats through the vast creation. From Him who created all, flow life and light and gladness throughout the realms of illimitable space. From the minutest atom to the greatest world, all things, animate and inanimate, in their unshadowed beauty and perfect joy, declare that God is love.

Appendix

Page 33. TITLES. Pope Innocent III declared that the Roman pontiff is "the vicegerent upon earth, not of a mere man, but of very God." See *Decretals of the Lord Pope Gregory IX,* liber 1, title 7, ch. 3. *Corp. Jur. Canon.* (2d Leipzig ed., 1881), col. 99.

For the title "Lord God the Pope" see a gloss on the *Extravagantes* of Pope John XXII, title 14, ch. 4, *Declaramus.* In an Antwerp edition of the *Extravagantes,* dated 1584, the words *"Dominum Deum nostrum Papam"* ("Our Lord God the Pope") occur in column 153.

Page 33. INFALLIBILITY. See Philip Schaff, *The Creeds of Christendom,* vol. II, *Dogmatic Decrees of the Vatican Council,* pp. 234-271; *The Catholic Encyclopedia,* vol. VII, art. "Infallibility"; James Cardinal Gibbons, *The Faith of Our Fathers* (Baltimore: John Murphy Co., 110th ed., 1917), chs. 7, 11.

Page 33. IMAGE WORSHIP. "The worship of images . . . was one of those corruptions of Christianity which crept into the church stealthily and almost without notice or observation. . . . So gradually was one practice after another introduced in connection with it, that the church had become deeply steeped in practical idolatry, . . . almost without any decided remonstrance; and when at length an endeavor was made to root it out, the evil was found too deeply fixed to admit of removal."—J. Mendham, *The Seventh General Council, the Second of Nicaea,* Introduction, pages iii-vi.

For a record of the proceedings and decisions of the Second Council of Nicea, A.D. 787, called to establish the worship of images, see *A Select Library of Nicene and Post-Ni-*

cene Fathers, second series, vol. XIV, pp. 521-587 (New York, 1900); C. J. Hefele, *A History of the Councils of the Church, From the Original Documents,* bk. 18, ch. 1, secs. 332, 333; ch. 2, secs. 345-352 (T. and T. Clark, ed. 1896), vol. 5, pp. 260-304, 342-372.

Page 34. THE SUNDAY LAW OF CONSTANTINE. The law is given in Latin and in English translation in Philip Schaff's *History of the Christian Church,* vol. III, 3d period, ch. 7, sec. 75, p. 380, footnote 1. See discussion in Albert Henry Newman, *A Manual of Church History* (Philadelphia: The American Baptist Publication Society, 1933), rev. ed., vol. I, pp. 305-307; and in L. E. Froom, *The Prophetic Faith of Our Fathers* (Washington, D.C.: Review and Herald Publishing Assn., 1950), vol. I, pp. 376-381.

Page 35. PROPHETIC DATES. An important principle of interpreting time prophecies is the year-day principle—under which a day of prophetic time equals a year of calendar time. Some of the Bible reasons for this principle are as follows: (1) The year-day principle is in harmony with the principle of symbolically interpreting beasts as kingdoms, horns as powers, oceans as peoples, etc. (2) The Lord, speaking in Numbers 14:34 and Ezekiel 4:6, upholds the principle. (3) The 2300 days (years) of Daniel 8:14 cover the history of the Medo-Persian, Grecian, and Roman empires, as the angel explains in verses 19-26 ("at the time of the end shall be the vision"). These empires lasted many times longer than 2300 literal days. Nothing can fit except the year-day principle. (4) Daniel 11 is an expansion of the prophecy of Daniel 8, yet Daniel 11 is not symbolic. Three times it speaks of "years" (verses 6, 8, 13) as a parallel of "days" in Daniel 8:14. (6) The angel explained to Daniel that these prophecies concerned "the time of the end" (8:19, 26; 10:13, 14). If the "days" were literal, the prophecies would not make sense. (7) A day for a year was a common way of speaking in Old Testament Hebrew. See Leviticus 25:8; Genesis 29:27. (8) The book of Revelation unlocks the prophecies of Daniel, showing that their fulfillment was still future in the time of the apostles. Further, the year-day principle has been recognized and accepted as a valid biblical principle by many careful Bible students such as Joachim of Floris, Wycliffe, Joseph Mede, Sir

Isaac Newton, Bishop Thomas Newton, Alexander Keith and many others.

Page 37. FORGED WRITINGS. Among the documents generally admitted to be forgeries, the Donation of Constantine and the Pseudo-Isidorian Decretals are of primary importance. See *The New Schaff-Herzog Encyclopedia of Religious Knowledge*, vol. III, art. "Donation of Constantine."

The "false writings" referred to in the text include also the "Pseudo-Isidorian Decretals,"—fictitious letters ascribed to early popes from Clement (A.D. 100) to Gregory the Great (A.D. 600) and later incorporated in a ninth century collection purporting to have been made by "Isidore Mercator." The falsity of the Pseudo-Isidorian fabrications is now admitted.

Page 38. PURGATORY. Dr. Joseph Faa Di Bruno thus defines purgatory: "Purgatory is a state of suffering after this life, in which those souls are for a time detained, who depart this life after their deadly sins have been remitted as to the stain and guilt, and as to the everlasting pain that was due to them; but who have on account of those sins still some debt of temporal punishment to pay; as also those souls which leave this world guilty only of venial sins."—*Catholic Belief*, p. 196 (ed. 1884; imprimatur Archbishop of New York).

See *The Catholic Encyclopedia*, vol. XII, art. "Purgatory."

Page 39. INDULGENCES. For a detailed history of the doctrine of indulgences, see *The Catholic Encyclopedia*, art. "Indulgences," vol. VII; A. H. Newman, *A Manual of Church History* (Philadelphia: The American Baptist Publication Society, 1953), vol. II, pp. 53, 54, 62.

Page 44. THE SABBATH AMONG THE WALDENSES. Historical evidence exists for some observance of the seventh-day Sabbath among the Waldenses. A report of an inquisition before whom were brought some Waldenses of Moravia in the middle of the fifteenth century declares that among the Waldenses "not a few indeed celebrate the Sabbath with the Jews."—Johann Joseph Ignaz von Döllinger, *Beitrage zur Sektengeschichte des Mittelalters* (Contributions to the History of the Sects of the Middle Ages), Munich, 1890, part 2, p. 661. This source indicates the observance of the seventh-day Sabbath.

Page 49. EDICT AGAINST THE WALDENSES. A portion of the papal bull (Innocent VIII, 1487) against the Waldenses is given in an English translation, in Dowling's *History of Romanism*, bk. 6, ch. 5, sec. 62 (ed. 1871).

Page 53. INDULGENCES. See note for page 39.

Page 54, 60. WYCLIFFE. For the original text of the papal bulls issued against Wycliffe with English translation, see John Foxe, *Acts and Monuments of the Church* (London: Pratt Townsend, 1870), vol. III, pp. 4-13; Merle d'Aubigné, *The History of the Reformation in the Sixteenth Century* (London: Blackie and Son, 1885), vol. IV, div. 7, p. 93; Philip Schaff, *History of the Christian Church* (New York: Chas. Scribner's Sons, 1915), vol. V, part 2, p. 317.

Page 54. INFALLIBILITY. See note for page 33.

Page 64. INDULGENCES. See note for page 39.

Page 64. COUNCIL OF CONSTANCE. Recent publications on the Council are K. Zähringer, *Das Kardinal Kollegium auf dem Konstanzer Konzil* (Münster, 1935); Th. F. Grogau, *The Conciliar Theory as It Manifested Itself at the Council of Constance* (Washington, 1949); Fred A. Kremple, *Cultural Aspects of the Council of Constance and Basel* (Ann Arbor, 1955).

See John Hus, *Letters*, 1904; E. J. Kitts, *Pope John XXIII and Master John Hus* (London, 1910); D. A. Schaff, *John Hus* (1915); and Matthew Spinka, *John Hus and the Czech Reform* (1941).

Page 81. INDULGENCES. See note for page 39.

Page 146. JESUITISM. See *Concerning Jesuits*, edited by the Rev. John Gerard, S.J. (London: Catholic Truth Society, 1902). In this work it is said that "the mainspring of the whole organization of the Society is a spirit of entire obedience: 'Let each one,' writes St. Ignatius, 'persuade himself that those who live under obedience ought to allow themselves to be moved and directed by divine Providence through their superiors, just as though they were a dead body, which allows itself to be carried anywhere and to be treated in any manner whatever, or as an old man's staff, which serves him who holds it in his hand in whatsoever way he will.' "—p. 6.

Page 147. THE INQUISITION. See *The Catholic Encyclopedia*, vol. VIII, art. "Inquisition"; and E. Vacandard, *The Inquisition: A Critical and Historical Study of the Coercive Power of the Church* (New York: Longmans, Green, and Company, 1908).

For the non-Catholic view, see Philip van Limborch, *History of the Inquisition;* Henry C. Lea, *A History of the Inquisition in the Middle Ages,* 3 vols.

Page 166. CAUSES OF THE FRENCH REVOLUTION. See H. von Sybel, *History of the French Revolution,* bk. 5, ch. 1, pars. 3-7; H. T. Buckle, *History of Civilization in England,* chs. 8, 12, 14 (New York, ed. 1895), vol. I, pp. 364-366, 369-371, 437, 540, 541, 550; *Blackwood's Magazine,* vol. XXXIV, no. 215 (November, 1833), p. 739; J. G. Lorimer, *An Historical Sketch of the Protestant Church in France,* ch. 8, pars. 6, 7.

Page 167. PROPHETIC DATES. See note for page 35.

Page 167. EFFORTS TO SUPPRESS AND DESTROY THE BIBLE. The Council of Toulouse ruled: "We prohibit laymen possessing copies of the Old and New Testament. . . . We forbid them most severely to have the above books in the popular vernacular." "The dwellings, the humblest hovels, and even the underground retreats of the men convicted of having the Scriptures shall be entirely wiped out. These men shall be hunted for in the woods and caverns and any who shall give them shelter shall be severely punished."—*Concil. Tolosanum,* Pope Gregory IX, Anno chr. 1229. Canons 14, 2. This council sat at the time of the crusade against the Albigenses.

"This pest [the Bible] had taken such an extension that some people had appointed priests of their own, and even some evangelists who distorted and destroyed the truth of the gospel and made new gospels for their own purpose . . . [they know that] the preaching and explanation of the Bible is absolutely forbidden to the lay members.''—*Acts of Inquisition,* Philip van Limborch, *History of the Inquisition,* ch. 8.

At the Council of Constance in 1415, Wycliffe was posthumously condemned as ''that pestilent wretch of damnable heresy who invented a new translation of the Scriptures in his mother tongue.''

Opposition to the Bible by the Roman Catholic Church increased because of the success of the Bible societies. On December 8, 1866, Pope Pius IX, in his encyclical *Quanta cura,* issued a syllabus of eighty errors under ten different headings. Under heading IV we find listed: ''Socialism, communism, clandestine societies, Bible societies. . . . Pests of this sort must be destroyed by all possible means.''

In recent years a dramatic and positive change has occurred in the Roman Catholic Church. On the one hand, the church has approved several versions prepared on the basis of the original language; on the other, it has promoted the study of the Holy Scriptures by means of free distribution and Bible institutes. The church, however, continues to reserve for herself the exclusive right to interpret the Bible in the light of her own tradition, thus justifying those doctrines that do not harmonize with biblical teachings.

Page 173. THE REIGN OF TERROR. For a reliable introduction to the history of the French Revolution, see L. Gershoy, *The French Revolution* (1932); G. Lefebvre, *The Coming of the French Revolution* (Princeton, 1947); and H. von Sybel, *History of the French Revolution,* 4 vols. (1869).

See also A. Aulard, *Christianity and the French Revolution* (London, 1927), in which the account is carried through 1802—an excellent study.

Page 175. THE MASSES AND THE PRIVILEGED CLASSES. See H. von Holst, *Lowell Lectures on the French Revolution,* lecture 1; also Taine, *Ancient Regime;* and A. Young, *Travels in France.*

Page 177. RETRIBUTION. See Thos. H. Gill, *The Papal Drama,* bk. 10; E. de Pressensé, *The Church and the French Revolution,* bk. 3, ch. 1.

Page 177. THE ATROCITIES OF THE REIGN OF TERROR. See M. A. Thiers, *History of the French Revolution* (New York, ed. 1890, tr. by F. Shoberl), vol. 3, pp. 42-44, 62-74, 106; F. A. Mignet, *History of the French Revolution* (Bohn, ed. 1894), ch. 9, par. 1; Sir Archibald Alison, *History of Europe, From the Commencement of the French Revolution to the Restoration of the Bourbons*, vol. I, ch. 14 (New York, ed. 1872), vol. 1, pp. 293-312.

Page 179. THE CIRCULATION OF THE SCRIPTURES. In 1804, according to Mr. William Canton, of the British and Foreign Bible Society, "all the Bibles extant in the world, in manuscript or in print, counting every version in every land, were computed at not many more than four millions."

From 1816-1981, the American Bible Society alone published 98,200,951 copies of the whole Bible and 3,396,127,592 copies of portions of the Bible. In 1981 3,365,779 copies of the whole Bible were published by the ABS. Other Bible societies would add many millions more copies to these figures.

Page 179. FOREIGN MISSIONS. The missionary activity of the early Christian church had virtually died out by the year 1000, and was succeeded by the military campaigns of the Crusades. The Reformation era saw little foreign mission work. The pietistic revival produced some missionaries. The work of the Moravian Church in the eighteenth century was remarkable, and there were some missionary societies formed by the British for work in colonized North America. But the great resurgence of foreign missionary activity began around the year 1800, at "the time of the end" (Dan. 12:4). In 1792 the Baptist Missionary Society sent Carey to India. In 1795 the London Missionary Society was organized, and another society in 1799, which in 1812 became the Church Missionary Society. Shortly afterward the Wesleyan Methodist Missionary Society was founded. In the United States, the American Board of Commissioners for Foreign Missions was formed in 1812, and Adoniram Judson was sent out that year to Calcutta. He established himself in Burma the next year. In 1814 the American Baptist Missionary Union was formed. The Presbyterian Board of Foreign Missions was formed in 1837.

"In A.D. 1800 . . . the overwhelming majority of Christians were the descendants of those who had been won before A.D. 1500. . . . Now, in the nineteenth century, came a further expansion of Christianity. . . . Never in any corresponding length of time had the Christian impulse given rise to so many new movements. Never had it had quite so great an effect upon Western European peoples. It was from this abounding vigor that there issued the missionary enterprise which during the nineteenth century so augmented the numerical strength and the influence of Christianity.''—Kenneth Scott Latourette, *A History of the Expansion of Christianity,* vol. IV, *The Great Century, A.D. 1800–A.D. 1914* (New York: Harper and Bros., 1914), pp. 2-4.

Page 203. A DAY FOR A YEAR. See note for page 35.

Page 205. THE YEAR 457 B.C. For the certainty of the date 457 B.C. being the seventh year of Artaxerxes, see S. H. Horn and L. H. Wood, *The Chronology of Ezra 7* (Washington, D.C.: Review and Herald Publishing Association, 1953); E. G. Kraeling, *The Brooklyn Museum Aramaic Papyri* (New Haven or London, 1953), pp. 191-193; *The Seventh-day Adventist Bible Commentary* (Washington, D.C.: Review and Herald Publishing Association, 1954), vol. III, pp. 97-110.

Page 209. FALL OF THE OTTOMAN EMPIRE. Throughout the Reformation era Turkey was a continual threat to European Christendom; the writings of the Reformers are full of condemnation of the Ottoman power. Christian writers since have been concerned with the role of Turkey in future events, and commentators on prophecy have seen Turkish power and its decline forecast in Scripture.

For the "hour, day, month, year" prophecy, as part of the sixth trumpet, Josiah Litch worked out an application of the time prophecy, ending Turkish independence in August 1840.

A book by Uriah Smith, *Thoughts on Daniel and the Revelation,* rev. ed. of 1944, discusses the prophetic timing of this prophecy on pp. 506-517.

Page 232. ASCENSION ROBES. The story that the Adventists made robes with which to ascend "to meet the Lord in the air" was invented by those who wished to reproach the advent preaching. Careful inquiry has proven its falsity.

For a refutation of the legend of ascension robes, see Francis D. Nichol, *The Midnight Cry* (Washington, D.C.: Review and Herald Publishing Association, 1944), chs. 25-27, and Appendices H-J. See also LeRoy E. Froom, *The Prophetic Faith of Our Fathers* (Washington, D.C.: Review and Herald Publishing Association, 1954), vol. IV, pp. 822-826.

Page 269. A THREEFOLD MESSAGE. Rev. 14:6, 7 foretells the proclamation of the first angel's message. Then the prophet continues: "There followed another angel, saying, Babylon is fallen, is fallen, . . . and the third angel followed them." The word here rendered "followed" means "to go along with," "to follow one," "go with him." It also means "to accompany." The idea intended is that of "going together," "in company with." The idea in Rev. 14:8, 9 is not simply that the second and third angels followed the first in point of time, but that they went with him. They are *three* only in the order of their rise. But having risen, they go on together.

Page 352. SUPREMACY OF THE BISHOPS OF ROME. See James Cardinal Gibbons, *Faith of Our Fathers* (Baltimore: John Murphy Co., 110th ed., 1917), chs. 5, 9, 10, 12.

Page 352. THE SABBATH AMONG THE WALDENSES. See note for page 44.

Page 353. THE ETHIOPIAN CHURCH AND THE SABBATH. Until rather recent years the Coptic Church of Ethiopia observed the seventh-day Sabbath. The Ethiopians also kept Sunday. The observance of the seventh-day Sabbath has, however, virtually ceased in modern Ethiopia. For eyewitness accounts of religious days in Ethiopia, see Pero Gomes de Teixeira, *The Discovery of Abyssinia by the Portuguese in 1520* (translated into English in London: British Museum, 1938), p. 79; Father Francisco Alvarez, *Narrative of the Portuguese Embassy to Abyssinia During the Years 1520-1527*, in the *Records of the Hakluyt Society* (London, 1881), vol. LXIV, pp. 22-49.

Something for you . . .

☐ Send me a free copy of *Signs of the Times*, the international prophetic monthly.

☐ Enroll me in one of your free Bible courses.

☐ I want information about the Five-Day Plan to Stop Smoking.

☐ I would like more information about the Bible prophecies of Daniel and Revelation.

☐ Send me the address of the nearest Adventist Church.

Complete this coupon below, and mail to

Pacific Press Publishing Association
P.O. Box 7000, Mountain View, CA 94039

_____
Name

_____
Street or Box

_____
City   State   Zip   F